GLOBAL INEQUALITIES BEYOND OCCIDENTALISM

Global Connections

Series Editor: Robert Holton, Trinity College, Dublin

Global Connections builds on the multi-dimensional and continuously expanding interest in Globalization. The main objective of the series is to focus on 'connectedness' and provide readable case studies across a broad range of areas such as social and cultural life, economic, political and technological activities.

The series aims to move beyond abstract generalities and stereotypes: 'Global' is considered in the broadest sense of the word, embracing connections between different nations, regions and localities, including activities that are trans-national, and trans-local in scope; 'Connections' refers to movements of people, ideas, resources, and all forms of communication as well as the opportunities and constraints faced in making, engaging with, and sometimes resisting globalization.

The series is interdisciplinary in focus and publishes monographs and collections of essays by new and established scholars. It fills a niche in the market for books that make the study of globalization more concrete and accessible.

Also published in this series:

Global Knowledge Production in the Social Sciences
Made in Circulation
Edited by Wiebke Keim, Ercüment Çelik, Christian Ersche and Veronika Wöhrer
ISBN 978-1-4724-2617-8

Reimagining Social Movements
From Collectives to Individuals
Edited by Antimo L. Farro and Henri Lustiger-Thaler
ISBN 978-1-4094-0104-9

Islam and Public Controversy in Europe
Edited by Nilüfer Göle
ISBN 978-1-4724-1313-0

Community, Competition and Citizen Science
Voluntary Distributed Computing in a Globalized World
Anne Holohan
ISBN 978-1-4094-5298-0

Multiple Modernities and Postsecular Societies
Edited by Massimo Rosati and Kristina Stoeckl
ISBN 978-1-4094-4412-1

Global Inequalities Beyond Occidentalism

MANUELA BOATCĂ
Albert-Ludwigs University of Freiburg, Germany

LONDON AND NEW YORK

© Manuela Boatcă 2015

All rights reserved. No part of this publication may be reproduced, stored in a retrieval system or transmitted in any form or by any means, electronic, mechanical, photocopying, recording or otherwise without the prior permission of the publisher.

Manuela Boatcă has asserted her right under the Copyright, Designs and Patents Act, 1988, to be identified as the author of this work.

Published 2016 by Routledge
2 Park Square, Milton Park, Abingdon, Oxon OX14 4RN
711 Third Avenue, New York, NY 10017

Routledge is an imprint of the Taylor & Francis Group, an informa business

British Library Cataloguing in Publication Data
A catalogue record for this book is available from the British Library

The Library of Congress has cataloged the printed edition as follows:
Boatcă, Manuela.
  Global inequalities beyond occidentalism / by Manuela Boatcă.
    pages cm. — (Global connections)
  Includes bibliographical references and index.
  ISBN 978-1-4094-4279-0 (hardback : alk. paper) – ISBN 978-1-4094-4280-6 (ebook) –
  ISBN 978-1-4724-0598-2 (epub) 1. Equality. 2. Social stratification. 3. Imperialism.
  4. Globalization—Social aspects. I. Title.
  HM821.B63 2015
  305–dc23
                                                                                  2014030033

ISBN 9781409442790 (hbk)
ISBN 9781409442806 (ebk – PDF)
ISBN 9781472405982 (ebk – ePUB)

To Torsten, for understanding

Contents

List of Figures and Tables	*ix*
Acknowledgements	*xi*

Introduction	1

PART I MARX AND POLITICAL-ECONOMY APPROACHES

1	Class vs. Other: Coloniality as Anomaly in Karl Marx	25
2	World-Systems Analysis and the Feminist Subsistence Perspective	47
3	Orientalism vs. Occidentalism: The Decolonial Perspective	81
4	The World-Historical Model: Relational Inequalities and Global Processes	117

PART II WEBER AND HISTORICAL-COMPARATIVE MODELS

5	The West vs. the Rest: Modernity as Uniqueness in Max Weber	141
6	Citizenship as Social Closure: Weberian Perspectives and Beyond	177
7	After Uniqueness: Entangled Modernities and Multiple Europes	201
8	Conclusions: For a Sociology of Global Inequalities Beyond Occidentalism	227

References	*233*
Index	*263*

List of Figures and Tables

Figures

7.1	The "Velvet Curtain of Culture". Reprinted by permission of Foreign Affairs. © The Council on Foreign Relations, Inc. www.ForeignAffairs.com	208
7.2:	Map of EU enlargement 2004, 2007 and pending	215
7.3	From mental maps to imperial maps	216

Tables

3.1	Occidental global designs	115
5.1	Typology of carrier strata and relationship to the world of cultural religions	150
5.2	Typology of classes according to Max Weber	156
7.1	Typology of conflicts	207
7.2	Huntington's "Velvet Curtain of Culture"	209
7.3	Multiple Europes	219

Acknowledgements

This book started out as a *Habilitation* project in sociology at the University of Eichstätt-Ingolstadt in 2004. The quest for intellectual and political dialogue that accompanied it took me on exciting journeys (scholarly and otherwise) and to several academic homes, all of which have shaped and enriched the scope and the direction of the project.

Pursuing a research agenda that draws on world-systems analysis and postcolonial perspectives in Germany has for a long time been a lonely undertaking. Solace and challenge, eye-openings and encouragement mostly came from rewarding conferences organised by kindred minds elsewhere:

Throughout the research and writing process, the annual meetings of the Political Economy of the World-Systems Section of the American Sociological Association provided me with a greatly stimulating intellectual home away from home. My thanks go first and foremost to Ramón Grosfoguel, who introduced me to this forum at UC Berkeley in 2004, and to Tom Reifer, who extended the first invitation to the IROWS at UC Riverside that same year. I also thank Agustín Lao-Montes and Joya Misra, Khaldoun Samman, Eric Mielants and Terry Ann-Jones, Chris Chase-Dunn and above all Immanuel Wallerstein for making later meetings and conference proceedings the best testing ground for many of the ideas that went into this book, and for the invaluable exchanges that ensued.

The conference "From World Modernity to Multiple Modernities: Social Theory in the Context of Global Transformation", held at the Instituto Universitário de Pesquisas do Rio de Janeiro in 2005, sparked more possibilities for joint projects in both Germany and Brazil than I had ever thought a single event could accomplish. Many thanks to José Maurício Domingues, Josué Pereira da Silva, Sérgio Costa, and Wolfgang Knöbl for inviting me to join in the conversation, which provided crucial impulses for this book – and then some! – and for thus paving the way for my research stay at IUPERJ two years later. Both the conference "Critical Thought/Transformative Practice. Peripheral Conditions and the (Dis)Location of Latin America" I co-organised with José Maurício Domingues and João Feres Jr. at IUPERJ in 2007, as well as the co-edited volumes *Decolonizing European Sociology. Transdisciplinary Approaches* (with Encarnación Gutiérrez Rodríguez and Sérgio Costa) and *Globale, multiple und postkoloniale Modernen* (with Willfried Spohn) became possible as a result.

During my time in Eichstätt, Nina Baur and Willfried Spohn volunteered much-needed brainstorming and feedback sessions, as well as a wonderful basis for our joint work in Eichstätt, Berlin, and wherever the ISA Working Group Historical and Comparative Sociology took us. I will always be grateful for the faith both of you had in this project from the beginning, and for the ideas that ensued from our always constructive dialogues.

To Gabriele Dietze and Julia Roth I am indebted for the most inspiring exchanges on the gendering dimension of inequality processes and its neglect in many macrotheoretical approaches, as well as for thinking with me on a gendered critique of Occidentalism along the lines of the concept developed by our late friend and colleague Fernando Coronil.

I am particularly grateful to Walter Mignolo for the ongoing, mostly long-distance dialogue since our first meeting in Munich in 2003, as well as for consistently weaving me into his expanding decolonial network from the first meeting of the Duke-Bremen series in Germany in 2006 to the coloniality workshop in Hong Kong in 2011 and the many meetings in print in-between.

To my latest academic home at the Institute for Latin American Studies of the Freie Universität Berlin and in the Research Network desiguALdades.net I owe the good fortune of teaching and researching in an unrivalled interdisciplinary environment full of effervescent exchanges and shared intellectual commitments. My thanks to Sérgio Costa, Marianne Braig, Susanne Klengel, Stefan Rinke, and my favourite co-teacher Claudia Rauhut for engaging with arguments of this book at different stages and for providing a vibrant environment for discussion in formal and informal contexts. Sharp comments from and discussions with the graduate students in my classes on "Macrosociology of the 21st century", "Europe as a Process, a Project, and a Problem" and "Global and Regional Transformations" in Eichstätt, Rio de Janeiro, and Berlin have greatly helped me hone and clarify ideas presented in this book.

Special thanks go to Oliver Tewes for his committed research assistance throughout the last stages of writing, for sharing in both the enthusiasm and the frustration of various phases, as well as for making the careful editing of the manuscript into his own personal mission.

For comments and critiques of different chapters of this book, but especially for being that very rare species known as true friends well beyond our common academic and political allegiances, I deeply thank Santiago Slabodsky, mi hermano en espíritu, Julia Roth, one of a kind soul sister, and Vilna Bashi Treitler, the generous alter ego.

I am thankful for fellowship support from DAAD, FAPERJ and the German Research Community (DFG) during my research stay at IUPERJ in 2007–2008 as well as from desiguALdades.net during my sabbatical at the Freie Universität Berlin in 2010, all of which were decisive at different stages of the manuscript. Funding from desiguALdades.net, a Research Network sponsored by the German Ministry of Education and Research, thankfully ensured that editing and indexing this manuscript became a multi-person task rather than being heaped on a multi-tasking person.

Publishing a monograph with Ashgate has turned out to be as rewarding a work experience as co-editing the volume *Decolonizing European Sociology. Transdisciplinary Approaches* was in 2010. My heartfelt thanks go to Neil Jordan, whose promptitude, patience, invaluable advice and expertise on both occasions have become legendary among those of us who have had the pleasure of working with him. Many thanks also to Robert Holton for making *Global Connections* such an exciting series and for welcoming this book in it, and to Lianne Sherlock and Barbara Pretty for assistance with the submitted manuscript.

My steady companion throughout the long process of turning emerging ideas into a completed text has been my husband Torsten, whose unconditional support of my every project, including that of seeing this book into print, was coupled with his unmatched capacity to ground me and with the talent to paint our common world beautiful bright colours, regardless of the hardships. This book is dedicated to him, my *ohana*.

Introduction

What is New about Global Inequalities?

> Global inequality begins to matter
> Branko Milanovic, November 2012

In terms of press coverage as well as academic debates, talk of global inequalities is currently in full swing. Approaches vary widely between and within both realms as far as the questions asked, the answers given, the methodology used, and the political stance behind each. Yet the (tacit) consensus lies in the very topic: To the mainstream media, global inequality is news. To most academics in the global North, global inequalities are new.

As recently as the end of 2012, The Economist was still questioning whether inequality needed to be tackled at all, since globalisation and technical innovation had allegedly narrowed inequality globally. However, the fact that the gap between rich and poor had increased within many countries such as the United States and Great Britain since the 1980s made inequality "bad for growth" (*The Economist* 2012). At the same time, news of the decrease of income inequality in Latin America, viewed as the world's most unequal region for decades, made the headlines as "Gini back in the bottle" (*The Economist* 2012). That the unprecedented changes had suddenly rendered the United States more unequal than much of Latin America further spurred debates on inequality – in rich countries (Light 2013).

Even the more critical views have mostly been based on the premise that extreme global inequalities are only decades old. After the World Economic Forum's Global Risk report rated inequality as one of the top global risks of 2013, Oxfam published a media briefing denouncing extreme wealth and inequality as economically inefficient, politically corrosive, socially divisive, environmentally destructive, and unethical (Oxfam 2013). At the same time, the corresponding policy recommendation was to end extreme wealth and inequality by aiming to return to 1990 inequality levels – implying that the risks of political corrosion, social divisiveness and environmental destruction would thereby become acceptable. Similarly, a recent World Bank policy paper, tellingly entitled "Global Inequality: From Class to Location, From Proletarians to Migrants" suggested that we live in a fundamentally different world than the one Marx and Engels had described in the Communist Manifesto: unlike in the mid-nineteenth century, when inequality could largely be explained by income differences between workers and capital-owners within individual countries, in the twenty-first century, most global income differences are due to large gaps in average incomes between countries; as a result, international migration becomes the most powerful tool for reducing

2 *Global Inequalities Beyond Occidentalism*

global poverty and inequality, and replaces class struggle as a social and political issue (Milanovic 2011).

The need to update inequality approaches of the discipline's classics to fit a twenty-first century context is an even more frequent issue in current sociological discussions about global inequality. In most cases, the proposed updating involves or even equates upscaling the unit of analysis: Whereas Marx and Weber conceptualised inequality structures and the conflicts arising from them in the context of particular nation-states, present-day approaches have to take into account supranational and global levels of the production and reproduction of inequality. Thus, the critique of the methodological nationalism inherent in conventional inequality research makes the proper unit of analysis a crucial factor in the reconceptualisation. However, the transnationalisation of social inequality is frequently viewed as a new phenomenon that sets in with twentieth century globalisation. The proposed shift from methodological nationalism to methodological cosmopolitanism therefore becomes a necessary adjustment to the qualitative change that globalisation has operated in structures of inequality, but is of no consequence for the assessment of earlier or "classical" inequality contexts – for which the nation-state framework is still considered appropriate (Weiß 2005; Beck 2007; Pries 2008). Thus, new scholarly concepts coined in order to address issues of inequality in the context of globalisation are often mistaken for the newness of the phenomena themselves.

The present monograph in turn departs from the premise that the shift in the unit of analysis from the nation-state to the world as a whole reveals that global inequalities are not a new phenomenon. Instead, inequalities have been the result of transregional processes for more than five centuries. Systematic transregional migration is considerably older than the transnational migration hailed as both a new trend related to globalisation and as a new means of global social mobility. At least since the European expansion into the Americas, intercontinental migration, the Atlantic slave trade, and the unequal economic exchange between shifting metropolitan and peripheral areas have provided transregional entanglements that decisively shaped the inequality structures of both the former colonising as well as the former colonised regions – none of which were yet nation-states. The book therefore argues that viewing the trans*nationalisation* of inequality as a new phenomenon today requires (1) disregarding the large-scale, systematic cross-border processes that long preceded the emergence of the nation-state in Western Europe, (2) erasing the transnational experiences of non-European, non-Western regions as well as of non-Western or non-White populations from social theory and (3) disregarding the multiple entanglements between Europe and its colonies, dependencies and occupied territories throughout the centuries.

In drawing attention to the continuities and interconnections between historical and current patterns of global inequalities, as well as to the structural relations of power underlying them, this book is intended as one of many still necessary responses to the Gulbenkian Commission's plea to "open the social sciences" (Wallerstein et al. 1996). The Commission's 1996 report argued that the intellectual

Introduction 3

division of labour established among the social sciences in the nineteenth century reflected a corresponding geopolitics of knowledge production and reproduction with respect to different positions in global structures of economic, political, and military power. Within that division of labour, the task of sociology, and the primary intellectual concern of canonised classics like Karl Marx and Max Weber, had been to explain why it had been the Western world that had pioneered modernity, capitalism, or both. The task of dealing with "Oriental" and otherwise non-Western societies had instead fallen to anthropology and Oriental studies, concerned with why these parts of the world were not or could not become modern (Wallerstein et al. 1996: 25; Randeria 1999a; Patel 2006). Drawing on these findings, the present monograph zooms in on the enduring impact of the nineteenth-century intellectual division of labour on the sociological analysis of inequalities. It argues that, for sociology as a discipline of Western modernity, claiming universal relevance required erasing the particular historical circumstances of the European colonial expansion in the Americas, of the colonial and imperial conquest of the non-European world, as well as of the impact of slave labour on colonial plantations upon the development of Western societies from the elaboration of its categories of analysis. The grounding of central fields of – especially macrosociological – theory and research in the epistemological premises of the Western European context systematically produced methodological and geopolitical blind spots.

My approach, as all others, is geopolitically, intellectually and epistemically situated. I was socialised in a white middle-class Romanian household during the last decade of Ceauşescu's reign and raised by two teachers of Romanian literature and lovers of grammar and history who had had little to no opportunity of travelling abroad. After getting a degree in English and German languages and literatures in Bucharest, I went to Germany to study sociology. It was not before I had obtained a PhD in sociology that I acknowledged that I was a migrant and was in Germany to stay. I acquired increasing awareness of my lesser Europeanness in a Western European environment through the difficulties that the spelling of my last name posed to everyone outside of my country of birth and the uneasiness that my Romanian passport occasioned border authorities and myself. Acquaintance with dependency theory, world-systems analysis and the modernity/coloniality perspective during my research stay in the United States shortly before 9/11 provided me with an analytical framework into which peripheral experiences and structural dependencies at the global level made perfect sense, as did their marginalisation in mainstream social theory.

My position is therefore informed by a biographical and intellectual background in a state socialist regime, sociological training in Germany and the United States, and a long-standing research interest in the theoretical production of Eastern Europe and Latin America. It thus builds on several related and complementary positions: (1) on world-systems analysis' agenda for unthinking nineteenth-century social scientific paradigms and on the corresponding critique of the nation-state as an unquestioned unit of analysis (Wallerstein 1991c); (2) on postcolonial studies' critique of Eurocentrism in general and of Orientalism in particular (Said 1978); (3) on dependency theory's focus on the entanglements between patterns of inequality as reflecting colonial power relations between metropoles and colonies (Cardoso and Faletto 1969; Frank 1972); (3) on the decolonial perspective's conceptualisation of modernity/coloniality as eminently relational and joint products of Europe's colonial expansion in the Americas in the sixteenth century and of the resulting geopolitics of knowledge production (Coronil 1996, Mignolo 2000); (4) on several works locating Eastern Europe and the Balkans in-between colonial and imperial designs of the modern world as well as in-between Eurocentric and Orientalist frameworks of thought (Bădescu et al. 1995; Bakic-Hayden 1995; Todorova 1997).

The present work draws on these related positions with respect to the study of social inequality and their affinities with recent developments within postcolonial approaches to sociological theory more generally. It therefore conceives of peripheral, colonial, as well as neo- or postcolonial realities of the past 500 years as part of modernity's dark side, the inequality contexts of which can illuminate the blind spots of Western inequality theories. Accordingly, the hypothesis advanced in the following is that the difficulties currently experienced with the integration of further – but not necessarily new – dimensions and categories of social inequality as part of standard inequality studies arise from sociology's conceptualisation of capitalist modernity as due only to endogenous factors such as Western Europe's "Industrial Revolution", and the systematic omission of exogenous ones, such as colonial and imperial exploitation. Viewing categories like race and ethnicity as either new or secondary dimensions of social inequality rather than as integral to the specifically modern pattern of social stratification, and disregarding the global dimension of inequality processes accordingly pertain to what Raewyn Connell has labelled the "gestures of exclusion" of metropolitan theory (Connell 2007: 46).

Past Legacies and Current Problems

The sociology of social inequalities, central both to classical sociology and to present-day macrosociological concerns, is particularly illustrative of some of these structural gaps around which the discipline has been constituted since its beginnings.

The early sociology of social inequality was linked to the socioeconomic context of Western European industrial society, in which class divisions, labour migration, and mass poverty constituted the main social questions (Kreckel 2008). The consequent focus on class and status as core categories of inequality research, and of the nation-state as the corresponding unit of analysis, lent an Occidentalist bias and a methodologically nationalist framework to both mainstream social inequality research and prominent approaches to related issues such as social change, development, and the conceptualisation of modernity.

Late twentieth- and early twenty-first-century analysts of social inequality gradually expanded the standard categories of examination – in part to account

Introduction 5

for within-country inequalities, and in part to account for inequality on a global scale. They included gender, race, and ethnicity among the standard categories of inequality studies, and introduced new dimensions beyond income, educational attainment, and one's individual position in the labour market.

The core of mainstream inequality research today, however, is still represented by the study of intergenerational income and class mobility limited mainly to OECD countries. This continued focus reflects the field's debt to its original context of reference, Western European industrial society. The place of racial, ethnic, and gender inequality within the general field of inequality research still seems to be ill fitted, and none of the three is systematically articulated with global inequality patterns. Moreover, increasing support for the idea that globalisation widens the between-country inequality gap has only led to transferring the unit of analysis in studies of income inequality from the national to the global level. Still lacking is a coherent and comprehensive framework for the analysis of world inequality that departs from a developmental view of the world in which the West represents the epitome of the modern age.

Tellingly, interest in the study of global inequalities was aroused by the unprecedented increase in income inequalities in the United States and Great Britain since the 1980s (Korzeniewicz and Moran 2009). At the same time, theoretically and methodologically different approaches to global inequalities developed in the formerly colonised and peripheral parts of the world did not become incorporated into the apparatus of general social theory. Instead, they were considered particular responses to different and unrelated pathologies of the "non-modern" world and as such ungeneralisable and irrelevant to the world as a whole. Thus, today's mainstream inequality research is still characterised by an ongoing Occidentalist perspective and narrow empirical basis as well as a view of inequality focusing on differentials of wealth and income.

In the 2000s, debates largely revolved around World Bank findings assessing the relationship between inequality and economic growth in the previous decades. Whether they concluded that "growth is good for the poor" (Dollar and Kraay 2002) or that "inequality is bad for the poor" (Ravallion 2005), their explicit focus was on poverty as the issue that overrides inequality in poor countries and therefore was to be tackled first. Subsequent discussions accordingly centred on identifying the most accurate methodology and statistical measures for determining the impact of economic growth on the poverty rates of individual countries, while global inequality was understood as the gap between rich and poor at the world level. Mounting evidence of a steep increase in the income ratio between the world's richest and the world's poorest since 1980, as well as ever more data on rising inequality within the largest growing economies of China and India have mostly upstaged the ongoing World Bank discourse of mean income convergence between countries and declining global inequality between world citizens (Sutcliffe 2007; Duggan 2013; Milanovic 2012).

The same is true for the study of ethnic and racial inequality, oftentimes relegated to the new residual category tellingly labelled "non-class inequalities"

(Pakulski 2002). In the case of Europe, systematic analyses of racial inequality are prevented by lack of widespread acknowledgment of the relevance of the category of race and of the enduring presence of non-White populations on the European continent (Hine, Keaton, and Small 2009). In turn, acknowledgment of the fact that stratification patterns outside the Western industrial context tend to defy simple class analysis is more common:

> In the Andean highland, Indian has come to mean as much a class category as an ethnic one, but in the Amazon, it still implies autonomy and the existence of a different social world [...] In Mexico and in the Andes, ethnic categories originate in racist classifications of the sixteenth century, but have evolved into something much more complicated [...] As one moves up the stratification system, the significance of cultural signals recedes and that of phenotype increases. Upward mobility is fluid and possible but remains characterised by the advantages of racial whiteness. (Hoffman and Centeno 2003: 379f.)

In Brazil, despite recent improvement still one of the most unequal countries in Latin America, the bulk of the explanation for inequality is of a non-class nature:

> Blacks weigh less at birth than whites, have a greater probability to die before completing one year of age, have a lesser probability to frequent a day-care centre and repeat school years more often than whites, hence leaving school with inferior educational levels than whites do. Young blacks die in a violent form in bigger numbers than young whites and have lesser probabilities of finding a job. If they do find a job, they receive less than half the wage that whites do [...]. Throughout all their life, they receive poorer health assistance and end up living less and in greater poverty than the whites. (IPEA 2007: 281, my translation).

On average, Afro-descendants in Latin America have a shorter life expectancy, live in poorer conditions, have lower levels of formal education and have less access to public services than the Latin American population as a whole; this tendency is even more pronounced in the case of women (Antón et al. 2009; Costa 2011; Faguaga Iglesias 2011). Likewise, Africa's racial and ethnic differences largely mirror the classification policies of past colonial regimes. Accordingly, race and ethnicity, rather than class or status, provide the bulk of the explanation for the continent's inequality patterns:

> Namibia and Zimbabwe combine colonial settlements with pronounced indigenous underdevelopment, without much of the late apartheid cross-race industrialization of South Africa. But southern Africa apart, African inequality is more a pattern of exclusive ethnic circles, than the Latin American hierarchies of White-Mestizo-Indian and White-Mulatto-Black. (Therborn 2006: 31)

Gender issues surface more systematically in quantitative analyses, where gender features among the categories to be measured, yet is seldom decisive in the elaboration of the theoretical framework that preceded the analysis. Relevant theory-building in the field of inequality of sex and gender occurs within gender or women's studies, but most of the time it does not significantly affect the class-based "universal frames" of mainstream inequality research, which "validate the experiences of white males as a proper lens for reading the realities of groups as diverse as black women, poor Latinas, and white lesbians" (Allen and Chung 2000: 803). The same holds true even more for the treatment of sexual orientation. This has led feminist theorists to diagnose a "missing feminist revolution" (Stacey and Thorne 1985) for sociological theory as a whole in the mid-1980s and, more recently, to describe the division of labour between the sociology of class inequality and the feminist treatment of gender disparities as "sociological inequality discourse without gender and feminist theory without class" (Gottschall 2000: 15). The focus of the newer intersectionality research on multiple processes of discrimination on the basis of gender, class, race, ethnicity, and sexuality tries to bridge the divide thus established, yet often ends up dealing with subjective identity categories defined in terms of the respective class, ethnic, racial, and gender differences, rather than with the structural causes behind the unequal distribution of resources along gender, racial, ethnic, and class lines. The analysis is therefore often located on the meso and micro levels of identity and discrimination, rather than on macrostructures of inequality (Klinger and Knapp 2007; Roth 2013).

Some Current Solutions

Solutions to this categorial inadequacy/insufficiency of the social inequality research apparatus have included several strategies that targeted some or all of the deficits addressed above, mostly by effecting conceptual changes.

At a *philosophical level*, Amartya Sen's question "inequality of what?" sought to expand the scope of the very undertaking by suggesting that the narrow focus on income distribution be replaced with a broader understanding of human capabilities as conducive to both freedom and development (Sen 1992; for a critique see Domingues 2006). Referred to since then as the "capability approach", his focus on equality as capability to function as a human being has provided the basis for the United Nations' Human Development Reports and the elaboration of the Human Development Index.

The *theoretical level* saw a broad range of proposals. The conceptualisation of "inequalities" as plural (Kreckel 1983), while apparently banal, entailed in fact destabilising the centrality of class (*Klasse*) and strata (*Schichten*) as the main structuring principles of inequality in affluent societies on the one hand (Berger 2003: 474) and ethically informing the inequality discussion on the other (Therborn 2006, 2013). The ethical component also provided the basis for the recent shift in economic discourse from "inequality" to "inequity" (World Bank 2006;

Kreckel 2008). The more consequential reconsideration of the notion of caste both within and outside India (Hoffman and Centeno 2003; Randeria 2002; Patel 2006), meant to account for the allegedly non-modern in the midst of modern societies, partially drew on the severe critique of the older caste model of race relations in the United States (Hurst 2007).

Finally, on the *methodological plane*, the debate surrounding the relationship between globalisation and inequality has led theorists to further differentiate among *inequality, polarization, poverty*, and *misery* (Castells 1998: 71ff.) on the one hand – thus, however, maintaining the focus on the material distribution of resources – and either *relational* vs. *distributive inequality* (Kreckel 2004: 19ff.) or *vital, existential*, and *resource inequality* (Therborn 2006, 2013), thereby making hitherto secondary and lesser inequality dimensions such as life expectancy, health, knowledge, and recognition/discrimination into integral parts of the research on inequality, on the other. Likewise, Charles Tilly's (1998) comprehensive account of inequality-generating mechanisms stressed the relational and categorical aspects of inequality by distinguishing among *exploitation, opportunity-hoarding, emulation*, and *adaptation* as mechanisms of inequality production and reproduction between genders, races, ethnic groups, and classes, and advocated thus a return to classical sociology's dynamic, relational approach to inequality. Nevertheless, even the more prominent among these proposals have tended so far to be treated rather as innovative terms of individual authors than as contributions to a makeover of the mainstream conceptual framework of social inequality approaches. In terms of its capacity to assess new inequality phenomena in a changing global context, as well as to adequately explain the mechanisms of their production, the field therefore remains heterogeneous and highly divided.

Consequently, an analysis of global inequalities in light of the ideological tensions inherent to Western modernity would have to transcend its epistemic and theoretical frame of reference in order to complement the view on inequalities from within modernity with one from its "dark side" – not from its exteriority, but from coloniality (Klinger and Knapp 2007; Mignolo 2012).

The Mainstream Model: Transformative Modernity

The European modernity's repertoire of promises is usually drawn from key moments in Western history and their symbolic role within a linear trajectory intended to disseminate to the entire world. Tellingly, after the "overcoming of feudalism", this trajectory only features positively connoted entries: the Renaissance, the Reformation, the Enlightenment, the French Revolution, and the Industrial Revolution. Together, they embody the attainability of humanism, rationality, equality, scientificity, and progress. The ideals thus postulated consequently became the criteria by which the gradual reduction of social inequalities – the guiding principle of rational social organisation – should be measured.

Introduction 9

For the theorisation of social inequality, this meant fitting Karl Marx's theory of class antagonism and Max Weber's complementary three-layered model of social stratification along the lines of class, status and party to the entire world to the extent that it became modern. Thus, a one-size-fits-all model was posited in which the history of the world was either the history of class struggle (in the Marxian variant) or a mixture of class and status (in the Weberian interpretation). Inequalities of gender, race, ethnicity, religious denomination, age, and sexual orientation, when taken into account at all, were viewed as disparities of the second degree (Allen and Chung 2000; Bhambra 2007a). In the particular case of race and ethnicity, which had received explicit, although not elaborate treatment in the works of the classics, relegation to secondary status occurred either according to the Marxist tradition – i.e., as superstructure, or to the Weberian framework – i.e., as a form of status difference which would gradually lose significance in modern society. This analytical framework has been employed throughout most of the Western sociology of social inequality in the twentieth century. For a long time, racism and race relations were considered objects of study of colonial and postcolonial contexts, especially South Africa and the United States, while ethnicity and forms of ethnic nationalism outside of the classical countries of immigration were dealt with either as past phenomena or as results of post-World War II independence processes in ex-colonial countries. This perception gradually changed as of the 1970s, when Western Europe turned into the recipient of large migratory flows from the state socialist Second World and the decolonised Third World, ethnic conflicts broke out in the midst of Europe after the Communist demise, and political regionalism became a Western European phenomenon (Bader 1998: 96f.). The resurgence of nationalism and ethnic identity prompted a revival of interest in race and ethnicity as forms of social identity more generally and as dimensions of social inequality in particular. While assimilation into the national class structure of the receiving society had until that point been considered the eventual outcome of virtually every migration process, ethnic group formation now came to the fore as a permanent characteristic of post-industrial societies, in which ethnicity had replaced class as a principle of social stratification:

> The new word is "ethnicity", and the new usage is the steady expansion of the term "ethnic group" from minority and marginal subgroups at the edges of society – groups expected to assimilate, to disappear, to continue as survivals, exotic, or troublesome – to major elements of a society. There is something *new* afoot in the world, and [...] we may label it "ethnicity". (Glazer and Moynihan 1975: 25f., emphasis added)

The contribution of the European colonial expansion and decolonisation to the changed circumstances did not enter into the explanation except, at most, as an analogy with inner-European territorial conflicts over ethnicity and religion, i.e., as internal colonialism.[1] When exogenous factors were taken into account, they were only supposed to explain the coexistence of class and ethnic stratification in colonial societies as a result of intervention by the metropole, not, however, the social structure of the metropole itself, paradoxically seen as having developed – and stratified – endogenously (Hechter 1971).

Similarly, gender only became a legitimate category of analysis in its own right within Western sociology once it had successfully entered most other academic departments due to the feminist movement and been institutionalised in its turn as women's or gender studies. Within the analysis of social inequality, its place, as that of the other "non-class" factors, remains ill-fitted (Kreckel 1989, 2004).

Consequently, the theorisation of gender, race, and ethnicity did not manage to dismantle – or even unsettle – the canon of the sociology of social inequality to the extent of incorporating them as dimensions of social stratification on a par with those of class and status. Rather, with the rise of feminist theory on the one hand, and the revival of sociological interest in the issues of race and ethnicity on the other, the initial choice between Marxist and Weberian theories of inequality was translated into an intellectual division of labour along the lines of Weber's distinction of class and status: the sociology of social inequality deals with structural disparities, while gender, racial, and ethnic studies analyse what counts as merely cultural difference (Weiß 2001). Besides conceiving of gender, race and ethnicity as types of status [*Stand*] that result in either second-degree or "new" inequalities, this decoupling of tasks amounts to a "culturalisation of sociological analysis" (Eder 2001: 56) with repercussions on its social structural components as well.

At the same time, research on social inequality relations, especially income inequality, has been circumscribed by the focus on the nation-state as the unit of analysis. Studies of global inequality, to the extent that they have been undertaken at all, overwhelmingly consist of comparisons of wealth and income disparities between nations.[2] As such, they are primarily guided by the quest for empirical evidence for either the convergence or the divergence hypothesis, as indicated by long-term trends in the distribution of income between rich and poor countries. Yet neither a shift towards a focus on patterns of global stratification nor towards greater attention devoted to spatial relations across national boundaries follow from such studies. It is only relatively recently that this uncritical conflation of legally and administratively defined space with sociological units of analysis has been criticised as "methodological nationalism" (Smith 1995; Wimmer and Glick Schiller 2002; Beck 2004; Heidenreich 2006; Weiß 2005). The solution advanced has often been that of positing the world society as the study unit of both relational and distributive inequalities (Kreckel 2004: 45; 50) and thus viewing the North-

---

1 The internal colonialism approach had however been initially developed within the context of Latin America and the United States and therefore meant to explain postcolonial contexts and classical immigration contexts, respectively (see Hurst 2007: 178).

2 For an overview and critique see Bergesen and Bata 2002; Weiß 2005; Kreckel 2004, 2008; Turner and Babones 2006, Korzeniewicz and Moran 2009.

Introduction   11

South-divide as the main antagonism of the present world (instead of the class antagonism of yore). Despite internal differences, such criticisms, however, have tended to offer merely methodological solutions to what is regularly perceived as a methodological problem, and therefore not meant to question or transcend the limits of the Eurocentric tradition on which theories of social inequality in modern Western societies have been based. The linear, stage-by-stage development of (national or global) stratification patterns towards the gradual overcoming of inequalities – as present both in the modernisationist approach (Parsons 1970) and underlying the Kuznets hypothesis on the transition from the agrarian sector to urban industrialisation – remains a valid option:

> All these claims accept […] the view that sociology's central concept, society, has been equated with one of modernity's major socio-political references, the nation-state. They also agree with the fact that this equation between society and the nation-state takes an endogenous or internalist explanation of social change for granted and ask for a thorough revision of the self-sufficient image of society. Interestingly, then, these writers […] share the claim that the 'nation-state' has become the 'normal' form of society in modernity – with the interesting but underdeveloped proviso that this applies best to the Western world. (Chernilo 2006: 8)

Nor has the innovative potential inherent in different feminist theorists' demands for full-fledged incorporation of gender inequalities on the one hand and for the inclusion of supra- and subnational inequality contexts on the other, managed so far to substantially transform the analytical framework of studies of social stratification. Rather, the critique it prompted has trickled away into what tends to be considered subfields of the same. Tellingly for the lack of dialogue within social inequality studies, such developments coexist with their analytical opposites inside national cultures of scholarship. Thus, in the latter part of the twentieth century, the debate on social inequality research in the context of Germany involved rather minor modifications of the classical analytical model – to which, however, major importance was attached. An entire series of new stratification models thus produced claims that class and status are obsolete and inadequate categories for capturing the supposed transition from the industrial to the post-industrial or risk society in the West, yet they at the same time attempt to explain current relations of inequality in terms of the class- and/or status-derived categories of social milieu, life style, or everyday life conduct (Beck 1986; Berger and Hradil 1990; Schulze 1992). All of these supposedly new conceptualisations represent a mere watering down of the more rigid categories of class and status, or the advancement of a model of "class relations without classes" (Kreckel 2004: 222) that reinforces the above-discussed tendency towards the culturalisation of sociological analysis, at the same time as it contributes to the delegitimisation of macrostructural conceptions of inequality-generating mechanisms and collective actors (Eder 2001: 32). Consequently, such conceptualisations also leave structural inequalities along the lines of gender, race, and ethnicity untouched – not to mention undeveloped and undertheorised. In the process, they maintain the nation-state framework to which the classical dimensions of class and status were tailored.[3] The underlying implication is that these categories have either never been or are no longer relevant for Western societies, in which gender equality has been enforced, ethnicities are regulated through citizenship, and race has only become a problem since postcolonial immigration. It seems to follow that their incorporation into the analytical canon does not represent a structural necessity.

The modernity to which this analytical model refers therefore restricts itself to being a transformation to a qualitatively new stage – i.e., to encompassing the transition from feudal to industrial and post-industrial social structures and the corresponding changes of degree in inequalities of status and class within national societies. Criticisms to this perspective accordingly remain internal to modernity: Even while they aim at conceiving of modernity as a global(ised) structure, they define the respective "non-modern" out of existence in terms of its sociological relevance.

Telling, in this vein, are once again the inroads which the sociology of gender was able – and allowed – to make in the scope of the discipline as a whole: On the one hand, the substantial contributions of the gender perspective, including the sociology of sex and gender inequality, seemed for a while to point in the direction of a reconceptualisation of modernity as gendered, i.e., as a system in which access to privileges and rights is regulated according to gender and is as such systematically unequal. On the other, this qualification of the canonical definition of modernity was soon subsumed to the general one of modernity as transformation, in which the gendered distribution of modernity's positive achievements was just another stage to be overcome in the course of a "second modernity" (Beck 1999), not an integral part of modernity as such. The tendency of accommodating so-called "particular aspects" – such as gender – within the core categories of sociological analysis has thus not only allowed mainstream sociology to continue in a "pre-feminist mode" (Acker 1992: 65), but persistently results in the relegation of further "particularities" – like race, ethnicity, sexuality – to the second tier of sociological concerns.

Disparities caused by the subaltern position of the social actors in the epistemic hierarchy of the existing global balance of power remain hereby unaddressed, as do the differences between hegemonic and peripheral languages in the context of the world-wide knowledge production (Mignolo 2000; Connell 2007) alongside other, manifold asymmetries that accompanied the colonisation as the overall process of expansion, study, conquest and the imperial homogenisation of the western capitalist modern trend after 1492 (Hall 1997). Much like in terms of gender, but on a greater scale, sociology thus largely persists in what could be analogously called a "colonial mode" (Boatcă and Costa 2010; Seidman 2013; Steinmetz 2013),

---

3   For a detailed critique of the specific German debate on the dissolution of social classes see Geißler 2001 and Geißler 2002.

which only allows limited treatment of issues long defined as non- or pre-modern and which prevents a global encompassing perspective on historical power hierarchies – both crucial components for the theorisation of social inequalities. Postcolonial critique has been increasingly seen as an adequate corrective of such structural constraints. On account of the fact that, unlike the feminist critique, the postcolonial one is explicitly directed at core sociological categories, especially the sociological conceptions of modernity, it seems to harbour "the capacity to effect what is 'missing' in other 'revolutions'" (Bhambra 2007a: 873).

The Global Model: Colonial, Racial(ised), and Gendered Modernity

The glossing over of critical disparities of the modern world in the North Atlantic social scientific discourse has been a central concern for more than one theoretical perspective in recent years. For post- and decolonial theories, the abstract universalism of Enlightenment thought represents a discursive strategy for dealing with the geopolitical impact of the European "discovery" of the New World, as well as a strategy of rule. For one thing, the idea of a universal history subsuming the whole of mankind under one "project of (Western) modernity" with identical stages and goals provided the legitimating rhetoric for the further colonial expansion. At the same time, upholding European superiority in relation to the New World required, first – translating the negative experience of otherness into the positive idea of "discovery" – and, second – turning the European colonial relation into a "blind spot" (Hesse 2007: 657) within the Occidental self-image.

The Discovery of Otherness – Social Theoretical Implications

The glorification of the discovery, and, parallel to it, the establishment of Western hegemony occurred with the help of what Aníbal Quijano has termed the foundational myths behind the propagation of Eurocentrism: On the one hand, *evolutionism* – the notion that human civilisation advanced through a unilinear sequence of stages leading up to the Western model of capitalist modernity – and, on the other, *dualism* – the view that differences between Europeans and non-Europeans could be traced back to insuperable natural categories such as primitive-civilised, irrational-rational, traditional-modern (Quijano 2000a). They entered the conceptualisation of sociology as the two major cleavages characterising modern society, which it was the task of a discipline concerned with this new form of society to analyse and describe: Temporally, *the epochal break* accounted for the transition from agrarian tradition to industrial modernity, a process consequently seen as evolutionary. Spatially and at the same time ontologically, it was *cultural differences* that made sense of the features distinguishing Western European societies from the rest of the world according to the above-mentioned dual pattern (Hall 1992; Connell 1997; Bhambra 2007). The theorisation of these defining moments of Occidental modernity hence constituted as much a central concern for the classics of the discipline as they did for the main theorists of the latter part of the twentieth century.

The notion of Western Europe's *epochal break* with a feudal past in favour of a modern present permeated the whole range of approaches to societal change and reverberated throughout conceptualisations of social inequality, seen as changing accordingly from the former to the latter stage: For Marx, both feudalism and modern industrial society represented instances in the dialectics of class struggles making up the history of the modern world. In turn, Weber's distinction between status and class was meant to capture two moments in the inequality structures of pre-modern vs. modern society, respectively (Parkin 1971: 38; Böröcz 1997; Kreckel 2004: 64ff.), while allowing for a temporary overlap between the two. In Durkheim's view, class conflict in industrial societies was a mere indicator of the tensions inherent in the transition from mechanical to organic solidarity, in the course of which both class and racial (but not gender!) inequalities were meant to diminish and eventually disappear (Lehmann 1995; Hurst 2007: 209ff.). Reliance on the analytical categories of class and status, including their later derivatives – milieus, life styles, life conduct – for an explanation of inequality structures, social conflict, and social mobility, is thus premised on a linear sequence of change from an agrarian through an industrial and up to a post-industrial or service society, in which processes of class formation, identification, and dissolution play a central part. The prevalence of post-agrarian industrial employment, and, with it, the salience of class relative to other processes of group formation on the basis of ethnicity, racial affiliation, or religious denomination, have however been unique to Europe (Therborn 1995). At the same time, the persistent focus on class as the relevant model for the analysis of processes of stratification and patterns of social conflict throughout the twentieth century disregards the specifically Western European character of the class phenomenon as it downplays the importance of the ethnic and racial components of conflict and inequality and, with it, the dynamics of colonialism. On the one hand, European overseas settlement and conquest prompted massive emigration out of Europe from 1500 until World War II, and thereby eased both the pressures on income distribution and the social conflict *within* the continent. At the same time, outbound migration reinforced the inner-European ethnic homogeneity that successive waves of ethnic levelling occurring throughout Europe until the mid-twentieth century had succeeded to create (Therborn 1995). Class organisation and identification thus gained preponderance over ethnic allegiance. With the reversal of the migration trend in the latter half of the twentieth century toward large-scale immigration from Europe's ex-colonies into the metropole, and – to a lesser extent – with the breakdown of the Communist regimes in Eastern Europe, ethnic conflict came to the fore as a largely extra-European problem that increasingly posed a threat to Europe. The conceptualisation of European industrial society as "modern" and of non-European agrarian societies as "pre-modern" allows it to conceive of them as disconnected contexts of social inequality, to be explained and analysed in terms of class on the one hand and of ethnicity/race on the other. In turn, from a post- and decolonial perspective, ethnicity and race do not represent relatively "new" categories to be taken into account in the European context only since the 1970s, but ones that have gained more sociological visibility since that time on account of having become significant in the geopolitical core of the discipline – Western Europe (Boatcă 2010).

Cultural differences, constructed around the theorisation of Occidental superiority over the rest of the world and the uniqueness of the Western experience, were conceptualised on the basis of the nature-culture dichotomy – which underlay both evolutionism and dualism and at the same time provided the necessary linkage between them. Thereby, the reorganisation of the older principle of gender domination around the counterposed notions of nature and culture yielded the feminine nature – masculine culture binary, associating the former with immutable, irrational wilderness and chaos and the latter with its opposite – the dynamics of constructing a rational social order. Gender differences within Western Europe, as well as gender, racial and ethnic differences between the West and the non-West were consequently naturalised or culturalised according to the same cumulative principle: Women, children, the elderly, the poor, non-Whites, people of the periphery, and animals were sorted under the natural world, and hence seen as disorderly, unworthy of reward, legitimately exploitable, and in need of control. White men from or in the core entered the categorisation as culture-creators and nation-builders, in charge of the domination, control, or guardianship of the former (Dussel 1995; Pelizzon 2002; Tucker 2002; Federici 2004).

With the emphasis on Reason, which, alongside the notion of progress and the faith in scientific development, characterised European Enlightenment thought, the distinction irrational-rational became the overarching pair of this binary logic and as such central to the conceptualisation of modern civilisation. Part of the self-definition of modernity in this context had been the notion of the increasing pacification of society in the course of the transition from a pre-modern to a modern social order. The state monopoly on the use of violence, according to Weber a result of gradual rationalisation processes in the West, was therefore seen as characteristic of modern societies, while uncontrolled and irrational violent behaviour allegedly distinguished pre-modern ones. Violence, i.e., the illegitimate, private use of force, was therefore relegated spatially outside modernity, and temporally in its past (Connell 1997; Liell 2002; Boatcă and Lamnek 2003). As in the case of racial and ethnic issues, it was thus not incorporated into the analysis of modernity until the late twentieth century, after two state-sanctioned world wars inside Europe had induced the notion of the "failed century" (Scheerer 2001) of an otherwise linear pacification process. Once again, this exclusive focus on inner-European developments posits that both modernity and its Other are understandable in terms of endogenous causalities; it thus engenders systematic disregard for the violence that modern European states had perpetrated in the colonies and in other non-European settings at the same time as their national societies were being gradually pacified (Connell 1997; Knöbl 2006, 2012). Instead, viewing both private and state-induced violence – whether as conquest, colonial exploitation, or in its extreme form of genocide – as constitutive for the interconnected history of European modernity and European colonial expansion requires revising the stark antagonism underlying the distinction "peaceful-violent" (implicit in "civilised-barbarian") as a necessary supplement to "irrational-rational" and "traditional-modern". Rather than an irrational counterpart to the rationality being developed in the European metropoles, violence was both a prerequisite for the European colonial conquest and for the metropolitan exploitation of the colonies' resources towards the building of the affluent European modernity. The condition of possibility of the Amerindian as modernity's first legitimately exploitable Other therefore was that violence was sacrificial, i.e., part of the inevitable costs of civilising, modernising or developing the uncivilised, the non-modern, the underdeveloped – a view first articulated by Juan Ginés de Sepúlveda against Bartolomé de las Casas in the sixteenth century (Dussel 1995; Dussel 2007). While Marx and Weber were seldom explicit about whether violence is an exclusive attribute of pre-modern as opposed to modern societies, and while Weber's treatment of modernity and capitalism is not openly evolutionary in outlook, the rational-irrational dichotomy as a principle of differentiation between the West and the non-West is common to all of their approaches. The link between modernity and rationality in the works of the classics therefore rests on the experience of colonialism and the construction of irrationality it entailed.[4]

The Colonial Relation as Blind Spot

A reconceptualisation of the standard dimensions of social inequality in light of the power relations engendered on the colonial side of modernity does not restrict itself to a mere enlargement of the list from class and status to gender, race, ethnicity, sexuality, age, and religious denomination. Focusing instead on processes of othering as systematic and ongoing practices of gendering, racialisation, and ethnicisation allows us to grasp the dynamic, rather than the static aspect of social inequality and stratification. Othering as "the defining into existence of a group of people who are identifiable, from the standpoint of a group with the capacity to dominate, as inferior" (Schwalbe 2000: 777) became the quintessential mechanism for the production of exploitable natural, economic, and labour resources of the expanding capitalist modernity as of the sixteenth century. Thereby, socioeconomic conditions in the world-system's

---

4 "For many educated European men, the poor, women, and colonized were identified with unbridled passions. They were defined as wild, irrational, unable to control their impulses, and naturally prone to emotion. The very notion of reason developed in the context of these social definitions of irrationality and colonialism. Marx, Weber, and Durkheim participated in this discourse of colonialism and irrationality, as they defined non-modern peoples as less rational and less developed than modern Europeans. Women, too, were often labelled as representing the irrational. They rarely questioned the superiority of modernity, and often assumed it was inevitable" (Tucker 2002: 10).

Introduction 17

peripheries as well as supposedly non-modern social relations within core areas were relegated outside modernity and thus systematically rendered invisible for its analytical sociological frame (Connell 1997). Accordingly, chattel slavery and its consequences, racially segregated work forces both in the core and in the periphery, exploitative bourgeoisies and "dual economies" in Latin America, patriarchal gender relations in Africa and the Middle East, and the coexistence of forms of wage and non-wage labour in all colonised areas were seen as feudal remnants and proof of the periphery's backwardness up to the twentieth century. As such, they did not qualify as products of inequality relations under capitalism and did not go into its theorisation. Consequently, the radical reorganisation of differentiation criteria yielding the racial and ethnic structure of the European overseas colonies, first, and then of Western Europe's further emerging Others, such as "the Orient", "Eastern Europe", and Africa, is for its most part unaccounted for in the conceptualisation of inequality as *social difference* – which remains largely premised on a class structure.

The notion of *colonial difference*, on the other hand, has been employed to this very end both within Indian Subaltern Studies and Latin American decolonial thought, but given a different scope within each. While Partha Chatterjee (1993) developed the term in order for it to apply to an analysis of the racial practices of the colonial state in India as different from the modern (British) state, Walter Mignolo (1995) advanced it as the common denominator of coloniality as a worldwide phenomenon. Thus, inequalities ensuing from the production of the colonial difference since the European overseas expansion are prime examples for the "silences", "absences" (Santos 2004: 14ff.) or "blind spots" (Hesse 2007) that the definition of modernity as a particularly Western European achievement has created within sociological analysis.

The division of labour between core and periphery that resulted from this classification conceptualised *modernity* as the location of capital accumulation, political control, and scientific study of the rest of the world, while the *coloniality* of lesser economic and state power, traditional knowledges, and inferior humanity was analytically relegated to the undifferentiated residual category of the non-modern.

Seen from this theoretical vantage point, the modernity that a global sociology should study in order to encompass such multiplicity of processes in their historical unfolding and structural interconnectedness is not, as in mainstream sociology, merely transformative, but also, and necessarily, colonial, gendered, and racialised. Rather than second-degree categories in relation to class and status, such categories of analysis as gender, race, ethnicity, religious denomination and sexual orientation are basic structuring principles of an essentially capitalist and colonial modernity, around which enduring processes of othering have been defined since at least the sixteenth century.

If sociology was born of a need to understand modernity (Baechler 2007: 205), its analytical categories should duly reflect modernity's colonial as well as its racist character. Instead, as shown above, in most of its classic and contemporary approaches to social inequality, modernity exhausts itself in being either merely

18 *Global Inequalities Beyond Occidentalism*

progress or a variation thereof. Acceptable indicators of modernity thus defined range from industrial to post-industrial societies, from liberal to neoliberal market economies and political regimes, and from enlightened to postmodern worldviews. As such, they not only restrict the definition to what Enrique Dussel has called the Second Modernity (Dussel 2007: 242ff.) under the auspices of British hegemony in the world-system, but also reduce the categories by which inequality can be assessed to class, status or a derivative category. Race, gender and ethnicity are relegated, if at all, to lower ranks in a hierarchy of analytical principles that reveal the narrow scope of modernity's self-description.

The plea for a sociology of global inequalities advanced here consequently draws on the insights of gender studies, world-systems analysis, and post- and decolonial perspectives in order to suggest three substantive and interrelated modifications of the mainstream study of social inequality.

First, a shift from the focus on the nation-state as sole unit of analysis to a global focus encompassing worldwide centre-periphery relations alongside nationwide and regional inequalities and the connections between them; second, a systematic and explicit engagement with the theories of social change implicit in concepts of social inequality and the conclusions entailed for the corresponding definition of modernity and the modern; and third, an emphasis on the dynamics behind the emergence of categories along which inequality structures were historically constructed, i.e., on processes of othering such as gendering, racialisation, and ethnicisation, rather than on static categories such as gender, race, and ethnicity.

In the following, these necessary corrections will serve as a criteria catalogue with the help of which classical theories of social inequality and stratification, as present both in their initial formulation by Karl Marx and Max Weber, and in approaches building on them, will be examined with regard to their explanatory potential for a sociology of global inequalities. Besides its impact on sociology as a discipline that emerged as an institutionalised attempt at understanding precisely this modernity and still defines itself in these narrow terms, a critique of classical theories of inequality that consistently takes coloniality into account could accomplish a translation between the claim to universality inherent in its current theoretical canon on the one hand and the "blind spots" resulting from the particularity of a single epistemological perspective on the other, i.e., between the overrepresentation of modernity and the underrepresentation of coloniality. As such, it would be an essential contribution to the unthinking of dominant social theoretic paradigms and to the indisciplining of institutionalised structures of knowledge on which the larger processes of political, economic, social and epistemological decolonisation depend.

Structure of the Book

In the works of sociology's canonised classics, the issue of social inequality was not an aim in itself, but was always embedded in a larger theory of society, in its turn tied to a theory of modernity and capitalism. To both Marx's and Weber's theories of class corresponded not only the nation-state framework of their emergence, but also specific theories of social change in the West, such as industrialisation and rationalisation, as well as an understanding of the dynamics of the processes of class formation behind the production and reproduction of inequality, as in the case of proletarianisation in Marx or social closure in Weber. Today's theories of global or transnational inequalities in turn are first and foremost theories of globalisation – of which the issue of inequality is an illustration – rather than new approaches to inequality consistent with a theory of global society.

In the following, it is therefore argued that a reconceptualisation of inequality that is both theoretically informed and methodologically consistent would have to cater to the implications of shifts from national and Western structures to global structures in all three dimensions: the upscaling of the unit of analysis, the uncovering of interdependent processes of social change linking Western and non-Western areas, as well as the inclusion of dynamics of class formation corresponding to both. The book illustrates the way in which methodological shifts related to each of these dimensions have been proposed within different approaches. The first half of the book groups together theoretical models with a structure-analytical emphasis and dealing with the political economy of social inequalities, starting with Marx's approach. The latter half focuses on approaches with a cultural-theoretical emphasis and a historical-comparative methodology on the other, starting with Weber's approach. While reflecting the current division of labour between the macrosociology of structural inequalities and a macrosociology of cultural differences, this classification is not intended to positively sanction the division, but to trace the imprint that an alignment with either a Marxist or a Weberian approach to the macro level of social inequalities has left on present-day theoretical and analytical models.

Chapter 1 starts by placing Marx's sociology of social inequality within a late twentieth and early twenty-first century academic context and goes on to provide an overview of the political economy of inequalities commonly associated with the work of Marx and Engels in Western academia. It argues that Marx's sociology of social inequality was built on, but not reducible to, class theory. Accordingly, classes for Marx were primarily social relationships, and the various stages in the division of labour mirrored different relations of individuals to one another at the national level, and the relations of different nations at the global level. Yet, despite attention to the global dimension, Marx commonly did not go beyond the focus on the nation-state for the analysis of either capitalism in general or inequality more specifically. It is rather Marx' and Engels' largely ignored articles and letters on Asia, the Middle East, Russia, Ireland, and the Americas, that provide a framework within which to comprehend the relationship between Europe and its Other(s) as a dialectical one, and help situate capitalist modernity globally as the product of unequal relations between coloniser and colonised. In particular, Marx's treatment of New World slavery as a condition of possibility for European industrialism and for modernity more generally provides a key point of entry to Marx' understanding of coloniality as a set of anomalies meant to disappear in time, yet structurally embedded in the logic of capitalist production.

Late twentieth-century critiques of Marxian political economy directed at the "blind spots" of its definition of capitalism build the focus of *Chapter 2*. Starting in the 1970s, several critiques of the concept of primitive accumulation gradually converged into an explicitly Marxist reconceptualisation of gender relations *and* colonial exploitation under capitalism that actively incorporated developments outside of Europe. Among them, the chapter focuses on the world-systems perspective, which argued that non-wage, colonial modes of labour control were integral to and essential for the logic of capitalism, as well as on the feminist approach of the Bielefeld School of development sociology, which claimed that subsistence labour paralleled wage labour as a core pillar of capital accumulation. Focused on the attempt to decentre the role of the proletariat as the main exploited class, and that of wage labour as the defining moment of the capitalist system, these approaches shift attention to plantation slaves in the Caribbean on the one hand and housewives on the other as pillars of capital accumulation at the global level. In the process, they reveal the structural entanglements between metropoles and colonies as main determinants of global inequalities. According to these combined perspectives, the methodological implications of accounting for coloniality as structurally embedded in modernity, instead of as a set of anomalies, therefore include complementing the analysis of processes of proletarianisation in the core with that of bourgeoisification in the entire world-system, of ethnicisation of the labour force in the periphery, and of gendering as their underlying logic.

Discursive patterns of racialisation, ethnicisation, and gendering throughout the history of the modern world-system form the object of *Chapter 3*, which introduces the Latin American decolonial perspective and its dialogue with as well as departure from world-systems scholarship and postcolonial studies. In differentiating between Occidentalism as a discourse *from* and *about* the West, emerged as early as the European colonial expansion, and Orientalism as a discourse about the West's Other, emerged in the wake of the Enlightenment, the decolonial perspective stresses that the epistemic dimension of inequality processes had been coterminous with the emergence of capitalism itself, and is thus essential for an analysis of global inequalities. Building on the decolonial perspective's notion that evolutionism and dualism formed the basis of several Occidental global designs of the expanding modern/colonial world-system since the sixteenth century, the chapter distinguishes three interrelated patterns of racialisation/ethnicisation of difference, resulting from four major global designs of Occidental provenience. On the basis of postcolonial and Third World feminist positions, the chapter complements the decolonial perspective's focus on racialisation and ethnicisation by an analysis of the corresponding strategies of gendering as underlying the logic of Occidentalism.

Chapter 4 foregrounds a recent approach that also aims to account for the racial and ethnic dimension of inequality structures, while empirically establishing that they are the result of eminently relational processes between and within countries. Less centred on the historical reconstruction of the colonial past than the decolonial perspective, Korzeniewicz and Moran's model focuses in particular on the way in which the institutional arrangements of the recent past contributed to different levels of income inequality across the world. Central to their world-historical perspective on inequality and stratification is the methodological premise of shifting the unit of analysis from the nation-state to the world-economy as a whole. In this case, the shift spectacularly reveals that ascriptive criteria remain the fundamental basis of stratification and inequality in modernity and that, since the nineteenth century, citizenship, i.e., nation-state membership, has been the most important of these criteria. Placing this approach in relation to similar theoretical and methodological proposals in dependency theory, labour history, transnational inequality research, and decolonial migration studies reveals Korzeniewicz and Moran's analysis as one of the most promising frameworks for a political economy of global income inequalities today.

Just as Marx's class analysis did not stand alone, but was instead embedded in his theory of capital accumulation, Weber's views on inequality and stratification are intimately tied to his larger theory of the rise of the modern world. *Chapter 5* therefore reviews Weber's theory of modernity as an indispensable prerequisite for any analysis of his approach to social inequality. The specific rationalism which, in Weber's view, characterised Western civilisation as a whole, lays the basis for his theory of modernity as uniqueness vis-à-vis which the entire non-Western world falls short. In the process, Weber sharply dissociates Western capitalism from the colonial enterprise and, ultimately, the emergence of modernity from the history of colonialism. The second part of the chapter zooms in on Weber's approach to race and ethnicity in order to pinpoint the blind spots that Weber's analysis has bequeathed to the sociology of social inequality more generally and to the sociology of race and ethnicity in particular. Through a reconstruction of Weber's conceptual and political take on race and ethnicity in his chapter on ethnic groups, his treatment of the "Polish question" in Germany and of the "Negro question" in the United States, the chapter links Weber's general social theory with his particular views on racial and ethnic matters.

Taking as a point of departure Engin Isin's critique of Weber's conceptualisation of citizenship as an institution specific to the modern Christian Occident, *Chapter 6* briefly reviews several approaches to citizenship and (in)equality that directly or indirectly build on Weber's conceptualisation. While most approaches to citizenship in the West have tended to focus on the equalising effects of the modern institution of citizenship within states, a global perspective on citizenship reveals its role as a mechanism of social closure mobilised by prosperous states against non-citizens and thus as an inequality-generating institution. These findings resonate both with the world-historical model presented in Chapter 4 and with the necessary reconceptualisation of modernity as defined by ascribed characteristics that resulted from it. The chapter goes on to argue that those Weberian approaches that offer the widest analytical scope for examining the effects that social closure through citizenship has on the reproduction of existing inequalities are the ones that leave behind the comparative-historical framework Weber foregrounded and instead offer a global perspective. The chapter ends with current examples of new transnational actors in citizenship policies, whose impact makes an analysis of strategies of closure and usurpation beyond the state level imperative and additionally emphasises the need for a shift from the national to the global view.

Unlike Marxist political economy, Weber's theory of culture did not easily translate into a macrosociology of inequalities. At the macrostructural level, it was therefore primarily in civilisational analysis that Weberian sociology was most clearly applied to the study of global cultural dynamics. In briefly reviewing notions of the global dynamics of civilisations put forward by Shmuel Eisenstadt and Samuel Huntington, *Chapter 7* shows how an emphasis on tensions within and clashes between civilisations serves to reassert both the uniqueness of the West and its ontological autonomy. The chapter argues that, especially through the focus on conflict and tension between an initial modern civilisation and its sequels, civilisational analysis not only retains an Occidentalist bias, but also replaces the Marxist political economy of class conflict with what has been called a Weberian "political economy of cultural differences" (Zimmerman 2006). I propose instead that an understanding of the dynamics of modernity that de-centres the role of the West does not require a notion of multiple modernities emerging through dialectic tension from a European original, but an analysis of the multiple alterities within Europe which enabled both Western Europe's colonial and imperial expansion and its monopolisation of the definition of modernity. A corresponding model referred to as multiple Europes is detailed in the final part of the chapter. Finally, *Chapter 8* gives a short overview of the main arguments of the book and draws theoretical and methodological conclusions as to how a sociology of global inequalities would best transcend its current Occidentalist bias.

Toward the end of the twentieth century, Immanuel Wallerstein (1991c) had affirmed the need of unthinking social science in order to transcend the limits of the nineteenth-century paradigms that had informed the scope and methodology of such disciplines as sociology, anthropology, history, economics, and political science. Perceived as a growing tendency a mere decade or so later, the practice of unthinking central theoretical and methodological categories within sociology such as the unit of analysis, the plurality – or uniqueness – of modernity, and its boundaries with other social sciences and the humanities more generally has raised fears of the rise of an "anti-sociology" (Touraine 2007: 191). Yet, as shown above, the destructive tendencies implied in the choice of such a term are misleading. With respect to the analysis of social inequality, the act of unthinking is not the equivalent of an act of anarchy, but a sustained effort at arriving at a theory able to encompass different social realities. Such efforts have been undertaken independently in non-core areas of the world since the very birth of sociology as a discipline and up to our days. "Unthinking" or "undisciplining" the present theoretical models so as to make them reflect the impact that the geopolitical displacement of the sixteenth century has had on European thought categories therefore does not amount to undoing sociology as a discipline, but rather to filling in the blanks that have so far prevented it from becoming both global and truly "cosmopolitan".

PART I
Marx and Political-Economy Approaches

Chapter 1

Class vs. Other:
Coloniality as Anomaly in Karl Marx

For a few decades after World War II, Marxism – both as a political position and as a social scientific stance – was an adversary to be reckoned with. Accordingly, when not positively espoused, it had to be explicitly disavowed: While modernisation theorists advocated liberal capitalist development under the banner of a "Non-Communist Manifesto" (Rostow 1960), inequality researchers marked their distance from Marxism by advancing "anti-class theory" (Schelsky 1966). Marxism started occupying the centre-stage of politics and theory once again with the administrative decolonisation of most of Africa in the 1960s and 1970s, the subsequent proliferation of socialism in the region on the one hand, and the rise of Marxist structuralism, radical political economy, and dependency theory during the same period on the other. However, at least within the field of social theory, it had already forfeited this pivotal role by the end of the century.

Politically, the end of the Cold War, the dismemberment of the Soviet Union, and not least the bourgeoisification of the working class in the Western world made socialist movements negligible there, proving the thesis of the immiseration of the proletariat a mistake. Individualisation processes and the pluralisation of life forms under conditions of globalisation were instead declared the order of the day. Economic and political developments thus seemed to prefigure the "collapse of Marxism" (Wieviorka 2003) in theoretical and political terms and validate the "end of history" approach (Fukuyama 1992). At the same time, given the pluralisation and internal differentiation of Marxism itself into diverse and even competing approaches, the exact scope of the delegitimisation was not clear. Moreover, and in particular with respect to the analysis of social inequality, the Marxist tradition seemed to be deader in some countries – and their national cultures of scholarship – than in others.[1] A minimal academic consensus as to the core of Marx's sociology of social inequality is outlined below.

---

1   In a survey of mainstream German approaches to social inequality, Rainer Geißler (2002: 141) spoke of the "German *Sonderweg* of social structure analysis", in which the appropriateness of social classes and social strata as categories of analysis of postindustrial Western societies was seriously questioned during a decade-long debate. Geißler noted that no corresponding rejection of Marxist terminology can be found elsewhere in Europe, or, for that matter, in North America. While Anglo-Saxon sociology developed a macrosociological tradition in which Marxist and Weberian approaches were pitted against each other, but nevertheless counted as equally valid choices, German scholarship drew an

26   *Global Inequalities Beyond Occidentalism*

Class vs. Other: Coloniality as Anomaly in Karl Marx

Marx and Engels's materialist conception of history departed from the premise that all human history rests on the material basis of the existence of living individuals, their activity, and their consequent relationship to nature (Marx and Engels 1977a). In what they called the materialist method, the first act in human history was considered to be the production of material life, while the various *modes of production* of human physical existence, i.e., of the means of subsistence, were ever so many *modes of life*:

> As individuals express their life, so they are. What they are, therefore, coincides with their production, both with what they produce and with how they produce. The nature of individuals thus depends on the material conditions determining their production. (Marx and Engels 1977b: 242)

As such, the material conception of history was the result of the inversion of Hegel's idealist notion of history as the self-realisation of Spirit, or God. According to Hegel, the self-objectification of spirit as space yielded nature, whereas the gradual process of its self-objectification as culture amounted to the succession of world civilisations from the ancient Orient to modern Europe. Marx and Engels claimed to have stood Hegelian dialectic on its head, "or rather, turned [it] off its head, on which it was standing, and placed [it] upon its feet" (Marx and Engels 1962: 387): To Hegel's view that history, and, with it, all human activity was a mere manifestation of the Spirit acting through people, Marx countered that Spirit was nothing but human activity itself, and that history was a product of human labour:

> Hegel makes the predicates, the object, independent, but independent as separated from their real independence, their subject. Subsequently, and because of this, the real subject appears to be the result; whereas one has to start from the real subject and examine its objectification. (Marx 1997: 166)

Hegel conceptualised human nature in general and man in particular as "universal self-consciousness", arguing that the world achieves consciousness of itself as spirit through the philosopher's mind; alienation of human nature thus equalled alienation of self-consciousness of the world as spirit, until the attainment of absolute knowledge – the recognition of the whole of creation as spirit (Tucker 1978: xxi). By contrast, Marx held that man[2] was in the first place a social being

---

imaginary evolutionary line between Marx' economistic sociology and Weber's historical-comparative, culturalist approach, making Marxism an illegitimate choice.

2   Generic grammatical forms notwithstanding, Marx's constant reference to "man" as subject of history on the one hand echoes Hegel's use of the term, on the other reflects Marx's own gender bias in conceptualising the role of men and women in history. In the

and that consciousness was constructed by man's social practice – which was, through its very capacity to change the material world, objective practice.

Ludwig Feuerbach's "transformational criticism" of Hegel, which used an inverted reading of Hegelian philosophy to conclude that alienation in the religious sphere stems from man's projection of an idealised self-image onto an imaginary God, served Marx as a basis for his own analysis of man's alienation in the economic sphere. In an explicit departure from Hegel's view of history as the self-objectification of Spirit in culture, Marx therefore conceptualised history as the process of self-development of the human species through labour, across several stages leading up to communism. Against the Young Hegelians (including Feuerbach) and their abstract notion of Man as the universal motive force in history, Marx and Engels argued for a conceptualisation of men "within given historical conditions and relationships", in turn made up by "the productive forces and forms of intercourse at any particular time" (Marx and Engels 1977b: 182). Hence, Marx held that any study of human history should reflect the various stages in the history of economic activity and the social relations corresponding to them.

> In the social production of their existence, men inevitably enter into definite relations, which are independent of their will, namely relations of production appropriate to a given stage in the development of their material forces of production. The totality of these relations of production constitutes the economic structure of society, the real foundation, on which arises a legal and political superstructure and to which correspond definite forms of social consciousness. The mode of production of material life conditions the general process of social, political and intellectual life. It is not the consciousness of men that determines their existence, but their social existence that determines their consciousness. (Marx 1971: 20f.)

In Marx's view, the labour process itself was an objectification of human powers. Since man's essential nature was that of being a free, conscious producer, alienation was man's loss of control over his own activities, especially labour, and resulted in his loss of the role of subject and initiator of the historical process (McLellan 2003: 38). For Marx, not only was the relation of workers to the product of their labour *not* the basis for alienation, as Hegel would have it, but, as objectification of man's essential nature, it was the only genuinely human relation: "It is just in the working-up of the objective world ... that man first really proves himself to be a *species being*. This production is his active species life. Through and because of this production, nature appears as *his* work and his reality" (Marx 1978a: 76). In turn, commodity production under capitalism turned labour itself into an

---

following, the use of the masculine form mostly follows Marx's own, while gender-neutral terms are employed when assessing those parts of Marx's analysis referring to humankind in general. The issue of gender in Marx's and Engels' work is addressed later in the chapter.

28   *Global Inequalities Beyond Occidentalism*

object, while the relation of the worker to the product of his labour became one of alienation:

> Labour-power is, therefore, a commodity which its possessor, the wage-worker, sells to capital. Why does he sell it? In order to live. But the exercise of labour-power, labour, is the worker's own life-activity, the manifestation of his own life. And this life-activity he sells to another person in order to secure the necessary means of subsistence. Thus his life-activity is for him only a means to enable him to exist. He works in order to live. He does not even reckon labour as a part of his life, it is rather a sacrifice of his life. It is a commodity which he has made over to another. Hence, also, the product of his activity is not the object of his activity. (Marx 1978c: 205)

Historically, other forms of production, whether that of independent producers epitomised by the figure of Robinson Crusoe, subsistence producers in patriarchal industries, and even dependent producers rendering services and payments in kind under feudalism more adequately reflected the social character of labour by laying bare the social relations connecting the amount of individual labour-power with the value of labour's product. By contrast, commodity production substantially relied on wage labour, which disguised the fact that, in the bourgeois society for which this labour form was characteristic, the labour-power through which individuals manifest their lives had in itself become a commodity. In ancient slavery, the labour-power being traded was only part of the commodity that the slave as a whole represented, and as such it belonged to the slave owner; during feudalism, it made up only a part of the labour-power of serfs, who in turn belonged to the land owned by the feudal lord; it was only during capitalism that labour-power was a commodity, the only one which free labourers could sell to the capitalist in exchange for wages, and which thus ensured that every wage worker belonged to the entire capitalist class (Marx 1978c: 205; Marx 1978e: 256).

By focusing on the centrality of wage labour in bourgeois society in later works such as *Wage Labour and Capital*, the *Grundrisse*, and *Capital* itself, Marx implicitly built and followed up on the theory of alienated labour developed in the *1844 Economic-Philosophical Manuscripts*. While the arguments for a discontinuity between Marx's philosophical and his economic work have usually entailed considering "alienation" to be a concept restricted to his early, philosophical-humanist thought, with no reverberations into his economic writings, the logic underlying Marx's critique of capitalist labour points in the opposite direction.[3]

---

3   Marcuse's early assessment that "Marx's early writings are mere preliminary stages to his mature theory" (1986: 281) has been echoed several times throughout the literature – at times in a similar, at others in a qualified form (McLellan 1973: 39; Tucker 1978: xxxi; Pilling 1980: 161). For a discussion of the implications of the continuity vs. discontinuity thesis within Marx's work in general, see below.

In order to trace back the economic analysis of wage labour in Marx's late work to the central theme of alienation of the early writings, Robert Tucker prefaced his selection from *Wage Labour and Capital* by noting that

> If the thesis on 'alienated labour' was to be made scientifically cogent and if the expectation of coming proletarian revolution was to be based upon it, [Marx] needed to show the capital-labour relationship, which he took to be the core of the bourgeois socio-economic system, to be dialectically self-destructive, i.e., transitory by virtue of its inner dynamics of development. (Tucker 1978: 203)

In tracing the relation between labour power and property through various modes of production, Marx therefore laid the basis for examining the relationship between labour and capital in bourgeois society, which, again drawing on Hegel, he revealed as one of reification. Hegel's analysis of the relationship of lord to servant as a result of certain modes of labour rested on the insight that it was through the products of their own labour that workers acquired consciousness of themselves and that this consciousness later became objectified (Marcuse 1986: 116). For Marx, however, this dialectical process of reification (of the worker in labour) and its negation (self-realisation of consciousness in labour product) failed to do justice to social reality, since, according to him, the existing antagonisms could not be resolved at the level of abstract thought, as Hegel postulated, but only in relation to a given social and political order. In bourgeois society, the reification of social relations occurred via commodity production: "the mutual relations of the producers, within which the social character of their labour affirms itself, take the form of a social relation between the products" (Marx 1978f: 320).

Marx therefore rejected classical economic theory's naturalisation of the relation between capital and labour as a purely objective material relationship and instead built on Hegel in order to analyse both the categories of bourgeois economy more generally and the relationship of the capitalist to the wage worker in particular as expressions of the specific historical mode of labour control of commodity production (Marx 1978f: 319ff.). In this particular context, the historically determined mode of production and the social character of labour characterising it appeared as objective relations resulted from the expenditure of human labour power, the exchangeability of commodities thus produced, and commodity prices as expressions of the magnitude of their exchange value – a condition that Marx called the "fetishism of commodities":

> The character of having value, when once impressed upon products, obtains fixity only by reason of their acting and re-acting upon each other as quantities of value. These quantities vary continually, independently of the will, foresight and action of the producers. To them, their own social action takes the form of the action of objects, which rule the producers instead of being ruled by them. (Marx 1978f: 323)

Hence, both the alienation of labour through production for wage instead of life-activity, and the fetishism of commodities through the universalisation of exchange-value were forms of reification of labour-power. If one concealed the commodity-form that labour-power acquired during capitalism, the other concealed the qualitative aspect of value inherent in the concrete way in which products meet human needs, i.e., their use-value. Marx consequently pleaded for a conceptualisation of the social character of labour as two-fold, i.e., as comprising both the quantitative and the qualitative aspects of value:

> On the one hand all labour is, speaking physiologically, an expenditure of human labour-power, and in its character of identical abstract human labour, it creates and forms the value of commodities. On the other hand, all labour is the expenditure of human labour-power in a special form and with a definite aim, and in this, its character of concrete useful labour, it produces use-values. (Marx 1978f: 312)

The conflation of exchange value and use value under the unqualified general label of "value" as the result of abstract labour derived from the artificial separation of the objective conditions of living labour from the subjective living labour capacity, which thus appeared as alien from each other. The product of labour accordingly appeared as "a combination of alien material, alien instrument and alien labour" (Marx 1978e: 254), such that *living labour*, i.e., human activity in the work process, was in turn perceived as a means of realisation of objectified labour, i.e., of *use-values*. Although this exchange of objectified labour for living labour bore the resemblance of a free exchange between capital and labour, it in fact disguised the process of appropriation of the surplus labour of wage workers in the form of the surplus value *of capital* – and therefore again alien to the worker. Through its negation of labour and labour products as properties of the individualised worker, capital became "the predominant subject and owner of alien labour, and its relation is itself as complete a contradiction as is that of wage labour" (Marx 1978e: 261). Marx thus countered Hegel's notion that the social and political forms had become attuned to the principles of reason, by maintaining that the very existence of the proletariat contradicted the reality of reason that Hegel presupposed: Since the lot of the proletariat represented no fulfilment of human potentialities, but its reverse, the entire proletariat as a class was proof of the very negation of reason. In Marcuse's words,

> If property constitutes the first endowment of a free person, the proletarian is neither free nor a person, for he possesses no property. If the exercises of the absolute mind, art, religion, and philosophy, constitute man's essence, the proletarian is forever severed from his essence, for his existence permits him no time to indulge in these activities [...] The existence of the proletariat thus gives living witness to the fact that truth has not been realised. History and social reality themselves thus 'negate' philosophy. The critique of society cannot

be carried through by philosophical doctrine, but becomes the task of socio-historical practice. (Marcuse 1986: 261)

Both the separation of the producer from the means of production and the appropriation of surplus labour were the result of the previous process of expropriation of the agricultural population from the land, that Marx identified as the starting point of the capitalist mode of production, and that he labelled "primitive accumulation". Unlike Adam Smith and the classical political economists, who viewed the emergence of capitalism as a natural development arisen from an increasing division of labour between producers of specialised goods, merchants, and factory owners employing wage labourers, Marx stated that capitalism had been based on the violent dissolution of feudal economic structures and their transformation into capitalist forms of exploitation:

> the historical movement which changes the producers into wage-workers, appears, on the one hand, as their emancipation from serfdom and from the fetters of the guilds, and this side alone exists for our bourgeois historians. But, on the other hand, these new freedmen became sellers of themselves only after they had been robbed of all their own means of production, and of all the guarantees of existence afforded by the old feudal arrangements. And the history of this, their expropriation, is written in the annals of mankind in letters of blood and fire. (Marx 1978f: 433)

Against the political economists' naïve belief in the potential of the division of labour alone for bringing about capitalism, Marx held that there is no necessary or causal relationship between the employment of wage-workers and the development of a capitalist mode of production. Quite the contrary, the use of free workers for luxury production had sporadically occurred in pre-bourgeois economies without triggering a change in the mode of production (Marx 1978e: 259f.), i.e., without the transformative moment characterising modernity. In order to occur, the transformation of feudal into capitalist economic structures therefore had to involve a relationship between two different kinds of commodity-possessors: the owners of the means of production on the one hand, and the "free" labourers resulted from the violent process of expropriation, on the other:

> Free labourers, in the double sense that neither they themselves form part and parcel of the means of production, as in the case of slaves, bondsmen, & c., nor do the means of production belong to them, as in the case of peasant-proprietors; they are, therefore, free from, unencumbered by, any means of production of their own. (Marx 1978f: 432)

The social division of labour between the owners of the means of production and the owners of labour-power ensured a social inequality structure on the basis of which the capitalist mode of production acquired the dynamics of its reproduction.

32   *Global Inequalities Beyond Occidentalism*

For Marx and Engels, the structurally unequal access to the means of production had resulted in antagonisms reflecting the respective society's class structure at all stages of historical development. In capitalist societies, the main classes, the bourgeoisie and the proletariat, represented the main antagonism as they embodied the relationship between the owners of capital and the producers of surplus value, respectively. Other classes, such as the landlords, the middle class, the petty bourgeoisie, the peasantry and the lumpenproletariat, while remaining part of the capitalist class hierarchy, were not essential to its dynamics – which tended towards polarisation. Rather, they were residues of previous classes, from which future members of either the capitalist or the working class could be recruited:

> The lower middle class, the small manufacturer, the shopkeeper, the artisan, the peasant, all these fight against the bourgeoisie, to save from extinction their existence as fractions of the middle class. They are therefore not revolutionary, but conservative. Nay more, they are reactionary, for they try to roll back the wheel of history. If by chance they are revolutionary, they are so only in view of their impending transfer into the proletariat, they thus defend not their present, but their future interests, they desert their own standpoint to place themselves at the service of the proletariat. (Marx 1978g: 482)

According to Marx and Engels, the natural division of labour in the family, derived from the original division of labour in the sexual act, represents the basis of property and therefore of the unequal distribution of labour and its products, i.e. it is a very crude form of slavery already present at the stage of tribal ownership. As such, it will only develop further "with the increase of population, the growth of wants, and with the extension of external relations, both of war and of barter" (Marx and Engels 1977b: 168). Marriage, property, and the family on the other hand are "the practical basis on which the bourgeoisie has directed its domination" (Marx and Engels 1968: 463), such that the complete development of the slavery latent in early family forms will be realised only in the capitalist family structure, based on private gain, in which "The bourgeois sees his wife as a mere instrument of production" (Marx and Engels 1977a). Ascribing the status of objects or even victims of capitalist relations to women as a general social category across class distinctions, while reserving both that of subject and referent of discourse to (bourgeois) men is characteristic for the treatment of gender issues throughout Marx's work. The position of all women under capitalism is thus derived from the social and economic role of the wife in bourgeois marriage, defined – and denounced – as a "system of wives in common". As such, it only exists among the bourgeoisie, while being practically absent among the proletariat:

> Our bourgeois, not content with having wives and daughters of their proletarians at their disposal, not to speak of common prostitutes, take the greatest pleasures in seducing each other's wives. [...] it is self-evident that the abolition of the present system of production must bring with it the abolition of the community

Class vs. Other 33

of women springing from that system, i.e., of prostitution both public and private. (Marx and Engels 1977a: 235)

Hence, Marx's conceptualisation of women as social actors lacking political agency stems from his analysis of nineteenth-century capitalism as a system in which marriage was a form of female slavery to which most women had no alternative. Since bourgeois marriage entailed the use of women as male property, the abolition of marriage in the absence of the abolition of private property would only result in the "universal prostitution with the community" (Marx 1978a: 82). It is therefore only with the dissolution of the entire capitalist system in the wake of a proletarian revolution – i.e., as a result of *class* agency – that the inequalities between men and women would be thoroughly eradicated. Underlying Marx's conceptualisation of the capitalist family model – as with most nineteenth-century writing on gender issues – is a set of assumptions in which the Western European family pattern serves as the defining norm and heteronormativity as a model for human relations (Reiner 2008: 14, Gutiérrez Rodríguez 2010: 98f.).[4]

Marx's sociology of social inequality was thus built on, but not reducible to, class theory. The centrality of the concept of class antagonism pointed to the core meaning of Marx's definition of class, its relational character. Accordingly, classes were first and foremost social relationships, and the various stages in the division of labour mirrored different relations of individuals to one another at the national level, and the relations of different nations among themselves at the global level (Marx 1978b: 161). Despite attention to the global dimension, Marx however did not go beyond the focus on the nation-state for the analysis of either capitalism in general or inequality more specifically. While he did view the world market as the last stage in the evolution of the bourgeoisie and the international class struggle as the logical continuation of national class struggles, the framework within which the division of labour, the development of the forces of production, and ultimately the class antagonisms are located is nevertheless the nation (state) – as such, the only legitimate unit of analysis. It therefore was also within the national class struggle that classes moved from a mere commonality of economic conditions that characterised a class in itself (*Klasse an sich*) toward acquiring a collective

---

4   Credit for substantive incorporation of gender issues into the theorisation of capitalism was given rather to Engels alone, whose *Origin of the Family, Private Property and the State* is largely viewed as having paved the way for socialist feminism. Recent debates on the issue have swerved in the direction of considering Engels's contribution less meritorious than commonly assumed, and instead amending Marx's position to be essentially one of commitment to gender equality – which, however, being only achievable under communism, did not warrant extensive treatment during capitalist rule except as criticism of bourgeois relations (Reiner 2008: 25). Nevertheless, neither interpretation contests the fact that Marx's (and Engels') postponing of the goal of gender equality amounted to subsuming gender issues under class issues and limiting the agency for social transformation to class actors, i.e. the proletariat. For a detailed decolonial critique see Gutiérrez Rodríguez 2010 and below.

34 *Global Inequalities Beyond Occidentalism*

consciousness of common interests and political objectives as a class for itself (*Klasse für sich*), capable of bringing about revolutionary change.

> Economic conditions first transformed the mass of the people of the country into workers. The combination of capital has created for this mass a common situation, common interests. This mass is thus already a class against capital, but not yet for itself. In the struggle [...], this mass becomes united, and constitutes itself as a class for itself. The interests it defends become class interests. But the struggle of class against class is a political struggle. (Marx 1978d: 218)

The dynamics of capitalism's emergence and reproduction therefore triggers a dialectical process in the course of which the essential conditions for the existence of capital, alienated wage labour, becomes the premise for the system's demise by fostering the mass association of class-conscious workers against the bourgeoisie. The capital-labour relationship, reflected in the bourgeoisie producing above all its own grave-diggers, the revolutionary proletariat, thus eventually proves to be a self-destructive one (Marx 1978g: 483). It is at its most characteristic, the premise of dialectical transformation as the result of class consciousness, that Marx's conception became also the most vulnerable at the end of the twentieth century as a theory of history and social change.

Postsocialism, Postcolonialism and the Search for the True Marx

> There is no true Marx
> Immanuel Wallerstein (1991)

It becomes clear that for Marx, as later for Weber, the conceptualisation of social inequality was organically embedded in a theory of social change. As shown above, in the case of Marx it was a theory of evolutionary outlook centred on the concept of class: inequality of class was relevant for social change to the extent that the history of all hitherto existing societies was, in Marx and Engels' famous formulation, the history of class struggle (Marx 1978g: 473). As history progressed from primitive society through successive stages leading up to the communist social order, class antagonisms went from freemen versus slaves, patricians versus plebeians, and lords versus serfs up to the most polarised form of antagonism, characteristic of contemporary capitalism – bourgeois versus proletarian. Only with the disappearance of the private ownership of the means of production in the wake of the proletarian revolution was a classless society possible, and a fundamentally equal distribution of resources – "from each according to his abilities to each according to his needs" (Marx 1978f: 351) likely.

Yet, with the breakdown of socialist regimes throughout Eastern Europe in 1989/90, history seemed to have taken a wholly different course than Marx had predicted. Both the verdict of the death of Marxism as well as a series of existential questions as to the future of class analysis appeared justified at that point. In the words of a recent critic,

> If the Soviet Union adapted some of Marx's ideas as a legitimating ideology, didn't the collapse of the Soviet empire and the Soviet Union eliminate any further reason to study Marx? Does even one true believer still accept Marx's tragically mistaken theory of history, with its denouement in a proletarian revolution followed by a form of communist society that can never be? (Cohen 2005: xiv f.; see also Sanderson 2001: 69)

A way out of the conundrum – of pronouncing a classic dead and saving his face at the same time – was to declare Marx's theory of social change inessential to the core of his writings, seen as primarily concerned with the workings of capitalism and their consequences rather than with providing a philosophy of history.

At that point, the strict understanding of Marxism as a mere theory of capitalism had already left a clear imprint on the legacy Marx bequeathed to social inequality theory. Marx's sociology of social inequality had been unanimously considered a theory of class and, depending on his exegetes' own focus, accordingly celebrated for or imputed with the predominantly economic explanation it offered for social inequality. Economic determinism as well as the reduction of the structure of social inequality to two antagonistic classes at any time in history became the most common criticisms to Marx's approach (e.g., Bendix 1974). Revisionist Marxists, Communists and non-Marxist authors alike had long agreed that Marxist thought was essentially economic. As of the latter half of the twentieth century, the growing number of translations of the writings of the young Marx however gradually prompted the realisation that, aside from the primarily economistic Marx, there was the philosophical-humanist one. Much of the ensuing debate was ultimately carried out in terms of continuity or discontinuity within his work in general, and within his embedded theory of class in particular. Especially for structuralists, the economic determinism of the late Marx was a radical departure from the humanism of the young one, who therefore was himself not yet a Marxist (Althusser 1964). For Marxist humanists, on the other hand, Marx's work represented a unified whole, in which neither the notion of essential humanity, nor the agency of individuals on the political and ideological level could be derived from the economic one (Fromm 1956; Hall 1977).

Outside the frame of reference of the structuralist-humanist debate, the latter view has gained momentum in recent years due to a growing body of research arguing for the re-evaluation of the Marxist legacy that would dispel economism and the two-class theory as longstanding misconceptions and provide a more comprehensive framework for analysis by taking into account Marx's previously unpublished manuscripts (Dussel 2001; Hurst 2007: 190).

Two distinct, yet interrelated positions can be distinguished in this respect, both of which take an epistemological tension in Marx's work as a point of departure for its reassessment.

For world-systems theorists, it is Marx's alternating emphasis between the universalism of abstract theory and the specificity of the empirical reality of capitalism as an historical system that justifies speaking of "two Marxes". They however did not succeed each other chronologically, as the structuralists had assumed, but produced contradictory and coexisting historiographies as well as distinct future scenarios (Arrighi et al. 1989; Wallerstein 1991c, 1996). From this perspective, Marxist class analysis, when understood as class polarisation at the level of the capitalist world-economy, is not only still valid in the twenty-first century, but also historically and sociologically correct. Such understanding however requires the prism of the Marx interested in discrete historical processes and in the *critique* of political economy, rather than the Marx dedicating himself primarily to market interests within national contexts, and hence retreating into the classical political economy that he strove to overcome.

In turn, decolonial scholars differentiate between Marx's "two centuries". The first one, following his death in 1883, allowed access only to a limited amount of the original texts, and therefore prompted dogmatic and distorting interpretations, mainly Stalinism and Western Marxism. It is only Marx's "second century", which began intellectually with the publication of previously unknown manuscripts in German and their translation into English, and politically with the collapse of Eastern European socialist regimes, which will allow a complete rereading of Marx's work as a whole (Dussel 2001: 10). Thus, it will be possible to assess both the extent to which the philosophical and the economic analysis in Marx's work are integral parts of his ontology of capital, not mutually exclusive or reducible to each other (his "dialectical originality" – Dussel 2004: 348) and the epistemic perspective from which Marx articulated his radical criticism of capitalist ontology (his "analectic transcendence" – Dussel 2004: 366).

Both interpretations rely on the critical Marx as opposed to the one whose thought is in line with Enlightenment philosophy and the main tenets of liberalism. By retracing these approaches' claims at reinterpreting and further developing Marxist theory in light of twenty-first century developments, a sociology of social inequality could be outlined that adequately reflects the long-term consequences of a specific Marxist critique of political economy and its present-day variants. Thus, Orientalism, the insufficient treatment of gender and the disregard for racial and ethnic issues have featured prominently among the "blind spots" commonly imputed to Marxian theory in late twentieth and early twenty-first centuries (Wallerstein 1991; Schwalbe 2000; Tucker 2002: 104ff.; Uemura 2006: 10ff.).

The global dimension of inequality under capitalism was present in the work of Marx and Engels from the very beginning. Its emergence was explicitly and repeatedly linked to the "discovery" of the New World. Thus, as early as in the *Communist Manifesto*, the European colonial expansion, the development of the bourgeoisie, the Industrial Revolution, the rise of the world-market, and the international division of labour on which capitalist accumulation is based are articulated as parts of a coherent chain of events in Marx's writings:

The discovery of America, the rounding of the Cape, opened up fresh ground for the rising bourgeoisie. The East Indian and Chinese markets, the colonization of America, trade with the colonies [...] gave to commerce, to navigation, to industry, an impulse never before known. (Marx and Engels 1977a: 222)

In fact, Europe's colonial expansion in the sixteenth century is given considerable explanatory power in the emergence of global capitalism:

Modern industry has established the world-market, to which the discovery of America paved the way [...] The bourgeoisie has through its exploitation of the world-market given a cosmopolitan character to production and consumption in every country [...] In place of the old local and national seclusion and self-sufficiency, we have intercourse in every direction, universal interdependence of nations [...] The bourgeoisie, by the rapid improvement of all instruments of production, by the immensely facilitated means of communication, draws all, even the most barbarian, nations into civilisation [...] Just as it has made the country dependent on the towns, so it has made barbarian and semi-barbarian countries dependent on the civilised ones, nations of peasants on nations of bourgeois, the East on the West. (Marx and Engels 1977a: 224f.)

Similarly, the hierarchy of labour forms established under capitalism as a world-economy is consistently explained in relation to Europe's colonial enterprise. Thus, in *Capital*, the "dawn of the era of capitalist production", and, with it, the process of primitive accumulation of capital, are once again traced back to

the discovery of gold and silver in America, the expatriation, enslavement and entombment in mines of the aboriginal population, the beginning of the conquest and looting of the East Indies, the turning of Africa into a warren for the commercial hunting of blackskins. (Marx 1978f: 435),

thereby reinforcing the view that the development of modern capitalism was closely tied to European colonialism (Mintz 1978: 84; Jani 2002: 95 and below).

Hence, it was not the lack of treatment of global developments and disregard for the importance of colonisation processes that attracted Marx charges of Eurocentrism from various sides of the theoretical spectrum, but, rather, the centrality he awarded European experiences in the development of capitalism and the interpretation he gave extra-European events and social processes. While taking into account capitalist accumulation through overseas expansion and colonial exploitation, Marxist class theory rested on the fact that capitalism had developed in Western Europe, the proletariat had emerged there, and socialist revolutions would be occurring there first (Wallerstein 1991a). In turn, Marx's writings on the British rule in India, on China, Oriental despotism and the Asiatic mode of production more generally were taken as proof of his unilinear evolutionism, Eurocentrism, and, ultimately, Orientalism. The most widely quoted – and most heavily indicted – statements include the view that Indian society had no history but that of the successive intruders in its territory:

> India, then, could not escape the fate of being conquered, and the whole of her past history, if it be anything, is the history of the successive conquests she has undergone. Indian society has no history at all, at least no known history. What we call its history, is but the history of the successive intruders who founded their empires on the passive basis of that unresisting and unchanging society. (Marx 1978g: 659)

Similarly, for Marx, the "fanaticism of Islam" made the presence of Turks in Europe an obstacle to development (Marx 1968: 4f.) and China was, by virtue of the immutability of its social structure, a "living fossil" (Marx 1862, in: Avineri 1969: 442). On more than one occasion, the logical consequence they prompted was Marx's support of the European colonial endeavour and his exculpation of the destructive effects of capitalist penetration on native industries and local social structures in the name of social progress:

> England, it is true, in causing a social revolution in Hindustan, was actuated only by the vilest interests, and was stupid in her manner of enforcing them. But that is not the question. The question is, can mankind fulfil its destiny without a fundamental revolution in the social state of Asia? If not, whatever might have been the crimes of England, she was the unconscious tool of history in bringing about that revolution. (Marx and Engels 1979: 132)

Famously, for Edward Said, Marx's economic analyses therefore fall under the rubric of "standard Orientalist undertaking" (Said 1979:154) and are as such instances of a *manifest* (as opposed to a *latent*) Orientalism, the kind that

> kept intact the separateness of the Orient, its eccentricity, its backwardness, its silent indifference, its feminine penetrability, its supine malleability; this is why every writer on the Orient, from Renan to Marx (ideologically speaking) (…), saw the Orient as a locale requiring Western attention, reconstruction, even redemption. (Said 1979: 206)

Most of the time, however, both critics and Marxist scholars agreed that Marx and Engels did not have a full-blown theory of "the Orient" – references to which were restricted to Turkey, Persia, China, and Mughal India (Curtis 1997: 346) – let alone one of the entire non-European world. At the same time, their views on colonialism were seen as inseparable from their theory of capitalism as a world-historic necessity destined to override and transform modes of production and social organisation lacking internal revolutionary dynamics, such as the Asiatic mode of production (Tucker 2002: 104).

Drawing both on Said and on the work of the Indian Subaltern Studies group, Dipesh Chakrabarty took postcolonial criticism of Marx one step further, by arguing that the very indebtedness to European Enlightenment thought that informed Marxism's abstract categories made Marxist narratives of capitalist modernity insensitive to issues of historical difference. While Marx himself had at times offered fleeting glimpses of the coexistence of capitalist relations with elements that allegedly did not belong to its logic, such as "pre-capitalist" labour relations or forms of unproductive labour, the universal history of capital he advanced could only accommodate them as external, dialectical Others of the necessary logic of capital (Chakrabarty 2008: 67), not as integral parts that might amend and qualify this logic. For Chakrabarty, Marxism therefore remains an instance of European thought and as such "both indispensable and inadequate in helping us to think through the experiences of political modernity in non-Western nations" (Chakrabarty 2008: 16) – an assessment on which he subsequently grounded his plea for provincialising Europe. At the opposite end of the opinion scale are recent collective works (Bartolovich and Lazarus 2002) that view postcolonial theory itself as being grounded in Marxism and insist that it is the critique of colonialism as inextricable from the critique of capitalism, rather than the lapse into Eurocentrism, which is specifically Marxist (Bartolovich 2002: 6; Larsen 2002: 214f.).

Much like in the case of the structuralist-humanist debate, the wide variance of readings and the ensuing discussion about the right interpretation of Marx's political and epistemic stance towards the Western European colonial policy of his time led to a search for the "true Marx" that often entailed choosing artificially constructed sides, or one Marx over another. In his own position-taking on the issue of Eurocentrism and evolutionism in Marx's work, Stephen Katz (1990: 675ff.) distinguished four approaches with respect to Marx's writings on colonialism: first, a *non-Marxist* one that depicts the Eurocentrism of Marx and Engels' articles on India as representative of Marxism as a whole, and therefore is used to justify discarding Marxist critique entirely; second, the *neo-Marxist* treatment of dependency and underdevelopment as a reformulation of classical Marxism; third, an *apologetic* approach exonerating Marx from charges of Eurocentrism and racism on several grounds – among which the lack of empirical evidence regarding colonised areas, the intrinsic theoretical value of Marx's most problematic comments, and his ultimately humanist position in condemning the effects of the colonialism that he deemed necessary; and, lastly, the *alternative* attempt to derive Marx's theory of colonialism from sources other than his writings on Asia.

Katz himself joined structuralists, revisionist Marxists, and latter-day postcolonial theorists in the search for the "true Marx". In so doing, he subscribed to the fourth and last approach, which conceived of Marx's and Engels' writings on Russia and Ireland as the "actual" analyses of underdevelopment, on the basis of which Marxism can rightly be viewed as a precursor of contemporary studies of the Third World. In sharp contrast to the writings on India and China, which substantiate the historical materialist claim that the capitalist stage is inevitable and that social struggles in non-Western areas have to be Western-type class struggles, Marx and Engels's analyses of Russia and Ireland are singled out as explicitly non-evolutionist, anti-colonial (in the case of Ireland) and tellingly concerned with class struggles commonly not awarded revolutionary potential within historical materialism, such as the peasantry in the case of Russia (Nimtz 2002: 77). Marx's famous four drafts of the letter to the Russian socialist Vera Zasulich, arguing that a peasant economy such as the Russian commune could represent agrarian countries' path to socialism, and thus make a capitalist stage unnecessary there, corroborated the understanding that historical context did matter to Marxian theory (Boatcă 2003a; Katz 1990; Curtis 1997: 345; San Juan 2002: 228). In turn, Engels' view of Ireland as Britain's "first colony" and Marx' shift of political stance from advocating a socialist revolution in England to viewing Irish liberation as a precondition for the emancipation of the English working class (Marx 1969) further reinforced the claim that Ireland and Russia, rather than India and China, had been Marx' and Engels' non-Western case studies, and had provided the conceptual toolkit and the analytical groundwork for what would later be called the analysis of underdevelopment in colonial contexts (Nimtz 2002: 73; Jani 2002: 95; Cleary 2002: 120). For some, the case for these specific analyses making up the "true essence" of Marxism is additionally strengthened by the fact that, although they were concerned with countries that did not fit the standard definition of the Third World, they were explicitly linked to Marxist revolutionary politics through their focus on the transformation of non-capitalist structures dominated by the capitalist mode of production, "the pivotal point for any Marxist analysis of the third world" (Katz 1990: 678). In contrast, the "non-theoretical" and "strictly mercenary" (Katz 1990: 673) articles on the British rule in India, commissioned by the New York Daily Tribune, are not deemed an adequate starting-point for theories of imperialism. The difference, however, is blurred when one takes into consideration Engels' comments on the communal – as opposed to private – ownership of land as placing a hold on agricultural production and fostering the isolation of communities, which lent a basis for Oriental Despotism not only in China and India, but also in Russia (Curtis 1997: 355).

Katz's typology of approaches to Marx's writings on colonialism, however helpful, is thus not clear-cut in the end. The alternative stance, which looks for "the real Marx and Engels" (Nimtz 2002: 77) outside of their problematic articles on China and India, is easily conflated with the apologetic one, which aims at dismissing the Eurocentrism charge. As in the case of Marx's theory of social change, now overwhelmingly considered simplistic and historically flawed, professing a Marxist approach in the twenty-first century only seems possible by declaring Marx and Engels's Eurocentric comments and Orientalist analyses irrelevant or at least secondary to their overall theory of capitalism.

By contrast, the goal of the following is not to flesh out the true Marx or take sides in the debate, but rather to look for the most promising research agenda for the analysis of global inequalities that such debates have occasioned. To this end, instead of choosing between the Eurocentric and the non-Eurocentric Marx, considering his epistemic stance as rooted in the very dialectics of the modernity he was criticising proves a more viable option.

Dialectical Modernity and Anomalous Coloniality

According to Göran Therborn (1996), being the only tradition of thought to both hail modernity and attack it, Marxism was the theory of the dialectics of modernity as well as its practice:

> It simultaneously affirmed the positive, progressive features of capitalism, industrialization, urbanization, mass literacy [...] and, on the other hand, denouncing the exploitation, the human alienation, the commodification and the instrumentalisation of the social, the false ideology, and the imperialism inherent in the modernization process [...] Its theory centred on the rise of capitalism, as a progressive stage of historical development, and on its 'contradictions', on its class exploitation, its crisis tendencies, and its generation of class conflict. (Therborn 1996: 60)

Although Marx and Engels never explicitly used the term "modernity", their recurrent references to "modern (bourgeois) society", "modern relations of production", "modern productive forces", or "modern state power" do point to an underlying notion of capitalist modernity with both emancipatory and exploitative dimensions. The dialectics of balancing out the two as the reverse and the obverse sides of the same phenomenon has arguably been characteristic for both Marx's own writing and the later Marxist tradition (Therborn 1996: 61). It is the global dialectic of capitalist modernity that Latin American decolonial theorists would later conceptualise as modernity/coloniality, directly connecting modernity's "dark side" (Mignolo 2000, 2012) to the European colonial expansion into the Americas.

Seen from this vantage point, Marxian writings on colonialism and imperialism provide a framework within which to comprehend the relationship between Europe and its Other(s) as a dialectical one, and help situate capitalist modernity globally as the product of unequal and dialectical relations between coloniser and colonised (San Juan 2002: 229; Jani 2002: 90). As such, the articles and letters on Asia, the Middle East, Russia, or Ireland are equally relevant to Marx' and Engels' overarching theory of capitalism. On the one hand, the much-debated Marxian notion of England's historic "double mission" in India, directed both towards "the annihilation of Asiatic society and the laying of the material foundations of Western society in Asia" (Marx 1968: 126), and therefore seen as "destructive" and "regenerative" at the same time, mirrors the dual role of the bourgeoisie Marx and Engels describe in the *Communist Manifesto*: "revolutionary" in putting "an end to all feudal, patriarchal, idyllic relations" and "destroying the idiocy of rural life", yet also the agent of "destructive crises" in "dislodging old-established national industries" and "destroying a mass of productive forces" (Marx and Engels 1977a: 224f.)

42 *Global Inequalities Beyond Occidentalism*

through the conquest of new markets and the more thorough exploitation of old ones. On the other hand, the apparent contradictions that all Marxian analyses of non-Western contexts address – the regressive role of colonial rule in Ireland, the agency of Indian colonial subjects in overthrowing the British bourgeoisie, the "survival" of traditional economic sectors and pre-capitalist classes – are the direct result of exploitation and colonial/imperial domination as shared conditions and social relations characteristic of such contexts. The texts therefore contain an implicit or explicit theory of global social change, in which the European and non-European worlds, although clearly evincing dissimilar and contrasting patterns of class struggle and development, are nevertheless viewed as causally connected by the exploitation and domination of the former over the latter.[5]

This is nowhere more explicit than in Marx's letter to Paul Annenkov from 1846, in which Marx clearly spelt out how slavery in the colonies was the basis for the industrialisation of the European metropoles. It is therefore worthwhile to quote from it at length:

> Freedom and slavery constitute an antagonism. I do not mean indirect slavery, the slavery of proletariat; I mean direct slavery, the slavery of the Blacks in Surinam, in Brazil, in the southern regions of North America. Direct slavery is as much the pivot upon which our present-day industrialism turns as are machinery, credit, etc. Without slavery there would be no cotton, without cotton there would be no modern industry. It is slavery which has given value to the colonies, it is the colonies which have created world trade, and world trade is the necessary condition for large-scale machine industry. Consequently, prior to the slave trade, the colonies sent very few products to the Old World, and did not noticeably change the face of the world. Slavery is therefore an economic category of paramount importance. Without slavery, North America, the most progressive nation, would be transformed into a patriarchal country. Only wipe North America off the map and you will get anarchy, the complete decay of trade and modern civilisation. But to do away with slavery would be to wipe America off the map. Being an economic category, slavery has existed in all nations since the beginning of the world. All that modern nations have achieved is to disguise slavery at home and import it openly into the New World. (Marx and Engels 1982: 101f.)

We have here the same dialectics that regards freedom and slavery, and in particular industrial labour and slave labour, as opposites, while at the same time

---

5   For Erik Olin Wright (2002), exploitation, defined as "the process through which the inequalities in incomes are generated by inequalities in rights and powers over productive resources", is the pivotal concept of Marxist class analysis. Because it is based on antagonistic interests, forms of exclusion from access to resources, and appropriation of exploited labour, it is intimately linked to domination, conceptualised as the set of "social relations within which one person's activities are directed and controlled by another" (Wright 2002: 31ff.), and relying in turn on exclusion and appropriation of labour effort.

conceiving of them as indispensable to each other, and both as the obverse and reverse of capitalist forms of production. The map from which North America would be wiped off without slavery, in Marx's words, is a world map, and the capitalist world-economy constitutes the unit of analysis within which he placed his conceptualisation of slavery and industrial labour. Indeed, shifting the unit of analysis from the nation-state framework to the world-economy as a whole would be world-systems analysis' pivotal point in upholding the ongoing validity of Marx's theory of history in the twenty-first century (see Chapter 2). Yet neither was Marx himself consistent in his use of this angle, as world-systems theorists would later point out, nor was the world-economic focus the methodological currency in his time.

Especially for political economists, both slavery and serfdom however provided the standard against which free wage labour and capitalism were defined, rather than being seen as contemporaneous and compatible with it. For Adam Smith, a free market economy based on individual competition, free trade, and a high degree of division of labour was the most efficient economic system. By contrast, slavery was seen as creating an inefficient market with little to no incentives for competitiveness. Under this definition, Smith tellingly subsumed both plantation slavery in Europe's West Indian colonies and the "milder kind" – i.e., coerced labour found in Russia, Poland, and eastern Germany, in which "slaves ... were supposed to belong more directly to the land than to their master" (Smith 2009: 228), a labour regime which Engels would later label the "second serfdom" (Engels 1992, 1928). In turn, for Marx, the abolition of both serfdom and slavery was the first prerequisite for the emergence of a capitalist economy. In examining the conditions that had historically enabled money to become capital and labour to become wage-labour in *The Grundrisse*, Marx stressed that the capital-labour relationship had to take the form of a *free* exchange of objectified labour for living labour. In order to fulfil this condition, both the dissolution of "lower forms of living labour", among which he counted slavery and serfdom, as well as that of "happier forms of the same", such as communal labour, were necessary:

> The conditions under which the relation appears at the origin, or which appear as the historic presuppositions of its becoming, reveal at first glance a two-sided character – on one side, dissolution of lower forms of living labour; on the other, dissolution of happier forms of the same. The first presupposition, to begin with, is that the relation of slavery or serfdom has been suspended. Living labour capacity belongs to itself, and has disposition over the expenditure of its forces, through exchange. Both sides confront each other as persons. (Marx 1973: 464)

Although not explicit, Marx's map here is of a much smaller scale than in his letter to Paul Annenkov: it refers to "modern Western nations", where the industrial labour force was "doubly free" – from the means of production as well as from being bound to the land. Given that the world-economy in its entirety was capitalist, forms of unfree labour would eventually disappear, and, with them,

44 *Global Inequalities Beyond Occidentalism*

the process of othering to those performing the work: Unlike slaves or serfs, free workers enter the capital-labor relationship *as persons*. Accordingly, the occurrence of slavery at individual points within the capitalist mode of production was possible "only because it does not exist at other points; and appears as *an anomaly opposite the bourgeois system* itself" (Marx 1978e: 255, emphasis added). Specifically, for Marx, plantation owners in the Americas were capitalists only in virtue of being "anomalies within a world market based on free labour" (Marx 1973). Like other apparent contradictions, social conditions, labour relations and phenomena emerged as a result of colonial and imperial rule, they entered Marxian theory as anomalies to the capitalist mode of production. With both slavery and plantation owners appearing as anomalous and as structurally embedded in the logic of capitalist production at the same time, it ultimately is coloniality itself that is conceived as an anomaly within an internally still dialectical modernity (Boatcă 2013a, 2014).

Among the central arguments of the Marxist theory of capitalism, the problem of the contradictory social reproduction of the capitalist system has received the least systematic treatment within Marx's own work, which focused primarily on the historical materialist explanation of capitalism's dynamics (Burawoy and Wright 2006: 462). It however became a prominent subject of debate during the Marxist revival of the 1960s and 1970s, as the concept of class exploitation became central to Western Marxist sociology, while other apparent contradictions captured by Marx's concept of the Asiatic mode of production, the possibility of a Russian, non-capitalist road to socialism, and the political potential of the peasantry, that had been widely debated in Eastern European, Latin American and Asian strands of Marxism as early as the mid-nineteenth century (Boatcă 2003a; Burawoy and Wright 2006: 468; Therborn 1996; San Juan 2002: 225ff.), acquired more visibility in the core in the context of the global resurgence of Marxism.

By allowing one to differentiate between a structural regional level – in this case, Western Europe – where the contradiction between forces and relations of production had predominantly led to class polarisation and class struggle, and a global one, where polarisation resulted in an international division of labour with the different structural positions characterised by development, underdevelopment, or uneven and combined development, Marx' and Engels's writings on colonialism and imperialism thus acquire relevance for both the analysis of global inequality relations and for the theory of social change underlying it (Arrighi 2002; Wright 2002).

Consideration of gender inequality in the work of Marx and Engels parallels their treatment of colonial contexts and is as such equally decisive for an assessment of the epistemic stance characterising Marxian writing. On the basis of the references made by Marx in the *Communist Manifesto*, the *German Ideology*, and *Capital* to such issues as the bourgeois marriage, the position of women under capitalism, and sexual relations more generally, the prevailing opinion has for a long time been that Marx's work, much like the one of other classics of the discipline, reflected and was informed by a male, heterosexual, European perspective (Carver 1998: 206; Tucker 2002: 4).

Criticism to this very effect has been directed at Marxist theory not only in relation to its disregard of women's agency under capitalism more generally, but also of that of racial and ethnic groupings within or outside Western Europe, national liberation struggles in colonial contexts, and not least women of colour in the "Third World" during decade-lasting debates over the relationship between gender, ethnicity, race, and class. At least two different outcomes can be distinguished. On the one hand, the institutional recognition of the multiplicity of levels of difference alongside all of the above-mentioned dimensions in the 1980s and 90s, mirrored in the establishment of university departments on gender, racial and ethnic studies, was followed by the de-politicisation of the feminist movement, the simultaneous culturalisation of both feminist and national liberation movements, and the corresponding abandonment of a decidedly Marxist analysis of capitalism (Gilroy 1981; Solomos and Back 1988; Feldman 2002; Bartolovich and Lazarus 2002; Mies 2007).

On the other hand, several critiques of the concept of primitive accumulation starting in the 1970s gradually converged into an explicitly Marxist reconceptualisation of gender relations *and* colonial exploitation under capitalism that actively incorporated developments outside of Europe. Although they originated in (and are currently represented by) several theoretical and substantive directions, two main strands will be addressed in the following: (1) the world-systems perspective, arguing that non-wage, colonial modes of labour control were integral to and essential for the logic of capitalism, and (2) the feminist approach of the Bielefeld School, claiming that subsistence labour paralleled wage labour as a core pillar of capital accumulation. At the same time, the thrust of both their arguments can be summarised as the attempt to decentre the role of the proletariat as the main exploited class, and, accordingly, that of wage labour as the defining moment of the capitalist system. Both approaches also dovetail well with postcolonial, de-colonial and Third World feminist perspectives, in that they formulate their critique of Marxian political economy in terms of the "blind spots" of the conventional definition of capitalism.

Chapter 2

World-Systems Analysis and the Feminist Subsistence Perspective

> Why, then, has the vocabulary of those events become so handy for today's transnationalists? Is one entitled to wonder whether this means the world has now become a macrocosm of what the Caribbean region was, in the 16th century? If so, should we not ask what took the world so long to catch up – especially since what is happening now is supposed to be qualitatively so different from the recent past? Or is it rather that the Caribbean experience was merely one chapter of a book being written, before the name of the book – world capitalism – became known to its authors?
>
> Sidney Mintz (1998)

While no single text exhaustively captures any of the positions, two titles can be said to adequately characterise the approaches under discussion as well as point to the different emphasis each places on a particular blind spot – as opposed to the emphasis on the proletariat common to orthodox Marxism: Sidney Mintz's article "Was the Plantation Slave a Proletarian?" (1978) for the world-systems perspective, and Claudia von Werlhof's chapter "The Proletarian Is Dead: Long Live the Housewife!" (1984) for the subsistence approach.

Slaves vs. Proletarians

Sidney Mintz's discussion of chattel slavery in the Caribbean was among the first texts to use the theoretical framework of Wallerstein's world-systems analysis in order to explain the persistence of non-wage forms of labour control in the capitalist world-economy. Both Mintz's 1978 article and his 1986 book on the role of sugar in the history of capitalism had as a central reference point Marx's contention that plantation owners in America were capitalists existing "as anomalies within a world market based on free labour" (Marx, in: Mintz 1986: 59) and the difficulties of subsequent Marxists in making sense of the place of modern slave economies in world economic history. If free proletarian labour had emerged in Europe through the dispossession of the masses during the process of primitive accumulation, what process – and what economic system – did the simultaneous emergence of slave labour on the plantations of Britain's and France's Caribbean colonies belong to?

Since Marx had lumped slavery and serfdom together as relations of production to be superseded in the transition to capitalism, their existence in peripheral countries was conceptualised in terms of "feudal remnants" in

48   *Global Inequalities Beyond Occidentalism*

subsequent debates among Marxists. The attribute "feudal" soon became an umbrella term for traditional, precapitalist, or non-modern – structures.[1] In Latin America in particular, this became the conventional Marxist reading of economic underdevelopment, explained in terms of the persistence of such "lower" forms of labour despite capitalist penetration.

According to Mintz, the contrast Marx had drawn between slaves in the Americas and proletarians in Europe was less about the substance of the labour forms as such, which Marx himself had considered to be different only in degree – "the veiled slavery of the wage-workers in Europe needed, for its pedestal, slavery pure and simple in the new world" (Marx, in: Mintz 1978: 86). Rather, the distinction was meant to clarify what such labour forms revealed about the nature of the capitalist system. In order to shed light on the relation between the two categories of workers, Mintz therefore focused on the nature of slavery.

Taking into account Marx's caveat that only those free workers who sold their labour power as a commodity in a capitalist market had historically also been members of the proletariat (as opposed to occasional free workers in pre-bourgeois economies), the essential elements of the definition of the proletarian became

> That a free labourer has nothing to sell but his effort, that he sees and offers to sell that effort as a commodity to its prospective buyer, and that he has nothing but his labour-power to sell. (Mintz 1978: 83)

In turn, the plantation slaves that Mintz examined against the background of this definition were chattel slaves, "persons purchased or inherited and owned as property, who were used as labourers on large agricultural estates producing commodities for (mainly) European markets" (Mintz 1978: 82). As such, however, they were neither slaves in the sense of a slave mode of production, nor anomalous proletarians in a capitalist system. Instead, as Mintz showed for the entire Caribbean region from the sixteenth to the late nineteenth centuries, they were one of the several categories of (predominantly) unfree labourers employed on cotton, tobacco, sugar, and coffee plantations according to the extent to which they met the labour needs, climatic conditions, and topography of each particular case, alongside the successive demands of the capitalist world-economy for tropical commodities (Mintz 1977: 256ff.). Thus, while the first Hispanic sugar-cane plantations in the Antilles employed enslaved indigenous people and Africans between 1500 and 1580, the mass destruction of the native population and the abundance of land made the mixture of European indentured labourers and African as well as Native American slaves a more lucrative labour arrangement on British and French plantations a century later. It was only at the end of the seventeenth century that slavery represented the preferred form of labour exaction, soon to be replaced by a mix of enslaved, indentured and coerced labour in the

---

1   For a discussion of the feudalism debate in the context of modernisation theory, dependency theory and world-systems analysis, see Boatcă 2003a, Boatcă 2006.

eighteenth. While Mintz explicitly limited his periodisation to sugar plantations in the Caribbean as the same time as he allowed for a certain degree of generalisation to Brazil, parts of Mexico and the US South, his findings have more recently been corroborated not only in the case of Cuba (Tomich 1991), but also for both sugar and coffee plantations in Brazil and Colombia (Schwartz 1992; Cardoso 2008). This sequence of different labour patterns in the Caribbean continued until after the formal end of slavery with the emergence of a rural proletariat and the eventual elimination of manual labour from the sugar-cane plantations. Meanwhile, policies of labour migration contributed to preserving the link between tropical colonial labour and non-white labour well into the twentieth century by ensuring that the workers needed to "ease" the transition from enslaved to free labour were recruited from other European colonies such as India and Java or states with weak labour regulations, such as China (Mintz 1977: 264; Mintz 1998: 122; Tomich 1991: 304).

Over and above their intrinsic value, the arresting fact about Mintz' analysis of plantation slaves in the Caribbean and the case studies undertaken in its wake is the extent to which they unsettle central notions of Marxist theory (Boatcă 2013, 2014). Among them are the uniform character of slavery as a "lower form of labour" and its incompatibility with the free labour characterising the capitalist world market, as well as the basic evolutionary assumptions deriving from this conceptualisation: the abolition of slavery in the transition to capitalism and the inevitability of proletarianisation as the accomplishment of the shift to wage labour. According to both Mintz's and to newer studies, however, not only was (plantation) slavery *not* the norm in Europe's New World colonies, or exclusively based on imported African labour – except for a very limited period in the seventeenth century; it was not homogeneous, either. It instead encompassed several "slavery regimes" (Schwartz 1992; Cardoso 2008: 75) involving different degrees of coercion of workers in different regions – less coercion in poorer areas such as the Brazilian Northeast, and more in richer ones and on large plantations – as well as the concomitant use of enslaved and free labour in one locale. The alleged "transition" to free labour after the abolition of slavery further complicated this already fuzzy pattern, by forcing planter classes in Cuba and Brazil to employ peasants, indentured servants, and wage workers in order to compensate for the shortage of enslaved labour (Tomich 2004: 70f.) on the one hand, and by creating the possibility of simultaneous, multiple sources of income from such diverse employment regimes as share-cropping, tenancy, wage work, and private ownership for one individual (Frank 1967: 271f.), on the other. Even if such "permutations of labour relations" (van der Linden 2008: 27) as in the latter case were not the rule, documented proof of their occurrence nonetheless serves to demonstrate that chattel slavery was neither an anomaly or anachronism, nor a homogeneous phenomenon, but rather a highly flexible and sophisticated institution capable of accommodating the fast changing demands of the expanding world-economy throughout the centuries.

50 *Global Inequalities Beyond Occidentalism*

To the concrete question making up the title of his article, "Was the Plantation Slave a Proletarian?", Mintz's answer however remained elusive, as did his rectification of the Marxist view in light of the realities of Caribbean slave systems. While arguing that proletarians and slaves were linked by the world-economy and as such should not be defined or analysed in isolation from each other, Mintz concluded that the contrast Marx had drawn between free and enslaved labour, although not incorrect, was "extreme" (Mintz 1978: 97) and did not do justice to specific historical conditions. His book-length analysis of the rise of the sugar industry under capitalism, *Sweetness and Power*, allowed him to revisit the issue a decade later and specify both the linkages and the contrasting patterns in the emergence and the gradual transformation of slaves and proletarians:

> Like proletarians, slaves are separated from the means of production (tools, land, etc.). But proletarians can exercise some influence over where they work, how much they work, for whom they work, and what to do with their wages [...]. Slaves and forced labourers, unlike free workers, have nothing to sell, not even their labour; instead, they have themselves been bought and sold and traded. Like the proletarians, however, they stand in dramatic contrast to the serfs of European feudalism, and they are propertyless. (Mintz 1986: 57)

If an extreme contrast between forms of labour control had to be drawn, Mintz thus insisted that it should be one between serfdom in feudal Europe on the one hand and slavery and wage labour in the entire capitalist world-economy, on the other – a conceptualisation that entailed viewing both slaves and proletarians as instances of *modern* labour arrangements, corresponding to a *capitalist* mode of production. As such, plantation slavery in the Caribbean bore a number of essential features commonly associated with industrial production: discipline, processing under one authority, strictness of scheduling, the separation of production and consumption. If viewed as a remarkably early instance of Europe's industrial history overseas, plantation slavery thus becomes a model for the industrial capitalism later to be implemented on a large-scale in the metropoles, and the Caribbean turns into one of the first colonial laboratories of a globally conceived modernity.

Despite the different histories and the distinct geographical localities of the origin and functioning of chattel slavery and wage labour, Mintz claimed that

> their economic functions in the world trade system, especially from the mid-seventeenth to the mid-nineteenth century, were overlapping, even interdependent. The linkage between Caribbean slaves and European free labourers was a linkage of production and hence also of consumption, created by the single system of which they were both parts. Neither group had much to offer productively but its labour. Both produced; both consumed little of what they produced. Both were divested of their tools. [...] they really form one group, differing only in how they fit into the worldwide division of labour others created for them. (Mintz 1986: 57)

Mintz thus echoed debates undertaken in Latin America, China, Russia, and parts of Eastern Europe as early as the late nineteenth and throughout the twentieth century on the role of the peasantries, the dependency of local labour force on foreign industrial production, and the existence of a world proletariat (see Love 1996: 175; Boatcă 2003a). Unlike most of them, however, he did not stop at noting the incongruity between Marxist theory and social reality in non-industrial peripheries or at suggesting new terms to characterise these realities, but fitted them into the explanation of a global capitalist logic.

A central argument to this end was that slave-powered plantations had significantly contributed to the growth of homeland economies. Not only did they enable the direct transfer of capital to homeland banks for reinvestment, but they presented ready markets for the metropole's industrial products, especially machinery, cloth, and torture instruments. Moreover, Mintz pointed out, they provided low-cost food substitutes for the working classes of the industrial metropole:[2] as they entered the food diet of European labourers, tropical commodities such as tobacco, tea, coffee, chocolate, and sugar reinforced the double linkage of production and consumption between slaves in the colonies and proletarians in the metropoles, by increasing the latter's productivity and accounting for ever more of their caloric intake. At the same time, they underpinned the growing gender gap of the labouring poor by disproportionately contributing to women's and children's meals, while the more costly protein food was reserved for the adult male(s) (Mintz 1986: 148f.). How the parallel production and consumption of European commodities by slaves in the colonies and of Caribbean commodities by European wage-earners occurred in the absence of direct interaction between the free and the enslaved remained, for him, one of the most important chapters in the history of world capitalism (Mintz 1977: 265). As such, it was decidedly more than a mere instance of historical particularism concerning one specific world region and one unique socioeconomic context.

Proletarians vs. Housewives

What in Mintz's view had lent the issue of plantation slavery a general, rather than a narrow regional scope, making it relevant for an understanding of the logic of capitalism as a whole, was the fact that it was, alongside wage-labour, an indispensable element of the functioning of the world-economy. The mutual provisioning with commodities that linked plantation slaves to factory proletarians thus ensured the reproduction of both categories of workers and of the capitalist

---

2 Mintz's argument in this context owes of course much to the work of Trinidadian historian Eric Williams (1943), whose thesis that the slave trade had been the main factor responsible for the capital accumulation which financed Britain's Industrial Revolution had sparked a great amount of controversy in US and British academia for decades after publication.

world-economy which had created them: "Slave and proletarian together powered the imperial economic system that kept the one supplied with manacles and the other with sugar and rum" (Mintz 1986: 184).

Around the same time as Mintz, German feminist scholars would make a similar, yet even bolder claim with respect to the issue of housework: when related to the entire world-economy, housework, and, with it, the women's question, proved to be the most general, not the most particular, of all social questions, because it contained all others:

> unless the 'women's question' is seen as fundamental, the understanding of the development of non-European societies and their relationship to Europe since the end of the Middle Ages (and later to the USA and other countries of the so-called centre) has to remain superficial. (von Werlhof 1988: 14)

While explicitly conceiving of women's work as the "blind spot" in the critique of political economy and arguing that both women and colonies had been excluded from theories of modern capitalist societies, the German feminist theorists however did not plead for a mere inclusion of these issues into existing explanatory models. Instead, they aimed at a reconceptualisation of the process of capitalist accumulation that would make the relationship between *general human labour* and capital the central contradiction of the capitalist mode of production – rather than the narrower one between *wage labour* and capital (Mies 1988a: 3).

General human labour, in this understanding, included not only housework, but also other forms of non-wage work by subsistence producers in both the First and the Third Worlds. The approach thereby challenged the classical Marxist standpoint according to which non-capitalist subsistence economies, along with all other pre-capitalist sectors, would gradually disappear in the face of the expanding capitalist mode of production, thus making wage labour the rule all over the world-economy. This linear and irreversible process of proletarianisation and pauperisation of the labour force, such as it had taken place in the capitalist centres, was supposed to occur after the period of primitive accumulation. However, subsistence theorists argued that primitive accumulation was an ongoing process through which non-wage workers and subsistence producers are being tapped for surplus labour and surplus product in addition to the process of capital accumulation through the exploitation of the actual wage work (Mies 1988b: 43).

Known throughout the 1980s and the 1990s as the subsistence approach, this feminist materialist perspective had grown out of the Bielefeld School of development sociology, which built on the 1960s and '70s debate on the articulation of modes of production in French anthropology (Meillassoux 1975) as well as on the international domestic labour debate (Dalla-Costa and Jones 1973). Dissatisfied with both approaches' solutions for conceptualising subsistence labour in relation to capitalism – as pertaining to a separate economic system in the first case, or as a "forgotten" category of Marxist theory in the second – the Bielefeld subsistence approach joined the world-systems perspective being developed in the

1980s in arguing that housework, together with other forms of non-wage labour, depended on the logic of the world-economy for its reproduction.

Claudia von Werlhof's chapter "The Proletarian Is Dead; Long Live the Housewife?", first published in German in 1983 together with other key contributions by the feminist theorists of the German subsistence approach (von Werlhof et al. 1983), was soon afterwards included in the edited volume *Households in the World Economy* (Smith et al. 1984), the first publication to document the cooperation of the Bielefeld group with the Binghamton world-systems circle. Against domestic labour theorists, von Werlhof and her co-authors had previously argued that housewives in the centres and small peasants in the peripheries of the world-economy had not been merely neglected in Marxist analyses of accumulation, but had been the very precondition for the "rise" of the male, white wage worker and of the capital-wage labour relation to the centre-stage of theories of capitalism (von Werlhof 1988; Mies 1988a: 7). The focus on subsistence labour, especially in the form of housework, therefore grounded what the Bielefelders considered to be the analytically more fruitful "view from below" on which von Werlhof would base her argument for the *general* scope of the women's question as opposed to the *particular* character of the category of the proletarian.

Contrary to the main tenets of both Marxist and liberal theories of capitalist development on the model of the proletarianisation of the Western labour force, von Werlhof maintained that:

> the proletarian wage labourer is a minority phenomenon during a particular phase of capitalism and is limited to a few areas of the earth [...] Eighty to 90% of the world population consists of women, peasants, craftsmen, petty traders, and wage labourers whom one cannot call "free" or "proletarian". (von Werlhof 1984: 135)

Privileging these previously excluded workers in the study of the current capitalist tendencies at the level of the world-economy necessarily led to the insight that the free wage worker was neither the "pillar" of capital accumulation that Marxist theory had made him out to be, nor the revolutionary, progressive, or modernising social actor on whom all theories of modern social change relied. Claudia von Werlhof's radical thesis instead proposed that

> everything is just the opposite of what it appears to be. Not the 10% free wage labourers, but the 90% unfree non-wage labourers are the pillar of accumulation and growth, the truly exploited, the real 'producers', the 'norm', and represent the general condition in which human beings find themselves under capitalism. (von Werlhof 1984: 138)

While the unfree workers encompassed peasants, craftsmen, petty traders, unfree wage labourers, and housewives, it was this last category that, according

54 *Global Inequalities Beyond Occidentalism*

to subsistence theorists, epitomised non-wage work as the basis of capitalist production. Not only was the economic function of housewives under capitalism as closely interrelated with that of proletarians as Mintz had shown it to be the case for slaves in the Third World and proletarians in the First; housewives and proletarians were the very "Siamese twins" of First World economies (von Werlhof 1984: 139). As in the case of slaves, the contrast between housewives and proletarians was one between extreme ends of a continuum of capitalist relations of productions; yet, despite the conventional view, which upheld the proletarian as prototype of the capitalist worker, neither the individual categories nor their combination into an "economic couple" – the Western, white, middle-class nuclear family dependent on a "family wage" – frequently occurred in "pure" form.[3] The contrast between the two could therefore only be reconstructed on the basis of their respective ideal types:

> The proletarian is apparently free, equal, fraternal, and so on. The housewife is the reverse of that: She is in reality unfree in a double sense: (1) She is not free to choose or change the place and type of work or her particular job freely; she is bound to the apartment, the husband, and the children; (2) she is also not free from all means of production, so one cannot say that she merely possesses her labour-power, which in a certain sense is the case with the proletarian. (von Werlhof 1984: 139)

Through the systematic division of labour which makes the prototypical male proletarian into the sole supplier – and consequently possessor – of money, and the prototypical housewife into an unpaid labourer entitled only to "board and lodging", the economic position of the housewife resembles more closely that of slaves and serfs in the Third World than that of proletarians in the First (von Werlhof 1984: 140). New with respect to the social inequality structure thus generated was not the sexual division of labour as such – otherwise a universal feature of both capitalist and non-capitalist societies. Instead, the newness consisted in the centrality of a social category's access to money – which Marx had labelled the "queen of all commodities" – for determining one's position within the capitalist division of labour. The low social status of housewives, subsistence theorists thus argued, is not due to the low esteem in which housework was held, but to the low esteem of unpaid labour in general, with which the position of the housewife is associated (Bennhold-Thomsen 1988a: 161).

The same could therefore be concluded with respect to unpaid or underpaid workers in the Third World. When conceptualised as private-owning producers, as

---

3 "Only very few housewives are 'pure' housewives. Almost everyone – both women and men – are for some time of their life or from time to time also wage labourers, or they sell homemade products out of home (above all, in the Third World). [...] The wage labour of women is organized and treated as an extension of their housework and, moreover, for this reason correspondingly badly paid" (von Werlhof 1984: 141).

in the Marxist-Leninist approach to political economy, peasants and craftsmen in the so-called developing countries reasonably fit into the category of "remnants" of a pre-capitalist mode of production, meant to be gradually proletarianised during capitalism. Drawing on fieldwork undertaken in Latin America and India, subsistence theorists however argued that such economic sectors had only emerged in the Third World as a result of capitalist development, hence that they had been from the very beginning subordinated under capital and as such had to be analysed together with the capital valuation process (Bennholdt-Thomsen 1988a: 53; Baier 2004: 73ff.). Likewise, the overexploitation of and violence against women in the Third World, far from being a remnant of "archaic systems of patriarchy" or a marker of backwardness in such regions, was the very product of capitalist development (Mies 1988c: 137ff.; Bennholdt-Thomsen 1988b: 159). In particular, the making of the peasant housewife through the separation of male commodity production (cash-crop production and wage labour) and female subsistence production (homework and out-contracting) in the Third World exhibited marked similarities with the split between (male) public and (female) private spheres within the European bourgeois households in the eighteenth and nineteenth centuries. In the case of the Indian lower classes, the process was still taking place:

> some of the so-called "backward classes" (service castes like shepherds, potters etc.) have been able to rise in recent years to the status of middle peasants or even rich peasants. Previously their women did agricultural labour, but once they have achieved a certain economic status they subject their women to seclusion and strict patriarchal norms. The women cease to work on the land as a sign that they are no longer of the inferior class. They become "housewives". (Mies 1988b: 42)

The creation of the housewife as a systematic and historically specific process characteristic of capitalist development thus turned out to be the common denominator of both instances of sexual division of labour – the Western European and the non-European one. Consequently labelled "housewifisation" (Germ. *Hausfrauisierung*) (Bennholdt-Thomsen 1988a: 159), it however encompassed not only the generalisation of housework as the defining feature of women's work, but also, and more importantly, the gradual generalisation of non-wage labour at the level of the entire capitalist world-economy. The Bielefeld subsistence theorists thereby built on the concept of marginalisation developed within Latin American dependency theory (Quijano 1966; Cardoso 1971; Kowarick 1975) in order to counter the Marxian understanding of pauperised peasants and urban poor as an industrial reserve army of capitalism that would eventually be absorbed into wage labour – and therefore (successfully) proletarianised. The Latin American theorists had argued that dependent capitalism in the periphery would merely lead to the marginalisation of the peasant masses, yet would not be able to assimilate them into wage labour. The Bielefeld group amended this position in two important respects: First, they maintained that the creation of large marginalised masses in the periphery was not an instance of aberrant, dependent capitalism, but an integral part of the capitalist mode of production proper (Mies 1988: 29). Second, they claimed that this development had been modelled on the economic position of the housewife both in the centres and in the peripheries of the capitalist world-economy. The processes of marginalisation or pauperisation diagnosed in different parts of the world could therefore be best understood in analogy to the logic of housewifisation: "The housewife *is* labour power in capitalism: in a world in which money is the measure of all, she can be paid the least and need not be paid at all for the bulk of her work" (Bennholdt-Thomsen 1988: 166).

The first proviso amounted to the notion that treating the majority of the world population as a residual economic category was untenable. Showing how World Bank policies of land reform in development countries ended up producing more, rather than less, pauperised peasant masses, Bennholdt-Thomsen (1988: 56) identified the subordination of small producers to the market through credit mechanisms as the main tendency in agriculture in the latter half of the twentieth century, and thus the active "underdevelopment" of forms of production through the very action of capitalist development agencies. The second proviso, to be expanded upon in Maria Mies' later work (1996), was tantamount to viewing housewifisation as the strategy of defining subsistence work into nature, and both as characteristic tendencies of the capitalist world-economy that represented the very opposite of proletarianisation. Given women's child-bearing capacity and capitalism's dependence on living labour, the production of human labour-power was the central task around which the role of women under capitalism had been defined. Accordingly, the economic role of the housewife had been constructed as one based on "natural" propensities and subsistence production that did not involve the money economy. In a system centred around the ceaseless accumulation of capital, therefore, the most profitable forms of labour would not be wage work, but precisely unremunerated housework and forms closely approximating it, such as enslaved and enserfed labour in the (ex-)colonies, as well as peasant labour and housework in both centres and peripheries of the system.

> Slave-work today, unfree forms of wage labour, home-industry, peasant production and the like all lie on this continuum of capitalist production, which is today becoming more and more like a slide inclining towards housework. For all have one thing in common: dependence on the market and, generally, on money, or, more exactly, on a wage. (von Werlhof 1984: 141)

Accordingly, not proletarianisation, but housewifisation was the dominant tendency in the world-economy, as exemplified by the rise of the import in "guest-workers" in Western Europe, the high numbers of women employed in offshore manufacturing, and the increased transfer of industries to the Third World. The model of the future, subsistence theorists argued, was the world-housewife or the worldwide "industrial reserve army", the "marginal mass" – not, however, the proletarian.

In her now classic critique of Western feminism writing on the Third World, Chandra Mohanty would later point to Maria Mies' work on the effects of housewifisation as one instance of a politically focused analysis that derives theoretical categories from the context being analysed without falling into the trap of cultural reductionism, victimisation of or generalisation about Third World women (Mohanty 1991). The almost complete absence of works by Mies and her co-authors from social theory and gender studies curricula in Germany today attest precisely to the degree of discomfort that their radical theses, geopolitical and political focus, and the theoretical categories thus derived caused mainstream analyses of inequality under capitalism.

Methodological Implications: Anomalies Revisited

In essence, the arguments put forward by Mintz and the Bielefeld feminist theorists were not entirely new. As already noted, the notion of a world proletariat had been more or less explicitly formulated several times at the close of the nineteenth and the beginning of the twentieth centuries, while the existence of other forms of labour besides wage labour within the capitalist mode of production had been central to Latin American dependency theory, the Bielefeld school of development sociology, and US-based world-systems analysis during the 60s and 70s. However, by highlighting the contribution that modern slave economies on the one hand and subsistence production on the other had had to the emergence and maintenance of capitalism as a global mode of production, the two succeeded in modifying Marx's conceptualisation of the process of primitive accumulation so as to account for the creation of patterns of *global inequality*.

In turn, disagreement with the Marxian understanding of primitive accumulation at a world scale had first led both dependency theorists and world-systems analysts to a reconceptualisation of *global development*. For the dependentistas, capitalism represented an asymmetrical power relation structured around the developed, industrialised West, that constituted the centre of the system, and the underdeveloped, agricultural Third World, economically exploited by the centre and constituting the system's periphery (Cardoso and Faletto 1969). In this view, development and underdevelopment were not different "stages" in a continuum, but, like centre and periphery, relational notions co-existing in time and mutually reinforcing each other. Taking as a point of departure the fact that the international division of labour established since the European colonial expansion in the sixteenth century had gradually reorganised the economies of the colonies according to the needs of the European colonial centres (e.g., the extraction of raw materials in exchange for industrial goods), dependency theorists spoke of the "development of underdevelopment" (Frank 1966) as the process actively and systematically producing backwardness in the periphery. Latin America's underdevelopment was therefore not a matter of the region's "semifeudal" or "pre-capitalist" character, but a result of its

58 *Global Inequalities Beyond Occidentalism*

incorporation into the capitalist system as a raw-material producing area since colonial times (Frank 1967).

In his 1967 analysis of underdevelopment in Chile and Brazil, dependency theorist André Gunder Frank had accordingly concluded that the employment of workers in forms of serfdom, tenancy, sharecropping, and unpaid labour alongside forms of wage labour was no proof of a mixture of feudal and capitalist economic structures, but a direct consequence of the subsumption of Brazilian agriculture under the interests of metropolitan industries (Frank 1967: 230ff). Although he viewed all of these relations of production as being determined by a single, capitalist world system, he went on considering them "non-capitalist" in essence. In discussing worldwide capital accumulation through super-exploitation of slaves and the indigenous populations in India, Latin America, and the Caribbean immediately following these areas' colonisation, Frank therefore pleaded for replacing Marx' notion of "primitive accumulation" by "primary accumulation". According to him, the latter was the more adequate label for the exploitative practices that had continued until long after the industrial revolution and up to the present day[4] (Frank 1978).

Contemporary capitalism therefore at least partly depended for its reproduction on the conversion of use values – resulted from what Frank considered non- and pre-capitalist relations of production – into exchange values for the capitalist circulation of commodities. Gender relations entered the argument by logically fitting into the discussion of primary accumulation through subsistence labour:

> the most widespread and important incidence of ... capitalist accumulation of capital on the basis of primary accumulation through 'non-capitalist' relations of production is the unrequited production and reproduction performed by the wife and mother within the bourgeois and working-class families! For, if capital had to pay the housewife for the total contribution she [...] makes to the ability of the worker to produce surplus value, and if capital did not have her as a further underpaid labour force and reserve army of labour to boot, capitalist accumulation of capital would be difficult, if not impossible. (Frank 1978: 247)

Although Frank did not pursue the gender aspect any further, the parallel he drew between types of subsistence income as provided by housewives in households within the core and village production in peripheral areas by grouping them under "primary accumulation" was a crucial step in the reconceptualisation of both.

---

4 "Thus, the process of divorcing owners from their means of production and converting them into wage labourers was not only primitive, original or previous to the capitalist stage. It also persists through the capitalist stage. Primary *non-capitalist* accumulation feeds into the capitalist process of capital accumulation; but the latter continues not simply because capitalist development of wage labour divorces producers from their means; it also continues *despite* this divorce through the maintenance and even re-creation of working relations that are not strictly 'wage-labour'" (1978: 244, first emphasis added).

World-Systems Analysis and the Feminist Subsistence Perspective   59

He however concluded that the process of incorporating pre-existing forms of production into the capitalist system might involve the "trans-*formation* of relations of production from one 'non-capitalist' form to another, or the utilisation of pre-existing forms of production to contribute to capital accumulation in combination with different circuits of circulation" (Frank 1978: 251). This definition of transformation as the relevant criterion for the existence of capitalism therefore ended up leaving both subsistence production in the household and non-wage agricultural labour outside of the capitalist sphere.

According to Frank, however, the validity of any interpretation of Marx's understanding of capitalism would ultimately come from its capacity to do justice to the fact that

> the sugar slave plantations of Brazil in the 16th century, of more and more Caribbean islands in the 17th and 18th centuries, and of Southern U.S. cotton slave plantations in the 19th century were essential parts of a single system and historic process, in which they contributed materially to the primitive, and then industrial accumulation of capital concentrated in particular parts of the system and times of the process. (Frank 1978: 256f.)

It is at this particular juncture that the interests of the theorists of global development converged with those of researchers of global inequality relations, as becomes apparent both from Mintz's inquiry into the link between chattel slaves and proletarians and the Bielefeld group's analysis of the relationship between wage labourers and subsistence producers. A theory of capitalism accounting for the development of underdevelopment in the periphery as well as for the global inequality structures it generated would therefore have to incorporate slave plantations, serf labour, housework and other types of subsistence labour into its definition, instead of declaring them anomalies to the Western pattern of industrial development on the one hand and proletarianisation on the other.

Focusing on the wide variety of phenomena that orthodox Marxist theory turned into anomalies consequently became a point of access for the reconceptualisation of both world capitalism and world inequality. By noting that the key role Marxism attributed to urban industrial proletarians had meant explaining away the very existence of peasants, minorities, women, and the whole peripheral zone as a consequence, such that "[n]ine-tenths of the world became 'questions', 'anomalies', 'survivals'" (Wallerstein 1991a: 160), proponents of the world-systems perspective for the first time pointed to the fact that the necessary corrections had to be of a *methodological* nature.

Bourgeoisification

For one thing, the unit of analysis for patterns of capitalist development as well as of processes of class formation was not the nation-state or any other political-cultural unit, but the historical system corresponding to the modern capitalist world-economy. Earlier historical systems had been characterised by the existence of a single division of labour linking various areas through economic exchange on the one hand, and by a common political structure (as in the case of world-empires) on the other. In turn, a world-economy is not politically unified, such that the accumulated surplus can only be redistributed unequally through the market. Hence, a world-economy's mode of production is of necessity capitalist. Drawing on dependency theorists' relational notions of (under)development and the centre-periphery structure, Immanuel Wallerstein defined "relations of production" as (1) pertaining to the whole system of a European-led world-economy in existence since the sixteenth century and as (2) encompassing free labour in the system's core and coerced labour in its periphery (Wallerstein 1974).

Much like dependency theorists and the Bielefelder feminists, Wallerstein held that both Marx's notion of primitive accumulation and Rosa Luxemburg's modified version of it had contributed to the construction of anomalies of a capitalist system essentially based on free wage labour. For Marx, the incorporation of non-capitalist spheres of production, both in the form of particular social strata such as peasants, and entire geographical regions such as colonial areas, was important only during the stage of the primitive accumulation of capital, i.e., in the mercantile period. For Luxemburg, in turn, they were essential throughout the stages of capitalist development (mercantile and industrial) as markets for the consumption of industrial products, as an extra source of means of production, as well as of labour power, yet remained external to capitalism. Wallerstein therefore pointed out that the single major stumbling block of all debates on the advent of capitalism in non-Western areas was the existence of free labour as the defining characteristic of the capitalist mode of production – which, however, stemmed from an undue generalisation of Marx's analysis of the English case:

> The situation of free labourers working for wages in the enterprises of free producers is a minority situation in the modern world. This is certainly true if our unit of analysis is the world economy. It is probably true, or largely true, even if we undertake the analysis within the framework of single high-industrialized states in the twentieth century. When a deduced "norm" turns out not to be the statistical norm, that is, when the situation abounds with exceptions (anomalies, residues), then we ought to wonder whether the definition of the norm serves any useful function. (Wallerstein 2000: 142f.)

The methodological shift in the unit of analysis from particular nation-states to the level of the entire world-economy made it possible to view precisely the *mixture* of free and unfree forms of labour control, instead of free labour alone, as constituting the essence of capitalism: while free labour was characteristic of skilled work in core areas, coerced labour was employed for less skilled work in peripheral ones (Wallerstein 1974: 127). Thus, in the capitalist world-economy emerged with the establishment of Europe's overseas colonies in the sixteenth century, slavery, serf labour,[5] share-cropping, and tenancy were alternative capitalist modes of labour control, all of which employed labour-power as a commodity. Understood as expressions of various relations of production within a global capitalist system, anomalies such as capitalist plantation owners or chattel slaves thereby became "not exceptions to be explained away but patterns to be analysed" (Wallerstein 2000: 143).

At the same time, viewing capitalism as a mode of production of the entire world-system meant that its key actors no longer coincided with the ideal-typical members of the capitalist classes of industrialised core countries, i.e., the bourgeois and the proletarian; nor were the corresponding processes – from the bourgeois revolution through industrialisation to proletarianisation – an adequate description of reality. World-systems analysts concurred with subsistence theorists in their criticism of modern economic discourse in either the Marxist or the liberal variant, both of which upheld the capitalist bourgeois as "the central dynamic force of modern economic life" (Wallerstein 2000: 325f.) on the one hand, and the proletarian wage labourer as "the base of society, of democracy; [...] the allegedly equal and grown-up contract partner of the entrepreneur; the citizen, the 'human being', the member of society, the free individual" (von Werlhof 1984: 133) on the other hand. On the basis of this criticism, subsistence theorists argued that privileging the figure of the proletarian and processes of proletarianisation on the model of industrial England obscured *housewifisation* as the central process actually characterising the development of world capitalism. World-systems analysis in turn drew attention to *bourgeoisification* as a neglected dimension in the dynamics of the capitalist world-economy:

> We are all very conscious that the proletariat, or if you will, waged workers, have not simply been historically there, that they have in fact been created over time [...] This shift is called by some "proletarianization" [...] There are many theories about this process; it is the object of much study. We are also aware, but it is less salient to most of us, that the percentage of persons who might be called bourgeois [...] has no doubt augmented steadily since perhaps the eleventh century, and certainly since the sixteenth. And yet, to my knowledge, virtually no one speaks of "bourgeoisification" as a parallel process to "proletarianization". Nor does anyone write a book on the making of the bourgeoisie [...] It is as though the bourgeoisie were a given, and it acted upon others: upon the aristocracy, upon the state, upon the workers. (Wallerstein 2000: 333)

In both Marxist and liberal theories of history, the role of every bourgeoisie, irrespective of its geohistorical context of emergence, matched the one it was supposed to have played in nineteenth-century Britain, i.e., overthrow the

---

5   Wallerstein's term for the modern variant of serf labour, which, for the very reason of being part of the capitalist mode of production, was essentially different from its feudal European form, was "coerced-cash crop labour" (Wallerstein 1974: 110ff.).

aristocracy, seize state power and industrialise the country. Atypical phenomena such as the "aristocratisation of the bourgeoisie" in sixteenth to eighteenth century Europe, "the betrayal of the bourgeoisie" in non-European contexts in the twentieth, or the "administrative bourgeoisies" in post-decolonisation Africa had not unsettled the developmentalist assumptions underlying this conceptualisation, but had instead been treated as further anomalies. The shift of focus from the reified notion of the bourgeoisie as an "unexamined *essence*" (Wallerstein 2000: 334, my emphasis) to bourgeoisification as an historical *process* of the entire world-system made it possible to discern that not only had there been more historical instances of the economic and political rise of the "middle classes" that did not conform to the British model than instances that did; during the historical evolution of the capitalist system, there have also been ever less possibilities for bourgeoisies to become aristocracies by turning capitalist profit into rent, and therefore less factual control over the means of production than in the case of the classical bourgeoisie. Increasing bourgeoisification was "the end of the possibility of aristocratisation" (Wallerstein 2000: 340), or of the opportunity to convert profit into monopoly profit. In the process, the overall trend had therefore been toward the emergence of ever more administrative or salaried bourgeoisies, themselves living off wages.

> Over time [...] capital has tended to concentrate. [... E]nterprise structures have gradually become larger and involved the separation of ownership and control, and the emergence therefore of new middle classes. Where the "enterprises" are in fact state-owned rather than nominally private, as tends to be the case in weaker states in peripheral and especially semi-peripheral zones, the new middle classes take the form, in large part, of an administrative bourgeoisie. (Wallerstein 2000: 340)

Viewed in the longue durée, proletarianisation and bourgeoisification are thus strikingly analogous processes, both of which involve the transformation of social actors from individuals controlling the means of production and living off resources accumulated in the past – land or machines in the case of peasants and artisans, rent in the case of the aristocracy – to social actors controlling neither capital nor means of production and relying on present earnings.

By highlighting the phenomenon of bourgeoisification, world-systems analysts did not claim that it was *the* central process in the capitalist world-economy, as subsistence theorists did for housewifisation. Yet the conclusions of both approaches converged in dismissing proletarianisation as the governing tendency, and, consequently, as the main instance of class formation in the current capitalist system. This, in turn, called for a second methodological shift, which made the common denominator of the world-systems and the feminist subsistence perspectives even more apparent.

Householding

As proponents of both approaches noted, the centrality of free labour for the definition of capitalism had not only awarded proletarianisation a key role, but had also entailed a differentiation of economic activities in terms of the degree of their productivity. Accordingly, productive forms such as industrial labour had routinely been seen as more compatible with a capitalist mode of production than labour forms considered less or non-productive. The "enormous and very useful loophole in the definition of capitalism" (Wallerstein 2000: 142) thus created accordingly relegated housework and other types of subsistence activities to pre- or non-capitalist labour arrangements. Although subsistence theorists agreed with world-systems authors that this definitional loophole was a common trait of Marxist and liberal theories of capitalism, they maintained that it was the capitalist mode of production itself that made the "social invisibility" (Bennholdt-Thomsen 1984: 262) of subsistence production possible: by subordinating subsistence production to the production of commodities, and by relegating the former to the private sphere, capitalism artificially separated production from its basic goal, the reproduction of life. This separation was subsequently naturalised as the difference between work and non-work, thus allowing for the construction of the social role of the housewife.

For world-systems analysts, the issue entailed both theoretical reconceptualisation and methodological consequences. As an alternative to measuring the individual's position in a society's inequality structure, British theorists had proposed in the early 1980s that the social stratification patterns of the total population should be derived from the socioeconomic position of the male breadwinner, supposed to be the receiver of a family wage. The subsequent gender-and-class debate centred on arguments for and against considering women's position in the labour market when measuring a family's class position by taking the household as a unit of analysis (Goldthorpe 1983; Britten and Heath 1983). Against both sides in the discussion, world-systems theorists argued that, while the unit of analysis of people's incorporation into the labour force was indeed the household (i.e., not the individual), the concept should not be mistaken for that of the nuclear, wage-earning family (Wallerstein and Smith 1992a: 13). As such, it would not only reinforce the false premise that capitalism entailed a transition from traditional subsistence households to nuclear, wage-dependent ones, but also promote a transhistorical view of the household as an institution. In the preface to one of two collective volumes on households in the world-economy, the editors instead maintained that households were no primordial, transhistorical structures, but institutions constitutive of and inherent in the capitalist world-economy. As such, they relied on five distinct sources of revenue – only one of which was wage labour. Market sales of homemade products (i.e., profit from petty commodity production), rental returns from interest, dividends, and lease payments, state or private transfer of welfare and insurance benefits or substantial gifts from kin, and subsistence work (from the production of food to self-manufacture and

64 *Global Inequalities Beyond Occidentalism*

maintenance services) were counted among further strategies of systematically deriving or supplementing annual household income, *all* of which are articulated with wage earnings for most households in the world-economy today (Wallerstein and Smith 1992a: 8f.). In previous work on urban wage earners in Southeast Asia and Brazilian favelas, members of the Bielefeld group had come to similar conclusions as far as transfers from the subsistence sector were concerned, which complemented low wages on a regular basis (Evers 1981; Elwert et al. 1983). They had however not viewed subsistence work and private transfers as two different sources of income, but had grouped both under subsistence and opposed them to monetary income, under which both wage labour and petty commodity production were subsumed. Their resulting typology therefore illustrated the varying degrees to which households combined the two apparently contradictory economic strategies, rather than viewing the very range of strategies as characteristic for capitalist households in general.[6]

In a world-systems perspective, households were defined as "systems of reproduction of labour power [...] that are able to provide labour to capital precisely because they ensure the combination of income from wage labour with that from non-wage labour so as to form an adequate pool of resources guaranteeing the replenishment of labour power" (Smith et al. 1984: 8). As such, they were clearly differentiated from nuclear families, in that they were neither necessarily kinship-based, nor necessarily co-residential. Such a broad definition consequently allowed for subsuming under the notion of household not only units of sharing unrelated by blood lineage, but also units of consumption larger than individual dwelling units which fulfilled collective income-pooling functions, as found in West African, Brazilian or Malaysian contexts (Augel 1984; Elwert 1984; Bennholdt-Thomsen 1984).

Multiple criticisms had also been voiced in the case of North America and Western Europe with respect to both the theoretical implications and the empirical inaccuracy of assuming that the nuclear family was a ubiquitous, stable and homogeneous entity that could account for the class position of all of its members (Mann 1986; Kreckel 1989, 2004). Yet, in choosing to go back to analysing individual class positions in order to avoid the pitfalls inherent in this conceptualisation of the family, the critics also relinquished the methodological possibilities offered by larger units such as the household as an income-pooling unit.

---

6 In arguing against the mainstream tendency of explaining away non-Western social realities, including non-wage labor, by declaring them anomalous or exceptional, Wallerstein had pointed to the fact that the defining norm of a capitalist system has to be reconsidered when its definition produces more anomalies and residues than standard cases: "If we find, as we do, that the system seems to contain wide areas of wage and non-wage labor, wide areas of commodified and non-commodified goods and wide areas of alienable and non-alienable forms of property and capital, then we should at the very least wonder whether this 'combination' of the so-called free and the non-free is not itself the defining feature of capitalism as a historical system" (Wallerstein 1991c: 250f.).

The methodological shift from the individual or the nuclear family to the income-pooling household as a unit of analysis of labour market participation and class membership led to the characterisation of the multiple processes that ensured the individual and collective reproduction within such units as "householding" (Wallerstein and Smith 1992a: 13). The implications went far beyond what at first sight seemed to be the rather trivial conclusion that income from wage labour is in most cases insufficient for reproduction and has thus to be supplemented. On the one hand, in viewing subsistence labour as an integral part of processes of householding in the capitalist world-economy, world-systems analysts concurred with the Bielefeld subsistence theorists that housework as a specifically gendered economic activity was a product of capitalist development, not a vestige from a pre-capitalist past. On the other hand, by showing how apparently "non-capitalist" relationships and processes like short-term and seasonal work or informal economies both in the core and in the periphery were responsible for a substantial supply of the world's labour force, "householding" researchers undid the hitherto accepted link between wage labour and (racial and ethnic) whiteness. Instead, they argued that certain combinations of sources of household income were only made possible through the ethnicisation of the work force within the boundaries of a given state (Wallerstein 2000: 306f., 350). The extent of the rereading of world capitalism and global inequality relations made possible by the theory behind the notion of ethnicisation would however only become apparent in the context of work on coloniality in the Americas as well as on inequality proper (Quijano and Wallerstein 1992; Balibar and Wallerstein 1996; see below).

Thus, the analytical shift from the nation-state to the world-system amounted to the assessment of tendencies of capitalist polarisation between the world-economy's core and periphery instead of national bourgeoisies and national proletariats, respectively. Accordingly, the shift of focus from the individual to the household meant that existing combinations of forms of income across working-class households correlated with either core or periphery structures in ways that reflected the polarisation at the level of the entire world-economy.[7] While agreeing that the process could adequately be described as housewifisation, Wallerstein and Smith (1992b: 256ff.) cautioned, as Claudia von Werlhof had, against conceiving it as exclusively gender-based, and additionally distinguished between two models of housewifisation:

First, the peripheralised household type (either in the world-system's periphery itself or embedded in the core), was characterised by different forms of incomplete proletarianisation ranging from a combination of low wage income

---

7 Wallerstein and Smith additionally explain how the shifts in household patterns correlate with the expansion/stagnation phases of the capitalist world-economy (Kondratieff waves), dealt with in detail in Wallerstein's earlier work (Wallerstein 1974, 1979). While at least as important for the functioning of households as the system's core-semiperiphery-periphery structure, the issue extends beyond the *emergence* of inequality patterns addressed here, and is therefore not explicitly tackled.

with subsistence activities in the past, to a growing trend toward a mixture of wages and petty market operations in the present. Examples included the retail sale of factory products such as matches, the renting of living quarters space and services, as well as various illegalized transactions, usually subsumed under the (misleading) umbrella term "informal economy" and analysed as a growing trend towards "marginalisation". Second, the core working-class household type (however, estimated using only US data), for which wage income was also found to be insufficient even when available as double income of a cohabitating couple.[8]

In view of this evidence about the core-periphery distribution of working-class household patterns, the classical proletarian household solely dependent on a family wage turned out to make up for only a tiny, rather affluent minority of households throughout the world. From a world-systems perspective, the increase in the numbers of such households would therefore be proof of a tendency toward bourgeoisification, much rather than toward proletarianisation:

> The ultimate paradox is that it is the well-to-do professional or executive who is most often the true full-time wage worker; the proletarian is condemned to remain a partial wage worker. Thus we do live out the social polarization predicted by nineteenth-century social science in ways quite different from the patterns they thought would express this polarization. (Wallerstein and Smith 1992b: 261f.)

Hence, world-systems scholars find themselves in agreement with subsistence theorists as far as the subject of polarisation processes is concerned. Neither is the proletarian the model of the future for global capitalism, nor is s/he the cheapest type of work-force for global capital (in fact, far from it).

In spite of the substantial modifications and significant methodological corrections they operated on Marx's theory of capitalism, both the world-systems and the feminist subsistence approach viewed the Marxian account of the polarisation of capitalist classes as essentially correct. For both, the key aspect of a rereading of Marx in light of global inequalities consisted in reframing capitalism as a *world*-economy as well as in understanding capitalist development as a set of processes benefiting core regions at the expense of peripheral ones. This would not only resolve the issue of the constantly growing list of anomalies with respect to

---

8 The second model was additionally subdivided into two patterns of supplementing wages: On the one hand, the pattern of the poor, for whom possibilities of return to subsistence farming no longer existed in the core, involved compensating low wages with welfare payments; on the other, the pattern of the well-to-do working class entailed increasing amounts of self-provisioning labour, i.e., a type of subsistence production, in order to diminish household cash expenses: "the productive workers (male and female) contribute surplus-value twice, once as a wage worker and once as self-provisioning consumer" (Wallerstein and Smith 1992b: 261).

the state-centred view of capitalism, but would at the same time reconcile the main theses of Marxian theory with global social reality:

> As long as Marx's ideas are taken to be theses about processes that occur primarily within state boundaries and that involve primarily urban wage-earning industrial workers working for private industrial bourgeois, then these ideas will be easily demonstrated to be false, misleading, and irrelevant – and to lead us down wrong political paths. Once they are taken to be ideas about a historical world-system, whose development itself involves "underdevelopment", indeed is based on it, they are not only valid, but they are revolutionary as well. (Wallerstein 1991a: 161)

In focusing on what they viewed as the processes underlying capitalism's tendency towards class polarisation, the two perspectives not only discarded the classical proletarianisation thesis in favour of that of housewifisation (in the case of the feminist subsistence theorists) and of that of a mix between incomplete proletarianisation and bourgeoisification (in the case of the world-systems perspective); they at the same time emphasised the *processes* involved in inequality relations, rather than the *static categories* whose reified character had more than once formed the focus of heated debates in the twentieth century, and that standard empirical analyses of inequality still focus on.

At first sight, the merits of such a measure seem to lie in the mere suffixation of the terms that designate theoretical categories and social roles so as to indicate processes (i.e., the social role of the housewife becomes the process of housewifisation, while the class category of the bourgeoisie becomes the process of bourgeoisification). Yet the advantages this move offers primarily reside in calling attention to the historical dimension of global inequality structures. Nevertheless, given that in both cases the explanation was grounded in the functioning of the overarching structure of the capitalist world-economy and primarily accounted for processes of economic inequality that had supplanted or overridden the proletarianisation Marx had predicted, economic determinism was a frequent criticism directed at world-systems analysis (for an overview and response see Wallerstein 2004).

The concept of geoculture, developed in analogy with that of the geopolitics of the world-system, came as a (late) corrective and partial response to the perspective's critics. Defined as "the cultural framework within which the world-system operates" (Wallerstein 1991b: 11), a geoculture accepted by the elites as well as the large majority of the masses was considered to have been a result of the French Revolution:

> In the case of the modern world-system, […] its geoculture emerged with the French Revolution and then began to lose its widespread acceptance with the world revolution of 1968. The capitalist world-economy has been operating since the sixteenth century. It functioned for three centuries, however, without any

68 *Global Inequalities Beyond Occidentalism*

> firmly established geo-culture. That is to say, from the sixteenth to the eighteenth
> century, no one set of values and basic rules prevailed within the capitalist world-
> economy, actively endorsed by the majority of the cadres and passively accepted
> by the majority of the ordinary people. (Wallerstein 1995a: 189)

In contrast to the static view of society that had prevailed up to the late eighteenth century, Wallerstein argued, the French Revolution managed to impose the novel notion that political change was normal. In so doing, it proved much more successful than the English Revolution or the Reformation and Counter-Reformation before it, which, in global terms, had had a rather limited local impact. In turn, the fundamental cultural transformation occurred as a result of the French Revolution reverberated throughout the capitalist world-economy in Haiti's revolution of the enslaved, Ireland's and Egypt's (failed) independence movements against England and the Ottoman Empire, respectively, as well as in the first wave of decolonisation across the Americas (Wallerstein 1991a: 13ff.). Since Enlightenment thought postulated development and universal progress as the natural outcomes of evolutionary change, putting into practice the normality of change – such as it was assumed to be true of the countries of the core – has been interpreted to mean "the increased homogenization of the world, in which harmony would come out of the disappearance of real difference" (Wallerstein 1991a: 22). Thus, the universalist ideology that promoted freedom, equality and fraternity for all citizens evolved in the nineteenth century alongside the racism and sexism responsible for curtailing the same rights for non-citizens as well as for those considered less developed, modern, or civilised than the norm. Although Wallerstein ultimately understood the geoculture of the world-system as a set of *ideologies* made up of universalism on the one hand and racism and sexism on the other, he did not consider it to be superstructural, but, on the contrary, to be underlying and informing the economic base, i.e., to be its "underside" (Wallerstein 1991b: 11). The notion dovetailed well with the feminist subsistence theorists' plea for incorporating "views from below", Third World feminists' proposal of rewriting the history of slavery and colonialism from "oppositional locations" (Mohanty 1991), and the growing number of "standpoint theories" of race and gender that foregrounded epistemic claims in the 1980s and 90s. As a consequence, the incorporation of the geocultural aspect was meant to enable world-systems analysis to account not only for inequalities along economic dimensions, but also for those concerning ethnicity, race, and gender.

The Ethnicisation of the Labour Force

This approach worked out best in the case of ethnicity, understood as "the set of communal boundaries [...] serving to locate our identity and our rank within the state" (Quijano and Wallerstein 1992: 550). Since all the states emerged with the European colonial expansion in the Americas were new creations, so were all the major ethnic categories, in turn linked to the position of sovereign states within the interstate system and of social groups within states. Thus, while the crude sociocultural hierarchy between Europeans and non-Europeans mirrored the economic and political power differential between coloniser and colonised countries, the various ethnic categories within each state reflected and at the same time justified the division of labour created in the wake of the colonial occupation of the Americas: slavery for Black Africans, various forms of serfdom for Native Americans, and indentured labour for the White European working class. As both state and ethnic boundaries varied in time, these early forms of ethnic allotment to position in the work hierarchy were transformed in order to fit the economic requirements of particular sociohistorical contexts, thus yielding fewer ethnic categories in moments of acute social conflict and more during times of economic expansion and complex divisions of labour. Regardless of such variation, the underlying pattern, that Wallerstein (2000: 307; 349) labelled the "ethnicization of the work force", was viewed as a mechanism that, up to the present day, allows capitalism to reconcile the two pillars of its geoculture, universalism and racism/sexism, i.e., the ideology of equality and the reality of inequality. Here, too, the key institution that facilitated the mechanism's functioning was the household of part-time wage labourers, as the one more likely to employ other forms of income to compensate for low wages than the fully proletarianised household:

> Wherever we find wage workers located in different kinds of household structures, from more highly-paid workers located in more "proletarianized" household structures to less highly-paid ones located in more "semiproletarianized" household structures, we tend to find at the same time that these varieties of household structures are located inside "communities" called "ethnic groups" [...] Even without a comprehensive legal framework to enforce this, as in South Africa today, or in the United States yesterday, there has been a very high correlation everywhere of ethnicity and occupation, provided one groups "occupation" into broad and not narrow categories. (Wallerstein 2000: 307)

The correlation turned out to be threefold when viewing households in their capacity as agencies for (primary) socialisation (Wallerstein and Smith 1992a: 20). By socialising children into norms of ethnicity and constantly reinforcing these norms for adult family members, households assume responsibility for the *particular* social identity of ethnic groups, which a state education system, bound by the *universal* principle of equality before the law, cannot legitimately enforce. To the extent that it correlates with norms for specific ethnic groups, socialisation towards greater or lesser wage-dependence, greater or lesser reliance on subsistence production, or towards various degrees of active involvement in market activities not only affects choices household members make with respect to the relations of production they enter, but also provides a nonmeritocratic, and thus anti-universalist basis for justifying inequality: When ethnicity can be linked both to the type of household structure and to the way household members relate to the overall economy, evidence for the poor performance of some ethnic strata in the job market appears to be statistically documented (Quijano and Wallerstein 1992: 551).

70   *Global Inequalities Beyond Occidentalism*

The constant ethnicisation of occupational categories according to current needs and the legitimacy this process conferred to the overexploitation of the majority of the work force were however conceptualised as manifestations of racism, not as processes understandable through the workings of ethnicity alone. For one thing, racism was viewed as a capitalist system's compromise between the need to devalue the work of certain social groups in order to minimise the costs of their labour power and the risk of political protest thereby entailed. The flexible ethnicisation of the labour force was therefore merely the concrete form in which racism operated in a capitalist world-economy (Wallerstein 2000: 349; Quijano and Wallerstein 1992: 551). At the same time, ethnicisation produced a racist discourse, in that the devalued segments of the work force appeared as on the whole racially inferior to the dominant ones, regardless of the particular ethnic hierarchy that the process of ethnicisation generated in individual locations. While the upper end of the hierarchy mostly included a White privileged segment and its lower end a Black underprivileged one, it was the constant (re)creation of reified racial and ethnic entities that characterised capitalism as a racist system:

> Some groups can be mobile in the ranking system; some groups can disappear or combine with others; while others break apart and new ones are born. But there are always some who are "niggers". If there are no Blacks or too few to play the role, one can invent "white niggers". (Wallerstein 2000: 350)

The world-systems perspective therefore offered no analytical framework for disentangling race from ethnicity and separating the inequality relations stemming from them. While it did conceptualise ethnicity (i.e., a category) as chronologically prior to racism (i.e., an ideology), the latter was viewed as being implicit in ethnicity since the sixteenth century, but as having been explicitly formulated only during the nineteenth century as a defining feature of the emerging geoculture of the system (Quijano and Wallerstein 1992: 551). In world-systems terms, racism therefore remained an ideology. As such, it had practical effects contingent upon its functionality for the capitalist system, yet it was not analysable as a systematic practice, i.e., as racialisation, or as a separate phenomenon, i.e., as racial inequality.[9]

To the extent that sexism represented, alongside racism, the counterpart to universalism – as one of the system's key ideologies, created with a view to minimising labour costs as well as the risk of political unrest – the same was true for gender. At the same time, the world-systems notion that the capitalist production of gender inequality occurred mainly through the process of housewifisation fed into the various debates about the anomalies of capitalist development: patriarchal relations in the household were considered a constitutive component of the

---

9   For recent work on racism that agrees with the world-systems basic views on the topic, yet further differentiates between race as a social construction, racialisation as the process by which race becomes socially relevant, and racism as the causal condition making racialisation possible, see Bashi Treitler 2013.

modern world-economy, not a remnant of an earlier stage of development. Unlike Marxist feminist scholars, who had tried to reconcile the capitalist exploitation of labour and the patriarchal subordination of women by conceiving of capitalism and patriarchy as two separate and contradictory systems of exploitation (Eisenstein 1981; Hartmann 1981), world-systems analysts claimed that "our reconceptualization of the household places the question of the subordination of women at the centre of any account of accumulation on a world scale" (Smith et al. 1984: 13). Yet, on this point, as in the case of racism, the balance sheet is not clear-cut: On the one hand, the concepts of housewifisation and householding did encompass the creation of the economic role of the housewife both in its historical dimension and in its present-day empirical manifestations, as well as the function of non-wage und unpaid labour for capitalism. On the other hand, further aspects of gender inequality outside the household as well as the distribution of goods and power inside it remained thereby unaddressed.

Gendering as Semiproletarianisation

Despite its innovative focus on the historical nature of patriarchy and the latter's embeddedness with capitalism, the perspective on gender advanced by world-systems analysis had little impact on contemporary feminist scholarship, Marxist or otherwise. Similarly, world-systems work on gender and its dialogue with the feminist subsistence theorists of the Bielefeld school remained largely confined to the research on households undertaken in the 1980s and 1990s, leading critics to condemn the gender-blindness of the world-systems perspective a mere decade later (Misra 2000; Dunaway 2001).

A partial recuperation as well as a further development of the structural – yet not the geocultural – explanation world-systems analysis had offered for gender inequity occurred in the context of its theorists' engagement with or critique of postcolonial (and) feminist literature. In holding the "post-tradition" (i.e., the postmodern, poststructuralist, and postcolonial feminist interventions) of the 80s and 90s responsible for having replaced political economy with identity politics in the treatment of gender relations, and the "dual-systems" theory for dissociating capitalism from patriarchy, world-systems feminist scholars agreed with a growing number of – predominantly Marxist – critics. They however considered the specific methodological as well as theoretical contributions of world-systems analysis, rather than political economy more generally, to be the key to a Marxist analytical framework of global gender inequality that would transcend the ahistorical, depoliticised and essentialist approaches to gender prevalent in women's studies and feminist theories (Forsythe 2002; Feldman 2002; Pelizzon 2002). The shift in the unit of analysis,[10] both at the level of the world-economy and the level of the

---

10   Drawing on the definition of world-systems analysis as "the study of long-term, large-scale social change", Nancy Forsythe contrasted feminist theories and world-systems analysis in terms of the scope of their accounts on historical change as follows:

72   *Global Inequalities Beyond Occidentalism*

household, was seen as one of the central interventions to that end. The result was, once more, a focus on the dynamics behind inequality processes rather than on static inequality categories.

Building on newer work by the feminist subsistence theorists, several authors accordingly argued that the definition of households as an income-pooling unit, while crucial in identifying subsistence labour as (productive, capitalist) work, obscured the inequalities of income and social standing between household members. Moreover, it diverted attention from non-income economic activities such as water collection or fuelwood gathering, as well as from the pooling of non-material resources such as the female body's reproductive capacity, women's ecomedical knowledge, or their emotional carework (Dunaway 2001, 2003; Pelizzon 2002). By ensuring household subsistence, these characteristically *unremunerated* activities directly subsidised capital, i.e., they were types of resources, not of income.

According to Sheila Pelizzon, one of the structures that had made it possible to transfer the costs of the reproduction of wage-workers from the capitalist enterprise (or the state) to the household was gendering – "a socially created division that carried a notion of hierarchy that transcended all social domains and classes of people" (Pelizzon 2002: 202). Its institutionalisation had occurred parallel to the formation of the capitalist world economy in the "long sixteenth century", during which the incorporation of ever more colonised areas as part of the system's periphery and the corresponding rise in the cost of production for long-distance trade had prompted the lowering of wages in Europe on the one hand and the search for cheap labour forces both in Europe and in its colonies on the other. The construction of women's labour as non-work and the establishment of plantation slavery had both been solutions to these changed circumstances of the world-economy. In accordance with the parallel feminist subsistence scholars drew between the exploitation of women and that of colonies through patriarchal capitalism (Mies et al. 1988; Mies 1996), the definition of gendering was thus not restricted to women's subordination, or to the economic dimension of their domination. Instead, the process was seen as encompassing three constitutive and complementary aspects: the legal and economic marginalisation of women through their piecemeal exclusion from the professions, crafts, and high-profit trade; the denial of public space to women and their consequent relegation to household

---

"For feminists, the unit of analysis appropriate to the study of social change has at its centre the body, and the historical body must be located spatially and temporally, in particular practices; but that unit of analysis is less 'the truth' about social change than a heuristic tool for responding to women's movements as agencies of social change. Feminist situated knowledge about social change is always partial; its virtue is heuristically, not logically, derived. The world-systems pairing of abstract/concrete, displacing universal/particular (or case), allows us to make a claim about stability (in knowers or known) without precluding either the ontological status of the subject in the real world or its variability through time, space, and social location" (Forsythe 2002: 162).

World-Systems Analysis and the Feminist Subsistence Perspective   73

activities; and the social construction of women as intellectually weak, morally loose, and in need of supervision (Pelizzon 1998: 230ff; Pelizzon 2002: 204).

The logic behind the last point, part of the larger process that feminist scholars had repeatedly identified as the separation of Man from Nature (Ortner and Whitehead 1981; Merchant 1980; Mies and Shiva 1993), closely followed the Cartesian principle of the radical division between mind and matter that justified appointing men as "masters and possessors of nature". The same logic also placed social categories constructed as nature under the control of those constructed as culture in the corresponding binary pair. Besides women and women's work, gendering as defining-into-nature had thus additionally entailed categorising children, the elderly, non-Whites of both sexes, the poor, and colonial subjects

> as unreliable, incompetent, weak, fearful, inadequate, in need of control, and therefore legitimately exploitable and unworthy of reward. Conversely, (White) men have generally been gendered as the opposite of these characteristics – smart, strong, capable – and they and the work that they do have been generally deemed worthy of reward, albeit in varying degrees. (Pelizzon 2002: 203)

Through this focus on a pervasive epistemic logic informing the system's economic structures, the world-systemic conceptualisation of gendering was closer to the radical feminists' notion of intersectionality (Crenshaw 1991; Hill Collins 1999) than to social interactionist approaches to "gendering" or "doing gender", despite terminological similarity with the latter. This was in the first place a matter of the structural level of analysis: Interactionist models highlighted the production and reproduction of gender and gender inequality at the individual or institutional level at most, i.e., they traced the process of gendering to the micro or mesostructural level. Conversely, in providing the system with an epistemological foundation, the dichotomous logic of "othering" gender *and* race that radical feminists identified behind both cognitive structures of scientific discourse and everyday social practices characteristic of capitalism was largely metastructural. Yet, in being state-enforced as well as institutionally reproduced, the logic characteristically trickled down to the macro and meso levels:

> Within a dichotomous logic, social and natural phenomena are classified and compartmentalized into oppositional categories: White/Black, smart/dumb, rich/poor, man/woman, rational/emotional […], master/slave, heterosexual/homosexual, adult/child, and science/nonscience. The normal/deviant construct overlays this entire enterprise. Moreover, these oppositional categories intersect so that the qualities on the favorable side of these dichotomies coalesce to form the "normal". "Real" men, for example, are constructed as White, smart, rich, rational, masters, and potential scientists. In contrast, those groups deemed farthest away from the norm […] become derogated. Representations of and practices targeted toward African American women, African American men, White women, and other groups depend on varying patterns of convergence of

74   *Global Inequalities Beyond Occidentalism*

> dichotomies [...] distinguishing them from elite White men as the essentially
> normal and normative group. (Hill Collins 1999: 270)

However, in the world-systems conceptualisation of gendering, the emphasis definitely lay on the principle's *economic* functions rather than on the *epistemic* apparatus it generated. As such, gendering was viewed as an adequate means of explaining the emergence of households as institutions based on a sexual division of labour between male wage labour and female subsistence activities. Instead of representing the logical consequence of large-scale proletarianisation and of the rise of the nuclear family dependent on a family wage in its wake – as in orthodox Marxist theory – gendered households thus appeared as a structural solution for maintaining wages at a low level without destabilising the system. On the one hand, through confining women to housework, the economic and social polarisation between the sexes reduced competition in the wage labour market by half and relegated part of the reproduction costs to subsistence labour – i.e., it minimised the costs of labour for capital; on the other, the political exclusion of women from the public domain displaced social tensions from the public to the private sphere, i.e., it undermined class solidarity and thus minimised the risk of political unrest (Pelizzon 1998, 2002: 208).

Shifting attention to the ways in which gendering worked within and outside the household, Wilma Dunaway (2001; 2003) turned to the concept of the semiproletarian household as one of the foremost mechanisms through which the surplus created in non-commodified production was appropriated by capital (Wallerstein 1995b). Initially employed in the explanation of the ethnicisation of the labour force, the semiproletarian household was an umbrella term for distinguishing households which had to combine wage income with several other forms of income in order to make ends meet (viewed as the prevailing type of households worldwide) – from the more affluent, strictly proletarian households:

> Seen from the perspective of the employer of wage-labour, it is preferable, other things being equal, to employ persons who are less rather than more dependent on wage-income (let us call such households *semiproletarian* households). A wage-worker in a semiproletarian household is more able to accept a low real wage since this worker may be able to assume that, via self-exploitation, other compensating forms of income will be available to him or her. The more proletarian (that is, wage-dependent), the *household*, the more the individual wage-worker is compelled to demand higher real wages (a so-called living wage) (Wallerstein and Smith 1992a: 16)

In order to render women's inputs into the production process visible, Dunaway argued, it is however necessary to link the exploitation of semiproletarian households with the analysis of capitalist commodity chains: While commodity chains are the main mechanism regulating unequal exchange at the global level, household structures ensure the maximal exploitation of underpaid and

World-Systems Analysis and the Feminist Subsistence Perspective 75

unpaid labour between the nodes in the chain as well as within individual nodes, i.e. they are "microcosms of the structural inequities of the capitalist world-system" (Dunaway 2001: 12). In the course of the incorporation of new areas into the system, this "double register" of global and local dynamics accordingly entailed two dialectical labour recruitment strategies: the proletarianisation of (male) wage labourers for capitalist commodity production on the one hand, and the semiproletarianisation of female labourers for unremunerated, mainly reproduction activities on the other (Dunaway 2001; 2003, 2014). This yielded several patterns of distribution of female wage and non-wage labour in the twentieth century, according to the structural location within the capitalist world-economy: Whereas wage labour is characteristic for women in the core, it is only gradually becoming a source of income for women in the periphery, most of whom continue to supply non-wage labour inputs to the production process – as through petty commodity production or piece-rate labour – in addition to receiving (low) wages. On the other hand, non-wage labour, although still common throughout the world, tends to involve skilled or white-collar work in the core and predominantly unskilled or low-skilled physical work in the periphery – either in the form of industrial homework or resource gathering. Given the central role that natural resources play in women's subsistence work, from childbirth and childrearing to food production and processing, the devaluation of the entire nexus women/labour/ nature under capitalism allows it to render women's economic contribution throughout the commodity chain structurally invisible (Dunaway 2001, 2003, 2014). In other words, the concrete form the epistemic principle of gendering takes in the case of women's labour is their permanent semiproletarianisation:

> Because it accumulates greater profits off the backs of women, the world-system does not seek to transform females into wage labourers. The system profits at maximal levels by semiproletarianizing women and by shifting to women and households most of the costs of commodity production. (Dunaway 2001: 22)

As a structure for the reproduction of capitalist hierarchies, gendering in general and semiproletarianisation in particular thus fulfilled the very functions Wallerstein described as applying to both racism and sexism, i.e., that of reducing the costs of production at the same time as minimising the risk of political disruption. On the one hand, Pelizzon and Dunaway subscribed to the subsistence theorists' notion of housewifisation as the dominant tendency of present-day capitalism. On the other hand, they however viewed the actual moment of the creation of the housewife as a late step in the centuries-long process of gendering that, as in Claudia von Werlhof's model, included the ongoing devaluation of subsistence activities and reproductive labour. Their approaches therefore also concurred with Maria Mies' (1996) elaborate demonstration of how the rise of the ideal of the housewife and mother in Europe and the US in the wake of the European colonial expansion had had as its counterpart the enslavement of women in Europe's African, Asian, and Caribbean colonial possessions. In the sugar colonies, the active discouragement of enslaved women from becoming mothers had been an integral part of this double movement of defining women into nature. Thus, during the so-called sugar-revolution, beginning around 1760 and lasting for over a century, plantation estates went from being smallholdings with few slaves who reproduced naturally, to big plantations with large slave populations. Because of the labour power 'lost' during an enslaved woman's pregnancy and breast-feeding, it thus became cheaper for slave owners to purchase further captives as slaves than to allow children to be born to enslaved mothers. "Local breeding" only started being encouraged after the abolition of the slave trade:

> These more than a hundred years that "slave women in the Caribbean were neither wives nor mothers" were exactly the same period that women of the European bourgeoisie were domesticated and ideologically manipulated into wifehood and motherhood as their "natural" vocation [...]. While one set of women was treated as a pure labour force, a source of energy, the other set of women was treated as "non-productive breeders" only. (Mies 1996: 92)

Whether defined as gendering, semiproletarianisation, or housewifisation, the process described in all three approaches aimed at identifying the causal link with the patriarchal-capitalist mode of production, in which the naturalisation of women in colonised areas occurred in parallel with and close connection to the civilising of the European women, yielding what Mies called "the double-faced process of colonization and housewifisation" (Mies 1996: 97). The three approaches' common denominator was the view that the devaluing of women and nature that had ultimately led to the social and cultural invisibility of women's economic inputs had been dictated by the capitalist logic of maximising the accumulation of profit. Unlike in most other feminist materialist approaches, this logic was understood as operating in the longue durée of modern capitalism, i.e., since the European colonial expansion in the sixteenth century, as well as at the level of the entire capitalist world-economy – instead of individual nation-states.

The focus on gendering as semiproletarianisation however also went beyond the original world-systemic notion of the role sexism played in processes of householding. By stressing that capitalism had not only externalised to women the costs of the reproduction of the labour force and the subsidisation of wage income, it also called attention to greater costs and risks than those shifted to men (Dunaway 2001: 18ff; Dunaway 2003: 193ff.). Because women and their work are underrated, they not only have to work longer hours than men for equal pay, but also make up a larger share of the world's poor, thus incurring greater health and ecological risks. As already documented by Sidney Mintz with respect to patterns of food consumption during industrialisation, in lower class or peripheral households, costly protein food is disproportionately allocated to adult males, followed by male children. The impact of global ecological stresses leading to food and water scarcity is thereby significantly greater for women and girls, as recent data on malnutrition and child mortality easily illustrate (World Bank 2011; Asian Development Bank 2013).

The theoretically informed approaches on gendering as semiproletarianisation thus corroborate statistical evidence on gender inequality raised in the past decades by ecofeminism, regional inequality surveys, and the World Bank (Shiva 1989; McMichael 2000; Hoffman and Centeno 2003; World Bank 2011), which often sum up such results under the heading "feminisation of poverty". Unlike the latter, however, approaches on gendering do not consider this to be a new phenomenon, but one having its onset with the emergence of agricultural capitalism and being structural in nature. Global ecological stresses in the present are seen as affecting the core, the semiperiphery and the periphery in different ways; the patterns of households' pooling of resources and income according to gender are viewed as having varied widely according to the gender hierarchy prevailing at the time of the respective region's incorporation into the capitalist world-economy. Nevertheless, for world-systems theorists of gendering, the main cleavage accounting for global inequality is that of men vs. women, not core vs. periphery. This applies at all levels of the commodity chain, starting with the household:

> If we are to capture the workings of the household, therefore, we must recognize that there are two classes of people among the exploited: the doubly exploited (women) and those who are both exploiters and exploited (men). *To treat all peripheral households as though there are no gender differences in the experience of inequality is to ignore the worst effects of the world-system itself.* (Dunaway 2001: 18, emphasis in the original)

The focus on the double exploitation of women at the level of the entire world-economy is in itself double-edged. While it helps enforce a differentiated view of inequality within the periphery instead of promoting a polarised core-periphery account of inequality structures, it also completely loses sight of race and ethnicity in the process. Gendering, in Sheila Pelizzon's formulation, was supposed to encompass the joint derogation of social groups along the lines of gender, race, ethnicity, age, and ablebodiness. However, the reinterpretation of the parallel processes of the (predominantly male) proletarianisation and (predominantly female) semiproletarianisation to mean that male vs. female was *the* dividing line unduly overemphasises the gender dimension to the detriment of all others. Dunaway thus fell into the same trap that she criticised other attempts for ignoring, that of conflating inequality dimensions and reducing the corresponding processes, such as the one Wallerstein described as the ethnicisation of the labour force, to one aspect only – the semiproletarianisation of *female* work. This amounts to relinquishing to a large extent the potential inherent in the notion of geoculture as a set of ideologies including racism alongside sexism, and of the tensions with the system's ideological tenet, universalism.

Occidentalism as Geoculture

World-systems analysis' neglect of epistemic questions, and in particular of women's experience and knowledge as the basis for a radical critique of social theory, had been one of the main charges voiced by the perspective's feminist critics (Misra 2000; Feldman 2002). Through the idea of the naturalisation of gender differences, i.e., the defining of women "back into nature", both the epistemic and the ecological dimensions of what was perceived as a structurally gendered capitalist division of labour had been reconciled with world-systems' macrostructural approach to unequal exchange. However, the approaches based on this enhanced model did not get far in incorporating the processes of production and reproduction of racial and ethnic inequalities for which the notion of the geoculture of the modern world-system was supposed to account.

This task was to be reformulated and addressed anew within the Latin American decolonial perspective. Through a productive dialogue with world-systems scholarship and its roots in dependency theory, the decolonial approach foregrounded the view that the epistemic dimension of inequality processes not only could be used to make sense of the structures corresponding to the capitalist world-economy, but that it had been coterminous with the emergence of capitalism itself – i.e., it was not optional, but essential for any analysis of global inequalities. Therefore, Wallerstein's contention that the modern world-system had been capitalist for five hundred years, yet had only had a coherent geoculture since the French Revolution, left out half the story (Mignolo 2000: 56).

As detailed above, Wallerstein's notion of geoculture included the view that racism and sexism in their present form had emerged as a result of the political project of nineteenth-century liberalism in core countries: heralding universal human rights while withholding them from those deemed the "dangerous classes" within the core – which included women, the illiterate, and the propertyless – as well as from the "barbarians" living outside the core, whose exact hierarchisation was more complex:

> Who were the "barbarians"? The colonial peoples, to be sure; to the Whites, the Blacks and Yellows; to the West, the East; to the "historic" nations of Western Europe, the "nonhistoric" nations of Eastern Europe; to the Christians, the Jews. From the beginning, the human rights of "civilized" nations were predicated on the assumption that they were indeed "civilized". The discourse of imperialism was the other side of the coin. [...] It followed that any "rights of peoples" were reserved to a few specific peoples and were by no means the rights of all the other peoples. [...] The two sets of rights were therefore placed in direct conflict with one another in the nineteenth century; there was no way that the world could have both. (Wallerstein 1995a: 189)

Wallerstein traced the emergence of ethnic categories and the corresponding process of the ethnicisation of the work force, itself based on racist classifications, back to the European colonisation of the Americas in the sixteenth century. At the same time, he saw "full-fledged racism" (Quijano and Wallerstein 1992: 551) as a nineteenth-century phenomenon, just as indebted to Enlightenment thought as the Orientalism described by Edward Said, which Wallerstein's concept of racism included. However, if racism as an epistemic operation had first surfaced in the ethnicisation of the native population in the Americas, and was thus contemporaneous with the onset of modernity, then the geoculture of the world-system was not premised on eighteenth-century Orientalism. Instead, it had been Occidentalism – the self-definition of Christian Europe in contrast with, and as superior to, the "barbarian" New World in the sixteenth century – that had preceded the ideological separation of a dynamic West from a static Orient in the wake of the Enlightenment ideals of progress. An approach incorporating this critique would be gradually developed within the modernity/coloniality research program, more recently known as decoloniality. This is the topic of the next chapter.

Chapter 3

Orientalism vs. Occidentalism:
The Decolonial Perspective

> While from an Asian perspective it has become necessary to "provincialize" European thought, from a Latin American perspective it has become indispensable to globalize the periphery: to recognize the world-wide formation of what appear to be self-generated modern metropolitan centers and backward peripheries.
>
> Fernando Coronil (2004)

Operating within a modified world-systems perspective that drew from liberation theology, dependency theory, and Latin American philosophy, the modernity/ coloniality perspective initially emerged out of a critical reflection on Latin American cultural, economic and political realities. Central to the perspective since the 1990s was Aníbal Quijano's notion of the coloniality of power, later expanded to encompass labour relations and ontology as coloniality of labour and of being, respectively, as well as an alternative horizon, articulated as decoloniality. In their search of non-Eurocentric modes of inquiry into social reality, members of the modernity/coloniality group drew on critical theories of modernity and postmodernity in Europe and North America, South Asian subaltern studies, Chicana feminist theory, postcolonial studies, and Africana philosophy (Escobar 2007: 181). In the process, they operated substantive changes into core notions of some of these related perspectives, to the point of clearly delimiting themselves from both Occidental critical theory and postcolonial studies while self-designating as "decoloniality".

Within this perspective, and in a critique of both Edward Said and Immanuel Wallerstein, Walter Mignolo and Fernando Coronil argued that the Orientalism of the eighteenth and nineteenth centuries could not have been conceived without a previous idea of Occidentalism. In their view, the emergence of Occidentalism coincided with the onset of the Western European colonial expansion in the Americas (called the *Indias Occidentales* in the Spanish Empire). As a discourse dominating Western representations of the Other, the Orientalism that emerged following the Enlightenment had allowed Western European culture to gain "in strength and identity by setting itself off against the Orient as a sort of surrogate and even underground self" (Said 1979: 3). Scholarly, literary and scientific depictions of the Orient as backward, irrational, in need of civilisation and racially inferior produced during the next centuries had served as a background for representations of the Occident as progressive, rational, civilised, even biologically superior, thus justifying European colonisation and control. Yet it had been due to the rise of

Western Christianity as the dominant religion in Europe in relation to Judaism, Islam, and Eastern Christianity, as well as due to the concomitant Western European colonisation of the Americas in the sixteenth century, that the Occident had first become the measuring stick for a worldwide hierarchy of difference, of which eighteenth-century Orientalism would be but the most prominent instance. Such apparently disconnected events as the conquest of Muslim Granada by the Catholic Monarchs in 1492, the expulsion of the Jews from Spain and Columbus' "discovery" of the New World that same year are viewed as joint signals of the growing self-assertion of Europe as Christian and Western in the "long" sixteenth century, and at the same time as harbingers of subsequent practices of the production of difference from an Occidentalist standpoint: the production of religious difference within Europe and that of colonial difference in the conquered areas (Mignolo 2006a).

The juxtaposition, in the decolonial approach, of processes of *religious othering* underlying the persecution of Jews and Moors in the Iberian Peninsula on the one hand and of processes of *racial and ethnic othering* that accompanied the extermination and enslavement of the indigenous population and of Africans in the Americas on the other thus recasts and nuances the world-systems perspective on the geoculture of the capitalist world-economy in general and of racism in particular: What Quijano and Wallerstein had analysed as the ethnicisation of the work-force in the Americas according to the ethnic categories created after the conquest is thereby revealed to be the colonial side in the making of the modern world-system's geoculture, in place since the sixteenth century. This colonial underside is therefore meant to structure a system that, according to Walter Mignolo (2000), has to be understood as being "modern/colonial" at the same time.

Hence, in this perspective, Occidentalism as "the expression of a constitutive relationship between Western representations of cultural difference and worldwide Western dominance" (Coronil 1996: 57) does not represent the counterpart of Orientalism, but its precondition, a discourse *from* and *about* the West that sets the stage for discourses about the West's Other(s) – i.e., for Orientalism, but also for anti-Semitism, Islamophobia, racism, and sexism. Nor is Occidentalism a mere synonym for Eurocentrism, since it emerged not as a pan-European, but as an essentially pan-Western discourse, that constructed and downgraded both European and non-European Others to the extent that their "Westernness", i.e., their Occidentality, had become questionable in a given historical and geopolitical context:

> If racism is the matrix that permeates every domain of the imaginary of the modern/colonial world system, "Occidentalism" is the overarching metaphor around which colonial differences have been articulated and rearticulated through the changing hands in the history of capitalism ... and the changing ideologies motivated by imperial conflicts. (Mignolo 2000: 13)

Through the focus on the role of the Americas in the shaping of the world-system's geoculture, the Latin American modernity/coloniality theorists therefore operated two substantive changes in the analytical scope of the world-systemic framework: First, they emphasised the dialectical process through which the world-system had only succeeded in becoming *modern* to the extent that it had become increasingly *colonial*, i.e., by articulating "colonial differences" such as racial and ethnic categorisations alongside modern hierarchies of class as part of its self-definition. Conceptualising capitalism as "a modern/colonial world-system" as a consequence necessarily implied acknowledging the crucial importance of the modern idea of race emerged in the Americas for the production of new social identities such as "Indians", "blacks" and "mestizos", as well as for the redefinition of older ethnic categories such as European or White in contrast to the former (Quijano 2000a: 534). At the same time, the emphasis placed on the Western colonial – and especially, American – dimension of the capitalist system's expansion left the contribution of Ottoman, Tsarist or Habsburg imperial power to the establishment of inner-European and Eurasian ethnic and racial hierarchies unaccounted for.[1] In particular, the indiscriminate use of the terms "Eurocentrism" and "Occidentalism" in most works elaborated from the modernity/coloniality perspective – despite the particular attention devoted to the historical emergence and global reach of Occidentalism – attests to the insufficient differentiation of the impact of the system's geoculture within Europe.

The second important change in analytical perspective that the modernity/coloniality approach operated lay in the juxtaposition of different strategies of social classification in the centre as opposed to those in the periphery with the distinction between spatial and temporal strategies of racial and ethnic classification in capitalism's longue durée. Thus, Wallerstein's notion of the barbarians as the Others of nineteenth-century civilisation conflated two separate moments in the history of Occidentalism – the spatial racialisation of "barbarians" in the sixteenth century and the temporal racialisation of "primitives" starting in the eighteenth. In turn, their conceptualisation as successive ideological strategies of the modern world-system – or of what Mignolo (2000) labels "global designs" – allows for a step-by-step, ideal-typical reconstruction of the hierarchisation of colonial difference in terms of processes, i.e., racialisation or ethnicisation, rather than over-the-board ideologies, i.e., racism.[2]

---

1   For recent exceptions to this neglect of the impact of imperial powers in Eastern Europe and Central Asia in the decolonial perspective, see Mignolo and Tlostanova 2006, 2012 and Mignolo 2006b.

2   A similar take on processes of hierarchisation of difference, which also uses the concept of Occidentalism, is present in Venn (2006, 2009). In the context of an encompassing reconceptualisation of the postcolonial as a field of study, Venn defines Occidentalism as "the correlation of a conceptual space, a global, world-transforming project and a world order. It is the result of the co-articulation of ... the emergence of a technocratic modernity as dominant at the level of thought and practice, rational capitalism and its global

84   *Global Inequalities Beyond Occidentalism*

Although repeatedly addressed by most theorists of this perspective, gender does not figure in the argument as an essential component of social classification in Europe and its colonies. The incorporation of sexism/gendering into the larger framework of processes of othering is therefore unsystematic and partial at best, and remains as such acutely undertheorised (see exemplarily Quijano 2000b: 378; for a comprehensive critique see Lugones 2007; Tlostanova 2010).

Racialisation and Ethnicisation: Spatial and Temporal Components[3]

According to Aníbal Quijano, the worldwide propagation of Eurocentrism, that in time ensured the "European patent on modernity" (Quijano 2000a: 543), relied on two foundational myths: On the one hand, *evolutionism* – the notion that human civilisation proceeded in a linear and unidirectional way from an initial state of nature through successive stages leading to Western civilisation; on the other, *dualism* – the view that differences between Europeans and non-Europeans can be accounted for in terms of insuperable natural categories such as primitive-civilised, irrational-rational, or traditional-modern. As such, evolutionism and dualism formed the basis of several successive global designs of the expanding modern/colonial world-system, beginning with the evangelisation and the civilising mission, and up to developmentalism and globalisation, all of which were thought out and implemented from the standpoint of local Western European and, later, North American history. In this context, Mignolo's complementary pair of terms "local histories/ global designs" conveys the tension between the particular

---

implantation, and the Western form of colonialism" (Venn 2006: 8f.). He consequently traces the emergence of modernity back to 1492, highlights the idea of "temporality as linear progression" as a crucial component of Western modernity, and "ontological violence" as characteristic of Western colonialism. There are striking similarities with the modernity/coloniality approach more generally and with Coronil's and Mignolo's notions of Occidentalism in particular, as well as partly overlapping genealogies of thought between these theorists' model and Venn's. However, Venn does not seem to be aware of the Latin American theorists' earlier body of work on Occidentalism or the political economy of (post)colonialism. Instead, the engagement of (mainly English-language) postcolonial theorists with the concept of modernity and capitalist accumulation are discussed in Venn's writings as preliminary steps toward his own goal of establishing "the co-emergence of modernity, European colonialism and capitalism" (Venn 2006: 43, emphasis in the original). While a comparison of these two similar but parallel conceptions of Occidentalism might be rewarding, the focus of the present section is on the explanatory power derived from the centrality of the Americas in the analysis of global inequality structures and thus on the modernity/coloniality model. In the following, Venn's approach will therefore not be juxtaposed with related arguments, however similar.

    3   The following section represents an expanded and revised version of a book chapter published in German as "Lange Wellen des Okzidentalismus. Ver-Fremdung von Geschlecht, Rasse und Ethnizität im modernen Weltsystem" (Boatcă 2009).

epistemic perspective characterising a geohistorical location and the relation of power inherent in imposing that perspective at a global level. The present-day structural positions of core and periphery therefore not only mirror *economic* and *political* differences, but they at the same time enforce historically constructed *epistemological* divides between "developed" and "underdeveloped" societies. Once they accepted or even internalised the global design imposed upon them, peripheral and/or colonial societies become silenced in terms of the production of knowledge (Khatibi, in: Mignolo 2000).

In the following, I draw on the decolonial authors' complementary conceptualisation of Orientalism and Occidentalism and their articulations with global designs of the modern/colonial world-system in order to retrace the impact of strategies of racialisation, ethnicisation and gendering on Western discourses of difference since the European colonial expansion. Global designs are understood as organised around concepts of race, ethnicity, or both and as proceeding along a spatial, a temporal dimension or a mixture of the two, function of the dominant European (later, North Atlantic) worldview of the time. Moreover, it is argued that all of these concepts relied on the semantics of gendering outlined in Chapter 2, the logic of which they recreated, reproduced or echoed in the ensuing patterns of racial or ethnic othering. Hence, if the overtly weighted dichotomies of primitive vs. civilised, irrational and rational, nature and culture, magic and science, body and spirit – successively served to locate entire peoples, according to their degree of "Westernisation", on a temporal continuum at the far end of which stood modern Europe, this operation did not apply solely to the world-system's peripheral areas. The same paternalism which allowed treating non-Europeans in the colonies as "pre-Europeans" (Quijano 2000a: 556) who should be "modernized" with the help of pedagogical and other disciplinary measures, was also directed at women, whose systematic association with nature, corporality and magic (Mies 1996) applied both within the world-system's core and all the more in its peripheries. The subsequent construction, in Occidentalist discourse, of female identity as infantile, in need of control, and close to nature in virtue of its reproductive capacity brought it closer to the equally naturalised, "inferior races" and thus provided a rationale for the relocation of women's work into the background of the capitalist world-economy.

In much the same manner as the feminist subsistence theorists, Fernando Coronil (1997, 2000) therefore argued that a view of capitalism from the (post) colonies – the world's main providers of natural resources – allows both a fuller understanding of the role of nature and of the role of women's work in the making of European capitalism:[4]

---

4   While Marx and (few) subsequent Marxists did acknowledge the importance of land, i.e., nature, in the formation of wealth, they did not incorporate it in the analysis of capitalist production, centred on labour power as the only source of value. Coronil in turn suggested that uncovering the dialectical relationship between labour, capital, and land through a "grounded" view of capitalism rendered visible the economic, cultural and political processes

86   *Global Inequalities Beyond Occidentalism*

> Colonial "primitive accumulation", far from being a precondition of capitalist development, has been an indispensable element of its ongoing dynamic. "Free wage "labor" in Europe constitutes not the exclusive condition of capitalism but its dominant productive modality, one historically conditioned by "unfree labor" elsewhere, much as the "productive" labor of wage workers depends on the ongoing "unproductive" domestic labor of women at home. Instead of viewing nature and women's labor as "gifts" to capital [...], they should be seen as confiscations by capital, as part of its colonized other, as its dark side. (Coronil 2000: 358)

Since the incorporation of the first European overseas colonies in the sixteenth century, we can distinguish three patterns of racialisation/ethnicisation of difference in European discourses of otherness. They result from four major global designs of Occidental provenience and their corresponding gendering strategies.

Colonial Beginnings: The Christian Mission

The first pattern, which can be described as a *policy of spatial racialisation*, took hold as of 1492 and spans the two centuries after that date. Its defining trait, religious difference, had started dominating identity discourses once the Christian Reconquista of Islamic Spain on the one hand, and the European "discovery" of the Americas in 1492 on the other, set the stage for a reconfiguration of the Western European Christian identity.

For one thing, the rise in geopolitical importance experienced by Western Christianity both within Europe and in adjoining areas, prompted Occidentalist discourses of difference centred on religious identities. While Christians defined themselves as people with the "right" religion, Jews and Moors were gradually racialised from a Western Christian point of view as people of the "wrong" faith. The delimitation strategies thus derived involved the physical removal of – or considerable spatial distance from – the designated religious Others. Following the conquest of the kingdom of Granada, the last Muslim state in Western Europe, by the Spanish Catholic monarchs in 1492, Jews and Moors were expelled from the Iberian Peninsula by royal decree, while Jewish and Muslim converts to Christianity experienced increased persecution and discrimination for alleged

---

involved in the mutual constitution of Europe and its colonies, among which the American colonies played a special part: "Just as the colonial plantations in the Americas, worked by African slave labor, functioned as protoindustrial factories that preceded those established in Manchester or Liverpool with 'free' European labor [...], the American colonies prefigured those established in Africa and Asia during the age of high imperialism". (Coronil 2000: 358). Similar views are now expressed in newer world-systems literature, in which the systematic expropriation of the Americas' indigenous population links the commodification of land rights to the rise of industrial capitalism and groups both under a worldwide process of "global primitive accumulation" (see Araghi and Karides 2012).

Judaising, conspiring against Christianity, or secret practice of non-Christian faith (Mignolo 2000; Hering Torres 2006; Stam and Shohat 2012). The principle of the "purity of blood" (*limpieza de sangre*), gradually institutionalised as of the mid-fifteenth century, banned all individuals of "impure" descent, i.e., of Jewish, Muslim or otherwise non-Christian faith, from public and religious office, as well as from any position of authority within the university, the army, or the municipality (Gerber 1992: 127ff.).

On the other hand, the material reality, but above all the concept of the New World radically transformed the mental map of the Western European Christian world, for which the limits of known geography had until then coincided with the limits of humanity (Mignolo 2000: 283). The "discovery" of the American territories thus represented a double challenge to the Christian worldview: accommodating the Americas within existing cartography and accommodating Amerindians within humanity. Earlier European cartographies classified world regions in accordance with the Christian dogma, in which each of the three hitherto known continents corresponded to one of Noah's sons, thereby justifying the superiority of Europe over Asia and Africa (Mignolo 1995: 230). In turn, the New World was initially incorporated in the classification not as a separate continent, but as part of Spain's new colonial possessions, and as such labelled the West Indies (*Indias Occidentales*) – in order to distinguish it from Spain's older colonial dominion, the East Indies (*Indias Orientales*), i.e., the Pacific islands. Having displaced Spain and Portugal as "finis terra" in the Western European worldview, the West Indies thus became Western Europe's extreme West (Mignolo 2000: 58; Dussel 2005: 43), not, as in the case of Asia and Africa, its alterity. Within Occidentalist cartography, the New World therefore was assigned the place of Europe's spatial extension (later to be conceptualised as Europe's future, i.e., its temporal extension; see below).

At the same time, the indigenous populations in the West Indies, displaying no religious allegiance known to the Christian colonisers, were classified as "people with no religion", and as such a type of *tabula rasa* in terms of subjectivity, on which any religious outlook could be inscribed (Maldonado-Torres 2008: 210; Stam and Shohat 2012: 5). Unlike the Jews and the Moors, whose "wrong" religion placed them on an inferior stage of humanity, Amerindians thus entered the imaginary of the emerging modern world-system as savages, cannibals, barbarians – and therefore lesser humans. As inhabitants of Spain's colonial possessions, however, they were considered subjects of the Spanish crown and servants of God, whom the colonisers were called upon to educate and Christianise (Mignolo 2000: 30). As such, their existence was meant to reinforce the boundaries of the Christian world and, at the same time, provide it with a mission: salvation. By supplying an outlet for Western Christianity and especially Catholicism, the project of Christianising the indigenous population of the Americas additionally served to construct the distinction between Western and Eastern Christians within Europe:

> If *republica christiana* became located geographically in Europe, Europe would not only become more and more located in the West as opposed to the East

occupied by the Islamic world but would create a distinction between Western and Eastern Christians. Thus Indias Occidentales became both a geographical location and a location where the Western *republica christiana* would continue to grow. (Mignolo 2003: 326)

Indeed, the "Discovery Doctrine", the legal foundation for the conquest of the Americas, had its origin in the Roman Catholic Church during the crusades to "recover" the Holy Lands. As Stam and Shohat point out, the Discovery Doctrine was first applied to Muslim-dominated "infidel lands" (2012: 4). A 1455 papal bull granting Portugal the right to subdue and enslave "all Saracens and pagans" was later extended to the conquest of the Americas and reinterpreted accordingly. Theorists of world-systems analysis and modernity/coloniality agreed that the geosocial construct of the New World – i.e., the invention, rather than the discovery of America – was a constitutive act both for the consolidation of Europe as Christian and Western and for the corresponding conceptualisation of modernity (Quijano and Wallerstein 1992; Dussel 1995; Mignolo 2000, 2005). Yet, whereas the construction of the New World as an extension of Christian Europe entailed the – positively connoted – project of evangelisation, the conceptualisation of the American populations essentially involved delimitation strategies that would legitimise that project by constructing negative images of the New World Other. The 1550 debate of Valladolid on the humanity of the "Indians", revolving around the question whether they did or did not have souls (which could therefore be saved through Christianisation), makes this particulary clear. By framing the issue in terms of species membership, i.e., human or non-human, the demarcation undertaken between Christians and barbarians followed a racial logic that conformed to the very dualism of the nature-culture distinction. First articulated by Juan Ginés de Sepúlveda in the debate with Bartolomé de las Casas, the view that the enslavement of indigenous peoples was legitimate – i.e., was not a sin before God – because they were less than human, made of the Amerindians not only modernity's first racialised subjects, but also its first legitimately exploitable Others (Dussel 1995: 137; Dussel 2007: 195). As the argument about the need to Christianise the indigenous peoples gained ground, the racial logic which denied humanity to "peoples with no religion" and legitimised their enslavement as a consequence was transferred to other non-European populations, chiefly sub-Saharan Africans (Grosfoguel and Mielants 2006: 3). As a result, massive imports of African slaves served to replace the Amerindian work-force on the early colonial plantations, while Amerindians were henceforth employed in the *encomienda* system, in which a specified number of natives was forced to work in agriculture and mining in exchange for being instructed in the Spanish language and Catholic faith by the conquistadors. There gradually emerged a set of hierarchies internal to the colonised territories to which Robert Stam and Ella Shohat refer as a "racial/colonial order" (2012: 5) and Vilna Bashi Treitler as "the racial paradigm" (2013). Nelson Maldonado-Torres has described it as a "chain of colonial signification" functioning as a substitute for the natural chain of being:

when the Spanish and other *conquistadors* looked for slaves in Africa to replace or complement the indigenous workforce, both the available old forms of religious differentiation (derived in part from the Portuguese contact with Africa) as well as the new imperial and dehumanizing discursive forms that were crafted in the Americas intervened in the legitimation of African slavery. This justification, then, no longer needed to be based strictly on religious differences. The negro would come to be conceived as inherently a slave; slavery was part of the very being of the negro and vice-versa. As a result, the term "negro" would be used not only to refer to black-skinned subjects, but rather against all types of slaves and colonized peoples who threatened the colonial order, including indigenous people themselves. (Maldonado-Torres 2008: 233)

Assigning Black Africans to slavery and Native Americans to various forms of coerced labour thus represented the first steps toward the ethnically segregated work hierarchy that Quijano and Wallerstein would describe as the "ethnicisation of the labour force".

Thus, the religious differences that had started being articulated as differences of social status in the changing geopolitical context of sixteenth-century Europe were gradually consolidated as, on the one hand, *imperial difference* within Europe, by relegating non-Christian and non-European peoples such as the Turks and the Moors to an inferior status vis-à-vis the European Christians of the emerging Spanish empire; on the other hand, they were translated as *colonial difference* between Europe and the overseas colonies, by constructing the indigenous people of the New World territories as faithless barbarians to be Christianised by the colonisers (Mignolo 2000). What thus appears as a fairly clear-cut picture of the comprehensive hierarchisation of difference involved in the sixteenth century's policies of spatial racialisation was however further complicated towards the end of the sixteenth and in the course of the seventeenth centuries.[5] The expulsion of the Jews from Spain, the emergence of the new categories of Jewish and Moorish converts to Christianity – that became targets of "Anti-Semitism against Christians" ("Judenhass gegen Christen" – Hering Torres 2006) in the Iberian Peninsula, as well as the emergence of the category of "mestizo" for the population of mixed Iberian and Native American descent in the "New World" all contributed to the additional ramification of patterns of colonial and imperial difference alike. Briefly stated, the creation of the capitalist world-economy as a modern *and* colonial system went hand in hand with the establishment of a racial matrix having Western European Christians at its centre, Jews and Moors as internal Others (i.e., Europeans but non-Christians), and "Indians" and "Blacks" (non-Europeans, non-Christians) as external Others (Mignolo 2006: 20).

---

5   For a detailed view on and graphic representation of the further ramifications of the racial hierarchy on the basis of religious difference and/or "purity of blood" in sixteenth-century Europe (conversos, moriscos) and the colonies (mestizos, mulattos, zambos), see Mignolo 2009, especially Figure 1. See also Maldonado-Torres, 2008.

90 *Global Inequalities Beyond Occidentalism*

On the other hand, the creation of a racial hierarchy in the Occident and its New World extension echoed the reorganisation of the various gender relations on the European continent into a comprehensive gender hierarchy. This subsequently became the norm against which the – starkly different – social realities of the colonial peripheries were assessed. As Carolyn Merchant (1980) has amply demonstrated, parallel to the debate on the humanity of the Amerindians in the New World, a theological, scientific, and scholarly debate on the "nature" of women took place in Europe, at the end of which the view that women were essentially passive, sensual, fragile, and mentally inferior prevailed. As in the case of Amerindians and Black Africans, this shift was related to the capitalist transformation of economic roles: To the degree that the economy was being geared toward commodity production, women's role as economic resource for their families' subsistence turned into the one of emotional resource for their husbands (Merchant 1980: 155). As a consequence, marriage was re-signified as the social form which allowed controlling women's unbalanced nature and which was therefore the most adequate (i.e., desirable) social arrangement.

Thus, the decline in women's social status that Sheila Pelizzon (1998, 2002) and Maria Mies (1996)[6] associated with the specific capitalist processes of gendering and housewifisation, respectively, was tied to the European elites' attempt at restoring social order following "the crisis of feudalism": a lengthy period of internecine conflicts, falling agricultural profits, peasant uprisings and generalised social unrest during the late Middle Ages. As a result, at the same time that the peasantry started facing increasing taxation and exploitation by the nobility and the rising bourgeoisie in the newly established Absolutist States of France, England, Spain, and Austria, orthodox theologians began upholding the family, centred around the authoritative figure of the father, as the institution capable of restoring order and thus re-Christianise society:

> One method social control was to be achieved was by the inculcation of the idea that society reflects a notion of an immutable order willed by God. Individuals were supposed to develop the mental habit of assuming there was no other choice except that of social conformity [...] To this end, the authority of the father was equated with the authority of God, and God with that of an absolute monarch. By implication, this legitimated all other authorities – kings, nobles, landowners, priests. (Pelizzon 1998: 250)

Besides marking the religious celebration of motherhood and domesticity, the key role attributed to the (holy) family as a social ideal entailed an entire range of norms and regulations. They included the urban authorities' enforcement of the "conjugal order", the normative upgrading of domestic violence towards women as a socially desirable means of maintaining said order, and – most importantly – the gradual criminalisation of contraception, abortion, infanticide, and unwed

---

6 Both of whom build on the work of Carolyn Merchant in this respect.

Orientalism vs. Occidentalism 91

motherhood (Pelizzon 1998: 238f.; Federici 2004) – in short, of all forms of sexual independence.[7] Thus, 1492 was also the year in which the first ordinance forbidding women under the age of 50 to live alone and stipulating that they instead go into service until they were married was passed in Coventry, England – soon to be followed by stricter ones all over Western Europe (Peters 2004; Pelizzon 1998). Although exceptions to this norm still remained socially acceptable more than a century later, economic independence for single women was rendered increasingly difficult, while marriage became associated with economic prosperity and status in the community (Merchant 1980; Peters 2004). These trends were reinforced after 1550, when state policies were more specifically aimed at excluding women from skilled craft, guilds, and high-status occupations, and Protestant theology reinterpreted marriage and the household – rather than outside employment or political issues – as the main concern of women (Pelizzon 1998: 243). By 1600, the gradual banning of unmarried women and widows from most crafts and of all women from entering apprenticeships in many trades had limited employment opportunities for lower-class women to unskilled work, especially service activities, and to low-paid wage labour such as spinning (Merchant 1980; Pelizzon 1998). Prostitution, increasingly present in the cities both in the wake of the influx of pauperised peasants and of the declining work alternatives for women, was gradually stigmatised as morally repressible and its exercise restricted to special "women's houses" (Mies 1996: 81). Although women still figured in the public sphere throughout the sixteenth and well into the seventeenth century, this tended to concern only those public arenas ultimately linked with the household, such as markets.[8] In the meantime, a woman's sex had become a better predictor of her sphere of activity than her class membership (Merchant 1980: 150). It can therefore be said that, in the case of women, the policy of spatial othering involved confining them either to the private sphere or to delegitimised social spaces.

The same state-enforced endeavour aimed at the restoration of order provided the logic behind witch-hunting – which, as several authors have noted, was primarily, though by far not exclusively directed at women.[9] Rather than an

---

7   Silvia Federici (2004) additionally sees the progressive delegitimisation of abortive and contraceptive practices as part of a strategy of containing *unproductive sexuality* and thus subjecting the female body to the capitalist dictate of the reproduction of labour power. Through the control of women's reproductive capacity, "*the proletariat was expropriated from its body* as it had been expropriated from the land, where expropriation refers both to the destruction of specific faculties and their subordination to the aims of the nascent system of production" (Federici 2004: 16). For a similar argument, see also Linebaugh and Rediker 2000: 92.

8   Pelizzon (1998: 322) notes that "What the domestic ideology denied women in the end, was a right to freedom of movement – i.e., women were never supposed to be unsupervised by some man, or not under the immediate authority of some man. For example, this abbreviated the right to travel, or to live alone or assemble freely".

9   In his classic *La sorcière au village (XVe-XVIIIe siècle)*, Robert Muchembled (1979) distinguished between several phases of European witch-hunting and what we could call

instance of isolated trials, as before 1450, witch-hunting as a mass phenomenon was part of the above-mentioned re-Christianisation campaign of the sixteenth century. As such, it built on the already established practice of torturing and burning heretics at the stake, yet constructed witchcraft as the most sinful of heresies – the one posing a threat to the existence of the Christian world itself. On account of their alleged greater sensuality and sexual appetite, women were more readily associated with the figure of the witch whom the devil attracted through sexual intercourse (Merchant 1980). Tellingly for the interdependency of gendering and racial othering in the Occidentalist imaginary, the English ruling class commonly pictured the devil luring the witch into the sexual act as a black man (Linebaugh and Rediker 2000: 92). The crime of witchcraft was therefore a crime against God, "le crime de lèse-majesté divine" (Muchembled 1979: 74), and at the same time one that required and justified state intervention and control. While the notion that women were driven by sexual passions and were hence closer to nature had been present since the Renaissance, it had nevertheless presupposed a deferential view of Nature as a nurturing maternal figure (Mother Earth). By contrast, increasing scientific knowledge of the universe, geography, and the human body, as well as capitalist exploitation of new territories and their resources had gradually imposed a view of nature as an inanimate object, the exploitation of which was beneficial to Man and the taming of which was therefore not only legitimate, but also necessary (Merchant 1980; Mies 1996). In particular, the "discovery" of a New World inhabited by "faithless barbarians" and apparently devoid of human settlement greatly reinforced the Occidental image of nature as wilderness, to be accordingly Christianised and subdued. Thus, much like the enslavement of indigenous peoples in the New World on account of their lesser humanity, European witch-hunting on account of women's closeness to uncontrollable and disorderly Nature was the expression of a world-view taking shape in the sixteenth century:

> the persecution of witches was a way of publicly equating kings, God, elites, social order, and authority against a common enemy representing "disorder". At the same time the notion of "disorder", the common public enemy, could variously be equated with Nature, women, the poor, and non-whites (inasmuch as

---

their respective "gender profiling": While witchcraft trials had been relatively rare up to the fifteenth century and had mainly involved accusations of sorcery towards people, animals, and goods, their number increased dramatically in the latter half of the fifteenth century, especially in France, Switzerland, and Germany, and the charge disproportionately became that of sexual intercourse with the devil. If the number of women accused of witchcraft greatly surpassed that of men and children, the ratio went to up to four times as many women as men between mid-sixteenth century and the end of the seventeenth century. Witchcraft eventually became an almost exclusively female crime with the definitive gendering of women in the eighteenth century (Muchembled 1979: 74ff.). For data on the sex ratio of witchcraft trials spanning the time period between 1480 and 1700, see also Merchant 1980: 312.

> Europeans were now involved in the subordination and exploitation, or outright extermination, of non-Europeans). [...] What connected them was the ascription of a metaphysical femininity. They were therefore, knowable, conquerable, and exploitable, while the knower, conqueror etc. was metaphysically equated with the masculine. Thus, the world became gendered. (Pelizzon 1998: 276f.)

The emerging Occidentalist imaginary would subsequently employ gender both as a metaphor – resulting in the representation of New World territories as female virgin lands that the conquerors penetrated with the sword in hand – and as a means of subalternisation (McClintock 1995: 26; Mies 1996: 75; Schiwy 2007: 275). Gendered notions of "tropical" climates would soon serve as a foil for erotic Occidental depictions of the unknown and the wilderness waiting to be conquered and juxtaposed with Occidental fears of harmful diseases and the danger of contagion linked to the image of female prostitutes (Roth 2014). In the corresponding colonial map, the dividing line between the masculine European Self and its feminised New World Other was to be additionally drawn between literate people and people without writing, thus reinforcing the distinction between culture, the core, and Christianity on the one hand, and nature, the periphery, and non-Christians on the other.

Enlightenment: The Civilising Mission

In the eighteenth century, alphabetic literacy went from a cultural measuring stick to an essential requirement. Together with other characteristics of *Western* culture increasingly conceived as a mark of *universal* civilisation, it signalled the transition to the new global design of the civilising mission and, with it, to the *second major strategy of racialisation and ethnicisation.* Mechanisms of othering now operated along *temporal* rather than *spatial* lines: Unlike in the Christian worldview, the Enlightenment postulates of scientific progress and modernity, conceived as the overcoming of tradition, located the self-proclaimed European civilisation not only at the centre of Creation, but also viewed it as "the center and the end" of world history (Hegel 1955: 235). Secularisation thus brought about a shift of emphasis from the notion of a *spatial boundary* between Christians in Europe and barbarians in the colonies to the one of a *time lag* between modern civilisation and the primitive colonial world. In the Occidentalist imaginary, the earlier colonial task of Christianisation was thus superseded by the secular one of the civilising mission. The corresponding hierarchisation of difference now increasingly relied on evolutionist notions of human and societal perfectibility.

The normality of social change, a wide-ranging notion of freedom encompassing free trade, free labour, and free property, and the exploitation of natural resources, including women's bodies, were the parameters around which such perfectibility was being advocated.

Thus, the sequence of major political upheavals, from the seventeenth century Glorious Revolution and the eighteenth century French Revolution in Europe to the

94   *Global Inequalities Beyond Occidentalism*

wars of independence in both North and South American colonies in the eighteenth and nineteenth centuries gradually imposed the view that social change, rather than an exceptional instance of disorder, was normal, desirable, and conducive to progress (Wallerstein 1991a: 24). Evolutionary cosmology as advocated by Kant and Laplace in the 1780s and 1790s and the subsequent evolutionist turn throughout the natural sciences, which would culminate in Darwin's theory of the origin of the species in 1859, marked a similar shift in the determinist worldview that had characterised European scientific approaches up to the eighteenth century.[10] Change and development were thus accepted as the principles now governing both the social and the natural world. Enlightenment ideas such as faith in Reason and science, the commitment to the idea of progress, and the concurrent demotion of tradition served to postulate civilisation as the equivalent of modernity, and the French revolutionary ideals of freedom and equality as the highest civilisational goods. As the self-definition of the Occident was changing, so were the terms in which the othering of the colonised areas proceeded.

Against this background, slavery started being constructed as the very opposite: not only the obverse of freedom as a principle, but also the quintessence of the various forms of political, economic, and moral unfreedom against which civilisation had prevailed. If, during the seventeenth and the early eighteenth centuries, the enslavement of Europeans had repeatedly been advocated by political philosophers – including liberals such as Thomas Hobbes and John Locke – as a means of imposing discipline on the pauperised masses and thus of maintaining social order, by mid-eighteenth century, the institution of slavery was being vehemently denounced as a prime example of tyranny. Tellingly, references to slavery as a concrete historical institution in their writings were regularly drawn from European antiquity, not from contemporary New World reality. As Michel-Rolph Trouillot (1995) and Susan Buck-Morss (2000, 2009) have amply documented, Enlightenment thinkers from Locke to Montesquieu, Voltaire, David Hume or Jean-Jacques Rousseau condemned slavery philosophically, yet, when it came to the enslavement of black Africans, often upheld it practically or justified it on racial grounds. Even more tellingly, this shift in Occidentalist discourse occurred at the same time that the slave trade and the exploitation of slave labour in the colonies, triggered by the increasing demand for sugar, coffee, and cotton in Western Europe, reached unprecedented heights, while in Eastern Europe, serfdom was being reintroduced in order to satisfy the growing Western European demand for cereals.[11]

---

10   As Richard Lewontin remarked with regard to the state of the art in the European sciences, before the evolutionist turn, "Species were fixed, as was the position of the earth in the universe. Galileo's heresy was not that the earth was not at the center of the cosmos but that *it moved*. Men reason by analogy from the condition of their lives to the condition of the universe, and a static society could hardly believe in a dynamic cosmos" (Lewontin 1968: 208).

11   On account of its intensification, and by analogy with the emergence of Eastern European "second serfdom", Dale Tomich (2004: 56ff.) labelled nineteenth-century New

However, the paradox between political discourse and social reality was only on the surface. Such changes in the patterns of demand on the world market, together with the new patterns of consumption of tropical foodstuffs that industrialisation, urbanisation, and population growth had generated in Western Europe and North America, had led to the reorganisation of the international division of labour: Under nineteenth-century British hegemony, the direct political control over sources of production in particular colonies, which had characterised the mercantilist policies of Spain and Portugal in the sixteenth and Holland in the seventeenth centuries, was gradually abandoned in favour of a more complex mechanism of economic control over the flow of commodities between core and periphery more generally. As the search for cheap commodities – irrespective of the labour regime governing their production – became the main determinant of Western economic policy, "the slave as productive labour took precedence over the slave as commodity" (Tomich 2004: 62). The apparent contradiction between the discourse of freedom and the practice of slavery in the writings of Enlightenment thinkers was thus a logical reflection of the transformation of the capitalist world-economy from its mercantilist to its early industrial phase.

The corresponding change in the Occidentalist discourse echoed this transformation accordingly. While the logic of racial othering legitimising the enslavement of Blacks had closely followed the ontological order characterising the thought of Renaissance Christianity, the massive increase in slave production cemented the association between blackness, slavery, and inferiority. As a result, "By the middle of the eighteenth century, 'black' was almost universally bad. What had happened in the meantime, was the expansion of African-American slavery" (Trouillot 1995: 77). Towards the end of the century, the semantic overlap between dark skin and the slave status had been underpinned by legal regulations – thereby reasserting the irreconcilability between the freedom of the self-proclaimed civilised world and the unfreedom of its colonies: in France, which had declared slavery illegal on its territory in 1716, leading to the freeing of slaves upon arrival, African blacks were increasingly singled out as exceptions to the rule and "Negro" and "mulatto" immigration was finally prohibited in 1777 altogether; in England in 1772, a court ruled that slavery was "un-British", i.e., incompatible with the liberties guaranteed in England, and that the influx of "Negroes" should therefore be prevented; similarly, in 1773, Portugal forbade the entry of Blacks and Brazilian slaves, on account of their being unfair competition to domestic labour (Davis, in Buck-Morss 2009: 90ff.).

The racial discourse not only shifted thereby from questioning the humanity of religious Others to assigning different "degrees of humanity" to the colonised (the lowest of which to Black Africans); it also set the stage for an Occidentalist perspective which defined colonised and other non-Western populations back into a past that Europe had overcome. In the process,

---

World slavery the "second slavery". For a discussion of the strengths and limits of this analogy, see Boatcă 2013.

96   *Global Inequalities Beyond Occidentalism*

> spatial boundaries were transformed into chronological ones. Savages and primitives in space were converted into primitives and exotic Orientals in time. The question was no longer whether primitives and Orientals were human [...], but, rather, how far removed from the present and civilized stage of humanity they were. (Mignolo 2000: 283)

The systematic exercise of what Johannes Fabian has described as "the denial of coevalness" – "a discourse that consistently places those who are talked about in a time other than that of the one who talks" (Fabian 2006: 143) – became characteristic of this stage in the Occidentalist discourse. As the temporal dimension of othering took precedence over the spatial one, Blacks, indigenous and colonised people went from being seen as non-humans or subhumans to primitive humans, while slavery, serfdom, and other forms of unfree labour with which non-white labour was associated increasingly appeared not only as non-Western, but also as archaic and backward (Tomich 2004). Therefore, the ongoing redrawing of geographical borders now mainly entailed their simultaneous transformation into temporal stages of rationality and modernity. Both civilisation and modernity, as well as their respective products, civilised Man and modern Reason, were conceived as situated *geographically* in Europe and *temporally* at the peak of social evolution as a staged process of universal applicability.

Seeing Europe as the epitome of civilisation and as the end of world history entailed assigning to the remaining territories different degrees of progress on this predetermined path. In Hegel's nineteenth-century philosophy of history, the idea that historical progress followed a certain direction yielded a reshuffled map of continents according to their presumed position on the universal trajectory. Thus, for Hegel, if "Universal history goes from East to West. Europe is absolutely the end of universal history. Asia is the beginning" (Hegel 1830, quoted in Dussel 1995: 20).[12] Consequently, Europe is "absolutely the centre and the end of the ancient world and the Occident", while the New World, which "is new not only relatively but also absolutely", is viewed as representing the immaturity of the Spirit and thus as harbouring only the potentiality of future realisation. In contrast, Africa is credited with no history whatsoever;[13] being "submerged in the natural spirit", her Black inhabitants have no consciousness of God or the law, and are thus "human being(s) in the rough". As such, they do not regard slavery as improper, having experienced an even harsher type of slavery before European colonisation. According to Hegel, therefore, Black slavery under European rule, while still a form of unfreedom and unjust in principle, is historically justified and as such represents progress for the Africans.[14] If Africa is viewed

---

12   Unless otherwise indicated, all following quotations from Dussel 1995: 20–22

13   For a detailed and nuanced analysis of Hegel's claim that Africa is unhistorical, see Bernasconi 1998: 59f.

14   "slavery in the Indies is justified historically by the fact that among the Negroes too these slaves were slaves and were faced with an even harsher fate; by the fact that the

as having no history or culture of its own, in turn, Asia's culture, while older than Europe's, appears as static and unchanging, and thus as incapable of progress (Hegel 1995: 125f.). In the context of the expansion of Europe's colonial dominion into Asia and Africa in the eighteenth century, and especially after Napoleon's invasion of Egypt in 1798, the Orient and in particular the Arab Near East became the epitome of the backwardness, femininity, passivity, and conquerability that would make up the repertoire of Orientalist discourse throughout the nineteenth and twentieth centuries (Said 1979: 207). In the process, the "Muslim threat" characterising the Christianisation campaigns of the previous centuries was revived, while prior knowledge of Islam provided a basis for military incursions into the Orient at large and into Britain's and France's colonies in the Far East in particular.

Whereas Hegelian philosophy still conceptualised the development of world-history in religious terms, i.e., as the self-realisation of God and as a theodicy of liberty, the process described was ultimately one of Enlightenment, i.e., of the advance of secular reason (Dussel 1995: 20). Hegel's philosophy of history is thus indicative of the gradual replacement of the former hegemony of the Western Christian worldview by a more secular frame of mind, which, however, preserved its predecessor's missionary aspirations and entrusted Western Europe with *the civilising mission* of bringing progress to the rest of the world.

In considering Europe the end of universal history, Hegel had however only meant Western Europe. More precisely, he viewed "Germany, France, Denmark, the Scandinavian countries" as "the heart of Europe", while he counted among modernity's main achievements only such Western European events as the Lutheran Reformation, the Enlightenment, the French Revolution, and British Industrialisation, which he understood as manifestations of the universal Spirit (Dussel 1995: 26). Thus, hierarchies that structured Europe according to principles similar to those applied to the colonial world gradually started taking shape within Europe. If, as Aníbal Quijano (2000) contended, the propagation of Eurocentrism in the non-European world occurred with the help of evolutionism and dualism as its two founding myths, the same also served to propagate Occidentalism in Europe once the change in hegemony from the old Spanish-Portuguese core to the Northwestern one had been effectuated. On the one hand, the evolutionary notion that human civilisation had proceeded in a linear and unidirectional fashion from an initial state of nature through successive stages leading up to a singular Western

---

indigenous population is thereby relieved; by the fact that the Negroes are more capable of work, that the settlers have a property right over them, that the colonies would otherwise have to perish. Despite this justification, reason must maintain that the slavery of the Negroes is a wholly unjust institution, one which contradicts true justice, both human and divine, and which is to be rejected" (Hegel 1978: 68 quoted in Bernasconi 1998: 58). It should be noted that, by arguing that the indigenous population is relieved from slavery through the employment of Black Africans, Hegel reproduces the sixteenth-century notion according to which Amerindians had souls and could therefore be Christianised, whereas Africans were savages, wild nature, who could not.

form of civilisation justified the *temporal* division of the European continent: while the East was still considered feudal, the South had marked the end of the Middle Ages, and the Northwest represented modernity. On the other hand, the dualist idea that differences between Europeans and non-Europeans could be traced back to essential categories such as primitive-civilised, irrational-rational, traditional-modern (Quijano 2000: 543) allowed both a *spatial* and an *ontological* division within Europe. By being geographically inextricable from Europe, and at the same time (predominantly) Christian and white, the European Southeast and especially the Balkans could not be constructed as "an incomplete Other" of Western Europe, as in the case of the Far East, but rather as its "incomplete Self" (Todorova 1997). Moreover, its proximity to Asia and its Ottoman cultural legacy located it halfway between East and West, thus giving it a condition of semi-Oriental, semi-civilised, semi-developed, in the process of "catching up with the West".[15] In the same vein, the European South, epitomised by the declining Spanish empire and its Moorish legacy, was gradually defined out of the Western core both for its proximity to Arab/Berber North Africa and for its reputation as a brutal coloniser of the New World, which was constructed as the opposite of England's own benevolent colonialism (Cassano 1995; Santos 2006). To be sure, negative stereotypes of both the East and the South of Europe had existed long before the eighteenth century[16] and had mainly been linked to the perceived "Muslim menace" that the Middle East and North Africa, adjoining Europe's eastern and southern borders, represented for Christian Europe. Yet it is only with the emphasis on civilisation and progress as central elements of Occidentalism that racial discourses directed at the non-Western Europeans as *backward* with respect to the West acquired systematic character as elements of processes of racialisation internal to Europe.

Parallel to the construction of colonial difference overseas, we thus witness the emergence of a double imperial difference in Europe (stretching onto Asia): on the one hand, an external difference between the new capitalist core and the existing traditional empires of Islamic and Eastern Christian faith – the Ottoman and the Tsarist one; on the other hand, an internal difference between the new and the old capitalist core, mainly England vs. Spain:

> In this short history it is clear that the imperial external difference created the conditions for the emergence, in the eighteenth century, of Orientalism, while the imperial internal difference ended up in the imaginary and political construction

---

15 Maria Todorova speaks in this context of "Balkanism". Unlike Orientalism, which deals with a difference between (imputed) types – the European (Self) and the Oriental (Other) – 'Balkanism' as a discourse treats the differences within one type (Todorova 2004: 235) – the civilised Western European and the semi-civilised, semi-Oriental Eastern European.

16 For a discussion of Eastern Europe as Europe's racialised internal other, see also Wolff 1994; for Southern Europe, especially Spain, see also Greer et al. 2006, Mignolo 2006a.

of the South of Europe. Russia remained outside the sphere of Orientalism and at the opposed end, in relation to Spain as paradigmatic example of the South of Europe. (Mignolo 2006b: 487)[17]

A sharp distinction from all forms of tradition and backwardness, both within and outside Europe, would occur with the French Revolution. Here, too, an across-the-board notion of slavery, encompassing the slave status under ancient Roman and Greek law alongside feudal labour arrangements, served as the very prototype of unfreedom against which the French revolutionary ideal of liberty was projected.[18] In contrast, the granting of citizenship as the basis for universal equality of political and social rights in a modern social order was not only understood as an expression of liberty (i.e., the opposite of slavery), but also as the mark of civilisation. As such, citizenship was, however, to be acquired as the result of a civilising *process* – that is, gradually. In the immediate aftermath of the revolution, citizenship rights were therefore only granted to male property-owners, whose ability to pay taxes and military tribute, i.e., contribute to the maintenance of social order, qualified them as "active citizens". Women, foreigners, and children were in turn defined as "passive citizens" and denied all political rights (Wallerstein 2003: 653f.). While, in the case of women, this was considered a temporary provision, to be remedied by further educational measures, the grounds on which they were denied citizenship drew on the same charges as the witch-trials of the sixteenth century: being more exposed to "error and seduction" and more prone to "ardor in passions", their overall disposition could only generate disorder in public assemblies (Amar, cited in Wallerstein 2003: 654). Both Olympe de Gouges' 1791 "Declaration of the Rights of Women and the Female Citizen" and Mary Wollstonecraft's 1792 "A Vindication on the Rights of Women" pointed to the male dividend of the human rights and citizenship discourse – to no immediate avail. The constitution of 1793 extended active citizenship to all adult (not necessarily propertied) males,

---

17   Here, the distinction between Occidentalism and Orientalism also becomes clearer: "Occidentalism, in other words, is the overarching geopolitical imaginary of the modern/colonial world-system, to which Orientalism was appended in its first radical transformation, when the center of the system moved from the Iberian Peninsula to the North Sea, between Holland and Britain […] Orientalism […] was a particular rearticulation of the modern/colonial world system imaginary in its second phase, when Occidentalism, structured and implemented in the imaginary of Spanish and Portuguese empires, began to fade away" (Mignolo 2000: 59).

18   "This was a revolution against, not merely the tyranny of a particular ruler, but of all past traditions that violated the general principles of human liberty" (Buck-Morss 2000: 836). As Buck-Morss notes, the Marseillaise itself contains references to slavery as a central reason of the call to arms directed at the French citizens. Indeed, the second stanza is dedicated to the topic: "Que veut cette horde d'esclaves,/De traîtres, de rois conjurés?/Pour qui ces ignobles entraves,/Ces fers dès longtemps préparés?/Français, pour nous, ah! quel outrage/Quels transports il doit exciter!/*C'est nous qu'on ose méditer/De rendre à l'antique esclavage*" (my emphasis).

100   *Global Inequalities Beyond Occidentalism*

thus leaving women to derive their membership in the social community from their relationship to men (Hanagan 2002: 167). Seen in this light, the institutionalisation of the division between private and public spheres, habitually considered a characteristic of the specifically modern form of social organisation, is revealed to have been closely associated with the gendering of economic roles upon which the state-propagated, bourgeois family model was based. Additionally defined as vulnerable through the exclusion from the military and as close to nature on account of their reproductive capacity, women would now find themselves increasingly outside of the male domain of culture, in turn associated with wage work and the tasks to protect and provide. The culturally and normatively binding female ideal of the time found its expression in the social role of the housewife (and mother), whose consignment to the private sphere of the household entailed the simultaneous construction of the unpaid work done there as a natural resource and therefore as "non-work". Thus, the gendering of the private and the public spheres, although only legally sanctioned in the wake of the French Revolution, in fact built on the social definition of reproduction as a non-economic activity and as an exclusively female one, which had initiated with the degradation of women's social and economic standing in the sixteenth century.[19] By relegating women, children, and foreigners in the (however recent) past of the civilising process that adult men had supposedly accomplished, the implementation of universal principles was thus constantly creating its own particularisms.

And more would become apparent soon. In the French colony of Saint-Domingue, where the revolution of the enslaved led by Toussaint L'Ouverture resulted in the abolition of slavery in 1794, skin colour took precedence over property as a criterion for the granting of citizenship. Since not all whites were property-owners, but relatively many free mulattos were, the colonial assembly included the former in the right to vote even before this was accomplished in continental France, but excluded both slaves and mulattos from franchise after a series of heated debates (Blackburn 1988: 183ff.). According to a logic strikingly similar to the one that, in the sixteenth century, had questioned whether the Amerindians had souls that would allow them to be Christianised by the colonisers, the argument used by both the white planters and the poor whites of Saint-Domingue at the close of the eighteenth century was that slaves and free mulattos were not part of "the nation" and could therefore not become citizens.[20]

---

19 For views according to which the Enlightenment ideal of female passivity and domesticity was a result of the rise of scientific, especially medical knowledge of the human body and of the subsequent naturalisation of sex differences in the eighteenth century, see Nye 1993, Schiebinger 2004. For the counterargument that traces the naturalisation of women's reproductive role back to the sixteenth century, and sees eighteenth-century science as a latecomer to this task, see Pelizzon 1999, Federici 2004.

20 Tellingly, Saint-Domingue's first constitution as the independent republic of Haiti aimed at erasing precisely the racial differences that had made such hierarchisation by skin colour possible. To that end, it ruled that all Haitians, including white women and

For the same reason, and despite its globally transformative impact, the Haitian Revolution did not enter into the Occidentalist imaginary as an event on a par with the American and French revolutions (Stam and Shohat 2012: 96).

The same logic found further support in the contention of late eighteenth and nineteenth-century ethnologists that "Negroes" were not of the same species as the Europeans. As Maria Mies has documented drawing on work on the Caribbean, Burma, and Western Africa during this period, patterns of equality between the sexes among the enslaved population[21] were interpreted by the British colonisers as signs of backwardness of "the Negro race", whose degree of civilisation was seen as lagging centuries behind the European one:

> Men and women are not sufficiently differentiated yet in Burma. It is the mark of a young race. Ethnologists tell us that. In the earliest peoples the difference was very slight. As a race grows older the difference increases. (Hall, quoted in Mies 1996: 93)

Egalitarian views of the male-female relationship among the colonial subjects became a problem especially after the abolition of slavery. As long as the import of African slaves had been cheaper than the natural reproduction of the labour-force on the plantations, enslaved women in the Caribbean had been systematically prevented from forming families and having children (Mies 1996: 91ff.). In turn, after the abolition of the slave trade in 1807, the "local breeding" of the labour force became a more lucrative option. Since, according to the colonisers' civilizing mission, the adequate policy against the alleged primitivity of gender relations was the introduction of the European model of the bourgeois marriage, the ex-slaves' resistance to the monogamy norm and the nuclear family pattern came with high economic costs for the colonial administration. Especially the enslaved women's active birth strikes – such as occurred in the British Caribbean in the beginning of the nineteenth century and in German South West Africa at the turn of the twentieth – seriously affected the planters' designs for the supply of cheap labour power. At the same time, state legislation against "racially mixed"

---

members of naturalised ethnic groups such as Germans and Poles were to be referred to by the generic term "black", thus turning the term into a political rather than a biological category (see Fischer 2004: 233). The constitution thus seized upon the above-mentioned mechanism of deriving a universal term by generalising from a particular one, but in so doing reversed the prevailing hierarchy: As Sybille Fischer (2004: 233) cogently remarked, "Calling all Haitians, regardless of skin color, black ... both asserts the egalitarian and universalist institutions and puts them to a test by using the previously subordinated term of the opposition as the universal term".

21   "each woman could live with a man as long as she pleased; the same also applied to the man. Slave women saw the marriage tie as something that would subject them to the control of one man, who could even beat them. The men wanted more than one wife and therefore rejected marriage" (Mies 1996: 92).

102 *Global Inequalities Beyond Occidentalism*

marriages, varying widely in scope across the colonial world,[22] came to include the loss of citizenship and voting rights for both partners and their offspring in Germany's African colonies in 1908; in turn, informal sexual relationships between White male colonists and Black women were encouraged as long as they did not produce offspring (Mamozai 1982: 129). Both measures were primarily aimed at preventing the non-White population from acquiring property and thus from receiving voting rights; their most salient side effect, however, was forcing Black women into concubinage and prostitution, while reducing white women to housewifery and motherhood (Bush 1981; Alexander 1991). What Maria Mies described as "the double-faced process of colonization and housewifisation" (1996: 97) therefore did not necessarily take place in two different locations, the colonial zone on the one hand and the metropolitan one, on the other. Rather, the emergence of bourgeois marriage and family as protected institutions was causally linked to the disruption of clan and family relations of the "natives", to which the former were frequently contrasted within the colonial context itself:

> not only did the few European women who went to the colonies as wives and, breeders for race and nation' rise to the level of proper housewives on the subordination and subjection of the colonized women, so too did the "women, 'back home'"; first those of the bourgeoisie, later also the women of the proletariat, were gradually domesticated and civilized into proper housewives. For the same period which saw the expansion of colonialism and imperialism also saw the rise of the housewife in Europe and the USA. (Mies 1996: 101)

Consequently, to the extent that subsistence production outside Europe was declared a "backward" and "underdeveloped" labour form, the bourgeois family model propagated in Western Europe made it possible to stigmatise female housework as "non-work" and to define women into the norm of non-wage work altogether. Not only the naturalisation of women, but also that of peasants and slaves in the colonies thus occurred temporally and (ideo)logically parallel to the process of housewifisation of bourgeois women and to that of the proletarianisation of male non-wage workers in the industrial centres. Both were conceived as dimensions of the larger civilising process itself (Mies 1996; von Werlhof et al. 1983).

Scholars of the colonial world therefore seem to be in agreement that it was the conjunction of Europe's expansion into Asia and Africa, Darwinian evolutionism, and theories of the racial superiority of the white male (having the "beastliness" of the African woman as a counterpart) that eventually coalesced into nineteenth-century scientific racism (Mies 1996: 95; Quijano and Wallerstein 1992: 551). The mechanisms of othering thus employed blended the logic of gendering into the ones of racial and ethnic inferiorisation by equating primitiveness and exoticism with femininity and puerility. What Edward Said had identified as the set of features

---

22   For a recent comparison of taboos and legislation against interracial unions in nineteenth-century Cuba, Brazil and the United States, see Morrison 2010.

Orientalism vs. Occidentalism 103

used in describing the Orient as Other – "its eccentricity, its backwardness, its silent indifference, its feminine penetrability, its supine malleability" – applied to slightly varying degrees to African women, Oriental men, and the non-Western more generally:

> Along with all other peoples variously designated as backward, degenerate, uncivilized, and retarded, the Orientals were viewed in a framework constructed out of biological determinism and moral-political admonishment. The Oriental was thus linked to elements in Western society (delinquents, the insane, women, the poor) having in common an identity best described as lamentably alien. Orientals were rarely seen or looked at; they were seen through, analyzed not as citizens, or even people, but as problems to be solved or confined. (Said 1979: 207)

Whereas the social construct of skin colour replaced religious denomination as an identity marker and also as an indicator of a person's position within the hierarchy of methods of labour control outside Europe, citizenship, at first defined in relation to (male) gender, property status, literacy, but not least social and ethnic extraction, fulfilled the same function in the newly emerging secular nation-states of Western Europe. While the typologies thus established legitimated the hierarchy of labour payment according to a person's degree of proximity to this standard of citizenship, institutional mechanisms ensured the normalisation of the resulting "Others". The work of the Africans and Native Americans in the colonies, such as that of women and children in the entire world economy, was treated as inferior, and that of housewives even as "non-work". National constitutions, schools, hospitals, prisons, and guidebooks were in charge of emphasising the universal norm, isolating or treating deviation, and preparing the young generation for the role of the citizen as defined by Occidental standards. As decolonial philosopher Santiago Castro-Gómez has argued for Latin America, the disabled, homosexuals, and dissidents fell just as much short of the economically profitable and socially compliant national subject, as women, the illiterate, non-whites, or the enslaved:

> The acquisition of citizenship is [...] a filter through which only those are allowed to pass, whose profile fits the type of citizen required by the project of modernity: male, White, paterfamilias, Catholic, property-owner, literate and heterosexual. Those who do not meet these requirements (women, servants, the mentally ill, the illiterate, Blacks, heretics, slaves, Indians, homosexuals, dissidents) remain outside the 'lettered City' [...], sentenced to punishment and therapy by the same law that excludes them. (Castro-Gómez 2000: 149, my translation)

Especially in those parts of Latin America that had previously been central to the Spanish empire before the eighteenth century, and which still had a sizable indigenous population – such as Mexico, Central America, and the Andean region –

104 *Global Inequalities Beyond Occidentalism*

the inculcation of Western norms through public education was part of extensive policies of cultural assimilation that largely built on modified versions of the former colonial policies.[23] In contrast, in Argentina, Chile, and Uruguay, but also in the Unites States, where no successful "de-Indianisation" was deemed possible, the virtual physical extermination of the natives and the conspicuous absence of Blacks from state discourse silenced the question of the political participation and social enfranchisement of the non-White population (Quijano 2006: 199ff.). Thus, the civilising mission brought about a dual pattern of hierarchisation of difference according to both racial and ethnic criteria.

Post-war and Turn of the Millennium: Development and the Global Market

The Occidentalist discourse further complicated in the second half of the twentieth century, when it experienced a cognitive, yet not a factual, blur. The end of World War I had brought about the delegitimisation of the notions of progress and the advance of reason as necessary outcomes of social evolution (Connell 2007). In addition, the end of World War II had meant, on the one hand, the juridical and administrative decolonisation of large parts of Asia, Africa, and the Caribbean, and, on the other, the delegitimisation of biological racism. Scholarly explanations of macroeconomic disparities, intra- and interethnic conflict, migration and citizenship issues, or income inequality among racial and ethnic groups resorted instead to a naturalised notion of culture. Geographically remote cultures were accordingly treated as closed entities with incompatible sets of values and norms that situated them on different, but likewise irreconcilable temporal stages in a linear process of economic and social evolution. Their interaction therefore necessarily equalled a clash. This discursive shift from biological to cultural racism (Balibar 1996) accompanying an apparent shift in emphasis from differentiation on the basis of *race* (that supposedly included biological criteria) to differentiation on the basis of *ethnicity* (forged around cultural characteristics) marks the transition to the third and last Occidentalist pattern to be mentioned here, and which can best be described as the combined strategy of *ethnicisation along both spatial and temporal dimensions*. It is in these terms that both successive and partly overlapping global designs of the latter part of the twentieth and the beginning of the twenty-first centuries were framed.

---

23 As Quijano notes, these policies were not straightforwardly assimilationist but retained their colonial overtones: "However, said strategy never ceased to alternate and combine with discriminating policies against the "indio" as well as with the othering of the "indio". In this way, de-Indianisation could not encompass the majority of the "Indian" population, which could only incorporate itself or be incorporated to a partial, precarious and formal extent in the process of nationalising society, the culture, and the state" (Quijano 2006: 201, my translation). The consequences of these ambiguous neocolonial policies for today's patterns of ethnic and racial inequality in the region are discussed in detail below.

The first one, represented by *developmentalism*, featured most prominently in the United States' foreign policy after 1945 and received substantial academic support from modernisation theory. The bipolar geopolitical structure of capitalism vs. socialism characterising the aftermath of World War II and the subsequent process of decolonisation taking place in Asia, Africa, and the Caribbean prompted yet another conceptual reorganisation of the capitalist system's geoculture around the categories of the First, Second, and Third Worlds, respectively. The array of new Third World nation states emerged as a result of the dissolution of European empires consequently aroused competition for potential economic and political spheres of influence between the military leaders of the First and the Second worlds – the United States and the Soviet Union. In the conceptual apparatus of the modernisation approach, the nineteenth-century notion of evolutionary process was reduced to a transformation from tradition – viewed as the specific problem of Third World countries – to modernity – embodied by the United States and Western Europe and thus located in the First World. In response to the need to discredit the Communist model as a viable alternative for the new nations, the multidisciplinary US modernisation school identified the problem of Third World countries in their alleged "traditionalism" and viewed the solution to it in modernisation – understood as a stage-by-stage replication of the economic development of Western Europe and North America (So 1990). Drawing on evolutionary as well as functionalist assumptions, modernisation theory saw societies as becoming increasingly similar in the course of a slowly operating process of social change considered unidirectional, progressive, and irreversible. It thus revived basic premises of nineteenth-century evolutionary theory, such as the stage theory of development and the clear-cut distinction between traditional and modern societies, yet focused almost exclusively on the latter. Moreover, it subsumed such economically and culturally diverse regions as contemporary China, the Middle East, and medieval Europe under the "traditional" label (Rostow 1959). At the same time, modernisation theory replaced the notion of development as a by-product of an immanent historical process with the one of development strategy, deliberately triggered and controlled by political actors with the help of state-led policies. In "The Stages of Economic Growth", one of the most widely debated works of the modernisation school, and tellingly subtitled "A Non-Communist Manifesto", economist W. W. Rostow (1959) diagnosed the lack of productive investment as the main problem of Third World societies and was among the first to suggest that the obvious solution was to provide US aid to these countries – understood in terms of capital, technology, and expertise. Similarly, Daniel Lerner's *The Passing of Traditional Society. Modernizing the Middle East* (1958) typically identified in the sequence of stages of urbanisation, growth of literacy, and industrialisation a normative modernisation process by which Middle Eastern societies were supposed to replicate Western economic, social and political developments. In this twentieth-century variant, development therefore became coterminous with planned economic growth and political modernisation, to be implemented with the help of development agencies and foreign aid projects especially created for

106 *Global Inequalities Beyond Occidentalism*

the purpose. From an Occidentalist perspective, the world map was this time divided into developed and underdeveloped peoples: The former were commonly identified with unified and historically consolidated nation-states; the latter were seen as the mark of ethnic groups either not yet constituted into a modern nation-state or having recently acquired statehood as a result of decolonisation. Communist countries, constituting the deviant Second World in this model, eventually joined in this rhetoric by referring to themselves as "developing countries".

This state-centred view of the development process bore numerous consequences. Not only did it make the nation-state the default unit of analysis – and thus relinquished the global perspective that had been characteristic of nineteenth and early twentieth century social science, including the evolutionist conceptions from Comte through Spencer and Marx;[24] it also circumscribed the scope of alternative visions, such as Latin American dependency theory, which argued, against modernisation theory, that the differences between developed and underdeveloped states were the result of the structural dependence of peripheral, raw-material exporting countries upon industrialised central ones. Latin American dependency theorists advocated a socialist revolution based on the Cuban model both as a solution for eliminating the periphery's dependency on the centre's economy and as a way toward autonomous national development. In so doing, they however failed to transcend the nation-state framework dictated by the very developmentalist ideology they were attempting to counter (Grosfoguel 1997: 532). In both types of approaches, the categories of developed and underdeveloped countries ultimately appeared to connote natural differences between developed and underdeveloped peoples (Quijano 2000c: 80).

By contrast, the modernity/coloniality model, which takes the world-system as a unit of analysis, stresses the fundamental difference between processes of nation-state formation in Western Europe as opposed to the Americas: In Europe, nation-building has been the end result of a combined process of democratisation of society, the homogenisation of the population on the basis of common history, and the political organisation of a modern nation-state (Quijano 2000a, 2006). In both North and South America, however, the process of decolonisation begun with the region's independence from British and Iberian colonial rule did not give rise to homogeneous nation-states, but to what Aníbal Quijano has called

---

24   In Raewyn Connell's (2007) analysis of the formation of the sociological canon, the two major objects of sociological theory and research that the author identifies as characteristic of the late nineteenth- and early twentieth-century sociology are the idea of progress and what she calls the idea of "global difference" – the difference between the civilisation of the metropole and the primitiveness of the colonies. This finding is consistent with the periodisation undertaken here, that sees the global design of the civilising mission and its corresponding strand of Occidentalism as stretching until the former half of the twentieth century. According to Connell, it was only with Parsons' generation that the experience of the periphery started being erased from mainstream social theory, which increasingly centred on the West and its modernity, and thus on Western(-like) nation-states.

"independent states of colonial societies" (2000a: 565). In the United States and in most countries of the Southern Cone (except Brazil), indigenous serfs and enslaved Africans represented demographic minorities, while wage labourers and independent producers accounted for the bulk of the local economic production after decolonisation; in turn, in most other Ibero-American societies, serfdom was the social condition of the majority of the indigenous population, who made up the largest segment of the population in Mexico, Central America, and the Andes, while Afro-descendants predominated in Brazil and the Caribbean (Quijano 2006: 201; 203). The white bourgeoisie in Latin America, whose profits derived from slave-holding and serfdom, consequently had no interest in organising local production around wage labour (for which European and Asian workers were imported after the abolition of slavery), or in the democratisation of the political process. Unlike in the European case, the homogenisation of Latin American societies had thus entailed the extermination of the indigenous population and the political exclusion of Afro-descendants and mestizos, and as such could not have led to nationalisation or democracy.[25]

The notion that the process of decolonisation undergone by Latin American societies had occurred only at a juridical and administrative level – leaving intact colonial structures of social and cultural domination as well as the economic and institutional bases on which colonial control depended – lay at the centre of Quijano's concept of "coloniality of power" (2000b, 2007). In the context of conceptualising the world-system as a modern/colonial one, the implication therefore was that, much like modernity and in close interconnection with it, coloniality as a set of political, economic, and sociocultural hierarchies between colonisers and colonised emerged with the conquest of the New World in the sixteenth century. Coloniality is thus distinct from premodern forms of colonial rule in that it translates administrative hierarchies into a racial/ethnic division of labour; and it is more encompassing than modern European colonialism alone, in that it transfers both the racial/ethnic hierarchies – i.e., the "colonial difference" – and the international division of labour produced during the time of direct or indirect colonial rule into post-independence times (Mignolo 2000: 54ff.; Quijano 2000b: 381n1). In mandating Latin American countries – or any other former colonised nation – the one-size-fits-all trajectory from "tradition" to "modernity", the global design of developmentalism disregarded the region's historical experience of coloniality and the specificity of the state

---

25 "In no Latin American country today is it possible to find a fully nationalized society, or even a genuine nation-state. The national homogenization of the population could only have been achieved through a radical and global process of the democratization of society and the state. That democratization would have implied [...] the process of decolonizing social, political, and cultural relations that maintain and reproduce racial social classification. The structure of power was and even continues to be organized on and around the colonial axis. Consequently, from the point of view of the dominant groups, the construction of the nation, and above all the central state, has been conceptualized and deployed against American Indians, blacks, and mestizos" (Quijano 2000a: 567f.).

108   *Global Inequalities Beyond Occidentalism*

structures derived from it, in which the acquisition of citizenship was out of reach for the great majority of the population, that had been defined as an "inferior race" over and above the labour regime in which it functioned. For decolonial theorists, the full democratisation of the newly independent states would have required a thorough transformation of the power structures set in place by colonial rule. What, in an Occidentalist perspective, is framed today as a "new" indigenous question of countries in the region hence merely represents the carry-over into the twenty-first century of this unresolved "disencounter between nation, identity, and democracy", i.e., the coloniality of power:

> Why were the "indios" a problem in the debate on the implementation of the modern nation-state in these new republics? [...] the "indios" were not simply serfs, as the "Blacks" were slaves. They were, first of all, "inferior races" [...] This, exactly, was the indigenous question: it was not sufficient to remove the weight of non-wage forms of labour such as serfdom from the "indios" in order to make them equal to the others, as had been possible in Europe during the liberal revolutions [...] Who would then be working for the masters? (Quijano 2006: 196, my translation)[26]

Within Occidentalist perspectives, the question of democratisation, although also present in the normative canon of modernisation theory, only took centre-stage toward the end of the twentieth century, as the ideology of developmentalism was slowly translated into the language of *globalisation* – a very similar, yet distinct global design. Especially after the demise of Communism in Eastern Europe and the end of the Cold War, the Occidentalist discourse moved in the direction of the withering away of the state as an agent of development on the one hand and toward a strengthening of the self-regulating global market on the other. Politically, this ideological move was accompanied by the advance of neoliberalism and a corresponding trend toward privatisation and anti-statism. The resulting shift from nationally organised to globally managed economic growth (McMichael 2005) further enhanced the call for the – voluntary or coerced – democratisation of the non-Western world that was supposed to make the liberalisation of its market

---

26   To be sure, the homogenisation of European populations with the explicit or implicit end of national state-formation had also entailed various forms of forced ethnic change and waves of ethnic cleansing, especially during the emergence of Eastern European nation-states in the nineteenth and twentieth centuries, as Göran Therborn's (1995) detailed analysis has shown. Yet such violent forms of homogenisation had mainly been either a result of war – such as the extermination of the Jews throughout the continent during World War II, or the consequence of voluntary or coerced migration in the aftermath of war – such as the expulsion of millions of ethnic Germans from post-war Poland. In turn, the relative ethnic integration that the whole of Europe had eventually achieved by the mid-twentieth century did conform to the continent's tradition of Enlightenment and liberal revolutions (Therborn 1995: 43ff.). In the case of Europe, unlike in Latin America, the global design of developmentalism therefore built on the experience and social reality of local history.

economies possible. This time, the policy applied both to the Third World and to what used to be the Second: On the one hand, within the so-called Third World, several instances of successful economic growth, most particularly the "Asian Tigers" in Southeast Asia, served as proof of the model's viability; on the other, Eastern Europe and the Caucasus became the object of comprehensive programs of "transformation research" meant to account for the successful transition from socialist government and central planning to liberal democracies and market economies. Eastern European transformation research thus took over part of the ideological tool-kit that modernisation theory had applied to the entire ex-colonial world, and particularly to Latin America in mid-twentieth century. At the same time, the language of globalisation, whether coined in terms of the liberalisation of market economies, democratisation, or transition from the Second to the First World, revealed the same teleological understanding of world history on which nineteenth-century evolutionary models were premised, while adhering to a similar progressivist logic as the one inherent in the successive Western models of "development" represented by Christianisation, the civilising mission or modernisation. In the latest Occidentalist map, Western democracies and their liberalised market economies, representing the condition of possibility for the further advance of neoliberal globalisation, are pitted against non-Western and/or non-democratic forms of government and local economies, in turn conceived of as historical anachronisms.[27]

On the other hand, discourses of neoliberal globalisation operated a significant change in conventional Occidentalist strategies of constructing binary oppositions between the West and its Other(s). The borders between the First, Second, and Third Worlds were gradually blurred, all the more so in Europe thanks to the process of full integration of the former state socialist world into the world-capitalist one. State controls of national economies were increasingly weakened to the benefit of transnational economic activities and financial flows. Together, such developments have invalidated both the geopolitical polarities characterising earlier global designs and the affirmation of radical difference between the West and the Rest stemming from them. According to Fernando Coronil, this categorial

---

27   As Göran Therborn (2003: 296) rightly pointed out, historical anachronisms have tended to be the rule in the very midst of the Western world to which the definition of linear processes of modernisation and development is supposed to apply. Yet, if the preservation of a landed aristocracy and gentry, as well as of monarchy as a form of government are not considered impediments to British modernity, and the maintenance of slavery was no contradiction of the objectives of the American Revolution, the reverse seems to apply in the case of the non-Western world to the extent that it does not adhere to the standard definition in political, economic, as well as social terms. That liberal democratic rule, market economies based on wage-labour, and class divisions only remain minimal requirements for the modernity of peripheral or ex-colonial countries is thus just another proof of the asymmetric power deriving from the Occidentalist perspective from which the respective definition is being coined.

110   *Global Inequalities Beyond Occidentalism*

reshuffling therefore justifies labelling this latest global design "globalcentrism", in order to distinguish it from the Western bias of previous Occidentalist patterns:

> While the gap between rich and poor nations – as well as between the rich and the poor – is widening everywhere, global wealth is concentrating in ever fewer hands, and these few include those of subaltern elites. In this reconfigured global landscape, the "rich" cannot be identified exclusively with metropolitan nations; nor can the "poor" be identified exclusively with the Third and the Second Worlds. The closer worldwide interconnection of ruling sectors and the marginalization of subordinate majorities has undermined the cohesiveness of these geopolitical units. (Coronil 2000: 361)

Mainstream social science has tended to take the apparent dissolution of the West-Rest dichotomy at face value and analyse it either as "the end of history" (Fukuyama 1992), i.e., the end of ideological alternatives to (neo)liberalism and globalisation or, in the case of Europe, as an instance of post-Westernisation, i.e., as a type of convergence pattern that reduces social polarisation and instead promotes cosmopolitan orientations (Delanty 2003; Beck 2004). Conservative approaches have instead emphasised the resurgence of the cultural and religious threat posed by Islam to Europe and by the Latino population to the dominant Anglo-Protestant identity in the US (Huntington 1995, 2004). Thus, essentialised notions of Western civilisation and religious identity are on the one hand reasserted but on the other hand counterposed to an array of ethnicised Others no longer situated outside the West or at its borders, but in its very midst. Consequently, for theorists of modernity/ coloniality, globalcentrism not only represents a continuation of the Occidentalist logic in place since the sixteenth century, but a "particularly pernicious imperialist modality of domination" (Coronil 2000: 369) at that:

> Since the conquest of the Americas, projects of Christianization, colonization, civilization, modernization, and development have shaped the relationship between Europe and its colonies in terms of a sharp opposition between a superior West and its inferior others. In contrast, neoliberal globalization conjures up the image of an undifferentiated process without clearly demarcated geopolitical agents or target populations: it conceals the highly concentrated sources of power from which it emanates and fragments the majorities which it impacts ... The subjection of non-Western peoples [...] , like the subjection of subordinate populations within the West, appears as a market effect, rather than as the consequence of a Western political project. (Coronil 2000: 369)

Indeed, the weakening of collective bonds triggered by processes of denationalisation of industries and services and the large-scale privatisation of the economy disproportionately impacted the non-Western world and its indigenous populations, now faced with increasing labour precariousness, growing social polarisation, and less state protection. On the one hand, the widening economic

Orientalism vs. Occidentalism 111

and social gap between a privileged white and/or Western minority and the great majority of Blacks, indigenous, and non-Western peoples attests to the ongoing relevance of the category of the Third World – the geographical referent of which has however become so dispersed as to justify the plural "Third Worlds" instead. On the other hand, this has resulted in a variety of "diced identities" among the non-Western majority (Escobar 2004: 214). For Latin America, the process has been described as a "crisis of social identities" (Quijano 2006: 208) in the wake of which existing class identities were gradually replaced by ethnic, regional, or informal ones. While this has especially been the case for the large rural populations of Andean and Meso-American countries, where peasants (*Sp.* campesinos) increasingly opted for self-identification as "indigenous people" (*Sp.* indigenas), the declining role of the state as a guarantor of social rights and public services has made processes of re-identification with indigenous communities and dis-identification with the state decisive for social and political claims of indigenous movements throughout the subcontinent, most prominently in Chiapas, Guatemala, Bolivia, and Chile.[28] At the same time, decolonial theorists view the capacity of the best organised Latin American social movements to redefine the national question from below, i.e., from the perspective of black and indigenous communities, and to transform the very logic of political democracy, as the most important challenge to the Occidentalist pattern of domination. In the case of Ecuador's Confederation of Indigenous Nationalities (CONAIE), the explicit counter-neoliberal agenda includes, alongside opposition to free-trade agreements with the US and to involvement in the US-financed Plan Colombia, "the construction of a Plurinational and Pluricultural State and the installation of a Plurinational Democratic Government that acts on behalf of the interests of all the nationalities that make up Ecuador" (cited in Walsh 2010b). This entails the state enforcement of multiple citizenships comprising indigenous nationalities. In the case of Colombia, what Arturo Escobar (1995) has termed "the politics of place"

---

28   In terms of the possibilities of comparing the historical trajectory and present political claims of the various indigenous movements, Quijano's (2006) analysis makes it very clear that neither is the term "indigenous" designating a homogeneous historical identity (for which members of Amerindian groups still use the original designations, such as Aymara, Quechua, Mapuche etc.), nor are the various "indigenous movements" in Latin America interchangeable, as the case of Bolivia's worker-peasant movement easily demonstrates: "There isn't, in fact, an "indigenous movement" unless in a nominal, abstract sense. And it would be misleading to think that the term "indigenous" denominates anything homogeneous, continuous and consistent. Just as the word "indio" served during colonialism as a common identifier of many, diverse and heterogeneous historical identities in order to impose the idea of "race" and as a mechanism for domination and control that would facilitate the division of exploited labour, the word "indigenous", although proof of the rejection of the colonial classification and of the reclaiming of autonomous identity, not only is no liberation from coloniality, but does not indicate a process of homogenization, either" (Quijano 2006: 214f., my translation). For an anthropologically informed analysis of disproving the homogeneity thesis in the case of Bolivia, see Canessa 2007, 2012.

has been illustrated by the political-ecology framework adopted by the social movement of black communities of the Pacific, which has been relating claims to ethnic and cultural identity to claims to territory as a space for the exercise of ethnic identity, to local autonomy, and, at the same time, to their own vision of development, thus asserting rights to cultural and economic, as well as ecological difference (Escobar 2004: 223f.). The resurgence of the idea of development as sustainable and human development in the context of neoliberal globalisation, while appearing to do justice precisely to the issues of equity, democracy, bio-diversity and preservation of natural resources emphasised by the Latin American black and indigenous movements, does not in fact transcend the Occidentalist logic of mid-twentieth-century economic developmentalism (Quijano 2000c: 81). As decolonial scholar Catherine Walsh recently pointed out, the very notion of development is missing from the cosmologies, conceptual categories, and languages of indigenous communities. The alternative philosophy of "buen vivir" (living well), common to both indigenous peoples and descendants of the African diaspora in Latin America[29] and emphasising the communion of humans with nature, the protection of social memory and cultural patrimony, as well as an economic system based on solidarity and the equal distribution of development benefits, has been incorporated into the 2008 Ecuadorian constitution as a result of the struggle of indigenous movements in the past two decades (Walsh 2010a). However, its conceptualisation as a derivative of Western notions of sustainable development, and in particular as a state strategy, reveals the limitations to which the implementation of indigenous perspectives is of necessity subjected in the absence of the thorough transformation of the Occidentalist framework in which structures of cultural, political and not least socioeconomic power are embedded. The explicit goal of Ecuador's national plan for *el buen vivir* to construct a Plurinational and Intercultural State thus translates as the implementation of what Walsh has called "functional interculturality", i.e., an institutional strategy that promotes dialogue, tolerance and inclusion without addressing the root causes of inequality, and instead makes cultural diversity functional to the system (Walsh 2010a: 21). Such a strategy therefore stops short of initiating a "critical interculturality" that presupposes the profound questioning and according transformation of the system.

The distinction between functional and critical interculturality as operated by Walsh allows us to clarify the extent to which the notion of interculturality in the modernity/coloniality approach represents a departure from the postmodern Western policies of diversity and multiculturalism. While the promotion of multiculturalism at the level of state policy and discourse relies on the principle

---

29 A related notion explicitly conceived as an alternative to neoliberalism and linking knowledge, nature, and life-being is the one of *"vivir bien"* (to live well), a political philosophy and ethical maxim that orients the present Bolivian government of Evo Morales and the foundation of his proposal for a real South American Community of Nations, analysed in detail in Walsh (2010b).

of recognition and tolerance of racial, ethnic, religious, or sexual Others, and is thus closer to Walsh's concept of functional interculturality, the notion of critical interculturality introduced here – especially as defined and implemented by indigenous movements in Latin America – involves a questioning of the sociopolitical reality of (neo)colonialism reflected by the existing models of state, democracy, and nation and a transformation of these structures so as to guarantee full participation of all peoples in the exercise of political power (Walsh 2002). The terms consequently stand for widely divergent agendas: multiculturalism, tantamount to the postmodern identity politics of so-called "minority particularisms" in search for inclusion in the dominant system, aims at deconstructing present cultural hierarchies in exchange for a juxtaposition of cultural models that leaves the dominant model unquestioned. Examples are the discussions on the white Anglo-Saxon Protestant culture in the US, the republican model in France, and *Leitkultur* (lead culture) in Germany. By contrast, interculturality is conceived here as an ethical, political and epistemic project with the goal of decolonising forms of social organisation, institutional and government structures, as well as perspectives of knowledge originating in the sociohistorical context of the European modernity and imposed as universal during colonial and neocolonial times. Cautioning about the fact that the state-promoted strategy of multiculturalism masks the permanence of social inequalities while maintaining the sociopolitical structures that triggered and reproduce such inequality, Walter Mignolo argued that

> The State wants to be inclusive in order to maintain the neoliberal ideology and the primacy of the market. In contrast, the project of interculturality in the discourse of the indigenous movements is proposing a transformation. It is not asking for recognition and "inclusion" in a State that reproduces neoliberal ideology and internal colonialism, but rather it is reclaiming the necessity that the State recognize colonial difference (ethical, political, and epistemic). It is asking that it recognize the participation of indigenous peoples, intervention in parity and recognizing the actual difference of power – this is, the colonial difference and the coloniality of power still existent – of indigenous peoples in the transformation of the State, and of course, in education, the economy, and law. (Mignolo 2002: 226)

Meanwhile, both twentieth-century global designs discussed here, developmentalism and globalisation, rely on gendering as a strategy of subalternisation employing metaphors of femininity, submissiveness, passivity, and irrationality in order to characterise tradition, underdevelopment, and despotism, and counterpose them to representations of modernity, development, and democratic regimes. In particular, the stereotype of (female) passivity, a crucial element of eighteenth- and nineteenth-century Orientalism, was revived and revamped during the four "decades of development" that the United Nations proclaimed for the period 1961–2000, in the course of which the so-called Third World was dealt the part of a juvenile recipient of specific development policies aimed at relieving the socioeconomic pathologies of stagnation and underdevelopment. With the shift of emphasis toward "sustainable development" since the last UN development decade, the gendering pattern explicitly translated into control over nature and the local, both of which were to be brought in agreement with the allegedly universal interests of the global market. As seen above, in the face of Western notions of biodiversity and protection of the species, in which state and utilitarian criteria dominate, local knowledge systems and ecological strategies of indigenous populations are either marginalised as unscientific and irrational or, on the contrary, idealised as an example of (Third World) women's harmony with nature. In both cases, however, indigenous perspectives tend to remain unaddressed in the shaping of global environmental policy, as the example of "buen vivir" has shown. Questioning the extent to which the evolutionist outlook central to the self-definition of the modern world is complicit with a model of global economic growth that promotes the exclusion of the great majority of the world's population from the development process and the depletion of the world's natural resources has therefore more than once raised the issue of available alternatives and their respective scope. In the decolonial approach, the solution for transcending the (neo-)developmentalist logic does not lie within the epistemic scope of Occidental capitalist modernity, but would have to encompass the perspectives and modes of living that make up global coloniality, i.e., not provide alternative development, but alternatives to development (Escobar 1995).

Besides being successive, the global designs emanating from Occidentalism have consistently proven cumulative in character. Their coexistence is not only apparent in the eighteenth-century revamping of the global design of Christianisation into a secularised form that would become the civilising mission (Mignolo 2000: 280), but also in the relatively recent resurgence of the conceptual pairs Christian-barbarian, civilised-uncivilised, Occidental rationality-Oriental irrationality in the context of the "war against terrorism". The accompanying revival of the "Islamic threat" in the shape of Islamophobia (Mestiri, Grosfoguel and Soum 2008), the gendering of this threat in the Western moralistic outrage at the social figure of the veiled Muslim woman as the epitome of passivity, traditionalism, and unfreedom (Dietze 2009), alongside the renewed mobilisation of stereotypes against Hispanics in the US by analogy with Islamic terrorists all attest to the pervasiveness of ethnicisation as the othering strategy most closely corresponding to the current phase of Occidentalism. The combined logic of racial, ethnic and gender othering therefore remains pervasive. In this respect, ideological long waves of the modern world-system, although connected to its economic long waves, prove more durable than the latter.

Table 3.1 below summarises in a schematic fashion the characteristics of each global design according to the aforementioned periodisation and distinguishes between (1) the dimensions along which processes of racialisation/ethnicisation were undertaken, (2) the common denominator of processes of racialisation, ethnicisation, and gendering corresponding to each global design in particular,

Orientalism vs. Occidentalism 115

(3) the main gendering metaphor employed in the respective contexts, and (4) the stereotypical characterisation of each period's respective Others that most closely corresponds to the Occidentalist strategy for that period. The rightmost column additionally gives (5) an overview of the binary oppositions first emerged as a result of the different global designs, which, as mentioned above, did not necessarily supersede each other, but at times coexisted or, as in the case of the civilised-barbarian opposition, were revived at various later moments in the Occidentalist imaginary.

Table 3.1   Occidental global designs

Period	Global design	Racial ethnicisation	Gendering	Othering	Binary opposition
16th–17th c.	Christian mission	Spatial	New World is virgin	"people without religion"	Christian vs. barbarian
18th–19th c.	Civilising mission	Temporal	The exotic is feminine	"people without history"	Civilised vs. primitive
20th c.	Development	Spatial/temporal	Tradition is passivity	Underdeveloped people	Developed vs. underdeveloped
21st c.	Global market	Spatial/temporal	The local is irrational	Undemocratic people/rule	Democratic vs. undemocratic

Source: Compiled from: Mignolo 2000; Quijano 2000a; Grosfoguel 2005; Schiwy 2007.

The critique voiced by the decolonial approach at world-systems' analysis is at the same time directed toward Marx's own understanding of social difference, to which world-systems analysis largely remains faithful. By tracing the geoculture of the capitalist world-economy back to the emergence of the first pattern of Occidentalism in the sixteenth century and revealing its racialising logic, the Latin American theorists show that it was not the class differential triggered by the industrial revolution which had established the dominant patterns of inequality and stratification in the modern world-system. Rather, it was the racial differential, preceding the former by two centuries, that had hierarchically structured the system's colonial "underside". For an assessment of global inequalities, they claim, it is therefore not sufficient to analytically locate the process of class polarisation at the level of the entire world-economy instead of nation-states, as Wallerstein does, but also, and fundamentally, to account for the racial categorisation underlying processes of ethnicisation of the labour force since the conquest of the Americas. Briefly, both Marx's and Wallerstein's explanations for capitalist inequality are seen as mainly premised on class – or social difference, and thus as accounting solely for modernity. What is lacking is a comprehensive model incorporating race – or colonial difference – in a complementary model that would adequately describe its historical and present-day counterpart, coloniality:

116 *Global Inequalities Beyond Occidentalism*

> While class refers mainly to economic relations among social groups and is, thus, strictly related to the control of labor in the spheres of the colonial matrix of power, race refers mainly to subjective relations among social groups and is related to the control of knowledge and subjectivity. Thus, liberation and decolonization projects in the Americas today must have the colonial matrix of power, and not the industrial revolution, as a key point of reference. (Mignolo 2007: 487)

The decolonial perspective thus differs from Western orthodox Marxism in that it locates the question of race, not of class, at the root of global capitalism, while at the same time replacing the unqualified postmodern notion of difference by the ones of imperial and colonial difference. The latter are seen as intimately linked with the establishment of power structures on the basis of religious and cultural hierarchies both within Europe and between Europe and Central Asia, as well as of racial hierarchies in Europe's overseas colonies since the fifteenth century. At the same time, the perspective shares one of Marxism's main blind spots, a systematic incorporation of the logic of gendered difference into the explanation of capitalist exploitation. With few exceptions, an understanding of how a racialised gender system alongside systematic racialised gender violence has informed the Occidental global designs of the "colonial/gender system enmeshed in the coloniality of power into the present" (Lugones 2007: 207) is still to be coherently articulated with analyses of (de)coloniality undertaken within this framework.

The decolonial approach ultimately contends that colonial relations have not ended with the juridical and administrative decolonisation taking place at the end of World War II, but are still at work in processes of political intervention, economic exploitation and epistemological patronage exercised by the West on the Rest. In this sense, the process of decolonisation (of economic relations, social structures, political discourse and not least of knowledge) does not only involve deconstruction, but also, and especially, a structural transformation through the construction of a historically informed alternative of civilisation and society (Walsh 2002). Its aim thereby does not consist in a shift of focus from Western universal models onto essentialised particularisms, but in the disclosure and subsequent makeover of the structure of global power relations established in the context of Western European imperial and colonial expansion and its enduring effects at the local, national and international levels.

Chapter 4
The World-Historical Model: Relational Inequalities and Global Processes

A model that also aims to account for the racial and ethnic dimension of inequality structures while empirically maintaining that they are the result of eminently relational processes between and within countries has been developed by Roberto P. Korzeniewicz and Timothy P. Moran (1997, 2005, 2009). Central to their "world-historical perspective" on inequality and stratification is, as in the classical formulation of world-systems analysis, and in equally explicit opposition to modernisation theory, the methodological premise of shifting the unit of analysis from the nation-state to the world-economy as a whole. At the same time, through the emphasis placed on the consequences of European colonisation, expropriation, and enslavement of Native Americans for the inequality patterns prevailing in the Americas and for the region's indigenous populations in particular, their perspective is closer to the modernity/coloniality approach than to classical world-systems analysis. Yet, while Korzeniewicz and Moran's model exploits the tension between the modernisation paradigm and the underdevelopment literature in a manner similar to Quijano and Mignolo, it is less centred on the historical reconstruction of the colonial past than the de-colonial perspective and more on the way in which the institutional arrangements of the recent past, especially the nineteenth century, contributed to different levels of inequality across the world.

Inequality Equilibria: Institutional Innovation and Comparative Advantage

To this end, they focus on the contrast between the development of "institutions of private property" in today's high-income countries on the one hand and that of the so-called "extractive institutions" in low-income, formerly colonised countries on the other. Both modernisation theory and a significant part of the more recent state-centred research on social inequality maintain that economic growth and low levels of inequality are a function of efficient industrial production, economic liberalism, free labour, and democratic structures that promote economic redistribution. High inequality in poor countries that relied for a long time on agriculture and mining under coerced forms of labour (i.e., slavery, but also serfdom or debt peonage) and allowed access to political rights to only a small minority of the population has been offered different causal explanations. In the case of modernisation theory, it has been viewed as a consequence of "traditional structures". In turn, in the case of the institutional literature on inequality and development, it has

118   *Global Inequalities Beyond Occidentalism*

been traced back to the "legacy of colonialism". Common to both approaches is that the inequality patterns of today's wealthy countries, featuring universal franchise, mass education, and a welfare state on the one hand, and poor countries, characterised by limited access to public education, a long history of restricted franchise, and land policies favouring white elites on the other, are presented as having emerged independently of each other (Korzeniewicz and Moran 2009: 42).

In turn, Korzeniewicz and Moran's goal is to account for inequality as a complex set of related interactions between nations over time. As such, they match Quijano's approach to a great extent, yet their model is better fitted to the task. Despite its ambitious scope, Quijano's attempt to disclose the interrelationship between *modernity* and *coloniality* by using the example of the different processes of nation-state formation in the Americas did not translate into revealing the *inequality structures* thus derived as interdependent ones. In particular, by counterposing the European pattern of nation-building through ethnic homogenisation and democratic inclusion to the prevailing Ibero-American one, based on the extermination of the natives and the political exclusion of Afro-descendants and mestizos, Quijano's model insufficiently accounted for the high levels of inequality in countries in which Native Americans and Afro-descendants were demographic minorities, such as Chile, or where serfdom of the indigenous population was of limited scope and duration, as in the United States (Quijano 2000a: 565).[1] His model thus deductively conveyed the notion that the inequality patterns of most Latin American countries could not be analysed in terms of their European counterparts, nor would replicate the latter's trajectory at a later stage of development, as modernisation theory predicted; the concrete mechanisms shaping the long-term interrelation between Western European and Latin American inequality contexts, however, were merely hinted at in his concept of "coloniality of power", rather than made explicit.

In a more inductive manner, Korzeniewicz and Moran in turn depart from the social, political and economic mechanisms characteristic of inequality patterns in order to arrive at the interdependence between their contexts of emergence. On the basis of the Gini coefficients of 96 countries, they show that national inequality patterns can be grouped into two distinct and relatively stable clusters, characterised by high or low levels of inequality, respectively. Not surprisingly, the high inequality cluster (above a Gini of 0.5) contains the prominent examples

---

1   Tellingly, the highly similar argument that the density of the indigenous population in a particular area is a decisive factor in the establishment and maintenance of patterns of racial and ethnic exclusion by a small white colonial elite, and thus in the creation of structural obstructions to free enterprise and market activity, is a frequent element of the state-centred literature on inequality, e.g.: "a dense indigenous population may have produced a poor climate for market investment because legal rights and protections were systematically denied to large sectors of the population. The failure to protect civil and property rights for broad cross-sections of society can stifle entrepreneurial activity and undermine economic development" (Mahoney 2003: 77).

of inequality research, South Africa and Brazil, but also the bulk of Latin America, the Caribbean, and Africa. In turn, Australia, Japan, Canada, the whole of Western Europe and parts of Eastern Europe fall into the low inequality cluster (below a Gini of 0.3). The high-inequality pattern has been characterised by *systematic exclusion* on the basis of ascriptive criteria such as race, ethnicity, and gender in order to limit access to economic, social and political opportunity. By contrast, the low-inequality pattern has involved widespread *relative inclusion* through the extension of property and political rights increasingly derived from achieved (rather than ascribed) characteristics, such as one's education level, and the development of welfare states – which, in turn, further buttressed patterns of democratic inclusion. The authors find that membership in both clusters can be traced back in time to the eighteenth century, which prompts them to coin the term "inequality equilibria" for both cases. At the same time, the origins of the institutional arrangements typical of the low inequality equilibrium (LIE) are less apparent than those characterising the high inequality equilibrium (HIE), which clearly go back to colonial slavery (Korzeniewicz and Moran 2009: 31).

Against the state-centred view of most inequality studies as well as the modernisation paradigm, Korzeniewicz and Moran consequently advance a perspective considering the world-system in the long-term. Unlike other models in which the world-system was the unit of analysis and whose conclusions about patterns of global stratifications were only secondary to their analysis of development or modernity, their approach specifically targets between-country inequalities. This particular shift in the unit of analysis and in the temporal scope of prevailing inequality structures reveals that high-inequality equilibria historically constituted innovations in the world-economy, while low-inequality equilibria represented relative comparative advantages over these as well as over earlier arrangements. Far from the archaic and backward forms of labour and market organisation for which they are usually held, the various forms of coerced labour in general and slavery in particular had instead been highly profitable ones. Their implementation in Latin America and the Caribbean, i.e., the areas with the highest income inequality today, had rapidly turned the region into the world epicentre for the creation and accumulation of wealth from the period following European colonisation until well into the eighteenth century (Korzeniewicz and Moran 2009: 44). During the same time, Europe and the North American colonies – today's low inequality havens – although relying on manufactures and a free-labour system, were marginal, unprofitable and largely dependent on imports for meeting their economic needs. Korzeniewicz and Moran thus make an argument very similar to the one advanced in André Gunder Frank's notion of the development of underdevelopment as part of the process of primitive accumulation of capital. Frank's argument rested on the premise that, the richer a region had been at the time of its colonisation in terms of exploitable resources, the more underdeveloped it was in the twentieth century – as, for instance, Brazil; conversely, the poorer a colony had been upon its foundation, the more developed the area was in the present – e.g., New England (Frank 1972: 19). According to Frank, this dialectic of capitalist development had been contingent upon the emergence of an export economy in the richer colonies and of local manufacturing in the poorer ones, thus occasioning widely different class structures in the respective regions. More recently, Charles Bergquist (1996) had examined this very phenomenon under the heading of "the paradox of American development", which for him hinged explicitly on the systems of labour control employed in each area: While the resource-richest American colonies initially thrived on the exports of primary commodities produced under slave or indentured labour, as did Upper Peru and Bolivia on silver mining until the end of the seventeenth century, Saint-Domingue on sugar and South Carolina on rice until the end of the eighteenth, all are currently among the poorest and/or least industrialised; at the same time, Britain's New England colonies, which started out as the poorest in the Americas, had by the end of the colonial period become the richest and had set the standards against which the industrialisation processes of other regions had subsequently been measured (Bergquist 1996: 15).[2] Relational approaches such as those proposed within dependency and world-systems perspectives reject the culturalist logic behind the conventional explanation, which traces such divergent developments back to the character of British (or French) colonial institutions as against Spanish and Portuguese ones and the different cultural legacies they imprinted on their respective colonies: the Protestant work ethic favouring the emergence of modern capitalism in North America (except Mexico) on the one hand, the Catholic feudal institutions shaping the development of Latin America on the other. In particular, as Bergquist points out, the influence of British culture and institutions, as well as the ethnic composition of the colonisers had been the same in the case of both southern and northern British colonies in the New World; therefore, the reasons for the widely differing developments rather lie in the natural resources, labour supplies, as well as the labour systems developed according to these conditions in each particular location. The organisation of labour around wage-work and production for the domestic market in the New England and the mid-Atlantic British colonies, as opposed to the slave-based economies of the US South and the British Caribbean, geared toward export of raw materials to Europe, had consequently been a matter of strategic location in the existing trade system as well as of natural and human resources, not a matter of cultural values:

> It was not some unique cultural or racial attribute that explains their exceptionalism. It was their fortuitous location on lands lacking precious metals and with a climate unsuited to cultivation of the agricultural commodities Europe wanted. Their inability to produce primary commodities for export to Europe, their relative isolation from the main circuits of trade within the Atlantic system, allowed them to preserve and develop their unique free-labor system. (Bergquist 1996: 24)

---

2   See also Trouillot 1995: 100 for a similar argument and an overview of the relevant literature for the case of Saint-Domingue/Haiti.

The clearest proof of this argument lies in the economic and political evolution of the colonies of the southern mainland – or what would later become the South of the United States. During the colonial period, the "slave South" provided luxury commodities such as sugar, tobacco, and coffee to Europe. After independence, i.e., once industrial capitalism under British hegemony made commercial credit available for primary commodities such as cotton and the Atlantic slave trade was abolished, the South organised ever tighter around enslaved labour, encouraged local reproduction of the slave population and the internal trade in enslaved labour (McMichael 1991; Tomich 2004). Already in the eighteenth century, the industrialised North, much like Europe, had become a quasi-metropolis to the slaveholding South, a role that would be reinforced after the South's defeat in the Civil War and the imposition of the North's political institutions and legislation on the South. Among these political characteristics, the North's relatively egalitarian distribution of land and the extension of suffrage to male proprietors that went with it, were, however, primarily derived from the family and wage-labour system on which the North had specialised,[3] not from a higher regard for democratic values than in the South. In contrast to this internal division of labour between the US North and its South, Bergquist pointed out that the different trajectory of the former British and Spanish American colonies in the post-independence era could best be grasped by remarking that, unlike the United States, Latin America had "no North":

> No Latin American nation had a region where a free labor system in the colonial era had produced a relatively egalitarian, rapidly industrializing society in which liberal political ideas could flourish. Latin American liberalism enlisted a geographically diffuse but growing number of reformers drawn from elite and popular classes alike. (Bergquist 1996: 36)

Moreover, as already signalled in Quijano's treatment of democratisation in Latin America, among the region's promoters of economic liberalism, it had been the owners of large estates who had made up the most powerful classes far into the post-independence period. They had high stakes in Latin America's expanding role as a supplier of agricultural exports to industrialised countries and a vested interest in the maintenance of labour systems favouring the unequal distribution of wealth. Their protection of these interests had therefore stalled both the spread of free labour and industrialisation in the region for a considerable period of time.

---

3   As the racial rhetoric associated with slaveholding regimes across the Americas, and the explicit racial defence of slavery by Southern planters in the ante-bellum period demonstrate (see McMichael 1991), the reverse argument applies to the US South, and, by extension, to all colonies dependent on plantation export agriculture: "These societies failed to develop in the post-independence era in the way their once-poor, predominantly white, northern neighbors did not because they had too many blacks, but because they had too many slaves" (Bergquist 1996: 33).

The highly polarised, undemocratic system based on the exploitation of unfree labour thus created was therefore a response to this particular set of geographic and socioeconomic factors, rather than of any cultural or institutional legacy. The conclusion Bergquist reached pursuing this historical line of argument in turn constitutes the point of departure of Korzeniewicz and Moran's analysis between the *economic* legacy of colonialism and the differences between today's inequality patterns.

Interdependence through Creative Destruction

The historical blend between an industrial region characterised by institutions of private property and a primarily agricultural region organised around extractive institutions such as slavery is seen as largely explaining what Korzeniewicz and Moran call the United States' "hybrid case". Today, the United States combine patterns of inequality characteristic of both high and low inequality. This corresponds to its diverging Southern and Northern labour systems up to the end of the nineteenth century. The country has accordingly been shifting in and out of the low inequality cluster throughout the twentieth century – although it was constantly closer to the low than to the high inequality cluster. On the one hand, the *exclusionary* institutional arrangements of the high inequality pattern had been the result of "the inability of subordinate groups to radically transform the distribution of land and wealth in their favor" (Korzeniewicz and Moran 2009: 26), yet also of their ability to prevent even further polarisation of such distribution by the ruling elites. On the other hand, the *inclusive* institutions of the low inequality pattern had emerged in opposition to both exclusionary labour and property arrangements within the same state (such as slavery in the US South), and in opposition to more inclusive ones, that had historically produced still lower inequality patterns (such as those characteristic of Native American communities in the "open-frontier" areas of the nineteenth-century):

> if one side of the Janus face of the legal system as it developed in the United States in the nineteenth century entailed protection of white family farmers and settlers, in response to demands from below, the other side entailed the massive expropriation of non-whites. The establishment of LIE required the forceful elimination of even lower LIE. (Korzeniewicz and Moran 2009: 41)

Explaining the inequality pattern of the United States, treated as paradoxical by most state-centred inequality research, is relevant beyond the individual country case for several reasons. For one thing, the rise in inequality in the United States as one of the world's leading economic powers has been the reason behind much of the revived interest in inequality research in the past decades. More important, however, is the fact that the dialectical play between inequality equilibria that explains within-country institutional arrangements, including that of the United

States, is, according to Korzeniewicz and Moran, the very mechanism at the core of between-country inequalities, which they characterise as a high-inequality equilibrium in its own right. Hence, world inequality itself is an instance of the stable pattern of high inequality emerged in the areas where coercive labour forms prevailed. In turning their attention to inequality between countries, the authors recast Mintz's argument about the interdependence between Caribbean slaves and European free labourers to apply to the interaction between the particular historical contexts that produced today's high and low inequality clusters. According to them, different institutional paths in the distribution of economic resources are the outcome of processes of conflict and negotiation between social groups with different degrees of bargaining power. In turn, the consequences the resulting institutional arrangements entail have tended to change over time because of the very interaction between their contexts of emergence (2009: 51). Rather than assuming a simple correlation between equity and economic growth, as postulated by modernisation theory, the authors therefore suggest that the relationship between the two has changed over time. From high inequality generating more wealth under innovative extractive institutions such as plantation slavery in the New World, the relationship shifted to low inequality contexts gaining a comparative advantage over the former by means of different institutional or political practices – such as tax or wage-setting policies, extended access to education, or the regulation of international migration. Such a proposition however runs counter to more than just a modernisationist approach to economic development, as it undermines basic tenets of the sociological canon – above all, the sequence of tradition and modernity:

> Rather than simple industrialization, or a universal transition from tradition to modernity, successful economic growth historically has involved meeting a moving target of innovative practices. (Korzeniewicz and Moran 2007: 18)

What Frank had viewed as the characteristically capitalist dialectic of development and underdevelopment and Bergquist had treated as the paradox of American development *tout court*, Korzeniewicz and Moran thus analyse using Schumpeter's notion of creative destruction of innovation practices, which they interpret as a "constant drive toward inequality": The emergence of extractive institutions of high-inequality contexts such as plantation slavery and coerced cash-crop labour are analysed as significant innovations that provided competitive advantages to colonial and settler elites and allowed for an extraordinary accumulation of wealth and power in the area (Korzeniewicz and Moran 2009: 55). In such contexts, it was social hierarchies based on *ascribed characteristics* – chiefly, race – which allowed for the high degree of polarisation of the emerging labour structure along the lines of white supremacy vs. non-white subordination. Conversely, areas such as the New England colonies, in which the native labour force was scarce, but the amount of land available for cultivation abundant, encouraged the spread of private property across the adult male population. The latter areas thus maintained a pattern of relatively low inequality, which, in its turn, gained a comparative advantage over the high-inequality pattern after the onset of large-scale industrialisation. Although the low levels of inequality in such regions gradually came to be perceived as structured around *achieved characteristics* such as one's level of education or professional position, their long-term stability had nevertheless been safeguarded by restricting physical access to these regions on the basis of *ascribed categories*, especially national identity and citizenship, through the control of immigration flows. Following Charles Tilly's distinction between relational and categorical inequality (1998), Korzeniewicz and Moran therefore suggest that the ascription of national identity represents the basis of categorical inequality from a global perspective. Accordingly, both the rise of the welfare state and the increasing constraints on migration in wealthy countries had gone hand in hand with the consolidation of identities constructed around the nation-state and citizenship: "these strategies both universalized and simultaneously excluded on the basis of national identity" (2009: 85).

Contrary to one of the most widely held assumptions of inequality research from sociology's classics to Parsonian functionalism and modernisation theory, the authors thus claim that high and low inequality are not the result of traditional arrangements, in which the distribution of rewards occurs according to ascribed characteristics, and modern arrangements, where it occurs according to achieved traits, respectively, but that both are eminently relational constructions and as such the result of the process of creative destruction characteristic of world capitalism:

> between-country inequality is an outcome of the comparative advantages that some nations gain over others *in their interaction*. The relevant unit of analysis shifts from individual nations to a single process of creative destruction, and inequality between nations becomes an expression of the inextricable links between the "creation" that characterizes some places (or nations) and the "destruction" that prevails in others. (Korzeniewicz and Moran 2009: 74)

By viewing the process of creative destruction as a feature of world capitalism, the authors explicitly subscribe to world-systems analysis' most consequential methodological shift, i.e., the one from the nation-state to the world-economy. Yet by arguing that the unit of analysis is the very *process* of creative destruction (rather than an economic *structure* such as the capitalist world-economy), they move toward the methodological stance advocated in certain strands of transnational migration research, which foreground social processes in general and transnational flows of people in particular as phenomena requiring a relational concept of space beyond the one proposed within the world-systems perspective. The ensuing tension between the methodological premise and its different empirical application in Korzeniewicz and Moran's modified world-systems approach is explored in the next section.

The Unit of Analysis of Relational Processes

The shift of perspective toward a relational concept of space, viewed as capable of accounting for transnational inequality structures, has featured prominently among the solutions for overcoming methodological nationalism that various authors have advanced in recent years. Quite often, the plea for replacing nation-state centred "container concepts" with transnational or cosmopolitan "relational concepts" of space entails the explicit shift in the unit of analysis from individual societies to the world-economy proposed within the world-systems approach (Weiß 2005; Beck 2007; Pries 2008). However, the transnationalisation of social inequality is viewed as a new phenomenon that sets in with twentieth-century globalisation. According to its proponents, the shift from methodological nationalism to methodological cosmopolitanism therefore becomes a necessary adjustment to the qualitative change that globalisation has operated in structures of inequality, but is of no consequence for the assessment of earlier or "classical" inequality contexts – for which the nation-state framework is still considered appropriate.[4] For this snapshot in world history, the conclusions of transnational inequality research match those of Korzeniewicz and Moran to a certain extent. Thus, Weiß finds that class positions on a world scale are structured by the nation-state and its position in centre-periphery hierarchies and that those at the bottom of the inequality scale tend to be tied to disadvantaged locations lacking (welfare) state protection from the effects of the globalised economy (2005: 716). At the same time, she claims that, in a global class structure encompassing *transnational upper classes, the middle layers,* and *lower positions,* the nation-state, especially in its welfare variant, only constitutes a relevant structuring force for intermediate social positions, not, however, for those at the top and at the bottom of world society. Through the overemphasis on the *transnational* (inequality structures as well as social actors), the approach thus downplays the importance of – both core and peripheral – nation-states in assigning citizenship and deciding about the mobility of individuals in accordance with this particular ascribed characteristic. Ulrich Beck instead postulates that it is the combination of nationality and territoriality that *ascribes* an individual's social position on a world scale, given that a nation's rank and political status in the centre-periphery hierarchy decisively influence any status the individual may *achieve* within a national-territorial frame (2007: 689). However, for him, too, the social grammar of transnational forms of social inequality is a specifically "post-class" – and thus qualitatively and inherently new – development[5]

---

4 Thus, when speaking of the "anachronistic gaze of a territorially defined nation-state" (2007: 687), Ulrich Beck appears to assume that there used to be a time at which the national gaze *was* appropriate: It is only with increased transnational mobility that "the ability to cross borders has become an essential resource of social inequality in a globalized world" (2007: 690).

5 Beck's emphasis on newness leaves no room for interpretation: "We are witnesses to the emergence of a new kind of capitalism, a new kind of internationality, new kinds of social inequalities, new kinds of nature, new kinds of subjectivity, new kinds of

126 *Global Inequalities Beyond Occidentalism*

that defies the political and legal grammar of national boundaries as the premise of conventional social inequality research and reveals its ideological character.

> The pre-determined irrelevance of large global inequalities allows rich and powerful nation-states to offload the risks of their decisions onto poor states [...], a practice which is ultimately stabilized by the methodological nationalism of sociology which confirms and reinforces the national perspective of activities [...] What elsewhere would be considered problematic in terms of scholarship is here unreflectedly elevated to the level of a methodological principle: self research. (Beck 2007: 694)

Likewise, for Göran Therborn, the notion that achievement produces legitimate rewards represents first and foremost an ideologically charged element of liberal, individualist discourse, which leaves out the simultaneous production of unjust inequality: "it is blind to everything but the achieving actor, telling us nothing about her relations to others, not about the context of opportunities and rewards" (2006: 10). Instead of mutually exclusive national or regional contexts of ascription and achievement of rewards, Therborn therefore frames the interplay between national and international institutional arrangements as co-variation of internal equality and external inequality (2006: 15), in which the regulation of flows of people, but also flows of capital, trade, and information, plays a central role. While closer to the historical perspective advanced within world-systems approaches to inequality than both Weiß and Beck, his is more a desideratum for future research than an empirical result.

Korzeniewicz and Moran carry through on at least part of the desideratum of prominent research on transnational inequality by zooming in on the co-variation between the institutional arrangements that accounted for the low inequality of today's wealthy countries and those responsible for the emergence or increase of high inequality in today's poorer areas as instances of creative destruction. Once the analytical frame shifts from the nation-state to the world-economy, the apparent pattern of *relative inclusion* of the population through redistributive state policies, democratic participation, and widespread access to education in low inequality contexts is revealed to entail the *selective exclusion* from the same rights of large sectors of the population located *outside* national borders, (Korzeniewicz and Moran 2009: 78). The maintenance of national low inequality patterns of relative inclusion consequently requires the enforcement of selective exclusion on the state border, and thus the (re-)production of high inequality patterns between nations. Yet, while state borders are ages-old, the authors argue that it is the borders of *nation*-states that have primarily operated as instances of ascriptive exclusion since the nineteenth century, and that the nation-state itself has been the main

---

everyday co-existence with the excluded, indeed even a new kind of state organization, and it is precisely this kind of epochal transformation of meaning, which sociologists must understand, research and explain" (Beck 2007: 700).

The World-Historical Model 127

criterion for social stratification on a global scale ever since. To this end, they focus on late nineteenth-century mass migration across national borders, which led to significant convergence of wage rates between core and semiperipheral countries – mainly in Europe and the so-called settler colonies of North America, Australia and New Zealand, but which also tended to raise the competition for resources and employment opportunities within receiving countries, often located in the New World. The result was twofold: On the one hand, an increase in inequality in some national contexts, in which the large inflow of unskilled labour caused rising wage differentials relative to skilled labour; on the other hand, a decrease of inequality in the sending countries, where the income differential between skilled and unskilled workers declined and overall wages rose. Since the constitution of formal labour markets tended to exclude the participation of women, the overwhelming majority of the population accounting for the mass labour migration of the nineteenth and early twentieth century was male (Korzeniewicz et al. 2003: 24). The issue of gender inequality consequently remains mute for the rest of the analysis.

Methodologically, Korzeniewicz and Moran are thus quite close to recent transnational migration research, which advocates a mix of international comparison of individual nation-states, world-systems analysis, and transnational perspective in order to adequately account for twentieth-century world inequalities, and accordingly differentiates between the units of analysis, the units of reference and the units of observation of each (Pries 2008: 49). In this understanding, only transnational research can account for relational space, because its unit of reference is not the world-economy, but transnational social spaces. Empirically, however, Korzeniewicz and Moran's work is rather an applied world-systems perspective on large-scale, long-term social change, in which transnational inequalities are not (not even primarily) a twentieth-century phenomenon. Instead, transregional, transcontinental, and transnational inequalities represent the very premise upon which the functioning of the capitalist world-economy has been based since the sixteenth century, and which took a decisive turn in the nineteenth.

In the case of Europe, Göran Therborn's account of how the massive emigration toward the New World from 1500 until World War II eased both the pressures on income distribution and the social conflict *within* the continent empirically corroborates Korzeniewicz and Moran's thesis, while equally highlighting the nineteenth century as a period of large-scale migration from Europe to its overseas colonies. Thus, according to Therborn, migration to the New World provided a poverty outlet to some 50 million Europeans or 12 per cent of the continent's population between 1850 and 1930 (1995: 40). While almost all European states during this period were primarily sending countries, some experienced out-migration flows as high as 50 per cent of the national population – in the case of the British Isles – or one-third of it – in the case of Italy. At the time, this caused debates as to the rights of states to restrict *emigration.*[6] At the same time, outbound

---

6   In their overview of European history, Ostergren and Rice note that government opposition to emigration was a widespread phenomenon throughout Europe in the early

migration reinforced the inner-European ethnic homogeneity that successive waves of ethnic levelling occurring throughout Europe until mid-twentieth century had succeeded to create (Therborn 1995: 39ff.). Together, large-scale emigration and the high level of ethnic homogeneity attained by the 1950s had ensured that processes of collective identification as well as collective organisation within the continent occurred in terms of class rather than ethnic or racial allegiance. Labour unrest, the rise of scientific racism by the end of World War I, and social and economic protectionist measures in the wake of the Great Depression gradually made restrictions on *immigration* across countries of the core necessary, while strengthening notions of citizenship as a basis for entitlement to social and political rights (Korzeniewicz and Moran 2009: 84). The 1960s finally saw the decisive reversal of the European trend to outbound migration, such that, by 1990, Ireland was the only emigrant country in Western Europe (Therborn 1995: 41). All other Western European states became instead recipients of large migrant populations: first, from the recently decolonised Africa and from ever more dictatorial states in Latin America; subsequently, several waves of unskilled labour migrants contracted by government policies of post-war economic reconstruction from adjacent or formerly colonised countries; and, after 1990, hundreds of thousands of Eastern European war refugees. As a result, the ethnic and racial conflicts that accompanied the rise in immigration came to the fore as a largely extra-European problem that increasingly posed a threat to Western Europe in the form of ex-colonial subjects, guest workers (turned permanent), and incessant flows of labour migrants. As such, they appeared to be – and were often discussed as – forms of (ethnic and/or racial) stratification foreign to the *class* structure otherwise characterising Western Europe.

For the United States, Korzeniewicz and Moran (2008: 10) show a parallel first trend toward declining income inequality as restrictions on immigration increased in the beginning of the twentieth century. In turn, the 1965 reform of the US immigration policy, itself tailored to the active recruitment of labour migrants from Latin America and the Caribbean in response to the rising demand for unskilled labour throughout the world-economy, resulted in a sharp rise in income inequality. As in the case of Europe, the increase in inequality seemed to be a foreign-induced phenomenon directly linked to the inflow of (mostly uneducated) immigrants, thus prompting anti-immigrant sentiment and policies in response.

Against this background, the *ascribed characteristics* of nationhood and citizenship are considered to be as important for global stratification as class, usually considered a matter of *achievement*. Thus, Korzeniewicz and Moran argue that, while *class membership* has regulated the differential access to resources

---

nineteenth century: "In mercantilist economic theory a country's population was one of its chief resources and was to be preserved at all cost. Gradually, as free-trade and laissez-faire policies became more widely accepted, state governments relaxed restrictions on emigration" (Ostergren and Rice 2004: 88). See also Dowty 1987, quoted in Korzeniewicz and Moran 2009: 84.

The issue of citizenship had become part and parcel of the Occidentalist discourse of the civilising mission in the wake of the French Revolution. When viewed through a world-systemic lens, it is revealed to have been relevant not only for the relative social and political inclusion of the populations of Western European nation-states, but just as much for the selective exclusion of the colonised and/or non-European populations from the same social and political rights throughout recent history. On the one hand, the gradual extension of citizenship rights from propertied white males to all white males and to white women accounted for the development of the low inequality equilibrium within France as of the eighteenth century. On the other hand, the categorical exclusion of Saint-Domingue's black and mulatto population from French citizenship, irrespective of their property status, ensured the maintenance of a high inequality equilibrium between France and Saint-Domingue/Haiti. As has been documented for the postcolonial migration flows between several Western European countries and their former colonies, as well as for the US and its protectorates, the possession of the citizenship of the former metropole remains to this day a crucial factor deciding the timing and the destination of ex-colonial subjects' emigration as well as the strive for independence in the remaining colonial possessions. Thus, fear of losing Dutch citizenship has led to a dramatic increase in Surinamese emigration to the Netherlands in the years preceding Surinam's independence from the "motherland" (1974/75) and is the main reason behind the lack of political pressure for independence in the Dutch Antilles and Aruba today (van Amersfoort and van Niekerk 2006). Likewise, the extension of United States citizenship rights to the populations of all Caribbean colonies after World War II triggered a massive transfer of labour migrants from the Caribbean to the US. Migrants from non-independent territories such as Puerto Rico and the US Virgin Islands could thus enjoy both the welfare and the social rights that went with US citizenship, which constituted a strong incentive for migration across the lower social strata in their home countries. In turn, only the more educated, middle sectors of the working class from formally independent Caribbean states like

at the level of national populations, citizenship – i.e., *nation-state membership* – has restricted or undercut both the mobility and the access to resources of the poorest segments of the world population for much of the twentieth century. As a consequence,

> Inequality must be understood as it unfolds within world-historical institutions […] From a world-systems perspective, the same institutional mechanisms through which inequality historically has been reduced *within* nations often have accentuated the selective exclusion of populations from poorer countries, thereby enhancing inequality *between* nations. Shifting the unit of analysis to the world-system thus reveals that ascriptive criteria remain the fundamental basis of stratification and inequality and that national identity has been the most salient of these criteria. (2009: 88)

130   *Global Inequalities Beyond Occidentalism*

Jamaica, Barbados, and St. Vincent, who therefore did not possess metropolitan citizenship, chose to migrate to the US (Cervantes-Rodríguez et al. 2009).

The claim advanced within the world-historical perspective on inequality therefore is that, since the emergence of Western European nation-states in the nineteenth century, national identity, institutionalised as citizenship, has been the main mechanism ensuring the maintenance of the high inequality equilibrium between the core and the periphery. As such, it successfully replaced older criteria for global stratification such as the religious idea of divine rights and the racial principle of white supremacy to the extent that, in analogy to them, it has been naturalised – i.e., it has come to be seen as a natural instead of a socially constructed form of identity and category of social differentiation (Korzeniewicz and Moran 2009: 100).

Global Stratification by Citizenship

In sharp contrast to transnational inequality research, which has sought to devise theoretical criteria for and find empirical proof of processes of global or transnational class formation (Sklair 2001; Weiß 2005), Korzeniewicz and Moran therefore argue that national citizenship remains the main determinant of a person's position within the world inequality structure. Accordingly, global stratification is not the sum total of world elites, world middle classes, and the world poor (or of similar three-tiered models, such as the transnational upper class, the middle layer and the lower position discussed in Weiß 2005), but results instead from the social positions allocated by national identity in a global country hierarchy.[7]

Using a sample of 85 states, they combine country income deciles (as an indicator of within-country inequality) with estimates of per capita gross national income (as an indicator of between-country inequality), eventually ranking the distribution of income for 850 country deciles into 10 global income deciles. The rearrangement reveals that the two wealthiest global income deciles – those with an average per capita income of USD 7,898 or higher – encompass the entire population of Western European countries, the United States, Canada, and Australia. The whole of Norway and Luxembourg, and all but the bottom three deciles of the population of the United States and Canada are even contained within the top global decile, the one with an average of USD 28,570 or higher.

---

7   The authors' argument against the additive model dominating the analysis of social inequality throughout the twentieth century is not merely methodological, but theoretical as well. According to them, adding up the "elites", "middle classes" and "working classes" of different countries in search of a global stratification pattern entails the claim that the social formations thus identified occupy "the same objective position in terms of interest […]; from the point of view of the processes emphasized in this book, such a perspective was in fact a fundamental aspect of the very institutional creation of national states and interests organized around such 'social classes'" (2009: 99).

By contrast, between 70 per cent and 80 per cent of the population of Gambia, Ethiopia, Zambia, and Zimbabwe are located within the bottom global decile, having an average of USD 266 or lower (Korzeniewicz and Moran 2009: 92). Despite the limitations inherent in the use of GNI as a "proxy" for average income, as well as in the use of the notion of an "average" income as such, that the authors themselves address, the exercise convincingly demonstrates that both the middle classes and the working classes of rich countries are located in the wealthiest global deciles, mostly above the income level of the well-to-do "national elites" of poor countries. Thus, the average income of the poorest decile in Norway is still higher than that of the wealthiest decile in Russia, Hungary, Brazil, or Malaysia. Even within Europe, national distributions of income and the class categories usually corresponding to them can be as far apart as to have the poorest decile of Luxembourg (i.e., Luxembourg's lower working class) rank on average just above the richest decile of Croatia (i.e., Croatia's upper class), despite the fact that both countries are featured within the top income decile at the world level.

The data set thus empirically backs the authors' thesis that national citizenship represents the single most important variable for predicting a person's position within global stratification today. At the same time, it invites the ensuing view that international migration, which entails gaining access to at least the average income of the poorer country deciles of a much richer nation-state, becomes the "single most immediate and effective means of global social mobility for populations in most countries of the world" (2009: 107). Thus, migration not only represents a strategy of upward mobility for populations of ex-colonial countries possessing metropolitan citizenship, but also a means of eluding the ascribed position derived from the national citizenship of a poor state for populations able and willing to risk illegal, undocumented or non-citizen status in a rich state. Using the inequality data for six countries interlinked through considerable migration flows, the authors are able to show how anyone in the poorest seven to eight deciles of Bolivia or Guatemala can move up several global income deciles by migrating to Argentina or Mexico, respectively, and gaining access to the average income of the second-poorest decile there. Even more strikingly, anyone but people in the wealthiest decile in both Argentina and Mexico is able to skip several global income deciles by entering Spain or the United States' second-poorest decile through migration (Korzeniewicz and Moran 2009: 108f.). In all these cases, the upward mobility of migrant populations is considerably higher than either the within-country educational attainment or the economic growth of one's country of origin would have allowed during a lifetime (judging by the most successful examples of economic growth, such as South Korea in the 1980s or China today).

More recently, the finding has been reproduced using global data sets on urban wages across the world: Drawing on wage data collected by the Union Bank of Switzerland for the past 40 years in order to provide its clients with accurate international price and wage comparisons, Korzeniewicz and Albrecht (2013) reconstructed average wages, benefits, working hours and vacation days for over a dozen occupational categories in more than 30 cities worldwide. Occupations ranged from male construction labourers to unskilled female factory workers, to bus drivers and primary school teachers, to managers and engineers. Surveyed cities were located in Latin America, Africa, Asia, the Middle East, as well as the United States, Western Europe, Canada, Japan, and Australia. The authors found that, from 1982 to 2009, the average hourly wage in New York based on the surveyed occupations was more than 10 times higher than in Mumbai. The gap between the two cities was so large that it dwarfed opportunities for mobility within the whole of India. In other words, the rise in income that a worker in Mumbai could derive either from an improvement of her level of education or from India's economic growth are dwarfed in comparison to the upward mobility she can accomplish by migrating to New York City (Korzeniewicz and Albrecht 2013). Large disparities were consistent across cities and occupations, such that, in 1982, engineers in Mumbai, Buenos Aires and Madrid were found to have lower wages than even building labourers in New York. As the authors note, the focus on global patterns of wage inequality provides striking insights into long-term patterns of social stratification that once again confirm the continued importance of the ascribed characteristic of nation-state membership. Tellingly, globally and longitudinally consistent data to this effect is mostly available only from non-state actors, as in the case of the globally operating Union Bank of Switzerland, and as such only randomly accessible to social scientists.

However, as Korzeniewicz and Moran claim, the systematic naturalisation of categorical inequality through which the idea of national citizenship was constructed upholds nationally bounded measures, such as educational attainment and economic growth, as appropriate strategies for upward mobility. The patterns that had structured global inequality according to religious, ethnic or racial criteria in previous centuries are thus further reproduced:

> Categorical inequality and ascription are perhaps more fundamental than ever to the workings of global inequality: nevertheless (but this is not coincidental), such inequality coexists with a system of beliefs that asserts the primacy of individual achievement and opportunity, as pursued within nations, as the engine of everything. (Korzeniewicz and Moran 2009: 100)

In keeping with this analysis, authors of the modernity/coloniality group use the historicised notion of colonial and imperial differences in order to view global migration as a strategy of social mobility. To them, the construction of citizenship represents a late step in the Occidentalist production of otherness from barbarians to primitives and the underdeveloped: The much hailed principle of global citizenship, Walter Mignolo argued, only grants unlimited access across borders to the world political and economic elite, and thus to a tiny percentage of the world population. In turn, the citizenship rights of the majority of the world population more closely resemble the status accruing from black citizenship in the US South before the civil rights movement – i.e., restrictions to mobility and severely curtailed rights – than those of the global elite. Both the various types of frontiers and citizen mobility are thus closely related to the world-economic structures that the colonial and imperial differences contributed to creating and maintaining:

> What is important [...] is the directionality of migrations for which the very idea of citizenship is today at stake. It is obvious that there are more Nigerians, Bolivians, Indians, Ukrainians, or Caribbeans who want to migrate to Europe or the US than people in the US desiring to migrate to any of those places. We do not know of any stories of Anglo Americans dying in the Arizona desert when marching to cross the Mexican border. [...] You are not stopped at the gates (of frontiers or embassies) because you are poor, but because of your religion, your language, your nationality, your skin: whatever is taken as indicator of the colonial and imperial differences. (Mignolo 2006c: 316f.)

Thus, the reproduction of colonial and imperial racial hierarchies in countries of immigration today leads Mignolo to declare global citizenship a myth. The logic behind the processes by which racial hierarchies are re-created in postcolonial contexts becomes especially clear in the case of the racialisation of those Caribbean migrants, who, despite enjoying legal status as metropolitan citizens in France, Spain, the United States, the Netherlands, and the United Kingdom, experience "second-class citizenship" (Cervantes-Rodríguez et al. 2009: 7) upon arrival in the metropole, where they become the main targets of racial discrimination, social exclusion and criminalisation on the part of the dominant (white) population (see also Hine, Keaton, and Small 2009).

According to the colonial and/or imperial history that links the sending and the receiving countries, Grosfoguel (2003) consequently identifies three different types of migrant populations: *immigrants*, incorporated or perceived as part of the 'white majority' by the host population and able to experience upward social mobility in the first or second generation; *colonial immigrants*, whose countries of origin have not been colonised by the country to which they migrated, but who nevertheless are racially stereotyped by analogy with the receiving country's colonial subjects, like Dominicans and Haitians in the United States, Moroccans in the Netherlands, or Kurds in France; and, finally, *colonial/racial subjects of empire,* who have a long, direct colonial history with the host country, where racist discourses as well as the prevalent racial/ethnic hierarchy are frequently constructed in opposition to these (post)colonial populations. This is the case of Puerto Ricans, African Americans and Chicanos/as in the United States, Dutch Antilleans and Surinamese in the Netherlands, Algerians, Antilleans and Senegalese in France, Congolese in Belgium or West Indians and South Asians in the United Kingdom (see also Blakely 2009). The distinction is helpful in highlighting how the non-Western, often non-European and non-White origin of both colonial immigrants and colonial/racial subjects of empire plays a central part in the naturalisation of categorical inequality as well as in the regulation of social mobility available through transnational migration, and how both are linked to Occidentalism as the geopolitical imaginary of the modern/colonial world-system.

134 *Global Inequalities Beyond Occidentalism*

Against this background, Korzeniewicz and Moran's tentative notion of a "system of beliefs" as the framework within which the categorical inequality by citizenship is naturalised dovetails well with the modernity/coloniality group's account of Occidentalism as the naturalisation of social inequality at a global scale. It also additionally backs it up with empirical material. At the same time, despite obvious affinities to Coronil's and Mignolo's critique of Occidentalism, Korzeniewicz and Moran's self-designated "world-historical perspective" on social mobility and stratification leaves the very question of perspective unaddressed, i.e., the mechanism of knowledge production responsible for the "system of beliefs" they diagnose as coexisting with categorical inequality up to this day. While explicitly conceiving of patterns of inequality production as processes of selective exclusion, relative inclusion, and naturalisation, their approach fails to account for the agency of such processes: In establishing that categorical inequality is justified today by citizenship and was justified yesterday by white supremacy, the question of the logic of – as well as of the action behind – such legitimisation remains unanswered. This is consistent with their disavowal of a Marxist allegiance. Korzeniewicz and Moran instead formulate a double disclaimer against Marxist accounts of exploitation as adequate explanations for world inequality structures:[8] On the theoretical level, the authors argue that the lack of adequate data for assessing the centrality of transfers of economic surplus for the processes of innovation and exclusion that they describe as "creative destruction" makes exploitative relations between poor and wealthy regions an illegitimate interpretation (until further research). On the methodological plane, they consider Marxism's focus on the nation-state as the key site of struggle between bourgeoisies and working classes to be part of the very institutional arrangements underlying world inequality and, as such, an unsustainable stance that has additionally gained currency beyond Marxist analyses:

> In both its social-scientific and more popular versions, the prevalent mode of understanding the forces that shape inequality and stratification (and hence, the main way to delineate the relevant boundaries of a unit of analysis) is itself part and parcel of the process by which citizenship and nationhood were constructed and are constantly reconstituted as a justifiable basis for categorical differentiation. To question such a mode of understanding requires challenging the natural categories through which high levels of global inequality are legitimated. (Korzeniewicz and Moran 2009: 91)

Paradoxically, the result of trying so hard to avoid making exploitation a central part of the argument is that the authors end up begging the question altogether.

---

8 "Although the Marxist perspective on inequality and stratification certainly influenced the interpretations we advance in this book, we have chosen not to make arguments about exploitation a central component of our framework" (Korzeniewicz and Moran 2009: 58).

In their account of global stratification, capitalism itself is present only as a silent presupposition, which, aside from occasional references to works by Adam Smith, Karl Marx, and Joseph Schumpeter, appears in the text only as "the world-economy". Although this is a legitimate theoretical choice, it becomes clear that Korzeniewicz and Moran do not neglect agency to favour structure, but that the structure itself is left insufficiently explored (or unnamed), making global stratification a matter of historically constructed and interdependent institutional arrangements. As such, their explanation ultimately eschews the macro-micro debate altogether by consciously focusing solely on the mesostructural level.

This brings us back to the question of perspective. The world-historical approach certainly offers a solid methodological and empirical basis for explaining the enduring prominence of class and status as the primary dimensions for the analysis of social inequality in terms of an overgeneralisation from the Western European experience. Based on the evidence the authors supply for substantiating the need to shift the unit of analysis from the nation-state to the world-economy, one could argue that the methodological nationalism of class and status-centred approaches to social inequality stemmed from two interrelated tendencies of Eurocentric sociological production which made such overgeneralisation possible: First, the historical indebtedness of core categories of the sociology of social inequality, especially class, to the socioeconomic context of Western European industrial society and to the rise of the nation-state, rendered class conflict, proletarianisation, and social mobility within industrial nations more visible than colonialism, the slave trade, and European emigration into the New World. Second, this differential visibility made for the disproportionate representation of the former processes in mainstream sociological theory as opposed to the latter. Disregarding the massive dislocation of people triggered by the European expansion into the Americas since the sixteenth century, as well as the impact which subsequent migration processes have had on the ethnic homogenisation of core areas on the one hand and on processes of racialisation and ethnicisation in peripheral and semiperipheral ones on the other were essential in reproducing a Eurocentric/Occidentalist perspective. The establishment and maintaining of a sociology of migration devoid of colonisers as well as of colonial subjects and a sociology of inequality and stratification devoid of race and ethnicity until well into the twentieth century were the consequence (Boatcă 2010). The fact that Korzeniewicz and Moran do not foreground the epistemic claim inherent in their criticism, but instead stick to the theoretical and methodological implications derived from their empirical results, leaves their critique of Occidentalism as a "system of beliefs" undertheorised and their analysis of gender implicit.[9] Yet both

---

9 In an earlier piece co-authored with Angela Stach (Korzeniewicz et al. 2003), Korzeniewicz and Moran dealt with gender inequality as an additional, third dimension alongside between-country and within-country inequality. Although the gender issue receives equal treatment in the text, and does not feature as a derivative, second-tier inequality dimension as in most standard literature on social inequality, there is

136   *Global Inequalities Beyond Occidentalism*

a historicised notion of Occidentalism and of the gendering logic it entailed for global inequality patterns are present in their conclusions, alongside a questioning of the modern vs. traditional dichotomy underlying Eurocentric perspectives:

> The continued importance of nationality in organizing global stratification along ascriptive criteria raises another question: to what extent is our "modern" world substantially different from our "traditional" past? In our traditional past, elites often justified existing inequality as a consequence of the superiority of some races over others, or of men over women, and so forth, and "inferior" peoples were deemed to be in need of guidance and supervision to ensure their own welfare [...] But the well-off of our times continue to justify prevalent forms of inequality as an inevitable consequence of a rather natural order, now revolving around national citizenship, arguing that any relative advantages are purely the result of individual effort, and that inequalities, now between countries, are a consequence of the failure of poor peoples to advance their own interest. (Korzeniewicz and Moran 2009: 120)

Despite emphasising different analytical levels as well as distinct dimensions of global inequalities, the feminist subsistence theory, the modernity/coloniality approach, and the world-historical perspective therefore converge in making their respective critique of conventional development thought the basis of a reconceptualisation of capitalism as a world structure with important methodological implications for the reconceptualisation of inequality as a global phenomenon. That all three approaches should, within their respective focus, manage to encompass global economic disparities as well as racial, ethnic, and/ or gender inequalities without reducing one to the other or operating further hierarchisation between inequality dimensions currently places them among the most promising structure-analytical frameworks for an explanation of global inequalities. To date, these distinct analytical proposals however lead separate theoretical lives with little to no dialogue to point to an integrative approach capable of fitting the different emphases into a coherent whole.[10] The persistent divorce of global approaches to gender inequality from the rest of global inequality

---

no discussion of a logic connecting it to the rise of global inequality as in the feminist subsistence approach or feminist world-systems analysis. The opposite is in fact the case, as the authors conclude that market-centred growth since the 1970s has caused between-country inequality to increase rapidly, but has in turn led to a decrease of inequality between men and women by enhancing female labour force participation and access to education. If anything, it is rather within-country inequality that the authors see as negatively correlated with gender inequality (2003: 30).

    10   The all the more notable exception to this rule is Marcel van der Linden's recent excavation of the potential inherent in the feminist subsistence perspective for a history of world labour and of the possible merits of connecting this approach to world-systems analysis (van der Linden 2008).

research is in this context particularly striking, as it reproduces the division of labour between feminist theory and social structural analysis characteristic of twentieth-century sociology. As unsatisfactory as this may sound, bridging the divides between these approaches and uncovering their own blind spots remains a future task for which the above analysis has provided only a few out of the possible avenues.

PART II
Weber and Historical-Comparative Models

Chapter 5
The West vs. the Rest:
Modernity as Uniqueness in Max Weber

If neo-Marxism had featured prominently in both politics and theory in the 1960s and the 1970s, the last decades of the twentieth century have in turn witnessed a "Neo-Weberian Revolution" (Sanderson 1988). Geared primarily against what had been identified as the economic reductionism of Marxian and Marxist approaches alike, neo-Weberianism emphasised instead the role of the state and geopolitics in the rise and functioning of modern capitalism, as well as the multicausality, rather than just the economic logic, behind processes of social change more generally.

Much like the Marxist revival, which had revealed there to be "no true Marx" (Katz 1990, Wallerstein 1991), neo-Weberians claimed that there was "more than one Weber" (Collins 1986b). Talcott Parsons' rendition of Weber's work as an idealist alternative to Marxian materialism, and of Weber as primarily a theorist of social action, had reverberated throughout American sociology in the 1940s and 1950s, had decidedly influenced the resurgence of interest in Weber in Germany during the 1960s, and had gone into the construction of the sociological canon in many sociologies around the world (Sanderson 2001, Connell 2007). As of the 1970s, a growing number of authors however protested the artificial opposition between Marx and Weber thus created (Bendix 1974; Parkin 1979; Collins 1986b). They advanced a new interpretation of Weber as a conflict theorist who shared a good deal of common ground with Marx, and made Parsons' inaccurate translation of key Weberian concepts like *Herrschaft* as "leadership" or "legitimacy" – rather than as "domination" – and *Stand* as "status" rather than "estate" (Böröcz 1997) at least partly responsible for disregarding the links between Weberian and Marxian theory. "De-Parsonizing Weber" (Cohen et al. 1975) thus became an essential step toward the neo-Weberian revolution.

At the same time, this intellectual trend characterising US-American sociology in the 1970s reflected the political sentiment prevalent in the wake of the US war on Vietnam and the shift to the left in both politics and academia associated with it. The world economic downturn and the US military defeat in Vietnam shook confidence in modernisation theory and in the Parsonian functionalist logic it used in order to advocate the United States and England as models of development, and prompted instead the need to develop conflict models such as the ones present in both Marx and Weber in order to understand the growing importance of the state (Wiley 1985). Among other things, the gradual depolarisation of the constructed divide between the "materialist" Marx and the "idealist" Weber thus made room for the possible cross-fertilisation of both their theories of social inequality and stratification. In the

142 *Global Inequalities Beyond Occidentalism*

Parsonian-functionalist interpretation of Weber's work, which ignored the economic aspects of class and focused instead on status [*Stand*] as the main principle of social stratification alongside cultural values, the latter harboured no revolutionary potential; in turn, the conflict interpretation emphasised the similarities between Marx's notion of class for itself and Weber's notion of *Stand*, thus moving the latter to the centre-stage of politics and revolutionary conflict (Scott 1996, Wiley 1987). As Norbert Wiley has suggested, this trend toward a Marx-Weber truce has been partly responsible for the rise of comparative-historical research more generally, as well as for the latter-day understandings of Weber's notions of inequality and stratification (Wiley 1985). In the following, the conflict sociological interpretation is being used as a framework for reconstructing the main assumptions of Weber's view on social inequality. However, as in the case of the philosophical-humanist versus the economic determinist Marx, this is not to embark on the ongoing debate on whether Weber the conflict theorist prevailed over Weber the action theorist, or whether the "true Weber" is an altogether different one. Instead, the next chapters are geared toward the search for the most promising research agenda for the analysis of global inequalities that such debates have occasioned.

Modernity as Modern Western Rationalism

Just as Marx's class analysis did not stand alone, but was instead embedded in his theory of capital accumulation, Weber's views on inequality and stratification are intimately tied to his larger theory of the rise of the modern world. An understanding of Weber's theory of modernity is therefore an indispensable prerequisite for any analysis of his approach to social inequality.

Although Weber clearly placed greater emphasis on modernity as a series of specifically Western achievements than Marx had done, he did not use the term as such any more than Marx did. Alongside terms such as "the modern West", "modern European culture", and especially "modern rationalism" that he used to describe the objects of his study, it was frequently "modern capitalism" and "the modern capitalist enterprise" that he employed as proxies for modernity. Unlike Marx, however, his concern was not with capitalism as such, but with the uniqueness of the West – of which modern capitalism was but one component – as well as with explaining the origin of this uniqueness. While postcolonial critique has charged sociological classics from Comte to Marx and from Durkheim to Weber collectively or individually with Eurocentrism, evolutionary determinism, and ignorance of non-Western contexts, it was with reference to Max Weber's thesis of the "uniqueness of the West" that the notion of a Western sociology actively producing absences was first formulated (Hirst, 1975, in Zubaida, 2005: 112).

Thus, in his Prefatory Remarks to *Collected Essays on the Sociology of Religion* (written 1920), Weber begins by noting that, although scientific inquiry had existed outside the Western world and had given rise to such highly sophisticated developments as Islamic theology, Chinese historiography, Babylonian astronomy,

The West vs. the Rest

and Indian medicine, systematic, rational science was unique to the West and could be traced back to "the Hellenic mind", i.e., ancient Greece. In his view, a series of innovations in music, architecture, and art, such as the rational use of linear and spatial perspective in painting, were unknown outside the West, as was the Western universities' "rational and systematic organization into scientific disciplines" and the Western modern state's "organization of specially trained civil servants" (Weber 2005: 55), only precursors of which could be found elsewhere. Similarly, only "rudimentary developments" of the state as a political institution operating on the basis of "a rationally enacted 'constitution' and rationally enacted laws" (ibid.) had crystallised outside the West, where these distinguishing features now characterised the modern state. The singularity of the West in all these regards could not be overstated, as Weber stressed in *General Economic History*:

> Only the Occident knows the *state in the modern sense*, with a constitution [*gesatzter Verfassung*], specialized officialdom, and the concept of citizenship. Beginnings of this institution in antiquity and in the Orient were never able to develop fully. Only the Occident knows *rational law*, made by jurists and rationally interpreted and planned, and only in the Occident is found the concept of *citizen* (*civis romanus, citoyen, bourgeois*) because only in the Occident does the *city* exist in the specific sense of the word. (Weber 1961: 232)

In Weber's view, the same applied for capitalism. While the capitalist enterprise was a universal occurrence, having existed in all world civilisations from ancient China, India, and Egypt, through the Mediterranean and medieval Europe, modern Western capitalism alone was founded on "the rational-capitalist organization of legally *free labour*", which was either lacking in other regions of the globe or was present only in "preliminary development stages" there (Weber 2005: 58). According to Weber, the capitalist economic act in general, i.e., universal capitalism, involved not only the pursuit of profit, but "an expectation of profit based on the utilization of opportunities for *exchange*; that is, of (formally) *peaceful* opportunities for acquisition"[1] (Weber 2005: 56). In practice, however, capitalists have financed

> above all wars, piracy and all types of shipping and construction projects; as entrepreneurs in the colonies they have served the international policy goals of nations, [...] have acquired plantations and operated them using slaves or (directly or indirectly) forced labor; they have leased land and the rights to use honorific titles; they have financed both the leaders of political parties standing for re-election and mercenaries for civil wars. (Weber 2005: 58)

Weber called this type of entrepreneurs "adventure capitalists" and saw them as the main agents of "promoter, adventure, colonial, and [...] modern financial capitalism" (ibid.), i.e., capitalist enterprises of an irrational or speculative nature

---

1 Unless otherwise indicated, the emphases in Weber's texts are found in the original.

144   *Global Inequalities Beyond Occidentalism*

or of a violent character. These capitalists' use of coerced labour, Weber maintained, whether in the form of slavery, serfdom, cottage industries, or day labour, had only allowed for a very limited degree of rational organisation of work when compared to that of free industrial labour in the West. Even while acknowledging that modern capitalism had emerged alongside adventure capitalism, Weber thus viewed modern capitalism as an entirely different type, characterised by "the rational organization of industrial companies and their orientation to *market* opportunities, rather than to political violence or to irrational speculation" (Weber 2005: 59). The interconnection between the sovereign Western states' monopoly on legitimate violence within the national territory (which made the "peaceful opportunities for acquisition" possible) and the parallel legitimisation of political violence by the same states in Europe's colonies (in the name of the very rational organisation characteristic of modern capitalism) is blatantly absent from Weber's account. He therefore sharply dissociated Western capitalism from the colonial enterprise, and, ultimately, the emergence of modernity from the history of colonialism.

Instead, in order to explain the rational organisation of work characteristic of modern capitalism, he gave pride of place to "internal preconditions", i.e., developments internal to the West, such as the spatial separation of the household from the workplace (followed by the legal separation of personal from company wealth), as well as the emergence of rational accounting, which made the operation of independent business possible in the first place. According to Weber, the entire social order characteristic of the modern West, as well as the social conflicts specific to it, were a direct outcome of this type of organisational structure. As a result, not only modern capitalism was impossible outside the West, but the main pillars of a capitalist social structure as well as the class struggles out of which rational socialism could emerge in its wake were inexistent elsewhere, too:

> just as the concept of "citizen" is entirely missing except in the West and the concept of "bourgeoisie" is completely absent outside the modern West, so also the notion of a "proletariat" as a *class* is absent. Indeed, it could not appear outside the West precisely because a rational organization of *free labor* in *industrial enterprises* was lacking. "Class struggles" between strata of creditors and debtors, between those who owned land and those who did not (whether serfs or tenant sharecroppers), between persons with economic interests in commerce and consumers or owners of land – all these conflicts have existed for centuries in various constellations. Yet even the struggles typical in the West's medieval period between domestic industry entrepreneurs and their wage workers [the putting-out system] are found elsewhere only in rudimentary form. The modern opposition between large-scale industrialists, as employers, and free workers paid a wage is completely lacking outside the West. (Weber 2005: 60)

Weber thus offers a theory of Western exceptionalism based on a "denial of coevalness" vis-à-vis the entire non-Western world. As in the observation that the proletariat could not have emerged elsewhere, the typical Orientalist gesture involved in the denial of coevalness functions at the same time as a rationalisation of the conspicuous absence of modern capitalist traits in the non-Western world. Much like Marx, Weber defined modern capitalism in terms of the industrial organisation of free labour – and thus traced the rise of modernity back to the emergence of industrial capitalism. Yet, unlike Marx, Weber did not consider the question of capitalism as such to be the main factor in the explanation of the West's uniqueness. Rather, the central problem for him was that of accounting for the origin of the Western middle-class and its particular economic ethos, supported as it was (only) in the West by the rational structure of law and administration (Weber 2005: 59f.). Hence, according to Weber, the common denominator of the unique modern technological developments, state-building processes, capitalist organisation, calculable law and administration, and work ethic emerged in the West was the specific rationalism characterising Western civilisation as a whole.

The origin of the economic ethos of *modern Western* capitalism – as opposed to earlier manifestations of capitalism within and outside the West – had already constituted the subject matter of the *Protestant Ethic and the Spirit of Capitalism*, Weber's first attempt "to isolate the uniqueness of the modern West and to define its causal origins" (Kalberg 2005: 24). Contemporary competing explanations traced the emergence of capitalism to economic, technological or demographic factors or to an immanent process of social evolution. Against them, Weber instead argued that a work ethic based on *ideas* such as that of "a duty of the individual toward the increase of his capital, which is assumed as an end in itself (Weber 1992: 17) and "[t]he earning of money [as] the result and the expression of virtue and proficiency in a calling" (Weber 1992: 19) was what lent Western European and American capitalism its distinct rationality and what had been missing in earlier forms of capitalism. The notion that the "*ethically*-oriented maxim for the organisation of life" that Weber traces back to the basic religious ideas of ascetic Protestantism constituted the very *spirit* of modern capitalism was thus explicitly formulated as a contribution to an understanding of "the manner in which ideas become effective forces in history" (Weber 1992: 48). As such, it was directed against the Marxian view of ideas as a reflection of material conditions in the superstructure, to which it opposed the label of "ethical foundation and justification" (Weber 1992: 36). However, Weber did not thereby intend either to revert to the Hegelian notion that all human activity was a mere manifestation of Spirit – i.e., to substitute an idealist for a materialist theory of history – or to give primacy to any other causal factor in his search for the origin of modern capitalism. His emphasis on the ideas and values that went into the capitalist spirit was instead geared toward making the issue of the "economic ethic" of Protestantism an integral part of the analysis of the "economic form" emerging in the sixteenth and seventeenth centuries, so as to allow for multicausal rather than monocausal explanations of the rise of modern capitalism (Weber 1992: 125). Weber therefore considered the relationship between the Protestant ethic and the early capitalist institutions originating in the European cities to be a mutually favourable one, i.e., an "elective affinity" between a type of

146   *Global Inequalities Beyond Occidentalism*

religio-ethically motivated conduct and a mode of production, rather than a direct cause (Weber 1978a, Schluchter 2007: 82).

Alongside economic factors, ideas and values, Weber's multicausal explanations included historical events, social carriers, and power as pivotal causal forces, none of which, in his view, enjoyed primacy over the others (Kalberg 2005: 26). Among the factors he took into consideration, the notion of social carriers was particularly relevant for an understanding of his approach to social inequality. In order for ideas and values to become causal forces with enduring effects, they had to surface in patterns of social action of powerful social groupings such as classes, status groups, and organisations. If sects and churches thereby became the indispensable social carriers of the Protestant ethic, it was the middle class in particular that ensured its impact. Unlike Lutherans, who viewed the social division of labour and the occupational stratification deriving from it as expressions of God's divine plan and therefore as unchanging, Puritans gradually came to believe that "the providential purpose of the division of labour [Germ. *Berufsgliederung*, literally, division of occupations, M.B.] is to be known by its fruits" (Weber 1992: 107). According to the Predestination Doctrine, methodical work, economic competition, the pursuit of profit, and the attainment of wealth as a result of the rational performance of one's calling were signs of one's salvation. At the same time, the Puritan conception of the calling involved a practical-rational life conduct (*Lebensführung*) rooted in asceticism and directed against laziness and the sinful enjoyment of existence. According to Weber, such a conduct tended to be more characteristic of the capitalist middle-classes than either the nobility or the newly rich:

> The emphasis on the ascetic importance of a fixed calling provided an ethical justification of the modern specialized division of labor. In a similar way the providential interpretation of profit-making justified the activities of the business man. The superior indulgence of the seigneur and the parvenu ostentation of the nouveau riche are equally detestable to asceticism. But, on the other hand, it has the highest ethical appreciation of the sober, middle-class, self-made man. (Weber 1992: 109)

An ethical orientation that viewed the correctness of one's conduct according to religious precepts as a sign of God's approval was rooted in Old Testament norms common to both Puritan belief and of medieval and modern Judaism. Despite these apparent similarities, Weber however cautioned against mistaking the economic ethic of Judaism for an element of modern capitalism on equal footing with the Protestant ethic:

> The general tendency of the older Judaism toward a naïve acceptance of life as such was far removed from the special characteristics of Puritanism. It was, however, just as far – and this ought not to be overlooked – from the economic ethics of medieval and modern Judaism, in the traits which determined the

> positions of both in the development of the capitalistic ethos. The Jews stood
> on the side of the politically and speculatively oriented adventurous capitalism;
> their ethos was, in a word, that of pariah-capitalism. But Puritanism carried the
> ethos of the rational organization of capital and labour. It took over from the
> Jewish ethic only what was adapted to this purpose. (Weber 1992: 111)

Accordingly, pariah capitalism resulted in a different pattern of social stratification than modern capitalism, as Weber would repeatedly show using the historical example of the Jews as a "pariah people". On the one hand, the belief in being God's chosen people had led to the status segregation of the Jewish diaspora: Through the cultivation of the notion of the ethnic commonality of all Jews and of specific occupational traditions, the ethnic segregation had ultimately evolved into a caste situation of a legally precarious nature that allowed only limited political interaction (Weber 1978b: 934). On the other hand, the Puritans' notion of the chosen people belonging to the true church permeated the life conduct of the Puritan middle-class and thereby became "above all the only consistent influence" (Weber 1992: 117) of the economic-rational organisation of life characteristic of "modern economic man" (ibid.). For Weber, the same rational self-control and ethical restraint also distinguished the *middle-class* frame of mind of the Puritans from the adventure capitalists of the North American colonisation, "who wanted to set up plantations with the labour of indentured servants, and live as *feudal lords*" (Weber 1992: 117, emphasis added). The latter were therefore equally far from building a basis for the formation of capital through rational ascetic savings as both Jewish pariah capitalists and the old European "squirearchy". This was all the more the case for the ethical orientation derived from other world religions. While Christianity and Judaism had in common an origin as specifically bourgeois religions (*bürgerliche Religionen)*, Islam and all Asiatic denominations emerged as religions of the ruling stratum (*Herrenreligionen*) and as such lacked the middle-class, urban character of the Western capitalist ethos. In particular, the innerworldly warrior ethic characteristic of Islam, upheld by a status-oriented military aristocracy, only promoted heroic self-sacrifice in times of war, but not the long-term vocational asceticism that had allowed Protestantism to overcome the spirit of traditionalism in the economic and political spheres (Schluchter 2007: 80). In Weber's view, if Judaism never transcended the economic ethic of pariah capitalism, Islam thus remained feudal, petty bourgeois, or booty capitalist at best.

The contrast between the feudal and the modern economic ethos frequently served as the basis on which Weber illustrated the emergence of modern Western rationalism. Just as feudal agriculture, aimed at the mere acquisition of land as a means of entry in the nobility, diverged from the Puritans' engagement in agriculture, in turn geared toward *productive and commercial farming* (Weber 1992: 117), so the feudal knight's orientation to a code of personal honour clearly contrasted with modern economic man's rational calculation and "orientation toward a purpose [and] a common cause" (Weber 1978b: 1149). Thus, all forms of status group-oriented feudal ethic, including the Occidental one, stood in contrast

148   *Global Inequalities Beyond Occidentalism*

to the vocational ethic and the means-end rationality of modern capitalism. However, unlike any other, Weber held, Occidental feudalism contained important elements that challenged patrimonialism and allowed the development of rational economic action: the decentralisation of political foundation by means of a feudal hierarchy, the organisational principle of the corporate urban commune, the church as an autonomous institution, a rational lawmaking body, a bureaucratic power apparatus, and the idea of feudal contract. Therefore, while the Occidental feudal ethic is characterised by fealty on the basis of a free contract as well as a feeling of honour, "Oriental feudalism lacks fealty, Japanese feudalism lacks a patrimonial foundation, and only Occidental feudalism combines both" (Schluchter 2007: 99). Once again, the Orientalist rhetoric of lack actively produces absences in societies defined as non-modern. More importantly, however, the elevation of feudalism – a particular period in the history of some parts of Western Europe – to a universal stage in the history of world civilisations lends legitimacy to the search for structural absences outside the West and projects the postulated uniqueness further back in time.[2] In the process, the notion of modernity implicitly advanced is one of transformation – from the feudal to the modern.

Similarly, although the calculation of earnings in terms of money was common to all types of capitalism, the exact calculation necessary in rational industrial firms operating in private economies was possible only on the basis of free labour, and was as such an exclusive feature of modern industrial, i.e., Western, capitalism (Weber 2005: 60ff.). Consequently, free labour, freedom of the labour market, freedom in the selection of workers, and the substantive freedom of contract were just as central to obtaining a maximum of formal rationality of capital accounting as the rule of the rational administration and law or the separation of the household from the enterprise (Weber 1978a: 161f.). In Weber's view, it had been only in the context of the rise of the medieval Occidental city as a corporate body premised on the local political participation of free citizens that all these conditions had first been met. Consequently, "the ascent from bondage to freedom by means of monetary acquisition" (Weber 1978b: 1238), although also present in the Antiquity and in Russia, was most important in the medieval continental cities of Western Europe. The opportunity to purchase one's freedom

---

2   As early as 1960, anthropologists such as Marshall Sahlins had argued against generalising from the history of feudalism in the West on the grounds that many antique civilisations, from Rome to China, Sumer, and Mesopotamia, had been more developed at a far earlier stage, such that "Placing feudalism between these civilisations and modern nations in a hierarchy of over-all progress patently and unnecessarily invalidates the hierarchy; it obscures rather than illustrates the progressive trends in economy, society, and polity in the evolution of culture. Conversely, identifying the specific antecedents of modern civilisations throughout the world as 'feudalism' is also obviously fallacious and obscures the historic course of development of these civilisations, however much it may illuminate the historic course of Western culture" (Sahlins 1960: 31). For a discussion of debates on feudalism in Latin America and Eastern Europe, see Boatcă 2003 and Chapter 3 above.

The West vs. the Rest   149

intensified the economic activity of unfree petty burghers, leading to the rise of the rational accounting bourgeoisie, the urban burgher stratum. At the same time, the Christian tradition of religious communities premised on the oath-bound, fraternal association of *individual* believers, rather than on ritually sanctioned kinship ties, had fostered the decline of family loyalties in economic pursuits and the gradual legal separation of the household from the enterprise that accompanied the expanding need for credit and the innovations in bookkeeping methods (Bendix 1977: 74). In contrast, the caste and sib constraints of Indian and Chinese urban social formations thoroughly prevented the freedom of urbanites to form confederations of individual burghers as in North European cities. According to Weber, India's exclusive caste taboos and overwhelmingly rural population made the possibility that the city dwellers merge into a status group [*Stand*] with social and legal equality even more remote than in China (Weber 1978b: 1241). Although Weber stressed that the carrier strata of world-religions had varied in each individual case and over time, identifying the main carriers of the various religions made it possible to link particular social strata with the economic ethic that had come to characterise the respective religions (see Table 5.1):

> If one wishes to characterize succinctly [...] the types representative of the various strata that were the primary carriers or propagators of the so-called world religions, they would be the following: In Confucianism, the world-organizing bureaucrat; in Hinduism, the world-ordering magician; in Buddhism, the mendicant monk wandering through the world; in Islam, the warrior seeking to conquer the world; in Judaism, the wandering trader; and in Christianity, the itinerant journeyman. To be sure, all these types must not be taken as exponents of their own occupational or material "class interests", but rather as the ideological carriers of the kind of ethical or salvation doctrine which rather readily conformed to their social position. (Weber 1978a: 512)

Indeed, Weber's juxtaposition of the ideological carriers of religious doctrines is not a comprehensive comparative analysis of stratification. Rather, detecting an elective affinity between religion and carrier stratum is part of Weber's attempt at constructing a typology of rationalism based on the degree to which each cultural religion has "overcome magic" as well as on the ethical relationship it has constructed to the world (Weber 2004a: 35; Schluchter 1988: 99; 140ff.). According to him, the successful disenchantment of the world (*Entzauberung der Welt*) on which the modern world view was premised had been completely carried through only in ascetic Protestantism, which therefore represented the final stage in the elimination of superstition and magic. Similarly, the tension between religious duties and everyday social reality, characteristic of many religions, had fostered the rise of modern economic rationality only in the case of ascetic Protestantism, where the rational pursuit of profit had been interpreted as a sign of salvation and had accordingly prompted world mastery. In contrast, Confucianism, despite having a strongly rational character, had tended to cling to magic, to which it

150   *Global Inequalities Beyond Occidentalism*

attached "an unimpeachably *positive* significance for salvation" (Weber 2004a: 35). Confucianism was thus seen as lacking any natural scientific understanding of the world as well as any tension between this-worldly acts and other-worldly recompense. By advocating world accommodation instead of world mastery, it thus lacked the means to influence life conduct through forces other than tradition and family ties. In the case of Islam, it was the fluctuation between advocating world mastery as world conquest in times of war and world adjustment in ordinary situations involving no inner tension between salvational doctrine and salvational interest that had, in Weber's view, hindered the emergence of same relationship to the world which had prompted ascetic Protestantism's drive toward objective economic rationality (Schluchter 2007: 79ff.). Table 5.1 presents Weber's typology of carrier strata of world religions in a schematic fashion.

Table 5.1   Typology of carrier strata and relationship to the world of cultural religions

Religion	Carrier stratum	Relationship to the world
Ascetic Protestantism	Itinerant journeymen	World mastery
Judaism	Wandering traders	World indifference
Confucianism	World-organising bureaucrats	World accommodation
Hinduism	World-ordering magicians	World flight
Buddhism	Mendicant monks	World flight
Islam	World-conquering warriors	World-conquest and world adjustment

Source: Compiled from Weber 2004a: 35; Schluchter 1988: 99ff.

While a maximum of formal rationality could best be attained in a market economy, the central features of the rationalised modern economy more generally, such as the separation of the worker from the means of production, the specialisation of tasks, and the development of discipline were seen as common to both market and planned economies. Weber thus openly disagreed with Marx that the "separation of the worker from the tools of his trade" was a process specific to private industrial production. For him, ownership of the means of production of modern industry by either private industrialists or the state was by its very nature different from the artisan's ownership of his tools in the Middle Ages:

> As long as there are mines, furnaces, railways, factories and machines, they will never be the property of an individual or of several individual workers in the sense in which the materials of a medieval craft were the property of one

guild-master or of a local trade association or guild. That is out of the question because of the nature of present-day technology. (Weber 1972: 199)

He suggested instead that, besides the increase in technological complexity, it was first of all the greater efficiency of industrial production which led to the development of the discipline regulating factory work, state administration, as well as the army and the universities in modern rational economies. Discipline, defined as "the consistently rationalised, methodically prepared and exact execution of the received order" (Weber 1978b: 1149) was not only the basis of the process of "inescapable universal bureaucratization" of modern states, but also underlay the tendency of separation of industrial workers from the means of production in both capitalist and socialist states:

> This subjection to working discipline is so extraordinarily marked for the industrial worker because, in contrast to, say, a slave plantation or a socage-farm, modern industry functions on the basis of an extraordinarily keen process of *selection*. A modern factory proprietor does not employ just any worker, just because he might work for a low wage. [...] the machine is not working to capacity unless the man in front of it knows how to utilise it fully. [...] Every modern concern, in contrast to those of antiquity which employed slave labor, where the lord was bound to the slaves he owned [...], rests on the principle of selection, and this selection on the other hand is intensified to the extreme by competition between employers, which constrains the individual employer to certain maximum wages: the inherent necessity of the worker's earnings corresponds to the inherent necessity of the discipline. (Weber 1972: 201)

In the context of the separation of workers from their tools, the contrast with plantation slavery therefore fulfilled a different function for Weber than it had for Marx. In the case of Marx, the main outcome of the process of the expropriation of the agricultural population from the land was the emergence of a class of free wage-labourers that neither constituted the means of production, as both slaves and bondsmen had, nor owned any, as with subsistence producers. They were thus the first "doubly free" labourers in human history. Weber, too, utilised the juxtaposition with the slave economy much as he used the one with the feudal mode of production, i.e., in order to set the modern West apart from its own feudal past as well as from the non-West. Yet, in his case, the emergence of free labour was only one of the many consequences of the more significant process of the rise of rationalism as the unique feature of the modern West. Although market and planned economies resulted in markedly different standards of living, they were both instances of modern rationalism, whose pattern of rigorous discipline was modelled on the military. Accordingly, for Weber, the difference between capitalist and socialist economic action was only one of degree of formal rationality, whereas that between modern and pre-modern economies was one between rationality and lack of it, respectively:

152   *Global Inequalities Beyond Occidentalism*

> military discipline is the ideal model for the modern capitalist factory, as it was for the ancient plantation. However, organizational discipline in the factory has a completely rational basis. With the help of suitable methods of measurement, the optimum profitability of the individual worker is calculated like that of any material means of production. [...] This whole process of rationalization, in the factory as elsewhere, and especially in the bureaucratic state machine, parallels the centralization of the material implements of organization in the hands of the ruler. Thus, discipline inexorably takes over larger areas as the satisfaction of political and economic needs is increasingly rationalized. (Weber 1978b: 1156)

In contrast with irrational and speculative capitalism as well as with the feudal economy, modern capitalism was therefore, for Weber, uniquely characterised by a maximum of rationality, efficiency, and the systematic, dispassionate pursuit of profit (Weber 1992: 37). This however entailed an increasing depersonalisation and distancing from ethical norms and charitable orientations, the advancement of which went hand in hand with the expansion of bureaucratisation. Thus, bureaucracy was the better developed, the more "dehumanised" it became, i.e., the more it functioned according to the principle of *sine ira et studio* rather than on the basis of irrational and emotional considerations. Weber consequently feared that the bureaucratic state apparatus of modern capitalism would end up eliminating all ethical concerns from decision-making processes. Accordingly, if capitalism subjected workers to a form of "masterless slavery" (Weber 1978b: 1186) governed neither by ethical nor unethical, but rather by a-ethical bureaucratic principles, ethical values could not flourish and industrial societies would become increasingly stagnant. However, Weber thought that the social dynamism instilled by the logic of market competition under capitalism could mitigate the tendency toward bureaucratisation. This would in turn be more difficult under socialism, which promoted its own, even larger bureaucratic apparatus, thus placing the worker under the "dictatorship of the official" and further contributing to social stagnation (Weber 1972: 209). The emergence of a "closed caste" of functionaries, a fully rational, "organic social stratification", and social ossification might be the outcome, for "State bureaucracy would rule *alone* if private capitalism were eliminated" (Weber 1978b: 1402).

Modes of Stratification and Social Closure in Western Modernity

As early as the *Protestant Ethic*, Weber had emphasised that the history of rationalism had followed no single, progressive line, and that rationalism contained within itself a series of contradictions that fitted no simple developmental scheme: The high degree of economic rationalisation in industrial England was not accompanied by the rationalisation of law, which had instead attained its highest form in the Roman law of later antiquity and had prevailed during the modern era in the industrially underdeveloped, largely Catholic areas of Southern Europe,

The West vs. the Rest   153

rather than in Protestant industrial England (Weber 1992: 37f.). Nevertheless, Weber believed that the rise of rational discipline characterising modern capitalism imprinted a certain directionality to the transformation of social structural patterns, since discipline, being impersonal by nature, was intrinsically alien to charisma and status honour, yet akin to rational calculation and routinised skill: "the most irresistible force is *rational discipline*, which eradicates not only personal charisma, but also stratification by status groups, or at least transforms them in a rationalizing direction" (Weber 1978b: 1149). Accordingly, in the modern industrial West, stratification by class had become more widespread.

Yet, however more rational a social order based on class is considered to be than one based on status honour, in Weber's approach, stratification by status and by class do not stand for a chronological sequence on an evolutionary scale of linear progress. Rather, the dominant mode of stratification varies across civilisations and epochs such that

> When the bases of the acquisition and distribution of goods are relatively stable, stratification by status is favoured. Every technological repercussion and economic transformation threatens stratification by status and pushes the class situation into the foreground. Epochs and countries in which the naked class situation is of predominant significance are regularly the periods of technical and economic transformations. And every slowing down of the change in economic stratification leads, in due course, to the growth of status structures and makes for a resuscitation of the important role of social honor. (Weber 1978b: 938)

Both the differentiation between the two forms of stratification and the explicit disentanglement of each from a particular epoch or mode of production were meant as a reply to Marx, whose contention that "All history is the history of class struggle" awarded class phenomena universal relevance as a principle of social stratification. Conversely, for Weber, classes, status groups, and parties were all phenomena of the distribution of power in society. Classes emerged out of the *economic order*, i.e., of the distribution and use of goods and services, status groups were a result of the *social order*, i.e., of the distribution of social honour between groups. Parties, representing interests determined through class situation, status situations, or both, were the outcome of the *political order* related to the distribution of power among groups to influence communal decisions with respect to such interests. Consequently, a class did not in itself constitute a community (*Gemeinschaft*), nor was the emergence of *social* action from a common class situation a universal phenomenon:

> Every class may therefore give rise to some form of "class action", of one of the numerous possible kinds; but it need not do so. In any case, a class itself is not a community, and it is misleading to treat classes as conceptually equivalent to communities. […] men in the same class situation, faced with situations as emotionally charged as are those of economic life, regularly react by mass action

154   *Global Inequalities Beyond Occidentalism*

in the direction which best approximates their average interest – a fact which is as important for the understanding of historical events as it is basically simple. [...]

> If classes are not themselves communities, then, class situations arise only in the context of a community. The collective action which leads to the emergence of a class situation, however, is not in its essence an action undertaken by members of the same class but one involving relations between members of different classes (Weber 2004b: 185)

The modern proletariat was the most important historical example of a class situation resulting out of the structure of a concrete economic order and recognisable as such for its members. Other class situations resulting from highly polarised forms of the distribution of property had instead prevailed in the urban centres of Antiquity and during the Middle Ages. Within the economic order, therefore, what was decisive for the differential power distribution that allowed the owners of goods, but not the owners of mere labour power to profit from the price competition in the capitalist market was the availability of property – not the common class interests of each group. While Weber did see membership in a class as deriving from the commonality of class situation, he defined the latter as the condition in which

> (1) a number of people have in common a specific causal component of their life chances, insofar as (2) this component is represented exclusively by economic interest in the possession of goods and opportunities for income, and (3) is represented under the conditions of the commodity or labor markets. (Weber 1978b: 927)

Weber thus viewed the basic categories of all class situations, whether or not they come to involve class struggle, as being property and the lack of property, respectively, and the market principle as their underlying logic:

> The element which is always present in all cases where the concept of "class" is applied, however, is that it is the nature of chances in the market which is the common factor determining the fate of a number of individuals. In this sense, the "class situation" is ultimately a "market situation". (Weber 2004b: 184)

He further differentiated among three types of classes, all of which however were economically determined: *Property classes* (*Besitzklassen*) were primarily determined by property differences, *commercial classes* (*Erwerbsklassen*) by the marketability of goods and services, while *social classes* (*soziale Klassen*) were characterised by high individual and generational mobility. Members of each class were differentiated by whether they were positively or negatively privileged with respect to the determining dimension of the respective class. Thus, rentiers deriving income from the monopoly of high-priced consumer goods, sales, wealth, and capital – such as slave-owners – were the positively privileged members of the *property class*. In contrast, the unfree (*Besitzobjekte*, literally, objects of property) – such as slaves, alongside debtors, the declassed, and the paupers, were negatively privileged. Although examples of class conflict had historically pitted creditors and debtors or the propertied and the declassed against each other, Weber noted, a conspicuous instance disproving the universality of class struggle between the property and the propertyless was the lack of conflict between plantation owners and the "poor white trash" in the US, whose interests converged in terms of "anti-Negro" sentiment. Between the positively and the negatively privileged property classes stood the middle classes (*Mittelstandsklassen*), whose members lived off their property or their acquired skill.

This middle category partly overlapped with Weber's second category, *commercial classes*, characterised by the opportunity to exploit the market through natural or acquired skills as well as through monopoly of occupational characteristics. Thus, typical for the positively privileged commercial classes were entrepreneurs – including merchants, bankers, and professionals – while labourers, whether skilled, semi-skilled, or unskilled, were seen as typical for the unprivileged. The commercial classes' middle layer accordingly comprised self-employed peasants, craftsmen, public and private officials, and artists, but also the liberal professions, small entrepreneurs, and, last but not least, proletarians – to the extent that they had risen above the level of unskilled workers.

According to Weber, the upward mobility characteristic of *social classes* in general and of the propertied and the educated as the social classes' privileged layer in particular had increasingly become typical of the working-class as a whole in the unprivileged sector. Thanks to the acquisition of additional skills, such as through training on the job, unskilled workers could become white-collar employees, thus rising from the situation of a negatively privileged class to that of the middle classes, which, in the case of the social classes, further included the propertyless intelligentsia, civil servants, and the petty bourgeoisie. Pointing out that Marx had intended the unfinished last part of *Capital* to deal with the consequences of skill differentials among the working class for the emergence of class consciousness, Weber noted that the importance of semi-skilled workers had further increased since Marx's time, making a differentiated assessment of the working-class all the more necessary. This explains why, in Weber's model, proletarians featured both as part of the middle class of commercial classes and as the negatively privileged category of the social classes (see Table 5.2). As such, they were counterposed not only to a class of capitalist entrepreneurs and merchants profiting from investment and trade, as in Marx, but to one of rentiers living off securities, property, and land, i.e., dead capital. Consequently, in Weber's model, the bourgeoisie was no homogeneous or unified class, indeed the very label of "bourgeoisie" is not used to refer to the capitalist class, but only features as "petty bourgeoisie" in the middle sector of the social classes.

156 *Global Inequalities Beyond Occidentalism*

Table 5.2   Typology of classes according to Max Weber

	Property classes	**Commercial classes**	**Social classes**
Criterion of class situation	*Property differences*	*Marketability*	*Easy mobility*
Positively privileged	Rentiers	Entrepreneurs, merchants, bankers, proletarians	The propertied, the educated
	Middle classes (see also commercial classes)	Middle classes (farmers, craftsmen, officials)	Propertyless intelligentsia, white-collar specialists – Petty bourgeoisie
Negatively privileged	The unfree, debtors The declassed, paupers	(Un)skilled labourers	The working-class

If the differentiation of the concept of class into three subcategories was Weber's contribution to Marx's conceptualisation of the economic order, the introduction of the concept of status [*Stand*] added the social order as a further form of the distribution of power. Unlike classes, status groups [*Stände*] were viewed as hindering the consistent carrying through of the sheer market principle by being determined by the "positive or negative, social estimation of *honor*" (Weber 1978b: 932), rather than purely economic interests. Given Weber's understanding that "each kind of class situation, and above all when it rests upon the power of property per se, will become most clearly efficacious when all other determinants of reciprocal relations are, as far as possible, eliminated in their significance" (Weber 1978b: 930), the contrast in which status honour and economic property stood to each other (at least in theory) prevented the realisation of the market principle in the long run. This was most clearly the case when status groups monopolised certain goods, such as inherited estate property, certain forms of labour, such as serfs or bondsmen, or special trades, as with craft and merchant guilds. Consequently, by withholding goods, labour-power, and occupations from free exchange on the market, the direct translation of property ownership into class situation was in turn impeded. Although Weber noted that property often led to status recognition, ensuring a certain overlap between class distinctions and status distinctions, he pointed out that, unlike classes, status groups were communities (*Gemeinschaften*). As such, they shared a specific life conduct, formal education, and a similar degree of hereditary or occupational prestige, the consistence of which was enforced through several forms of social closure, such as restrictions on social intercourse, marriage partners, or political power monopolies. In principle, classes could be viewed as stratified according to their relations of production and *acquisition* of goods, while status groups were best described as stratified according to the principles of *consumption* of goods reflected in their particular life conduct (Weber 1978b: 938). Status groups were therefore much more likely to bring about social action in the form of closure than classes were to bring about class struggle.

The distinction between status and class was equally relevant for the contrast between the slave economy and modern industrial capitalism, since, for Weber, those "whose fate is not determined by the chance of using goods or services for themselves on the market, e.g., slaves, are not, however, a class in the technical sense of the term" (Weber 1978b: 928), but rather a status group of low social honour. As such, both they and the "adventure capitalists" who systematically employed slavery to generate profit remained located outside modern industrial capitalism, the criteria of which they did not fully meet. That status groups high in social honour – i.e., the very opposite of slaves – should consider the performance of common physical labour, as well as any rational economic pursuit more generally, as degrading and sanction it with disqualification of status was, in Weber's view, further evidence of the stark opposition between the principle of class stratification through market-regulated distribution of power and status stratification through honour:

> Commercial classes arise in a market-oriented economy, but status groups arise within the framework of organizations which satisfy their wants through monopolistic liturgies, or in feudal or in *ständisch*-patrimonial fashion. Depending on the prevailing mode of stratification, we shall speak of a "status society" or a "class society". The status group comes closest to the social class and is most unlike the commercial class. Status groups are often created by property classes. (Weber 1978a: 306)

Thus, although the prevalence of status and class did not follow a pre-established chronological sequence, in Weber's conceptualisation, the history of the West did describe a transition from feudal status societies to modern class societies, mediated through the rise of the urban burgher stratum in the medieval Occidental city. At least as far as European societies are concerned, Weber therefore followed both Marx and Hegel in mapping a transition from a premodern era, in which status prevailed, to a modern capitalist one, in which class relations became dominant (Scott 1996: xi). Accordingly, what Weber called "pure modern democracy" was devoid of any explicit status privileges for individuals. Stratification by status groups on the basis of conventional life conduct (*Lebensführung*) could, however, occur in long-standing democracies as well, as Weber illustrated using the example of men's submission to fashion in order to claim recognition as "gentlemen" in the United States (Weber 2005: 165). Moreover, the very tendency toward increased bureaucratisation in modern industrial society promoted the rise of a specific status group of functionaries that had to be systematically counterweighted by a democratic election of officials instead of their appointment for life (Weber 1978b: 1000f.).

The process of social closure however entailed consequences that reached beyond the mere stratification of status [*ständische Schließung*]. In purely economic terms, increased closure of a status group that enjoys preferential opportunities for special employment gradually leads to legal monopolies of

158   *Global Inequalities Beyond Occidentalism*

special offices for members of that group. In turn, the full realisation of social closure around a certain stratification of status honour – itself a consequence of a stable distribution of economic power – resulted in the transformation of status groups into "closed castes":

> Status distinctions are then guaranteed not merely by conventions and laws, but also by religious rituals. This occurs in such a way that every physical contact with a member of any caste that is considered to be lower by the members of a higher caste is considered as making for a ritualistic impurity and a stigma which must be expiated by a religious act. (Weber 1978b: 933)

Weber viewed the development of castes as an extreme consequence of status stratification, likely to arise only when the differences between status groups were "held to be ethnic" (ibid.). The qualification vis-à-vis "ethnic differences" as such stems from the fact, that, for Weber, ethnicity was a matter of belief, not blood relationship, and ethnic group cohesion depended on commonly held beliefs, rather than common social action.[3] Practices such as the exclusion of exogamous marriage and social intercourse, frequently used to uphold the belief in the blood relationship between members of an ethnic group, were also characteristic of caste situations such as had historically crystallised around the belief of the ethnic distinction of the Jews or other "pariah peoples". Thus, if the modern proletariat was the most important example of a class situation derived from the structure of the concrete economic order, the Jews were the outstanding historical example of a caste situation developed out of status closure. Decisive for the caste condition, and especially telling in the case of pariah peoples, was the fact that the caste structure bestowed more status honour on the privileged ethnic group and relegated others to subordinated positions in a systematic and hierarchical fashion. Instead, mere ethnic group segregation allowed each ethnic group to continue cultivating a belief in its status honour as the highest one. Ethnic distinctions thus became functional distinctions within a political association:

> A status segregation grown into a caste differs in its structure from a mere ethnic segregation: the caste structure transforms the horizontal and unconnected coexistences of ethnically segregated groups into a vertical social hierarchy of super- and subordination. Correctly formulated: a comprehensive association integrates the ethnically divided communities into one political unit. (Weber 1978b: 934)

Apart from their objective impact on the social structures in their respective cultural contexts, Weber considered these distinct principles of social differentiation, linked to their corresponding religious background, to have decisively influenced

---

3   Further into *Economy and Society*, Weber defined ethnic groups according to the very criterion of belief in a common origin (see below).

the development of rational, industrial capitalism. Thus, in his view, the hereditary caste system in India, resulting in a ritualistic segregation of the professions, had undermined guild associations and prevented the emergence of a citizenry and urban community paralleling those of the Western medieval cities (Weber 1978b: 1227). Similarly, the Jews' "pariah people" status in part accounted for Judaism's failure to develop into either a world-conquering "political" religion like Islam, or an ascetic salvation religion involved in actively reshaping the world, as strands of Christianity had (Weber 1978b: 1203f.; Schluchter 1988: 94).

Just as the emergence of closed castes was only an extreme form of ethnic group segregation, the development of status groups from ethnic segregation was not the rule, either. Rather, given the prevalence of class over status stratification during his own time, as well as the economic component of the development of exclusive lifestyles, Weber thought status group formation to be more often the result of class situations than of either political membership or the subjective belief in ethnic or racial commonality.

While classes belonged to the economic order and status groups to the social order, they constantly influenced one another as well as the overarching legal order of society, which in turn influenced them. Instead, parties, oriented toward influencing social action regardless of its (economic, social, or mixed content), would frequently recruit their following from class or status situations, as well as from a mixture of the two. They thus belonged to the political order and as such, their social action always involved "groups [*Gemeinschaften*] that have an associational character, that is, some rational order and a staff of persons available who are ready to enforce it" (Weber 1978b: 938). On account of being – unlike both status groups and classes – premised on association (*Vergesellschaftung*) for any type of social action, parties were therefore communities par excellence, whose structures differed according to the type of communal action (*Gemeinschaftshandeln*) they struggled to influence as well as according to whether the community was stratified by status or by classes.[4]

The fact that classes, status groups, and parties "presuppose a larger association, especially the framework of a polity, does not mean that they are confined to it. On the contrary, at all times it has been the order of the day that such association (even when it aims at the use of military force in common) reaches beyond the

---

4   The emphasis Weber placed on the community character of parties is largely lost in the authorised English translation, in which the terms "Gemeinschaft", "Vergesellschaftung", and "Gemeinschaftshandeln" are rendered by the seemingly unrelated "group", "association", and "social action", respectively. A closer rendering of Weber's emphasis would have to read: "As over against the actions of classes and status groups, for which this is not necessarily the case, party-oriented *community action* always involves an *associative relationship*. […] Parties are, therefore, only possible within *communities*, which in turn bear some kind of *associational character*, that is, some rational order and a staff of persons available who are ready to enforce it" (emphases added). For different translations of these three terms and the arguments behind them, see the corresponding entries in Swedberg 2005.

160   *Global Inequalities Beyond Occidentalism*

state boundaries" (Weber 1978b: 939). However, in Weber's view, this was valid for political factions in ancient Greece just as much as for those in medieval Italy and for nineteenth-century associations such as the socialist workers. Accordingly, there was nothing specifically modern about supranational forms of the distribution of power, nor had the European encounter with the non-West(ern) operated any significant change in the scope of such distribution from a regionally Western to a globally encompassing system of stratification. Rather, the onset of modernity had brought about an internal shift within the already existing types of stratification – from the predominance of status to the predominance of class.

Ethnic Groups (Ethnische Gemeinschaften)

Much like in the case of Marx, although by far not as virulently, Weber has been reproached with having provided the wrong prognosis on the trajectory of social change. Neither the massive bureaucratisation, the reign of formal rationality, nor social ossification came about as predicted in *The Protestant Ethic.* Weber's assessment of race and ethnicity as status categories that would disappear in the course of a modern self-identification increasingly based on class has often been viewed as belonging in the same category of wrong prognosis.

The source to which this interpretation is primarily traced back is the chapter entitled "Ethnic Groups" in the English translation of *Economy and Society*, which has long been considered to represent Weber's conclusive stance on the issues of ethnicity and race alike. In light of recent scholarship on the manuscripts that Marianne Weber edited and published as *Economy and Society*, it has however been argued that it is improbable that Weber would have even agreed with its publication (Mommsen 2005, Banton 2007). Although it was made available to an English-speaking public much later than Weber's sociology of religion, especially the *Protestant Ethic*, and enjoyed much less attention than the former for a considerable period of time,[5] Weber's chapter on ethnic groups left an indelible mark on both the sociology and the social anthropology of ethnicity and race in the twentieth century (Fenton 2003: 62).

Famously, for Weber, neither race nor ethnic membership by themselves constituted communities (*Gemeinschaften*), but both could facilitate community-building (*Vergemeinschaftung*) when subjectively *perceived* as common traits on account of shared physical features, customs, or a shared past. His definition of ethnic groups accordingly read:

---

5 At least in the English-speaking world, Weber was, as late as the mid-1980s, primarily known "for his general theory of social action and for specific theories of stratification, organizations, authority, power, and religion" (see Jackson 1983), and far less for his theory of ethnicity. Its subsequent recuperation remains partial, paying too little attention to Weber's early works and, to this day, fraught with problems deriving from anachronistic or plainly wrong translations (see below).

The West vs. the Rest   161

> We shall call "ethnic groups" those human groups that entertain a subjective
> belief in their common descent because of similarities of external habitus or of
> customs or both, or because of memories of colonization and migration; this
> belief must be important for the propagation of group formation; conversely,
> it does not matter whether or not an objective blood relationship exists.
> Ethnic membership (*Gemeinsamkeit*) differs from the kinship group precisely
> by being a presumed identity, not a group defined by concrete social action
> (*Gemeinschaftshandeln*), like the latter (Weber 1978a: 389)"

Even in the absence of an objective common descent, the belief in group affinity
on the basis of race or ethnic membership could thus lead to the formation of
political communities and even persist after such communities disintegrated.
Likewise, the existence or absence of intermarriage between different "racial" or
"ethnic" groups was, more often than not, due to social closure around "ethnic
honour" – which Weber considered to be closely related to status honour – rather
than to biological differences:

> 'Pure' anthropological types are often a secondary consequence of such closure:
> examples are sects (as in India) as well as pariah peoples, that means, groups that
> are socially despised yet wanted as neighbors because they have monopolized
> indispensable skills. (Weber 1978a: 386)

Similarities between membership in ethnic groups such as "pariah peoples" and
racial groups such as "Negroes" in the United States were therefore more directly
pertinent to Weber's thesis that group formation is contingent upon common
subjective beliefs than are differences between the two. Weber therefore never
distinguished between race and ethnic group, other than noting that excessively
heterogeneous "racial qualities" of members of a group could effectively limit
the belief in their common ethnicity. Instead, he stressed the importance of status
stratification through honour, that he saw as underlying both ethnic and racial
group formation, by using the example of the "one-drop rule" in the US:

> In the United States the smallest admixture of Negro blood disqualifies a person
> unconditionally, whereas very considerable admixtures of Indian blood do not.
> Doubtlessly, it is important that Negroes appear esthetically even more alien
> than Indians, but it remains very significant that Negroes were slaves and hence
> disqualified in the status hierarchy. The conventional *connubium* is far less
> impeded by anthropological differences than by status differences, that means,
> differences due to socialization *(anerzogene Unterschiede)* and upbringing.
> (Weber 1978a: 386f.)

Despite this and other references to the influence of the former slave condition
upon an individual's position in the modern status (i.e., racial) hierarchy, the
relationship between racism, colonialism, and slavery did not enter into Weber's

162 *Global Inequalities Beyond Occidentalism*

conceptualisation of racial or ethnic communities. Instead, he illustrated the compelling notion that memories of colonisation and migration underpinned group formation either through the experience of the colonisers[6] or that of voluntary migration that did not result in disqualification in the status hierarchy, such as in the case of (white) German-Americans. The shared experience of being colonised or enslaved is completely absent from the theorisation of racial and ethnic communities. Thus, Weber's examples bespeak merely one side in the power differential that gave rise to the status hierarchy: the white, European, male one. As such, the notion of group formation through memories of colonisation or migration remains unconnected to his argument that "racial antipathy" in the US was socially determined by the whites' tendency to monopolise social power and status, as well as to the example of patriarchal rule in the context of his discussion of the *connubium* – in which the father could grant equal rights to children born by a slave mother (Weber 1978a: 386).[7] His focus therefore lies on supplying a universally valid definition of ethnic differentiation as a form of status stratification using examples from a variety of historical contexts rather than on offering a historically informed analysis of the emergence of specific racial and ethnic groups. This approach is therefore consistent both with his relegation of slaves to a *status group* of low social honour (rather than to a lower *class*) and with his treatment of ethnic groups as characteristic of societies with a low degree of rationalisation, as opposed to the rationally organised and potentially more class-based societies of the West:

> If rationally regulated action is not widespread, almost any association, even the most rational one, creates an overarching communal consciousness; this takes the form of a brotherhood on the basis of the belief in common ethnicity [auf der Basis "ethnischen" Gemeinschaftsglaubens]. As late as the Greek city state, even the most arbitrary divisions of the polis became for the member an association with at least a common cult and often a common fictitious ancestor [...] It does not follow, therefore, that the Greek polis was actually or originally a tribal or lineage state, but that ethnic fictions were a sign of the rather low degree of rationalization of Greek political life. Conversely, it is a symptom of the greater rationalization of Rome that its old schematic subdivisions (curiae) took on religious importance, with a pretense to ethnic origin to only a small degree. (Weber 1978a: 389f.)

---

6   A standpoint with which Weber had already dealt in detail in 1894. See his article on the colonists in Argentina in Weber 1993: 286–303 and below.

7   In a similar vein, Michael Banton (2007: 24) has noted that "Weber's statement that belief in inherited difference creates a group fitted the circumstances of the whites in the United States South better than those of blacks, whose feelings of belonging together stemmed not from any attempt to monopolise social power but from another group's success in doing so. Group formation entailed a rejection of those not qualified for membership".

Consequently, the belief in common ethnicity belongs, together with irrational (or less rational) social action and the status order, to traditional social arrangements and forms of authority. Weber's definition of ethnicity has accordingly been found in line both with his theory of social action and with his typology of forms of domination: Ethnic groups that engaged primarily in "communal social action" based on feelings of belonging were characteristic of the status order under "traditional rule", whereas class members who engaged in "associative social action" grounded in rational economic interests were typical of forms of "rational rule" (Jackson 1983:10f.). Weber defined charismatic domination based on charismatic action in opposition to both the traditional and the rational types of rule. However, he pointed out that the process of routinisation of charisma into either one of the two led to "charisma of office" (*Amtscharisma*) in the rational order and to "hereditary charisma" (*Erbcharisma*) in the traditional one, i.e., to legitimacy through the holding of an office vs. legitimacy through the belief in the importance of blood relationship, respectively (Weber 1978a: 249ff.). The most important example of the former is the transmission of priestly charisma, which, especially in Catholic Christianity, allowed the bureaucratisation of the church by separating the powers of the office from the individual qualifications of the priest. The latter is best illustrated in Weber's view by the Indian caste system, the Japanese lineage state before bureaucratisation, and China before the rationalisation in the territorial states, all of which replaced the principle of qualification through achievement by the one of qualification through descent (Weber 1978a: 253f.). Thus, despite Weber's repeated disavowal of a staged theory of social evolution with respect to forms of social stratification, types of social action, or of forms of legitimate domination, it is tribal and lineage states and their corresponding ethnic fictions, communal social action, and traditional or hereditary charismatic forms of rule that repeatedly feature as examples of pre-rational, pre-modern social contexts. They are therefore examples of the larger tendency in Weber's work, in which non-Western contexts lend themselves to being associated with those aspects of Weber's theory that "emphasize the past" (Jackson 1983: 11). Modernisation theorists would later abstract from Weber's recurring historical examples the implicit contrast between modern Occidental rationality and its premodern counterparts within and outside the Western world and develop it into a clear-cut dichotomy between modern and traditional societies clearly located at different stages of development and moments in time.

His notion of social closure was in turn developed into a more encompassing model for the analysis of relations of domination and resistance that awarded an important role to the reactions of excluded groups (Parkin 1971). Conceptualised accordingly as reciprocal collective strategies of "mobilizing power in order to enhance or defend a group's share of rewards or resources" (Murphy 1988: 10), closure on the part of dominant group aimed at the monopolisation of opportunities, privileges and resources, while usurpation on the part of excluded groups sought the reduction of the share of resources claimed by dominant groups and the questioning of their privileges. Although the model explicitly linked closure and

164   *Global Inequalities Beyond Occidentalism*

usurpation to the distribution of power and to social stratification, it pivoted on the state as a decisive factor in struggles for social closure and thus only tangentially addressed processes of stratification at the global level. Thus, when discussing ethnic inequality, Frank Parkin did take a global perspective on historical instances of its emergence, yet only in order to make a point about the role of the state in creating or reinforcing processes of closure *within* its jurisdiction: "In all known instances where racial, religious, linguistic, or sex characteristics have been seized upon for closure purposes the group in question has already at some time been defined as legally inferior by the state. Ethnic subordination, to take the commonest case, has normally occurred as a result of territorial conquest or the forced migration of populations creating a subcategory of second-class citizens within the nation-state" (Parkin 1979: 96). Notions of social closure that more systematically address the global dimension would emerge in the context of theories of citizenship in the 1990s (see Chapter 6).

"From the Standpoint of Germanism": The Polish Question, the "Negro" Question, and the Nation[8]

Weber's analysis of ethnic communities has been on the one hand hailed for explicitly opposing biological explanations of the origins of ethnicity and thus anticipating the later literature on race and ethnicity as social constructs. On the other hand, it has been criticised for insufficiently addressing the historical origins of group formation as well as for disregarding the importance of multiple group memberships for the cohesion of a community (Banton 2007). Recognising the text's limitations however did not prevent later scholars from considering it the "canonical treatment of ethnicity" (Scaff 1998: 89, Stender 2000: 76) on which further research on the phenomenon could and should build.[9] Its prominence notwithstanding, the chapter was in fact far from exhausting Weber's views on

---

8   This is a revised version of an article initially published as "From the Standpoint of Germanism: A Postcolonial Critique of Weber's Theory of Race and Ethnicity" in *Political Power and Social Theory* 24, pp. 55–80. Copyright is owned by Emerald Group Publishing.

9   As Stender (2000: 68n8, 9) pointed out in his broad overview of ethnicity research in the US and Germany, the word "ethnicity" was first used by W. Lloyd Warner and Paul S. Lunt in 1941 in the first volume of the "Yankee City Series" and only subsequently entered Germany as a translation of the US term – which however was itself traced back to Herder's *Volksgeist* theory. This conceptual history is important in clarifying the fact that Weber himself neither coined nor ever used the word "ethnicity" (*Ethnizität*), which did not exist in his time, but referred instead to "ethnic commonality" (*Gemeinsamkeit*), "ethnic groups", and "ethnic communities", as explained above. In the English-language editions of his chapter on ethnic and race groups, first published in the late 1960s, these terms were nevertheless translated as "ethnicity", which not only confuses the term's history, but also obscures Weber's more differentiated treatment of the phenomena it encompassed. See also the entry on "ethnicity" in Swedberg (2005: 92).

race and ethnicity, as one of the earliest overviews convincingly showed (Manasse 1947). Most scholarship in the latter half of the twentieth century has however tended to overlook the bulk of Weber's statements on the issue and to concentrate instead on its succinct treatment in *Economy and Society*. That the entry on "ethnic groups" in the Max Weber dictionary should point to the existence of diametrically opposed views in the work of Weber himself is therefore not self-explaining: "While Weber took a stance against anti-Semitism and racial prejudices in general, it is common to find ethnic slurs in his early social science writings on the role of the Poles in Germany" (Swedberg 2005: 92).

How are Weber's views in the chapter compatible with ethnic slurs in his early work? And, if the latter have largely been left out of the canonical treatment of ethnicity following Weber, should they be seen as relevant for the Weberian tradition of social inequality research?

At stake are the following landmark dates: First, in the 1890s, Weber delivered a series of papers on the agrarian economy of the German East, in which he described the growing immigration of Catholic Polish labourers to West Prussia as the demise of the more developed Protestant civilisation of the German peasants before the physically and mentally lesser "Slav race". In his conclusions, he called for a closing of the state frontier to immigration from the East as a means of preserving German culture (Weber 1980). A second important moment is 1904. Shortly after having concluded the first part of *The Protestant Ethic and the Spirit of Capitalism*, Max Weber travelled to the United States, where he lectured on the topic of rural communities and modern economic development. There, he argued that, besides the economic contradictions occasioned by the advance of capitalism, the most pressing social problems of the US South were "essentially ethnic" (Weber 1998). Finally, at the meeting of the German Sociological Association in Frankfurt in 1910, Max Weber challenged Alfred Ploetz and his biologically determinist theory of race, using the example of the United States and arguing that race relations cannot be explained in terms of inborn racial qualities, but solely through cultural and economic factors.

Usually, the contradiction between the earlier and the later statements is resolved by Weber's biographers and reviewers by assessing his thought in terms of an evolution from an anti-Polish nationalism in the 1890s to a liberal and social pluralist anti-racism by the early 1900s (Manasse 1947, Tribe 1980, Kalberg 2005: 294n1). In particular, Weber's acquaintance with W.E.B. Du Bois during his trip to the United States and their subsequent exchanges, which included the publication of an article by Du Bois on racial prejudice as the "new spirit of caste" in the *Archiv für Sozialwissenschaft und Sozialpolitik*, are credited with a threefold influence on Weber's work: on Weber's distinction between class and status, on his analysis of "caste situation" as an extreme consequence of status stratification, as well as on his interpretation of the race element in the Hindu caste system (Manasse 1947: 200, Scaff 1998: 89). In the same vein, several authors have even assumed a "basic reversal" of Weber's political stance toward Poland, coupled with a move away from his early Social-Darwinist position on racial differences

166   *Global Inequalities Beyond Occidentalism*

(Mommsen 1974: 53; Roth 1993; Roth 2000: 129; Vernik 2011: 178). In Japan, where research on Max Weber has been exceptionally prolific, the shift has even been interpreted as a full-fledged conversion from the racist Weber of power politics to a humanist, unemotional Weber (Konno 2004: 22). Alternatively, a growing literature on the subject sees the evolution of Weber's thought as proceeding from a specific anti-Polish nationalism – which used religion as a proxy for race – in his early writings, to a cultural and economic racism cloaked as a comparative sociology of religion in his later work, especially as related to India and China (Abraham 1991; Zimmerman 2006, 2010; for China see Steinmetz 2010).

As in the case of Marx, the purpose of the present analysis is not to decide upon the truth value of any one of the available interpretations, but to expound the entire gamut of Weber's views on race and ethnicity as well as their relationship to his general sociological theory in order to assess their contribution to a research agenda for an analysis of inequalities at the global level. To this end, Weber's views on the three issues mentioned above will be checked for common denominators as well as reverberations with his wider argument.

The 1890s: Suppressing Polonism

As an astute critic has noted, Weber constructed his model of inequality relations at the very moment that the rise of imperial Germany rendered many of them obsolete (Wenger, 1980:. 373). The medieval estates were disappearing; industrialisation attracted large flows of labour migrants from the European East; and the local labour force was ever more proletarianised. European colonialism in Africa prompted an increased awareness of "the other" that translated as the infamous anthropological distinction between European *Kulturvölker* (culture peoples) and colonised *Naturvölker* (nature peoples), in turn associated with different degrees of humanity. Growing anti-Semitism was reflected in allegedly scientific support of racial concepts of German national identity as distinct from a Jewish race (Zimmerman, 2001: 242f.). With Germany's unification in 1871, existing anti-Catholic sentiment was institutionalised in Bismarck's *Kulturkampf* ("culture struggle") policies, meant to restrict the power of the Catholic Church and help define Germany as a secular state. As a result, the increasing presence of Catholic Poles in Eastern Germany was officially countered through the resettlement of German farmers in the region. The conservative Verein für Sozialpolitik, which Weber joined in 1888, had until then supported the Prussian state's resettlement policies only on class terms, that is, as a means of preventing the further proletarianisation of German farmers and an impending social revolution. It was Max Weber whose work in the Verein first made ethnic and cultural explanations central to the discussions of the Prussian East and who warned of the "danger of assimilation" from the standpoint of "reason of state" rather than on economic grounds (Zimmerman 2006: 61; 2010: 100ff.).

The West vs. the Rest   167

These views subsequently made the subject of other works during the same period. Central to Weber's controversial[10] inaugural lecture at the University of Freiburg (1895), entitled "Nationality in Economic Policy", was the question "What social strata are the repositories of Germanism (*Deutschtum*) and Polonism (*Polentum*) in the country districts?" (Weber 1980: 429). While he never provided a definition of either term, the systematic land purchase by the German state, the settlement of German farmers on Polish-owned land, as well as the closing of the German frontier to Polish workers had been part of Bismarck's official program of "Germanisation" of the Eastern provinces up to 1890, in which suppressing "Polonism" was an explicit goal. Weber was therefore employing known terms in order to address a known problem: the decline of the German landworker population in the face of Polish settlement on small farms and of the growing imports of cheap Polish labour on large estates. What was new, both with respect to the general discussion and to Weber's earlier treatments of the issue, was phrasing these *economic* developments in *ethnic* and *cultural* terms derived from each of the groups' religious affiliation: Since the census data available to him only differentiated by religion, not nationality, Weber interpreted the numbers indicating the decline of the Protestant population relative to the Catholic one to mean that it must be German day-labourers who move out of the estates on good soil, and it is Polish peasants who proliferate on low-quality land.[11] He traced this tendency back to "*a lower expectation of living standards*, in part physical, in part mental, which the Slav race either possesses as a gift from nature or has acquired through breeding in the course of its past history" (Weber 1980: 432). Although the Polish peasants, unlike the seasonal migrant workers, were German citizens at the time, Weber described the situation as an economic struggle "between nationalities" (1980: 428), ultimately decided through a selection process in favour of the nationality with the greater "ability to adapt" itself to given economic and social conditions. From this perspective, the Polish peasants living off subsistence production, i.e., not affected by price fluctuations on the market, were better adapted than the economically "more gifted" German farmers:

> The small Polish peasant in East Germany is a type far removed from the bustling peasant owner of a dwarf property, whom one may see here in the well-favoured valley of the Rhine as he forges links with the towns via greenhouse cultivation and market-gardening. The small Polish peasant in East Germany gains more land because he as it were eats the very grass from off of it, he gains

---

10 Although Max Weber himself has later expressed misgivings about aspects of his lecture, they did not refer to his upholding of the German nation, which is the focus of the following summary (see Abraham 1991: 47, Roth 1993).

11 Weber was of course aware of the methodological short-circuit inherent in using religion as a proxy for nationality, but decided that "only approximate accuracy" is good enough in the case of West Prussia, where religious affiliation "coincides within a few per cent with nationality" (1980: 429).

168   *Global Inequalities Beyond Occidentalism*

> not *despite* but *on account of* the low level of his physical and intellectual habits
> of life. (Weber 1980: 434)

Weber thus uses the Social Darwinist terminology of "adaptation", "selection process", and "race breeding" popular at the time in order to explain that a group's economic advance did not necessarily correlate with the "political maturity" needed in order to build up "the nation's power". Thus, in his view, Polish settlement and labour migration – allowed by Bismarck's follower Caprivi – led to the rise of "unviable Slav hunger colonies" (1980: 435) and drove out German agricultural labourers, instead of steering in the direction of the emergence of a strong proletariat on the model of England. The wish to protect "the German character of the East" (1980: 437) from such tendencies in turn led Weber to formulate his policy demands "from the standpoint of Germanism" and uphold "a German standard of value" against the international standards of social justice he saw political economy as promoting:

> The science of political economy is a *political* science. It is a servant of politics, not the day-to-day politics of the individuals and classes who happen to be ruling at a particular time, but the lasting power-political interests of the nation. And for us the *national state* is not, as some people believe, an indeterminate entity [...], but the temporal power-organization of the nation, and in this national state the ultimate standard of value for economic policy is "reason of state". (Weber 1980: 438)

Speaking at the close of the nineteenth century as a German economic theorist, a member of the bourgeois classes, and a son of a National Liberal member of the Prussian Diet,[12] Weber considered the "reason of state" in the case of German economic policy to be "the amount of elbowroom" conquered for the economic well-being of "the race of the future". He therefore called for the renewed closing of the Eastern frontier to Polish migrants, as under Bismarck, and for a state policy of systematic colonisation by German peasants on suitable land as a means of preserving German culture.

The same logic underlies Weber's 1894 article on Argentina's rising cereal exports after the devaluation of the Argentinean peso in 1889/90. In arguing both against the free trade doctrine and the "entirely unrealistic assumption of the international equality of cultures" (Weber 1993: 302), Weber insisted that Argentina's low production costs could to a great extent be traced back to the very low wages and cheap food that planters offered the "nomadic barbarians" that they hired for seasonal work. According to this low living standard, these workers "appear when the time for demand comes and disappear afterwards or

---

12   For an assessment of the significance of Weber's family history for a broader understanding of Weber's intellectual and political concerns, see Guenther Roth's 1993 review of volume 4 of the Max Weber Gesamtausgabe (Roth 1993).

after having drunk away their wages", while "in terms of housing [they] only know clay huts" (292). Economic competition with colonial economies such as the Argentinean one would therefore require *lowering* the level of German social organisation and culture in order to match that of Argentina's "half-savage trash" (129). Weber saw this very phenomenon as occurring with the Polish immigration in East Elbia:

> Should we be able and willing to work just as "cheaply", our rural workers would have to approach this type as well, and we can indeed find the first manifestations of this change if we observe the itinerant workforce and the import of Poles in the East. Briefly, the fact is that we are an old sedentary civilized people (*Kulturvolk*) on densely populated land with an old, highly distinctive and therefore sensitive social organization and typical national cultural necessities, which make it impossible for us to compete with these economies. (Weber 1993: 298f.)

Inherent in Weber's defence of the standpoint of Germanism in the 1890s is therefore a roundabout theory of ethnicity premised on the inequality of the cultural levels and the attitudes toward work of different "nationalities". As such, it is closer to a political position – against any type of internationalism in general, and against socialism in particular – than to a full-fledged theoretical apparatus. As Guenther Roth (1993: 152) has noted, Weber even turned against close collaborators when they "failed to bend in his direction": At the 1896 founding meeting of the National Social party, Weber cautioned its founder, Friedrich Naumann, that the new party's political platform required adopting a *national* stance with respect to the Polish question, instead of denouncing its promoters, as Naumann had done in *Die Zeit*. On such occasions, his anti-Polish rhetoric went beyond mere Social Darwinistic overtones and acquired racist traits phrased in typical colonial Occidentalist terms: "It has been said that we have degraded the Poles to second-class German citizens. The opposite is the case: We have turned them into human beings in the first place" (Weber 1993: 622). Clearly, Weber was in this case extrapolating from the distinction between *Kulturvölker* as civilised humanity and *Naturvölker* as barbaric humanity that he had explicitly mobilised in reference to the German versus the Argentinean economies (and that was commonly used in nineteenth-century German anthropology to refer to European and colonised peoples, respectively) in order to deny full humanity to populations within Europe. The modern, the civilised and the rational are thereby confined to an even more exclusive space within the European continent, which the imperial imaginary conceived as ending at Germany's eastern border and which I have labelled "heroic Europe" (see Boatcă 2010 and Chapter 7). The same national political position would lead Weber to withdraw from the Pan-German League in 1899, arguing that its immigration-friendly policies towards Polish workers were subservient to agrarian capitalists (Roth 1993: 159, Zimmerman 2006: 64).

The 1900s: The Problem of the Colour-Line

Weber's views on the matter had largely remained unchanged by the time he and Marianne Weber undertook their trip to the United States a few years later. Weber would put them to extensive use in his 1904 talk at the St. Louis World's Fair on the topic of rural society and modern economic development. While claiming that capitalism has different effects in old civilised countries with a dense population and strong rural traditions – such as Germany – than in new countries with vast amounts of land and no old aristocracy – such as the United States, Weber predicted that the same set of circumstances would eventually affect the latter as well. When that moment came, Germany's experience could therefore be a valuable lesson for the United States, in particular as regards policies addressing the rural social question, which, according to Weber, "cannot be cut with the sword, as was the slave question" (Weber 1998: 241). Expressed as an economic struggle between "two nations, Germans and Slavonians", Germany's rural social question was at the same time a cultural one:

> While thus under the pressure of conjuncture the frugal Slavonian small farmer gains territory from the German, the advance of culture toward the east, during the Middle Ages, founded upon the superiority[13] of the older and higher culture, has changed completely to the contrary under the dominion of the capitalistic principle of the "cheaper hand". (Weber 1998: 241f.)

That the absence of rural traditions and of an old aristocracy in the United States made the effects of capitalism stronger there than in Europe, did not, in Weber's view, prevent both American and German cultures from facing the same threat in the long run – economic competition from culturally "inassimilable" elements. As early as 1893, Weber had argued that migrant labour was less of a danger to German culture in the case of the importation of Chinese *coolies*, with whom Germans would not assimilate, than in the case of immigrant Polish workers. As he claimed in his Freiburg address soon thereafter, Poles tended to "soak up" national minorities, leading to the decline of Protestantism and the advance of Catholicism (Weber 1980: 432). With respect to its effects on the standard of living of civilised countries, the "Negro question" in the United States therefore paralleled the "Polish question" in Germany and would be additionally aggravated by Eastern European immigration to North America:

---

13   Weber's talk is not available in the original German, so his exact choice of terms is uncertain, but the context seems to confirm the translator's use of "superiority" as appropriate. Weber has employed its German equivalents *Überlegenheit* and *überlegen* in various comparative discussions, as in both his sociology of religion and law (e.g. 1922: 320 for the superiority of Christianity; 1922: 510 for the superiority of Anglo-Saxon law).

The West vs. the Rest 171

also the number of negro farms is growing and the migration from the country into the cities. If, thereby, the expansive power of the Anglo-Saxon-German settlement of the rural districts and, besides, the number of children of the old, inborn population are on the wane and if, at the same time, the enormous immigration of uncivilized elements from eastern Europe grows, also here a rural population might arise which could not be assimilated by the historically transmitted culture of this country; this population would change forever the standard of the United States and would gradually form a community of a quite different type from the great creation of the Anglo-Saxon spirit. (Weber 1998: 242)

In which direction Weber saw this "change of standard" to be pointing was spelt out in his 1906 article on the Russian Revolution, in which he spoke of how the "tremendous immigration of European, especially east European people into the United States, […] erodes the old democratic traditions there" (Weber 1989: 272). As late as 1906, Weber thus used similar racial stereotypes as in his early work on Polish labourers, only this time extrapolated to the entire European East, seen as lacking in both civilisation and democratic tradition and as such closer to a colonised *Naturvolk* than to an European *Kulturvolk* in the imperial imaginary.

The parallel with the "Negro question" would in turn be detailed in his study of the "psychophysics of work" in the context of a larger project on industrial labour in Germany that the *Verein für Sozialpolitik* undertook in 1908/09. The clearest proof of the relevance of "racial differences" for an assessment of the capacity to perform industrial work, Weber maintained, was the employment of "Negroes" in the North American textile industry (*"textilindustriellen Verwendung der Neger"*, Weber 1995: 110). That race should be the determining factor in such "extreme cases", however, did not mean that it could incontestably account for less conspicuous differences, such as those between ethnic and regional groups in Europe:

> The neurotic disqualification of American Negroes for certain tasks in the textile industry is easy to assess; but the infinitely finer, yet for the rentability of the respective workers decisive differences, which can be observed in European manufactures, are not. (Weber 1995: 238)[14]

Although he rejected the biological explanations that experimental psychology provided for the work capacities of various ethnic groups, Weber did not question the existence of ethnic differences in principle. Indeed, he assumed they were the rule in the case of Blacks in the United States and he would later repeatedly mention "the Negroes'" alleged unsuitability for factory work as "one case in economic history where tangible racial distinctions are present" (Weber 1923, in:

---

14   for a detailed examination of Weber's views on cultural attitudes to work, see Schluchter 2000; for further examples of his treatment of the "Negro question" in this context, see Zimmerman 2006: 67f.

Manasse 1947: 210n41).[15] With respect to the "finer" distinctions within Europe, he instead argued that, rather than *hereditary differences*, the temperament, disciplinability, and psychic constitution necessary for manufacturing work should be analysed as *differences of tradition*. Accordingly, whereas experimental psychology asked whether inherited or achieved characteristics were decisive for labour efficiency in general, economics, before taking into account any biological predispositions, inquired whether the characteristics that affected the different rentability of industrial workers could be traced back to the workers' social and cultural environment, tradition, and upbringing. In Wolfgang Schluchter's words, Weber thus counterposed the question of psychophysical *aptitude* to work to the one of cultural *attitude* to work (Schluchter 2000: 75).

Again, this approach can be seen as thoroughly consistent with the rejection of biological racism and the plea for a cultural and economic explanation of racial inequalities that Weber espoused in the famous debate with Alfred Ploetz one year after completing the study on the psychophysics of labour. A physician, biologist, and staunch Social Darwinist, whose work would later prove one of the main sources for Nazi eugenic policies, Alfred Ploetz had recently founded the journal *Archiv für Rassen und Gesellschaftsbiologie und Gesellschaftshygiene* and the German Association for Racial Hygiene (Deutsche Gesellschaft für Rassenhygiene). He had joined the German Sociological Association following the invitation of Ferdinand Tönnies (Weindling, 1989: 140). Against Ploetz, Weber argued that no sociologically relevant circumstances could be traced back to hereditary racial qualities, and gave the example of "the contrast between white and Negro in North America" (1971: 37). While hereditary qualities most likely were "strong factors at work", Weber insisted that the emergence of the unequal social standing of the two racial groups was primarily socially determined: "if it were possible for us today to impregnate persons from birth with black colour, these persons – in a society of whites – would be constantly in a precarious and peculiar situation" (1971: 37f.). At the same time, the equivalent view that Native Americans enjoyed a relatively higher social status in the United States than Blacks not because of superior innate characteristics, but because they had not been enslaved – a view which Weber would later express in *Economy and Society* – strikingly paralleled

---

15   In noting that Weber had reiterated the same view in the lectures he had given in Munich in 1919–20, Manasse chose to give Weber the benefit of the doubt in spite of the available counter-evidence: "I doubt whether these sentences are authentic in this form or, at least, whether they represent Weber's opinion at the time he was lecturing on economic history in Munich [...], also because I hesitate to charge Weber with an inconsistency in his notion of "race qualities" that *lasted for only a few decades*, at most" (1947: 210, emphasis added). Manasse's analysis is thereby not only one of the earliest overviews of Weber's views on race, but also the first overtly apologetic interpretation of his racist assertions, intent on proving that "Weber subjected his original intuitive conception of race to an ever-sharpening criticism", which resulted in "the almost complete destruction of his original conception" (Manasse 1947: 221).

The West vs. the Rest 173

the logic of a group's "ability to adapt" to social and economic circumstances that Weber had used in his analysis of the Polish workers. Just like the Poles, and in keeping with the claim that they were not fit for industrial work, the "Negroes" were viewed as better adapted to lower forms of labour than "Indians"; as in the case of "the Slav race", Weber left open the question of whether this condition was a matter of biology or of cultural custom:

> the reason constantly formulated by the whites for their different evaluation of the Indians is: "They did not submit to slavery" [...] Indeed, insofar as their specific qualities are the reason for their not having been slaves, it was their *inability to endure* the quantity of work demanded by the plantation capitalists – which the Negro could accomplish. Whether this was a consequence of purely hereditary peculiarities or of their traditions is doubtful. (Weber 1971: 38, emphasis added)

Incidentally, a biological argument would have been far more accurate in this case, since, as historians have long documented, among the reasons why millions of Africans had been traded into slavery on American plantations had been their immunity to many contagious European diseases, acquired through regular contacts with European traders in Africa since the fifteenth century (Curtin 1969). Resorting to a cultural argument to suggest that Africans were better fitted to lower labour forms than Native Americans therefore means implicitly mobilising the colonial racist tropes that Orientalised the native populations in the American colonies, yet placed Black Africans on an even lower rung of the racial hierarchy.

If, therefore, Weber wrote to W.E.B. Du Bois that "'the colour-line' problem will be the paramount problem of the time to come, here and everywhere in the world" (Weber 1904, in Scaff 1998: 90), apparently echoing Du Bois' own famous dictum that "the problem of the Twentieth Century is the problem of the color line", it is highly unlikely that they meant the same thing.[16] In light of the analogies Weber had repeatedly drawn to the situation of immigrant labour in Germany, his much-quoted statement about his 1904 visit to the United States – "the Americans are a wonderful people, and only the Negro question and the terrible immigration form the big black clouds" (quoted in Marianne Weber 1988: 302) seems a better indicator of his concerns: While Weber was an explicit and outspoken opponent of biological racism, his concern with "the power-political interests of the nation" consistently led him to check for economic and cultural "threats" to these national interests, such as immigrant workers and religious Others, and to treat them as culturally separate, inassimilable (and as such undesirable) social groups, thus using culturally racist arguments throughout. In the context of defining world power as

---

16 A detailed study of the possible intersections between Max Weber's and W.E.B. Du Bois' approaches on "the Negro question" against the background of Weber's early engagement with the Polish question in Germany has recently been undertaken by Chandler (2007).

"the power to determine the character of culture in the future" (Weber 1994: 76) during World War I, what Weber had described in his Freiburg lecture as the "standpoint of Germanism" would be restated as "the standpoint of those cultural values that have been entrusted to a people" (1994: 75) and which is the duty of a *Machtstaat* (power state) to protect. Insofar as Weber considered other countries to be *Machtstaaten*, great military states with a cultural "responsibility before history", this standpoint equally applied to them. Seeing, as he did, the problem of the colour line as paramount everywhere, was in this context an acknowledgment of the parallel threats that Weber saw both Germany and the United States as facing – not a plea for the social emancipation of Blacks in the US, as the one formulated by W.E.B. Du Bois. Thus, it is precisely because the threat Weber perceived in both cases did not come from a biologically distinct race, but from a lowering of cultural standards, that he could dismiss as unfounded the "one-drop rule" for determining race membership and condemn the anti-Black racism of the poor whites in the US South, yet refer to Black plantation workers as lesser humans in the same breath: On the one hand, the "numerous half-Negroes, quarter-Negroes and one hundredth-part Negroes whom no non-American can distinguish from whites" that he and Marianne Weber encountered at the Tuskegee Institute[17] were, for him, part of the "educated and often nine-tenths white Negro upper class" (quoted in Weber 1988: 296). On the other hand, what made the Negro question paramount was that, by comparison, "The semi-apes one encounters on the plantations and in the Negro huts of the "Cotton Belt" afford a horrible contrast, but so does the intellectual condition of the whites in the south" (idem). Clearly, Weber considered the second grouping – both uneducated blacks and poor whites – to have more in common with the Polish peasant's "low intellectual habits of life" or the Argentinean seasonal worker's "semi-barbarian" existence in clay huts than either with a Black intellectual like W.E.B. Du Bois – whom he mentioned in the debate with Ploetz as "the most important sociological scholar anywhere in the Southern States in America, with whom no white scholar can compare" (Weber 1973: 312) – or with members of the educated white upper class.

As late as 1917, Weber still championed the standpoint of Germanism underlying the "reason of state" policy – all the more forcefully so given the world war context. Placing the interests of Germanism (*Deutschtum*) above the task of democratisation, upholding both the privilege and the duty of the "master race" (*Herrenvolk*) to engage in world politics,[18] and protecting the Fatherland against "Negroes, Ghurkas and all manner of barbarians who have come from their hiding

---

17 For an elaborate analysis of Tuskegee Institute, see Zimmerman 2006, 2010.

18 "A *nation of masters* (*Herrenvolk*) and only such a nation can and may engage in 'world politics' – has *no* choice in this matter. Democratisation can certainly be obstructed – for the moment – because powerful interests, prejudices and cowardice are allied in opposing it. [...] Certain circles may have an interest in the inevitable political consequences. The Fatherland certainly does not" (Weber 1994: 129). Most commentators agree that Weber's use of the notion of *Herrenvolk* should not be mistaken for the National

places all over the world and who are now gathered at the borders of Germany, ready to lay waste to our country" (Weber 1994: 132) are statements characteristic of Weber's political writings of the period. In the conclusion to his book on Weber and the Polish question, Hajime Konno therefore noted that "observing and judging people from the vantage point of the West seems to have been Weber's lifelong method" (2004: 200, my translation).

Subsequent scholarship has accordingly tended to differentiate between Weber's political and his theoretical writings to the point of juxtaposing his "nationalist politics" to his "cosmopolitan sociology" (Roth 1993: 148). Most of the time, such differentiation was advocated on the basis of Weber's own postulate of value-freedom. However, in view of the particular (and particularistic) standpoint of Germanism that underlies both his theoretical and his political treatment of race and ethnicity – and at the same time belies his methodological postulate – Weber's sociology and politics can be shown to be closely intertwined. As Keith Tribe, calling for a reconstruction of Weber as a theoretician of power-politics, has noted in the 1980 introduction to the English translation of Weber's Freiburg address, "the question of power and the national state is one that retains a central importance until his death. The conditions under which this power is exercised, and the means adopted for the realization of a 'decisive national status' might alter, but the objects of this did not" (Tribe 1980: 422f.). Accordingly, while Weber's approach to the "Negro question" in the United States might not derive in a straight line from his earlier treatment of the Polish question in Germany, one certainly is inextricable from the other, and an awareness of both is needed in order to understand his analysis of the nation (Chandler 2007: 261).

That Weber's sociology should be so clearly indebted to narrowly defined and historically contingent cultural and political values underlying his notion of national identity has been alternatively seen as a reason for either discarding Weber as a classic (Abraham 1991) or re-reading him as a neo-racist (Zimmerman 2006). For an assessment of models of global inequality analysis, the compelling issue instead is ascertaining to what extent the geopolitical and historical contingency of Weber's standpoint has been successfully discarded or productively transformed in culture-theoretical, Weberian approaches to global inequalities.

Socialists' subsequent misuse of Nietzsche's concept, even though it still has clear imperialist connotations. See the corresponding entry in Swedberg 2005: 111.

Chapter 6
Citizenship as Social Closure:
Weberian Perspectives and Beyond

Especially in his section on the city in "Economy and Society", but also at various points in his sociology of religion, Weber had clearly traced the rise of citizenship – viewed as an institutionalised association of an autonomous status group (*Stand*) of individual burghers subject to the same law – back to the ancient Greek polis and the medieval Occidental city (Weber 1978b: 1240). According to him, the revolutionary innovation differentiating the central and northern European cities from all others had been the principle that "city air makes man free", according to which slaves or serfs employed for wages in the city soon became free from obligations to their master as well as legally free. Consequently, in time, status differences between free and unfree city-dwellers gave way to equality of individual citizens before the law. Although this was characteristic of medieval Occidental cities, Weber held, antecedents could be found in ancient Greece and Rome, but also in the Near East and in Russia, where town-dwelling slaves or serfs could purchase their freedom. For Weber, this possibility intensified the economic effort of unfree petty burghers, thus spurring capital accumulation through rational operation in trade or industry. Even more importantly, however, it constituted a preliminary stage in the achievement of political equality:

> The Occidental city thus was already in Antiquity, just like in Russia, a place where the *ascent from bondage to freedom* by means of monetary acquisition was possible. This is even more true for the medieval city, and especially for the medieval inland city. In contrast to all urban known developments elsewhere, the burghers of the Occidental city engaged in status-conscious policies directed toward this goal. (Weber 1978b: 1238, emphasis in the original)

In keeping with Weber's broader research agenda, intent on documenting the uniqueness of the West, his analysis of the city was thus geared toward the finding that the associational character of the Occidental city and the concept of the citizen either never developed in the Orient or existed only in rudiments there (Weber 1978a: 227).

For a long time, the link that Weber had repeatedly established between the emergence of the medieval Occidental city as an association of free citizens and the rise of the rational urban middle class in the West received little attention as an explanation for the development of rational, industrial capitalism. Some authors have suggested that the reason lay in the overemphasis placed on Weber's interpretation of the origin of capitalism in the Protestant ethic. In particular, for Engin Isin, the focus on religious ethics obscured the key role played by the broader and more significant notion that it was citizenship as a specifically Occidental institution that made capitalism possible (Isin 2005: 35). Previous critics had focused on Weber's views on the rationalisation of law and of the state administration as well as on the Protestant ethic as essential differences between Occidental and Oriental societies and cultures more broadly. Instead, Isin (2003: 314) stresses how Weber's very analytical concern with the uniqueness of a type of city consolidated the notion of ontological difference between types and thus turned into "political Orientalism" (Isin 2005). Not incidentally, Edward Said had referred to the use of types as an analytical device and as a way of seeing familiar things in a new light in terms of an "important and methodologically formative cultural force" (Said 1979: 259), which, among other things, had allowed Max Weber entry into the field of classical Orientalists.[1] A methodological critique of the heuristic use of ideal-type constructs had already been formulated by Parsons, who had cautioned that, through ideal-typification, each type (of social phenomena, groups or processes) becomes a unit of analysis in itself, while the systematic relation among units is obscured (Parsons 1966: 218).

In this context, Isin's detailed analysis and critique of Weber's Orientalism (2002b, 2003, 2005, 2013) built on the existing literature on the topic, yet considerably went beyond it. By pointing to both Weber's Orientalism and his unwarranted essentialisation of types of cities (to which he refers with Weber's term, "synoecism"), Isin connects Said's theoretical critique with Parsons' methodological caveat. He therefore zooms in on how Weber's development of a concept of Occidental citizenship through the juxtaposition against a "cluster of absences" in Oriental societies went into the explanation of the success or failure of the emergence of capitalism (Isin 2002b).

From among the five common features that Weber had identified as characteristic of the European city – fortification, market, autonomous justice, associative structure, and autocephaly – many were present in India, China, Judea, and the Middle East, as Weber himself had acknowledged. Yet, as noted above, he considered that it had been the associational character of the Occidental city, modelled on and mediated by the Christian congregation, that had brought forth the modern concept of the citizen (see Isin 2003; Domingues 2005). Since full membership in the ecclesiastic community was the prerequisite for urban citizenship, the fully developed ancient and medieval city of the West was first and foremost a sworn confraternity of individual burghers (Weber 1978b: 1246). According to Weber, the decisive thrust toward confraternisation into a city

---

1 "Although he never thoroughly studied Islam, Weber nevertheless influenced the field considerably, mainly because his notions of type were simply an 'outside' confirmation of many of the canonical theses held by Orientalists, whose economic ideas never extended beyond asserting the Oriental's fundamental incapacity for trade, commerce, and economic rationality" (Said 1979: 259).

corporation had come from Christianity and its unique quality of dissolving clan ties by replacing the ritual character of religious affiliation with a voluntary principle: "by its very nature the Christian congregation was a religious association of individual believers, not a ritual association of clans" (Weber 1978: 1247). As Isin notes, Weber thus traced the key element accounting for the rise of the modern citizenry as far back as early Christianity's overcoming of ritual taboos: "For without commensalism – in Christian terms, without the Lord's Supper – no oathbound fraternity and no medieval urban citizenry would have been possible" (Weber 1917: 37f., quoted in Isin 2003).

Conversely, in the case of Judaism, the absence of commensalism, alongside the ritual exclusion of connubium, had effectively prevented fraternisation between Jews and non-Jews in the medieval cities, resulting in the exclusion of the former from the developing burgher associations. Likewise, for Weber, the persistence of magical or animistic caste or sib constraints and of the corresponding taboos in "the Asian city" had constituted systematic impediments to the development of cities as confraternities of free town-dwellers throughout Asia, and therefore to the emergence of citizenship there. Thus, despite acknowledging similarities between all other aspects of city formation in the West on the one hand and Chinese, Indian, Japanese, or Near Eastern urban settlements on the other, Weber's comparative studies repeatedly concluded that ritual obstacles to confraternisation – stronger in the case of the Indian castes than for the Chinese and Near Eastern sibs – had accounted for the divergence between East and West in the long run. This type of argument still dominates sociological scholarship on the emergence of modern patterns of social stratification as well as of democratic ideals in the West. It can thus be argued that Weber's interpretation of citizenship as a distinctly Western institution "inaugurates a social science tradition where the origins of "city", "democracy" and "citizenship" are etymologically traced to the "Greek", "Roman" and "medieval" cities and affinities between "ancient" and "modern" practices are established and juxtaposed against oriental societies – Indian, Chinese and Islamic – as societies that failed to develop citizenship and hence indigenous capitalism" (Isin 2013: 117). Besides cementing the Orientalist construction of a binary opposition between East and West, Weber's analysis of citizenship amounts to inventing a unified and coherent tradition for each space: "a superior way of being political as 'simple and pure citizen' and an inferior tradition that never sorted out the contractual state or the citizen. For the occidental imagination such images are now such ways of seeing: that democracy was invented in the Greek polis; that the Roman republican tradition bequeathed its legacy to Europe and that Europe Christianized and civilized these traditions" (Isin 2013: 117). In the process, discontinuities and differentiations within the West are overlooked or ignored. Moreover, the necessary interrelations between the individual factors that had led to the emergence of citizenship in the Western context on the one hand and to different institutional arrangements for the concession of individual or collective rights in non-Western contexts on the other are left unaddressed. Thereby, the separate elements leading up to the emergence of citizenship in the

180   *Global Inequalities Beyond Occidentalism*

West are not dealt with in terms of their relational significance for one another, but are treated as a to-do list of "the Rest". Inevitably, such a procedure systematically encounters incomplete assignments and rudimentary developments everywhere outside the West, where a whole different set of socio-political, economic and cultural elements was at play.

As Bryan Turner had noted earlier with respect to Weber's analyses of Hinduism, Confucianism, and his unfinished study of Islam, Weber had portrayed religious doctrines "everywhere else" – i.e., outside the West – as opposed to social innovation and supportive of the status quo (Turner 1996). Especially in the case of India, he had viewed the rigid social doctrine, in which an individual's social position was seen as the effect of actions in a previous life, as legitimising the caste order, and therefore as leaving no room for a critique of wealth or for struggles against social inequality. The rigid caste order was thus a paradigmatic example of a structural impediment to social mobility that the institutionalisation of citizenship in the West alone had successfully overcome.

Beyond adding to the already vast critical literature on Weber's Orientalism as well as on the ideal-typical method, Isin's contribution is of particular importance for emphasizing the link between Weber's concept of citizenship and a theory of inequality. As the revolutionary innovation differentiating the Occidental city from the Oriental Rest, the principle that "city air makes man free" carried the additional meaning of a sequence of social change which, as it progressed from bondage to freedom, gradually abandoned ascribed criteria of social stratification in favour of achieved characteristics, ultimately describing an ideal-typical transition from tradition to modernity. According to Weber, the intended meaning and purpose (*Sinn*) of the institutionalisation of citizenship in the modern (Occidental) state – "the first to have the concept of the 'citizen of the state' (*Staatsbürger*)" – was that of providing "a certain counterbalance to the social inequalities which are neither rooted in natural differences nor created by natural qualities but are produced, rather, by social conditions". Taking into account the fact that "the inequality of the outward circumstances of life, particularly of property, [...] can never be eliminated altogether", Weber therefore suggested allotting parliamentary suffrage equivalent weight, "so as to counterbalance these other factors by making the ruled in society [...] the equals of the privileged strata" (Weber, 1994, 103f.).

The different religious logics to which he had traced social inequalities in the West and the Rest, respectively, turn out to be the structuring principles of the political organisation in the (allegedly) secularised European city:

> Equal voting rights means in the first instance this: at this point of social life the individual, for once, is *not*, as he is everywhere else, considered in terms of the particular professional and family position he occupies, nor in relation to differences of material and social situation, but purely and simply *as a citizen*. This expresses the political unity of the nation (*Staatsvolk*) rather than the dividing lines separating the various spheres of life. (Weber, 1994, 103, emphases in the original)

In the following, I briefly review several approaches to citizenship and (in)equality that directly or indirectly build on Weber's conceptualisation in order to assess their actual or potential contribution to a sociology of global inequalities. I argue that those Weberian approaches that offer the widest analytical scope are the ones that leave behind the comparative-historical framework and instead offer a global framework for examining the effects that social closure through citizenship has on the reproduction of existing inequalities. I end with current examples of new transnational actors in citizenship policies whose impact makes an analysis of strategies of closure and usurpation beyond the state level imperative.

Citizenship as Equalising Mechanism

In the mid-twentieth century, Weber's idea that the equality of citizens before the law represented an overcoming of particularities of birth became central to T.H. Marshall's sociology. Marshall considered the "modern drive toward social equality" (Marshall 1977) the latest phase in the evolution of citizenship. Extrapolating from the development of the British social welfare system, he saw this evolution as proceeding from the granting of civil rights in the eighteenth century, through that of political rights in the nineteenth and up to the concession of social rights in the twentieth. He defined citizenship as "a status bestowed on all those who are full members of a community" (Marshall 1977: 92), and saw a tendency towards an increase in the number of persons on whom the status is bestowed – and thus towards equality. In his view, citizenship therefore was the opposite of social class, which in turn only generated inequality. He thus advocated the extension of citizenship as the principal political means for reconciling the contradictions between formal political equality and the persistence of social and economic inequality under a capitalism system based on class divisions:

> The equality implicit in the concept of citizenship, even though limited in content, undermined the inequality of the class system, which was in principle a total inequality. National justice and a law common to all must inevitably weaken and eventually destroy class justice, and personal freedom, as a universal birthright, must drive out serfdom. No subtle argument is needed to show that citizenship is incompatible with medieval feudalism. (Marshall 1977: 93)

Despite severe criticisms directed at his evolutionary perspective, his unwarranted generalisation from the British case, and his view of the development of citizenship as an irreversible process, Marshall's model proved widely influential on further Weberian approaches to citizenship, only few of which directly addressed its nexus with inequality and stratification (see Bendix 1964).

Among them, Talcott Parsons, drawing explicitly on Marshall's work, referred to the institutionalisation of the basic rights of citizenship as an egalitarian tendency of modern societies, in which universalistic norms gradually replace earlier

182   *Global Inequalities Beyond Occidentalism*

particularistic solidarities of ethnicity, religion, and regional origin (Parsons 1965, 1966). In his view, this tendency stood for a shift from societies based on ascriptive criteria to societies based on achievement criteria, and the decisive thrust for its implementation had come from the French revolution:"Within the framework of a high level of national consciousness, the French Revolution demanded a community that included *all* Frenchmen and abrogated the special status of the *privilegiés*. The central concept was *citizenship*, the claim of the *whole* population to inclusion" (Parsons 1971: 79, emphasis in the original).

Parsons thus offers a textbook example of an Occidentalist conceptualisation of citizenship as traceable to a single historical event, the French revolution, as well as limited – both in its context of emergence and its scope – to continental France and its (white, male) population, not the French colonies and their inhabitants in the Caribbean or French India. Although his focus was on the US case and its special role in the institutionalisation of basic citizenship rights, Parsons considered it legitimate to extrapolate from Marshall's model, centred on Britain. The reason lay precisely in viewing the French revolution as a common tradition of both contexts, and thus of a broader modern West: "With all the differences between British and American societies, they have very similar values. After all, with an important infusion from the French Enlightenment and the Revolutionary tradition, the origin of our own values lies mainly in our British heritage" (Parsons 1965: 1016). He therefore took Marshall's sequence of citizenship rights to reflect not only a rough temporal series, but also a type of hierarchy of institutional steps towards the main aim of the French Revolution, the equality of membership status. Parsons viewed the French Revolution as having furthered civil rights, many of which had already been institutionalised in English and American law, as well as political rights, which he, like Weber, dated back to the ancient Greek polis. In turn, social rights had become important only in the mid-nineteenth century and had started being implemented in the twentieth (Parsons 1971). At the same time, Parsons echoed Weber's emphasis on confraternisation as a basis for claims to equality when stressing that the French revolution's slogan "embodied the new conception of community. *Liberté* and *Egalité* symbolised the two foci of dissatisfaction, political authoritarianism and privilege. *Fraternité* referred primarily to the broader context of belonging, 'brotherhood' being a primordial symbol of community" (Parsons 1971: 79f.). Again, both these accomplishments and the disparities that they addressed were presented as internal to a minimally defined West.

Following Weber's analysis of the city, Parsons also traced the solidary social community of modern societies back to the Christian community of faith. He pointed out that, in its secular modern form, however, the pattern of societal community had only been partially and unstably institutionalised in the nineteenth-century: in France, both the aristocracy and the Catholic Church maintained considerable privileges, while in Britain, franchise was extended only from 1832 on and aristocracy remained strong (Parsons 1971). In this case, he also noted that there had been several exceptions to the United States' claim of being a *voluntary* association of citizens, the clearest of which had been the case of enslaved Africans, who had been brought to the US by force and had long been barred from inclusion in the political community (Parsons 1965). However significant, these provisos were nevertheless coined in the language of "survivals" of an older system on its way to a modern society, in which privilege would play an ever-smaller part. As an "exception", the case of enslaved Africans also did not appear to warrant an inquiry into its structural impact on racial inequality in the US. The most consequential aspect of Parsons' analysis of the institutionalisation of citizenship in the Western world was therefore contained in his statement that "The critical issue of "privilege" was actually the hereditary ascription of status, which conflicted with the standards of either achievement or equality, or both" (Parsons 1971: 80). The notion of the incompatibility between the ascription of status and the achievement of more democratic arrangements, which went hand in hand with the model of a linear development from a traditional status order to a modern class order thereafter became mainstays of functionalist and modernisationist theories of inequality and stratification. As in the case of Marshall's legacy, however, the nexus between citizenship as a central category of social inequality and the stratification orders of the societies under scrutiny was mostly lost on subsequent approaches.

At the end of the twentieth century, Bryan Turner's critical synopsis of the scope of approaches to citizenship from Max Weber through T.H. Marshall, Michael Mann, and Talcott Parsons signalled the exhaustion of citizenship as a relevant concept in a world increasingly characterised by supra-national entities and allegiances (Turner 1990, 1993). Despite having undertaken a comprehensive analysis of Weber's Orientalism, to which he had later added a critique of Weber's Orientalist conception of citizenship,[2] Turner held both onto the central components of Weber's Occidentalist analysis and the evolutionary thrust of Marshall's even more particularistic, British-centred account. In his view, citizenship was "an essentially modern institution which reflects the profound changes which have occurred in western societies following the democratic revolutions in France and America and as a consequence of broader, more general social changes associated with the industrial revolution, such as urbanisation and secularization" (Turner and Hamilton, 1994, np). He therefore envisaged an ideal-typical historical trajectory, whereby citizenship "evolves through the establishment of autonomous

---

2   Turner's critique of Weber's Orientalism, undertaken as early as the 1970s, was simultaneously a critique of Parsons' legacy in the interpretation of Weber's work. Despite acknowledging ample evidence of Orientalism in Weber, he therefore argued that Parsons had greatly exaggerated the importance of religious work ethics in Weber's sociology to the detriment of the role the religiosity of certain classes or status groups played in social organisation. According to Turner, Weber thus avoided certain Orientalist assumptions and focused on the many empirical differences between Asian and European societies in terms of their socio-economic organisation, rather than compare ideal-typical abstractions in order to analyse the causal importance of religion (Turner 1996: 279).

184 *Global Inequalities Beyond Occidentalism*

cities, develops through the emergence of the nation-state in the eighteenth and the nineteenth centuries, and finds its full blossoming in the welfare states of the twentieth century" (Turner and Hamilton, 1994, np). Following Parsons' equally evolutionary notion that the development of citizenship involved a shift from particularistic to universalistic values, Turner concluded that, with globalisation, the importance of citizenship might decline in favour of a more universalistic notion of human rights:

> If sociology is the study of the transformation of *gemeinschaft* (organic and particularistic values and institutions) into *gesellschaft* (associations which are more universalistic in their definition of social membership) as a consequence of modernisation, we can conceptualise human-rights solidarity as a historical stage beyond citizenship-solidarity. Whereas citizenship as a doctrine has been a progressive feature of western societies in terms of universalistic values behind the welfare state, human-right concepts can be seen as a progressive paradigm which is relevant to a world-system. (Turner 1993: 470)

Hence, in spite of the manifold critiques of Orientalism, ethnocentrism, evolutionism, and unidirectionality directed at the Weberian postulate of the uniqueness of the West and at the inequality categories derived from it, neo-Weberian analyses of citizenship seemed to have come full circle: By taking the autonomous city-state of Western Europe as the locus of emergence of citizenship, they reinforced the notion of a linear trajectory leading from ancient Greece and Rome to revolutionary France and Western-style democracy. Likewise, in stressing the importance of industrialisation and urbanisation in the emergence of citizenship, they lent further support to the division of the world between a West and a Rest, all while professing a rejection of Orientalism. Finally, by concentrating on the way the allotment of citizenship levelled ethnic differences and appeased social conflict within nation-states, they provided what Bryan Turner (1990) has referred to as "internalist accounts" of the emergence of citizenship, and disregarded the importance of supra-national and transregional factors in the development of citizenship as nation-state protection. At most, the transnational dimension of citizenship was seen as deriving from recent developments like the formation of supranational entities such as the European Union, the increasing codification of human rights norms in the context of the emergence of new states, and the movement of migrant and refugee populations (Isin and Turner 2002; Mackert and Müller 2000). The global impact of nation-state membership was featured in these and similar Weberian approaches in terms of acknowledging that nationality constituted "the primary axis by which peoples are classified and distributed in polities across the globe" (Isin and Turner 2002: 4). At the same time, this was treated as "a simple matter of law" (ibid.), not as a centuries-old principle of global social stratification. Thus, much like the transnational approaches to migration discussed above, treatment of citizenship from a Weberian perspective assumed that global issues with respect to citizenship only have to be taken into account in the era of globalisation, but not in the context of the historical emergence of citizenship or at any other moment outside the present.

Citizenship as Social Closure

It is only with the revival of interest in Weber's notion of social closure in the 1990s that the issue of inequality and citizenship would be cast in a global perspective and would simultaneously make inroads into the historical development of the institution of citizenship. The main contribution to this effect came from Rogers Brubaker's acclaimed "Citizenship and Nationhood in France and Germany" (1992). In the book, sociology's hitherto neglect of formal citizenship was traced back to three factors: first, to what Brubaker called "the endogenous bias of the discipline" – the focus on processes and institutions internal to the national society; second, to the tendency within world-systems analysis, the "only explicitly global" approach in American sociology, to focus on political economy to the detriment of social and political structures; and, third, to the territorial bias in the study of the state, which had bred a sociology of the state focused on the transition from the medieval polity to the modern nation through the territorialisation of rule. Brubaker argued instead that "the division of the world's population into a set of bounded and mutually exclusive citizenries" (Brubaker 1992: 22) was in itself a neglected aspect of the development of the state system. He then built on Weber's notion of social closure in order to show how the nation-state enforces modern forms of closure anchored in the legal institution of citizenship.

Analytically, his goal was to uncover both large-scale structures and patterns of interaction of such processes. Already in stating that "In global perspective, citizenship is a powerful instrument of social closure, shielding prosperous states from the migrant poor" (Brubaker 1992: x), he pointed to the paradox that a shift from the national to the global perspective made apparent: the fact that citizenship is "internally inclusive" – i.e., it extends rights to all those defined as citizens – at the same time that it is "externally exclusive" – i.e., it restricts the access of non-citizens to the same rights. Thus, citizenship is both an instrument of closure and an object of closure, "a status to which access is restricted" (Brubaker 1992: 31). As in the case of Korzeniewicz and Moran's world-historical model, the shift in the unit of analysis of social inequalities through the focus on the global perspective offered unprecedented scope for an assessment of how citizenship relates to inequality patterns. By analysing citizenship in terms of status and its corresponding mechanism of status closure, Brubaker operated a momentous change in the common conceptualisation of citizenship as an institution of modern societies for which social mobility is viewed as characteristic. The double function of citizenship as an instrument and object of social closure, he argued, had been present ever since the French Revolution, which had created both the nation-state and its logical corollary, nationalism, in the same breath:

186   *Global Inequalities Beyond Occidentalism*

> A nation-state is a nation's state, the state of and for a particular, bounded, sovereign nation to which foreigners, by definition, do not belong. [...] By inventing the national citizen and the legally homogeneous national citizenry, the Revolution simultaneously invented the foreigner. Henceforth citizen and foreigner would be correlative, mutually exclusive, exhaustive categories. (Brubaker 1992: 46)

The subsequent generalisation of the principle of citizenship allocation in the modern world meant that every person ought to have the citizenship of at least one state. Yet, as Brubaker pointed out, this development stands in sharp contrast to the institution of citizenship in both the ancient Greek polis and medieval towns, where the possession of citizenship was not a given, but a privilege, while lacking citizenship was no anomaly. By contrast, every state today ascribes citizenship to certain persons at birth through either right of blood (*jus sanguinis*) or right of soil (*jus soli*) arrangements, or a combination of both. This mechanism, as Brubaker noted, was both "a striking exception to the secular trend away from ascribed statuses" and proved that "the state is not and cannot be a voluntary association. For the great majority of persons, citizenship cannot be but an imposed, ascribed status" (Brubaker 1992: 32). While naturalisation represents an option for acquiring citizenship later in life, it is not only anomalous and infrequent in most countries, but also mostly limited to legal immigrants to the territory, such that "by restricting immigration, states indirectly restrict access to naturalization" (Brubaker 1992: 34). Thus, closure based on citizenship acquired a circular quality whereby only citizens have free access to the territory, but only residents in the territory have access to citizenship. Despite marked differences in the degree to which states put this circularity of closure to use, Brubaker argued, it was thanks to it that they all remained "relatively closed and self-perpetuating communities, reproducing their membership in a largely endogenous fashion, open only at the margins to the exogenous recruitment of new members" (Brubaker 1992: 34).

Brubaker's notion of citizenship as social closure therefore broke with previous approaches to the study of citizenship in several important respects. On the one hand, the focus on the idea of citizenship as membership ascribed at birth prompted the unfamiliar view of the modern state as structurally different from a voluntary association, and of both as different from the institution of citizenship in ancient Greece and feudal Europe. Thus, his analysis explicitly emphasised the discontinuities, rather than the continuities in the historical trajectory of citizenship in the West.[3] On the other hand, both the ascription of citizenship and his historical and comparative analysis of the German case convincingly illustrated that the institution of citizenship was not essentially democratic. Instead, showing how German legislation had first proclaimed equality of all before the law, yet had codified membership of the *Stände* and their corresponding inequalities, prompted Brubaker to speak of the "pre-national, pre-democratic quality" (Brubaker 1992: 51)

---

3   See also Joppke 1995.

Citizenship as Social Closure 187

of the development of citizenship in Germany. In his view, Max Weber's plea against the "Polonisation" of the Prussian East, which Brubaker quoted as an instance of nationalist conservative attitudes to immigration, was an integral part of the German politics of ethnocultural nationality in the twentieth century. Nevertheless, Brubaker neither took the ascribed character of citizenship as counterevidence of the general trend away from ascription, nor did he question the modern character of citizenship and its democratising consequences in principle. Instead, he dedicated the rest of the book to the distinction between "civic" and "ethnic" understandings of nationhood in France and Germany, respectively, which he identified in the prevalence of either the jus soli or the jus sanguinis principle of citizenship allocation. It is for this distinction, rather than for its notion of citizenship as social closure, that the book has since been best known (Joppke 2010: 17f.).

Although still largely unacknowledged, the book's central contribution to a sociology of global inequalities undoubtedly lies in the conceptualisation of citizenship as an externally exclusive mechanism of social closure. In the conclusion to the book, Brubaker stressed that what is at stake in citizenship law is access to the territories, labour markets, and welfare systems of the world's wealthy states. While France and Germany had developed very distinct politics vis-à-vis the citizenship status of post-war labour migrants (who were therefore already in the territory), it is the citizenship status of *future* immigrants that makes a real difference both to the states and to immigrants themselves:

> the control of access pivots on the institution of citizenship. Noncitizens are routinely excludable; citizens are not. The citizenship status of potential immigrants therefore matters a great deal to the state. The citizenship status of actual immigrants matters much less. Noncitizens can routinely be refused admission to the territory; […] But noncitizens who have been admitted to immigrant status […] can no longer be excluded routinely from the territory, labor market, or welfare system. (Brubaker 1992: 181)

In a 2004 collection of articles that critically revisited the civic vs. ethnic nationalism contrast by looking at public discourse and recent legislation on naturalisation, Brubaker would briefly come back to the issue of citizenship as social closure and restate the point, without, however, developing it any further.[4]

---

4 "Civic understandings of nationhood are glossed as inclusive for one of two reasons. The most common is that the civic nation is based on citizenship, and therefore includes all citizens, regardless of their particularistic traits. But citizenship itself, by its very nature, is an exclusive as well as an inclusive status […] Access to citizenship is everywhere limited; and even if it is open, in principle, to persons regardless of ethnicity, this is small consolation to those excluded from citizenship, and even from the possibility of applying for citizenship, by being excluded from the territory of the state. This 'civic' mode of exclusion is exceptionally powerful. On a global scale, it is probably far more important,

His approach therefore remains very much within the realm of a historical-comparative analysis, the global implications of which are sketched, but not expounded. Decisive in this respect is the almost exclusive focus on Europe and North America, coupled with a thorough neglect of the consequences that social closure through citizenship has had for the non-Western world both during colonial times and today, as well as of the ways in which French and German colonial possessions have influenced the development of their respective politics of citizenship allocation.

A theoretically differentiated and explicitly Weberian approach to citizenship as a mechanism of social closure that builds on Brubaker's analysis has recently been developed by Jürgen Mackert (2004; 2006). Tracing the notion of social closure from Weber through Frank Parkin and Raymond Murphy, Mackert zooms in on Murphy's complementary pair of closure and usurpation as reciprocal means of mobilising power in order to enhance or defend a group's share of rewards and resources. Drawing further on T.H. Marshall's model, Mackert conceives of citizenship rights as "dimensions of exclusion" on the part of the state and "dimensions of usurpation" on the side of immigrants, respectively (Mackert 2004: 261ff.). Although identifying the two dimensions suggests a pattern of interaction, in effect, the categorical separation of state and immigrant dimensions obscures the role of state legislation in the creation of different categories of immigrants. Their context of emergence, including colonial and neocolonial practices of racialisation of immigrants, thereby slips between the cracks of the ahistorically conceived dimensions. Even more importantly for the purposes of the present analysis, by focusing exclusively on the mechanisms of internal closure through citizenship in the case of Germany, Mackert's analysis recedes from the global dimension that Brubaker had foreshadowed.[5]

The potential inherent in Brubaker's notion of citizenship as social closure for a sociology of global inequalities was thus largely left unexplored by the drift into the comparative-historical analysis of national citizenship policies in Western states or the focus on processes of internal closure vis-à-vis non-nationals in the territory. Moreover, citizenship studies' subsequent focus on the stereotypical contrast of "civic" versus "ethnic" nationhood in comparative contexts further downplayed Brubaker's more radical argument about the basically ascriptive character of citizenship as well as about the global consequences of this ascriptive mechanism.

---

in shaping life chances and sustaining massive and morally arbitrary inequalities, than is any kind of exclusion based on putative ethnicity" (Brubaker 2004: 141).

5   This focus has in turn proved productive in the analysis of other national contexts: Mackert's closure notion of citizenship has recently been applied to the case of Northern Ireland so as to explain the peace process under way since the mid-1990s as an institutional compromise between Unionist and Nationalist strategies of closure and usurpation (Koch 2003, O'Brien 2010). Here, too, the focus remains on the mechanisms of internal closure within the state territory.

Citizenship as Inherited Property

It is in the context of an explicit understanding of citizenship as a central factor in the maintenance and reproduction of global inequalities that the externally exclusive dimension of citizenship has been recently explored in some detail. Engaging several bodies of literature on citizenship studies, global inequality, and democratic theory, legal scholar Ayelet Shachar found that none systematically addressed the mechanisms by which citizenship is transferred, the implications of such transfer for the global distribution of wealth and opportunities, or the adequacy of national communities of citizens as a unit of analysis (Shachar and Hirschl 2007; Shachar 2009).

Drawing in part on Brubaker's notion of citizenship as both an instrument and an object of closure, Shachar therefore focused on how the intergenerational transfer of citizenship ascribed at birth resembles the intergenerational transfer of property at a global scale. According to her, birthright citizenship, whether ascribed under the jus soli or the jus sanguinis principles, functions as a kind of inherited property that restricts membership in well-off polities to a small part of the world population. As such, both inherited property and birthright citizenship grant legitimate title bearers the unconditional right of entry on the one hand and restricted access to scarce resources (e.g. land in the case of property, a welfare system in the case of citizenship) on the other. In the case of citizenship, Shachar labels the former "the gate-keeping function" of citizenship, while the latter represents its "opportunity-enhancing function": "Just as fiercely as it externally excludes nonmembers, citizenship can also act as an internal leveller of opportunity by providing the basic enabling conditions for members to fulfil their potential" (Shachar 2009: 35). Although less explicitly, she thus makes a similar case as Korzeniewicz and Moran (2009): while the institutionalisation of citizenship did ensure the relative social and political inclusion of the population of Western European nation-states, it also accounted for the selective exclusion of colonised or non-European populations from the same social and political rights, on the other.

More importantly, however, she notes that both inherited property and birthright citizenship are automatically transferred from one generation to the next. Although widely criticised in relation to both institutions, the hereditary transmission of privilege has been largely dismissed as feudal and inequitable with regard to property, yet maintained and even reinforced with regard to citizenship:

> Inherited entitlement to citizenship not only remains with us today; it is by far the most important avenue through which individuals are sorted into different political communities. Birthright principles strictly regulate the entail of political membership for the vast majority of the global population. Membership attributed through accident of birth secures the transmission of membership entitlement for a limited group of beneficiaries, either on the basis of bloodline or birthplace. These beneficiaries, in turn, gain the right to pass the benefit along to the next

> generation by inheritance, and so forth: it is this structure that effectively creates the "fee tail" in the transmission of citizenship. (Shachar 2009: 41)

Thus, both in its gate-keeping and in its opportunity-enhancing functions, citizenship is shown to bear striking similarities to the feudal entail, a legal means of restricting future succession of property to the descendants of a designated estate-owner practiced in medieval England. As such, the entail offered a tool to preserve land in the possession of dynastic families by entrenching birthright succession, while forbidding future generations to alter the estate inherited from their predecessors. By analogy, the entail of citizenship helps preserve wealth in the hands of designated heirs of membership titles – the state's citizens – by allocating political membership at birth in dramatically different opportunity structures (Shachar 2009: 38ff.). In Shachar's gripping comparison, for a girl born in 2001 in Mali, one of the poorest countries in the world, the chances of surviving to age five, having access to clean water, or getting an education were incomparably lower than for a baby born at the same time in the United States, where chances for boys and girls on all these counts are nearly identically high. Contrary to the claims of an entire Occidentalist tradition of citizenship theory from Weber through Marshall and up to Turner, citizenship and gender, the most decisive factors accounting for these extreme inequalities between individuals in poor and rich countries in the twenty-first century, are both statuses ascribed at birth.

By insisting that the birthright transmission of political membership represents a "blind spot" of citizenship theory with considerable implications for the global distribution of scarce resources, Shachar convincingly de-emphasises the contrast between jus sanguinis and jus soli arrangements, both of which rely on birthright ascription. At the same time, she – quite literally – agrees with Brubaker that the similarities between birthright citizenship and inherited property are but "a striking exception to the modern trend away from ascribed statuses *in all other areas*" (Shachar 2009: 13; 42, emphasis added).

Her analysis therefore remains premised on a Marshalian view of the modern history of citizenship as the gradual achievement of rights, while the solution offered tends to reinforce, rather than question, the role of nation-states as bounded communities in guaranteeing such rights: By further analogy to the workings of inherited property, Shachar suggests introducing a "citizenship tax", a levy on the privilege of birthright entitlement to the citizenship of wealthy states,[6] as a type of "infrastructure for reducing inequalities" (Shachar 2009: 138). As one of the added benefits of this global redistributive scheme and as proof of the fact that the effects of citizenship laws are borne both by the beneficiaries and by the excluded, she mentions compensations to formerly colonised countries for "unjust enrichment" during colonisation or occupation:

---

6   For a critique of Shachar's solutions see Stevens 2009, Boatcă 2012.

> those with stronger historical ties (through colonialism or conquest, for example) have a stronger claim to gain a say in [...] tackling the unjust fallouts of these cross-border coercive effects. [...] Certain countries which share tighter historical, economic, linguistic, or geopolitical ties may negotiate extended exchange or tax-substitution programs to reflect their contextual interrelationships [...] and interdependence. (Shachar 2009: 138)

At the same time, the birthright privilege levy is meant to counteract what Shachar identifies as the current trend towards the commodification of citizenship, which involves governments granting access to membership in return for cash or investment. For Shachar, turning membership into a marketable commodity involves the risk of "losing everything that makes citizenship meaningful and worth preserving today: security; identity; belonging; an equal voice in governance; a safety net; a basic public-minded commitment to a long-time horizon of intergenerational responsibility and continuity, to name but a few" (Shachar 2009: 60). Yet these core features of citizenship are precisely those to which the mechanism of external closure through birthright membership applies, and which could only develop by negating the colonial, military, or economic interrelationships and interdependence at a global scale for which the birthright privilege levy should compensate. Although she acknowledges international migration as a central means of global social mobility, which states offering "passports-for-cash" now mobilise in order to attract wealthy investors or highly skilled migrants, Shachar opts for maintaining birthright and against free movement – or for having the cake of "meaningful" citizenship and eating it, too.

Birthright Citizenship versus Citizenship by Investment

The notion of citizenship as inherited property runs counter both to Weber's view that citizenship represents a counterbalance to inequalities of property and to Marshall's claim that citizenship and a capitalist class system are opposing principles. It however does not relinquish the underlying Occidentalist assumption that citizenship as developed in the West through the legal (and physical) exclusion of non-European, non-White and/or non-Western populations from civic, political, social and cultural rights is a modern, progressive institution.

The increasing commodification of citizenship rights across the world in recent years makes the similarity between birthright citizenship and inherited property particularly salient. At the same time, it prompts the realisation that the ascription of citizenship represents no exception to a modern trend away from ascriptive mechanisms, as both Brubaker and Shachar surmised, but a core principle of global stratification. Resorting to market mechanisms in order to elude the ascription of citizenship is an increasingly visible, yet rare option available only to the wealthy few.

192 *Global Inequalities Beyond Occidentalism*

Conferring citizenship to investors contingent upon residence on a country's territory has been common practice in a number of states, including the UK, the US, Canada, Belgium, and Australia. The by far less common, but recently growing practice consists of extending citizenship status to investors without a residence requirement. Firmly implemented in St Kitts and Nevis and the Commonwealth of Dominica since 1984 and 1993, respectively, and recently set up in Antigua and Barbuda as well as Hungary in 2013, the so-called citizenship by investment (or "economic citizenship") programs have recently proliferated in Southern and Eastern Europe, too.

As one type of naturalisation procedure, citizenship by investment programs have a clearly economic rationale and are frequently used as an alternative development strategy in close connection to a colonial past and/or core-periphery relations in the present. For their first promoters, the programs were meant to bridge the transition from the export monoculture of the colonial economy to more diversified production after independence: St. Kitts and Nevis, a federation of two islands in the Caribbean, established its program one year after the islands gained independence from the United Kingdom in 1983. Initially, investment required to obtain citizenship was limited to a real estate option of 400,000 USD. After the islands' sugar industry was closed under pressures from the European Union and the World Trade Organisation, a second option was introduced in the form of a donation to the Sugar Industry Diversification Foundation (SIDF), a charity aimed at conducting research into the development of alternative industries to replace the sugar industry (Dzankic 2012a). Under the headline "Passports ... for a Price", Reuters pithily summarised the logic behind the move towards investment citizenship by noting: "For decades, the two-island nation of St. Kitts and Nevis exported sugarcane to keep its economy afloat. When sugar prices fell, St. Kitts began to sell an even sweeter commodity: its citizenship" (Reuters 2012). Similarly, the Commonwealth of Dominica, which gained independence from the United Kingdom in 1978, has established an investor citizenship program after adverse weather conditions and the decrease in the world prices of bananas, the country's primary crop, had seriously damaged its economy (Dzankic 2012a). Citizens of St. Kitts and Nevis can travel without a visa to more than half of the world's countries, including Canada and all of Europe. They pay no personal income taxes and can take up residence in any of the Caricom (Caribbean Community and Common Market) member countries at any time and indefinitely.

Within Southern and Eastern Europe, citizenship and residency programs have taken hold especially as a result of the 2008 financial crisis. Hungary, looking to refinance billions of dollars in foreign debt that will mature in the next few years, adopted an amendment to the immigration law introducing an investment citizenship option in December 2012. Foreigners who buy at least 250,000 EUR in special government residency bonds with a five-year maturity date are offered preferential immigration treatment and a fast track to Hungarian citizenship with no residence requirement or real estate purchase (Varga 2012). While Hungary boasts the lowest amount required of investors in Europe, a real estate investment of up to 650,000 EUR also buys foreigners residency rights – and, in some cases, full European citizenship – in Ireland, Spain, Portugal, Greece, Cyprus, Macedonia, Bulgaria, and Malta, whose investment programs have all been implemented since 2012 (CNN Money 2013; BBC News 2013). Visa-free travel to core countries, citizenship of a Schengen zone state, or even the right to work in the European Union thereby become available for the (moderately or very) wealthy, consequently linking the inequality of income and property to the access to property commodified in the form of citizenship. Some authors have therefore introduced the term "jus pecuniae" (Stern 2011; Dzankic 2012a) as a new type of criterion for the allotment of citizenship alongside jus soli and jus sanguinis. However, the commodification of citizenship that jus pecuniae involves neither follows an alternative, non-ascriptive logic – since investors already possess an ascribed citizenship, and the newly acquired one can be passed on to future generations by descent – nor does it represent a viable option for most of the world's population. Instead, it is either an option purposely designed for a very select few or – more frequently – is scandalised, stigmatised and, ultimately, criminalised when it threatens to become available to a wider number of people.

In most cases, the declared goal of economic citizenship programs is to attract wealthy investors, especially from China, but also, and increasingly, from Russia and the Middle East. While both the Hungarian and the Greek governments actively promoted the launch of their investment citizenship programs in China, Cyprus initially cut down the amount required for investment citizenship in order to compensate for the losses of the Russian business community in the recent Cypriot bank crisis (Focus Online 2013). At the same time, sharp criticism of economic citizenship programs as "an abuse of European Union membership" (Daily Mail, 2012) in the case of Hungary and as "cheapening citizenship" (Forbes 2013; Shachar 2014) in the case of Malta has been instrumental in reasserting EU core countries' leverage on semiperipheral ones, as becomes clear from the austerity measures and other sanctions imposed on Cyprus, Montenegro and Malta.

Thus, in the context of the debate on EU economic aid to Cyprus, the head of the German Christian Social Union (CSU) in the EU Parliament asked for a reform of Cyprus's citizenship law in order to ensure that not everyone who has a lot of money receives a Cypriot passport (Gammelin and Hulverscheidt 2013). It was also the German CSU that criticised the decision of Montenegro's government to implement a citizenship by investment program in the country. The CSU announced that it might request the reinstatement of visas for the citizens of Montenegro, implying that this decision might affect the previous "progress" the country had made in the area of border management and immigration control (*Vijesti* 12/08/2010, quoted in Dzankic, 2012a). In the wake of such reactions, the Montenegrin government has put the implementation of its citizenship-by-investment program on hold. In turn, Malta's brand-new citizenship scheme, with an initial investment threshold of 650,000 EUR, has been heavily disputed on a number of counts, including the European Commission's concerns that it would naturalise persons born and residing abroad without "genuine links to the country"

194 *Global Inequalities Beyond Occidentalism*

(*The Independent* 2014). As a result, the Maltese government has amended the scheme to include a more severe residence requirement and further investment in real estate and government bonds, raising the contribution to a total of €1,150,000. Despite many of the arguments exchanged by critics and promoters alike, at stake in such debates, however, is not the abstract worth of citizenship, nor the amount of cultural and social ties of members with the national community, but the consequences of the commodification of citizenship for migration to and the rights of potential migrants in core regions of the world-economy.

It is therefore important to note that, while any state's citizenship could theoretically be commodified by becoming the object of investor programs, it is only the citizenship of few states that lends itself to being commodified by virtue of being a scarce good awarding (relatively) rare benefits. From this point of view, states whose citizenship include the advantage of the above-mentioned visa-free travel to core countries or even the right to legal employment in them, offer what could be referred to as "premium citizenship" that is attractive to investors. States that are not part of the core, may, as in the case of St. Kitts and Nevis, use the residual benefits of having been a British colony – that today consist of being a member of the Commonwealth of Nations and of sharing, among other things, a visa-free travel area. This, however, hardly compares to the rights accruing from EU citizenship, which include free movement, residence and non-discrimination within the EU, the right to vote for and stand as a candidate in European Parliament and municipal elections, diplomatic protection outside the EU, etc. Thus, the colonial context has once again served as an ideal testing ground for "premium citizenship" as one of modernity's newest developments, the advantages of which are however only fully deployed in Europe.

In this context, Jelena Dzankic has recently pointed out that the Cypriot and Maltese programmes are more attractive for investors than those of the Caribbean islands for two reasons:

> the naturalised investor will be granted visa-free travel to 151 (Cyprus) or 163 (Malta) states. This is considerably more than they would have by virtue of possessing the best-ranked Caribbean passport, that of Saint Kitts and Nevis which allows visa-free entry to 131 countries. Second, and more importantly, since in the EU the regulation of citizenship is decided by each Member State for herself, an individual may now obtain EU citizenship for roughly the price of a Porsche 918 Spyder [...] This raises the question of whether it is proportionate and just that access to this array of rights is exchanged for the price of a sports car. (Dzankic 2014: 18)

At the same time, Dzankic's differentiation goes against her own earlier claim that "jus pecuniae" has become a third option for the acquisition of citizenship alongside jus soli and jus sanguinis. Citizenship for sale is not only unavailable to the majority of the world's population, but would not prove a viable economic strategy in any but "premium citizenship" states, among which European Union member states rank highest.

Thus, according to Henley & Partners, a private British consultancy that has coined the term "citizenship and residence planning", the European Union is home to nine out of the ten countries worldwide whose citizens enjoy the most freedom of visa-free travel (International Business Times 2013). The Henley & Partners Visa Restriction Index, produced in cooperation with the trade association for the world's airlines, IATA, ranks Finland, Sweden and the United Kingdom number one on account of a total score of 173 countries to which their citizens can travel visa-free (out of a maximum score of 218). Denmark, Germany, Luxembourg, and the United States share second place with visa-free access to 172 countries, followed by Belgium, Italy and the Netherlands at 171 (Henley & Partners 2013). Most passport holders in Africa, the Middle East, and South Asia have scores below 40, while mainland China has a barely slightly higher score of 44 – equal to that of Cameroon, Congo, Jordan, and Rwanda. This explains why EU residence permits are extremely attractive to Chinese investors, and much more so than for Hong Kong investors, who have access to 152 countries on account of holding a "Special Administrative Region of China" passport. The fine print to the Visa Restriction index lists all other overseas territories and colonial dependencies of the world in order to clarify that territories dependent on the United Kingdom, Australia, New Zealand, the USA, the Netherlands, and France are not considered separate nationalities, but "destinations" (Henley & Partners 2013) and thus do not get their own scores.

Henley & Partners, which has set up St. Kitts and Nevis' as well as Antigua & Barbuda's investment citizenship scheme and is now administering Malta's, hosts an annual Global Residence and Citizenship conference (with an additional Forum held in Malta in 2014) advertising the latest options available to wealthy investors in search for dual or "alternative" citizenships (Henley & Partners 2014). Among the benefits, it stresses that alternative citizenship is "an effective tool for international tax planning" – if one's state of origin imposes stricter tax rules – as well as for "more privacy in banking and investment". The highest worth, however, is attached to the insurance feature of citizenship: "a passport from a small, peaceful country can even save your life when travelling and in times of political unrest, civil war, terrorism or other delicate situations. For good reasons, many international business people and important persons who are active worldwide consider an alternative passport as the best life insurance money can buy" (Henley & Partners 2014).

Hence, while closure through citizenship as a globally operating mechanism is as old as the Western nation-state, closure and usurpation cannot be adequately analysed solely at the state level. Instead, the focus on state policies of closure through immigration and border control has to be complemented by an analysis of the usurpation of state authority "from above" by transnational managers of citizenship practices, frequently operating in offshore tax shelters: Henley & Partners, located in the British Crown dependency of Jersey, in turn one of the leading offshore financial centres, stands to make at least 60 million euros from its role as designer and principal contractor of Malta's revised citizenship scheme (*The Independent* 2014). Not only do state bureaucracies as administrators of investor citizenship lose importance in this context, but the state whose citizenship is being traded no longer is the site of wealth-preservation. Instead, wealth is transferred to private transnational actors who cash in on the conflict between the interests of states and those of very wealthy individuals.

Back Doors and Friendly Gateways: The Double Standard of Usurpation Strategies

As investment citizenship and residence programs open "global mobility corridors for the ultra-rich" (Bărbulescu 2014), thus usurping the mechanism of closure through citizenship "from above", strategies of usurpation that provide low-income migrants with far more limited paths to mobility are singled out as illegitimate and criminalised.

This double standard runs through the global logic of closure and usurpation. Usurpation strategies from above and from below are both geared towards more people gaining access to premium citizenship. However, the racial criminalisation of migrants to core regions – most prominently, to the European Union and the United States – only targets the so-called "poverty migration". The globally mobile ultra-rich seldom count or self-designate as migrants, but are instead called "global investors", "expats", or "foreign residents for tax purposes", while their migration process is more often referred to as "relocation" or qualified as "business migration". Yet, as visa requirements for the majority of the world's migrants become more restricted, investor citizenships and visas proliferate. The CEO of Arton Capital, a global financial advisory firm, summarised the investors' view of this transformation with the words: "It's a new world movement – global citizenship is not something you inherit at birth, it's something you have to work towards and invest in. This is the reason investment immigration is growing in popularity" (*China Daily*, 2014). Advertising for UK's newly revised "tier 1" investor visas, which largely benefit Russian and Chinese millionaires, the head of a British law firm explained that wealthy individuals see London as an "expat friendly gateway to Europe" (*Financial Times*, 2012).

For labour migrants, on the other hand, inherited citizenship and lengthy naturalisation procedures are legally (re)inforced as the only legitimate options. In this context, states relying primarily on jus sanguinis scandalise non-European, non-Western or non-white migrants' claims to citizenship as a type of "forged descent", while states where jus soli is the dominant principle denounce illegalised migrant paths to national citizenship as a form of "forged ascent". In either case, there are no friendly gateways waiting. Rather, the accusation is that of entering the world of wealth through the back door.

Thus, according to the French EU affairs minister Pierre Lellouche, one of the reasons France spoke out against Romanian efforts to join the EU's passport-free Schengen zone in 2010 was being concerned about "the distribution of Romanian passports" to Moldovans. The territory of Moldova was part of the Romanian Principality of Moldavia from the mid-14th thru the mid-19th century and part of Greater Romania between 1918 and 1940 as well as between 1941 and 1944.[7] Since many Moldovans are ethnically and linguistically Romanian and to almost 95 per cent Romanian Orthodox Christians, Bucharest adopted a law granting foreign nationals of Romanian descent the right to become citizens of the country as soon as Moldova gained its independence from the Soviet Union. Since then, Romania has processed an estimated 225,000 citizenship applications from Moldovans (Iordachi 2012).

The widely read, high-brow German magazine *Der Spiegel* illustrated the typical threat scenario mobilised in anti-immigration arguments with the words: "[T]he EU, which is already suffering from enlargement fatigue, is stealthily being expanded from the east – without a referendum or any agreements from Brussels, Berlin or Paris. The Moldovans are voting with their feet and marching into the EU's economic paradise – through the back door" (*Der Spiegel*, 2010).

As illicit intermediaries can even generate proof of Romanian ancestry where none exists, thereby spurring illegal trade in Romanian passports, EU fears of "creeping expansion from the East" have fed on exaggerated prognoses of the "stream of Moldovan migration" into Western Europe. Although evidence has shown that Romania's naturalisation program has created proportionately fewer EU citizens than similar efforts in France and the UK (Călugăreanu and Mogoş 2012), France's concern with Moldovan migrants was the first in a line of Western European states' arguments against Romania and Bulgaria joining the Schengen zone. In 2013, the then German minister of the interior, Hans-Peter Friedrich, announced that "the attempt [to join] will fail because of a German veto" if Romania and Bulgaria insisted on a decision, and he urged both countries to take further steps "to prevent migrants abusing the system" (quoted in *The Economist*, 2013). At the same time, leading EU officials have repeatedly expressed concern that the expansion of the Schengen zone to Romania and Bulgaria would trigger an influx of North African refugees from Greece, which currently has no land connection to the rest of the Schengen space (Brady 2012). As a result, Romania and Bulgaria's access to the Schengen zone is currently postponed indefinitely.

The ethnic profiling of Moldovans in the European Union is thus directed against immigrants suspected of having abused the right of blood in order to acquire citizenship. In turn, the ethnic and racial profiling of immigrants who

---

7 Formerly known as Bessarabia, the region was annexed by the Soviet Union during World War II and became an independent republic in 1991. According to Romanian officials, many Moldovans regard the Romanian passport as the key to the EU and try to acquire Romanian citizenship as fast as possible using both official and unofficial channels (Călugăreanu and Mogoş, 2012).

come to the US to give birth targets pregnant women accused of having abused the right of soil to the same purpose. In the latter case, immigration hard-liners describe a wave of migrants crossing the Mexican-US border in the advanced stages of pregnancy to have what are dismissively called "anchor babies" (Lacey 2011). The term refers to the automatic granting of US citizenship, in virtue of the 14th Amendment, to children born on US soil, who can in turn secure citizenship for their parents upon reaching the age of 21. However, many immigrants arriving to give birth in the United States are frequent border crossers with valid visas who travel legally in order to take advantage of better medical care. Moreover, although the total US immigration population continues to grow, unauthorised immigration has slowed in the past decade (Pew Research Center 2013). Nevertheless, several Republican attempts at amending the US constitution since 2010 have mobilised terms like "anchor babies", "birth tourism" and "accidental citizens" in order to end the automatic granting of citizenship, arguing that the provision attracts high numbers of unauthorised migrants (Feere 2010; *Huffington Post* 2013). Migrants themselves, however, stress that it is access to medical care and the prospect of better-paying jobs, not a (different) passport for their children, that prompts them to take the risk of unauthorised migration upon themselves and their families (Lacey 2011).

The increase in the commodification of citizenship in all of these instances not only reflects, but also reinforces the ongoing widening of the worldwide inequality gap. The emergence of official economic citizenship programmes as well as the illegal trade in EU passports in Eastern Europe and the Caribbean are similar strategies of eluding the ascription of citizenship through recourse to the market. Attempts to beat the ascriptive logic at its own game – i.e., by undermining the institution of birthright citizenship through illegalised trade in passports or illegalised migration – meet with critique, sanctions, and criminalisation from supra-state and financial institutions, encounter legal countermeasures, and are racially and ethnically policed. The scandalisation of "forged descent" in the case of Moldovan applications to Romanian citizenship and of "forged ascent" in the case of children born to cross-border migrants in the US is simultaneously a statement about the immutability of the ascription of citizenship through both bloodline and birthplace for the wider population, and ultimately a denial of equal opportunities for upward social mobility at the global level. Citizenship is thus not only a core mechanism for the maintenance of global inequalities, but also one on the basis of which their reproduction in the postcolonial present is being enacted.

The birthright transmission of citizenship is therefore no striking exception to a trend away from ascription, but a core principle of global stratification in a world capitalist system, as evidenced by Korzeniewicz and Moran above. It is in the context of global capitalism and its corresponding logic of accumulation that the institution of citizenship emerged; the economic and political interests of the core European countries that pioneered it were essential in defining its central features, and are decisive in maintaining premium citizenships restricted today.

Gate-keeping and opportunity-enhancing are hence just as much functions of the accumulation logic of global capitalism as they are functions of citizenship.

The comparative-historical analysis of the emergence of the institution of citizenship in different parts of the world in relation to the Western model or of national citizenship policies in Western states fails to target the logic of accumulation at the same time as it reinforces the principle of ascription that underlies it. Ultimately, a Weberian conceptualisation of citizenship focused on Western Europe's pioneering role in forging a community of equal members channels attention to processes internal to that community and the features that make it unique in comparison to its counterparts elsewhere. Even as it invites a comparative approach, such a focus however prevents both an understanding of the interrelations, including the relations of power, which made the singularity of the original context possible, and a global perspective on citizenship more generally.

Chapter 7
After Uniqueness:
Entangled Modernities and Multiple Europes

Weber's emphasis on cultural values and attitudes as determinants of social inequality in their own right, rather than as epiphenomena of an economic base, was widely celebrated as an overcoming of the economism that Marxist thought had bequeathed to social inequality analysis. Its potential for an explicit analysis of social inequalities was especially prolific at the micro and meso levels through such notions as status and life conduct, as well as habitus, cultural capital and social field.

Unlike Marxist political economy, Weber's theory of culture however did not easily translate into a macrosociology of inequalities. At the macrostructural level, it was therefore primarily in civilisational analysis that Weber's sociology of culture was most clearly applied to the study of global dynamics. Within this framework, Shmuel Eisenstadt's model of multiple modernties (Eisenstadt 2000a) has been hailed as one of the most influential approaches which further developed Weber's comparative research of world religions and which, for some, managed to overcome the Eurocentric assumptions of both Weberian and modernisationist perspectives in the process. At the same time, Samuel Huntington's widely debated "clash of civilisations" thesis, considered "one of the pivotal reorientations of civilisational analysis in the 1990s" (Tiryakian 2004: 36), drew on Weber's analysis of world religions in support of the claim that the major lines of division and the dominating source of global conflict in the future would be cultural ones (Huntington 1993, 1996a, 1996b).

Although both approaches have received considerable attention as well as substantial criticism, they are rarely considered together. Whereas Eisenstadt's multiple modernities perspective has generated an entire research program and has seen a range of further developments, Huntington's work has tended to polarise opinions and has mainly functioned as a one-man enterprise. In his plea for the renovation of the sociological tradition of civilisational analysis, however, Edward Tiryakian (2004) grouped Eisenstadt and Huntington within the third generation of scholars of the field initially inaugurated by Weber, Durkheim, and Mauss. In Tiryakian's view, both authors operated with a notion of tension in order to understand the dynamics of civilisations: Eisenstadt identified the dynamics of modernity within Axial Age civilisations by examining the tensions between "orthodox" and "heterodox" orientations and their followers, while Huntington located the dynamics in the tensions between civilisations, most notably between "Islam" and "the West". On account of the increase in population flows and intercivilisational encounters he saw as characterising the globalisation era, Tiryakian was critical of Huntington's view of a civilisation grounded in just one physical area. He however thought Weber had foreshadowed the "clash of civilisations" thesis and found evidence supporting it in a series of conflicts in the post-Cold War setting. Following Weber, Mauss, and Sorokin, Tiryakian's proposal for the civilisational analysis of the twenty-first century therefore involved taking civilisation "as a proper macro sociocultural unit of analysis, more encompassing than the nation-state but less sweeping than a 'world system'" (Tiryakian 2004: 43).

Advocates and critics of civilisational analysis alike have repeatedly pointed to the difficulties involved in the use of "civilisation" as both a term and a unit of analysis, and in particular to the racial connotations of notions of a superior Western civilisation (Melleuish 2004; Holton 2006; Zimmerman 2006). While more recent works in the field have given increasing attention to intercivilisational contacts and patterns of interaction (Arjomand and Tiryakian 2004; Ben-Rafael and Sternberg 2005), this focus on interconnections left the uniqueness of Western civilisation unchallenged, as a number of critics have noted (Randeria 2005; Spohn 2006; Bhambra 2007a; Patel 2013). In briefly reviewing Eisenstadt's and Huntington's notions of the global dynamics of civilisations, my aim in the following is to show how the emphasis on tensions within and clashes between civilisations serves to reassert both the uniqueness of the West and its ontological autonomy. I argue that, especially through the focus on conflict and tension between an initial modern civilisation and its sequels, civilisational analysis not only retains an Occidentalist bias, but also replaces the Marxist political economy of class conflict with what has been called a Weberian "political economy of cultural differences" (Zimmerman 2006). I propose instead that an understanding of the dynamics of modernity that de-centres the role of the West does not require a notion of multiple modernities emerging through dialectic tension from a European original, but an analysis of the multiple alterities within Europe which enabled both Western Europe's colonial and imperial expansion and its monopolisation of the definition of modernity.

Civilisations as Multiple Modernities

Shmuel Eisenstadt's complex relationship with the modernisation paradigm has met with diametrically opposed interpretations. Critics took his refutal of the worldwide convergence thesis, which modernisation theorists had advocated, as proof of an even narrower view – that the potential for modernisation was not to be found globally, but was specific to European civilisation (Randeria et al. 2004; Bhambra 2007a, Patel 2013). Supporters emphasised instead his heterodox position, informed by his East Central European Jewish and Near East Israeli experience, as well as his criticism of the Western-centric evolutionist premises of classical modernisation theorists (Casanova 2011; Spohn 2011). In view of this uneasy connection with modernisation theory, the multiple modernities perspective seemed to harbour both the root of utmost Occidentalism and the potential for its

After Uniqueness 203

overcoming. A closer look at the recurring themes throughout his work helps to clarify the picture.

In his 1966 *Modernization: Protest and Change*, Eisenstadt defined modernisation in typical Occidentalist fashion: "Historically, modernisation is the process of change towards those types of social, economic, and political systems that have developed in Western Europe and North America from the seventeenth century to the nineteenth and have then spread to other European countries and in the nineteenth and twentieth centuries to the South American, Asian, and African continents" (Eisenstadt 1966: 1). This definition was so much in line with classical modernisation theory that the authors of the corresponding entry in the 2001 Encyclopedia of Sociology quoted it up front as illustrative of the entire paradigm (Armer and Katsillis 2001).

The typically modernisationist and Occidentalist rhetoric of diffusion from the original Western location to other parts of Europe and eventually the entire world was equally present in Eisenstadt's conceptualisation of modernity as a civilisation, which characterised his writings from the 1980s onwards:

> Modernity, the modern cultural and political programme, developed in one of the Great Axial Civilizations – the Christian-European one (Eisenstadt, 1982, 1986) […]. This civilization, the distinct cultural programme with its institutional implications, crystallized first in Western Europe and then expanded to other parts of Europe, to the Americas and later on throughout the world. This gave rise to continually changing cultural and institutional patterns which constituted, as it were, different responses to the challenges and possibilities inherent in the core characteristics of the distinct civilizational premises of modernity. (Eisenstadt 2004: 48)

As the focus on *modernisation* as change shifted to one on *modernity* as transformation, and thereby from a process to a civilisation, the significance Eisenstadt attributed to the dynamics of conflict as a catalyst of change increased accordingly. In his civilisational analysis, he therefore stressed that the transformation of the utopian visions of heterodox sects (that had remained marginal within medieval and early modern European Christianity) had acquired centrality in the political arena in such specifically Western historical moments as "the Enlightenment and in the Great Revolutions, in the English Civil War and especially the American and French Revolutions and their aftermaths" (Eisenstadt 2004: 48).

According to Eisenstadt, the confrontation with Western Europe played an important part in the development of multiple modernities elsewhere, as did colonialism and imperialism as vehicles of such confrontation. These processes appeared however as a logical consequence of Western superiority, the power and violence components of which remained unquestioned and thereby positively connoted: "The variability of modernities was accomplished above all through military and economic imperialism and colonialism, effected through superior economic, military, and communication technologies" (Eisenstadt 2000a: 14). Structural dependencies and processes of hierarchisation that followed from Europe's colonial expansion did not enter into the explanation of how multiple modernities emerged and thus played no part in an understanding of their specificity. Through the decisive role attributed to the Western European model in the genesis of multiple modernities, Eisenstadt paradoxically reinforced the notion of a self-sufficient Western modernity that he had initially criticised. His theoretical shift from one modernity to several therefore involved no shift of paradigm, but remained instead immanent to a modernisationist perspective. The modernisationst rhetoric of lack – the systematic identification of deficits, residues and gaps – made the non-Western modernities thus diagnosed into mere extensions of the Western one, i.e., regional deviances from the cultural program of modernity as emerged in the West (see also Cooper 2005; Nederveen Pieterse 2010). That was also the case when the lack of "European" characteristics was interpreted as a chance for a new start and when the break with the European past was viewed as constitutive for further modernities. This becomes particularly evident in the case of what Eisenstadt saw as the first multiple modernity in the Americas, the United States:

> One of the most important structural differences between societies in Europe and the USA was of course the lack (except in the South) of a feudal aristocracy. A further factor was the social mobility enabled by the open frontier. Sombart and many others recognized that the perception or the awareness of mobility brought by the shifting frontier was an important factor which distinguished the American worker from the European one. (Eisenstadt 2000b, my translation)

The prominent role awarded to Western modernity as a reference point for continuity as well as discontinuity in the emergence of further cultural programmes is thus central to the multiple modernities approach – and as such unmistakeable to both its critics and its advocates. Although the approach did not plead for the subsequent Westernisation of the world, but for a multiplicity of modernities, its underlying premise was that colonialism and imperialism are merely triggering moments in the emergence of such multiplicity. The multiple modernities were therefore expected to eventually decouple from the European prototype – as well as from (neo)colonial structures – and become independent. Through the silencing of colonial violence underlying the Western expansion of white settlers in the USA, the brutal repression of the native population appeared merely as a positively connoted, open frontier. As such, it harboured the promise of social mobility (since it was a "shifting" frontier) – seen as characteristic for the first multiple modernity in the Americas. Also missing in Eisenstadt's analysis of the impact of European modernity on African, South American, Australian and Asian populations are colonialism and the exercise of violence accompanying it (Joas and Knöbl 2004). While Eisenstadt readily acknowledged that the crystallisation of European modernity and its later expansion were "by no means peaceful", the confrontations they engendered were presented as internal to each modernity. Likewise, although internal factors leading to clashes were seen as compounded by "international conflicts" and "imperial systems", their first as well as their most important violent effects were nevertheless considered to be the ones occurring within Europe: the first instance of the ideologisation of violence, terror, and war is seen as having materialised in the French revolution, while the extreme manifestation of the nation-states' link with such ideologies of violence is taken to have been the Holocaust (Eisenstadt 2000a). Thus, in Eisenstadt's view, although clashes and conflicts give the cultural and political program of modernity its dynamics, they are inherent to it and are consumed internally.

The Clash of Civilisations as the Next Pattern of Conflict[1]

Samuel Huntington's connection with modernisation theory, although no less complex than Eisenstadt's, has provoked less disagreement among his commentators. Most emphasised his consistent critique of the convergence hypothesis and therefore considered him a critic of modernisation theory. Others, however, pointed to his simultaneous endorsement of such key modernisationist notions as the necessity of a market economy for the emergence of democracy and the breakdown of traditional political order in the transition to modern societies. The latter hence saw him as part of a later, more sophisticated generation of modernisation theorists (So 1990).

Countering the notion that modernisation equals Westernisation was just as much an objective of Huntington's early work as of his later civilisational analysis. In his 1968 "Political Order in Changing Societies", he argued that economic modernisation, while undermining traditional political authority and institutions, does not always result in a modern, stable political order, but instead often breeds violence, instability, and authoritarianism (Huntington 1968). For political modernisation to result in stable liberal democracies, he claimed, the sequence of change would have to observe the Western pattern, in which the rationalisation of authority had preceded the differentiation of political structures and the expansion of political participation. Although he viewed the West as a model of modernisation, Huntington, like Eisenstadt, did not argue for its universality, but for the distinct combination of factors that accounted for the West's success – and thus for its uniqueness.

Unlike Eisenstadt, however, Huntington placed less emphasis on the West's modernity than on its "essence", a notion which became central to his thesis of the clash of civilisations (Huntington 1993, 1996a). In arguing that "the West was

---

1 The following sections are a thoroughly revised and expanded version of a chapter published as "Multiple Europes and the Politics of Difference Within" in *The Study of Europe*, edited by Hauke Brunkhorst and Gerd Grözinger, Nomos Verlag, Baden-Baden, 2010, pp. 51–66.

206   *Global Inequalities Beyond Occidentalism*

the West long before it was modern" (1996a: 72), Huntington aimed to trace the unique qualities of Western civilisation back to a premodern past whose essence, in his view, had to be preserved and defended in the face of declining Western power in the twentieth century. He thus considered the classical legacy of Greece and Rome, Catholicism and Protestantism, pluralism, individualism, and the rule of law to have been distinctive characteristics of Western civilisation centuries before it modernised, and counted Western Christianity as the most important single feature among them. The uniqueness of the West, however, was not considered to stem from any one of these characteristics alone, but from their combination:

> Individually, almost none of these factors was unique to the West. The combination of them was, however, and this is what gave the West its distinctive quality. These concepts, practices, and institutions have simply been more prevalent in the West than in other civilizations. They form at least part of the essential continuing core of Western civilization. They are what is Western, but not modern, about the West. In large part, they are also the factors that enabled the West to take the lead in modernizing itself and the world. (1996a: 72)

The thrust of Huntington's clash of civilisations thesis, formulated a few years after the collapse of state socialism in Eastern Europe, was directed particularly against those interpreting the end of the Cold War as the end of global conflict. Especially prominent in this regard was Francis Fukuyama's notion of the "end of history" (Fukuyama 1992), which took the triumph of liberal over socialist ideology in Eastern Europe to mean the end of significant conflict in global politics and the universalisation of Western liberal democracy. Huntington instead claimed that, in the post-Cold War world, global politics had become both multipolar and multicivilisational for the first time in history and that modernisation produced neither Westernisation nor a universal civilisation. Rather, it was conflicts between groups from different civilisations that became central to global politics. He defined civilisation as "the highest cultural grouping of people and the broadest level of cultural identity people have short of what distinguishes humans from other species" (Huntington 1996a: 43) and viewed human history as the history of civilisations. While he argued that contacts between civilisations had been intermittent or nonexistent during most of this history, he attributed systematic intercivilisational contacts to the "rise of the West" after 1500 and to the subsequent Western colonisation of or impact upon every other civilisation. Much like Eisenstadt, he saw the central role which European colonialism had played in the rise of the West as a consequence of Western military and technological superiority. If the state-sanctioned violence accompanying Western colonialism figured more prominently in Huntington's explanation than in Eisenstadt's, the aim – that of extolling Western virtues – was still the same. Thus, for Huntington,

> The expansion of the West was also facilitated by the superiority in organization, discipline, and training of its troops and subsequently by the superior weapons,

After Uniqueness 207

transport, logistics, and medical services resulting from its leadership in the Industrial Revolution. The West won the world not by the superiority of its ideas or values or religion (to which few members of other civilisations were converted) but rather by its superiority in applying organized violence. (Huntington 1996a: 51)

In reviewing modern Western history, Huntington found that the conflicts between princes, nation-states, and ideologies characterising Western wars since the seventeenth century as well as the two World Wars and the Cold War had been conflicts within Western civilisation with two or multiple poles of power. With the end of the Cold War, he claimed, the centrepiece of international politics however became the interaction between the West and the non-West, especially Western civilisation and Islam, as well as among Western civilisation, such that global politics was now both multipolar and multicivilisational at the same time (see Table 7.1).

Table 7.1   Typology of conflicts

Starting point	Epoch	Type of war	Geohistorical location
Peace of Westphalia (1648)	17th–18th c.	Wars of princes	↑
French Revolution (1789)	19th c.–World War I	Wars of nations	Western phase
Russian Revolution	World War II–Cold War	Ideological wars	↓
End of Cold War (1989)	Since 1989	Civilisational wars	West vs. non-West

Source: Compiled from: Huntington 1993, 1996a.

The new world order he outlined was one in which the most salient and dangerous conflicts would no longer take place between economically defined social classes, but rather between people belonging to different cultural entities, i.e., civilisations: "In class and ideological conflicts, the key question was "Which side are you on?" and people could and did choose sides and change sides. In conflicts between civilisations, the question is "What are you?" That is a given that cannot be changed" (Huntington 1993: 27). Thus, in Huntington's view, not only were cultural differences less mutable and hence less easily resolved than political and economic ones, but they had also proven more enduring than political and economic cleavages throughout history.

His treatment of Europe is illustrative in this regard. Already in his 1993 article, Huntington argued that the eastern boundary of Western Christianity around the year 1500 had replaced the relatively short-lived Iron Curtain as the

Source: Huntington 1993, 72 (3), p. 30.

Figure 7.1   The "Velvet Curtain of Culture". Reprinted by permission of Foreign Affairs. © The Council on Foreign Relations, Inc. www.ForeignAffairs.com

most significant dividing line in Europe. This civilisational fault line, that he referred to as the "Velvet Curtain of Culture", was seen as more pervasive than the political cleavage between Western and Eastern Europe during the Cold War (see Figure 7.1).

In Huntington's view, there had been, at least since 1500, two fundamentally different Europes, the Eastern and the Western one. The border dividing them had briefly changed during the Cold War, when it matched the boundary separating the First World from the Second. However, in "essence", differences in economic level, political culture and especially religion between East and West had remained unchanged during the state socialist regimes in the region. According to Huntington, the role of each of the two Europes in the construction of modernity had been decisive for the maintenance of the disparity. Whereas he saw Protestants and Catholics as having been actively involved in, as well as shaped by, feudalism, the Renaissance, the Reformation, the Enlightenment, the French Revolution, and

After Uniqueness 209

industrialisation, in turn, Orthodox Christians and Muslims, having historically "belonged" to the Ottoman or Tsarist empires, were considered to have been only "lightly touched" by these events (Huntington 1993: 30). The resulting conflict justified, in his view, treating the two parts of the continent as belonging to two different civilisations: Western Christianity on the one hand and Orthodox Christianity and Islam on the other. Their respective cultural logic allegedly also dictated the stability of democratic political systems after the fall of the Iron Curtain: stable democracies were considered a likely prospect for countries of the West, while the permanence of democracies in the East appeared questionable (see Table 7.2).

Table 7.2   Huntington's "Velvet Curtain of Culture"

Fault lines	North/West	South/East
Religion	Protestant/Catholic	Orthodox/Muslim
Economic progress	High	Low
Role in history of European modernity	Central	Peripheral
(Future) political system	Stable democracy	? (Democracy unlikely)

Source: Compiled from Huntington 1993.

Countries with large numbers of peoples that the "Velvet Curtain of Culture" divided into different civilisations, such as the Soviet Union and Yugoslavia, were considered "candidates for dismemberment" and referred to as "torn countries", which, by the time of the publication of Huntington's 1996 book, seemed like an accurate prognosis already come true. The fault line also ran right through existing states, from Belarus and Ukraine, splitting the latter into its Catholic Western and Orthodox Eastern parts, through Romania, where it separated Transylvania from the rest of the territory. However, his prototypical examples of torn European countries were Russia, representing the cleavage between Western ideology and Eastern Christianity, and Turkey, representing the divide between Kemalism and Islam. If Turkey's involvement with the West, embodied in its NATO membership, was seen as significantly weaker after the end of the Cold War, the possibility of Russia "becoming Western" was considered to bring about the end of Orthodox civilisation. For Huntington, "The civilisational paradigm thus provides a clear-cut and compelling answer to the question confronting West Europeans: Where does Europe end? Europe ends where Western Christianity ends and Islam and Orthodoxy begin" (Huntington 1996a: 158). With the expanding European Union as the West's "primary entity in Europe", he claimed, the identification of Europe with Western Christendom provided a reliable criterion for the admission of new members.

210 *Global Inequalities Beyond Occidentalism*

Huntington's model has been frequently and severely criticised on a number of counts. Within civilisational analysis alone, the critique was directed in particular at his essentialist notion of civilisation as well as at his disregard of the systematic interrelationships between Europe, Islam, and Byzantium during the Middle Ages that decisively influenced the formation of Western civilisation (Melleuish 2004; Arjomand and Tiryakian 2004; Arnason 2004). The primacy he awarded culture as a source of collective identity as well as of global conflict was however embraced both by the media and by many theorists of civilisational analysis. Huntington's detailed description of the fault lines along which the clash of civilisations was to take place has prompted serious inquiry into such questions as "Is Israel Western?" (Smooha 2005), "Is the Hindu-Muslim cleavage the paradigmatic case for conflicts in South Asia?" (Tambiah 2005) along with the identification of new "trajectories" such as "From East Europeans to Europeans" (Sztompka 2005) and of a new European collective identity (Martinelli 2005). In a prominent attempt to once again link the cultural explanation underlying civilisational analysis to the legacy of Max Weber, the articles collected in Huntington's co-edited volume *Culture Matters* rejected colonialism, dependency and racism as valid explanations for the economic situation and living conditions in most non-Western countries except the East Asian NICs. Instead, they traced global inequalities of income, education, life expectancy, and democratic rights back to the cultural values and attitudes of civilisations and ethnic groups. In particular, they pitted Puritan thrift and hard work, which Confucian cultures could at least "emulate", against African "distaste for work" and "suppression of individual initiative" or Islamic fatalism and suppression of enterprise (Harrison and Huntington 2000).[2] On the basis of an Occidentalist construction of Western uniqueness, such culturally reductionist approaches end up replacing the political economy of capitalist development by a political economy of immutable cultural differences that both revives old culturally racist stereotypes and prompts new ones.

Entangled Modernities and Multiple Europes

As Engin Isin has noted with respect to the issue of citizenship, claims to Occidental uniqueness in the wake of Weber's analysis have produced two types of dissenting responses: On the one hand, the attempt to prove that the necessary prerequisites for the emergence of modern institutions, thought to be lacking in the Orient, were actually present; on the other hand, the refusal to engage in any comparison between Occidental and Oriental institutions, followed by a denial of the existence of certain modern institutions in the Orient altogether. The fallacies of both approaches are immediately apparent: the former left the truth claims about the Western institution of citizenship unquestioned and analysed the Orient

---

2   For a detailed critique of the cultural determinism espoused in the entire collection, see Sen 2004.

in Western terms; while the latter reinforced the assumption of an ontological difference between Orient and Occident, which precluded any understanding of their age-old interconnections (Isin 2005).[3] A parallel argument can be made about the place of Europe in the civilisational analysis that draws on Weber's legacy: in Eisenstadt's multiple modernities perspective, European modernity, although no longer unique, remains the original one as well as the yardstick against which subsequent multiple modernities are measured; in turn, in Huntington's clash of civilisations model, the impact attributed to Western Christianity on the one hand and to Orthodox Christianity and Islam on the other in shaping the economies and political cultures within Europe cements the idea of an ontological difference between the West and the East of the continent.

The growing literature on cosmopolitanism has more recently offered a different view of the world order of the twenty-first century, in which processes of "re-bordering" (Rumford 2006) play a more important role than old binary oppositions such as the "West vs. the Rest" or centre-periphery. In the case of Europe, this shift has been therefore described as "post-Westernization" (Delanty 2007), a process in which intercivilisational dynamics produce a cosmopolitan Europe with different forms of and experiences with modernity, instead of making the borders between civilisations the regular zones of conflict between them:

> the cultural logic of Europeanization has brought a decrease in border conflicts and a general move in the direction of more cosmopolitan orientations. [...] In sum, the border is not just a conflict zone where a primordial clash of civilizations is played out. The border takes many different forms and includes sites of negotiation [...]. In such cases, the periphery has moved beyond the limits of border thinking and the simple polarities of self versus other are losing their force. (Delanty 2007, S. 10)

As important as the emergence of new borders and the cosmopolitisation of Europe are for refuting the thesis of the clash of civilisations, overemphasis on such phenomena however (mis)leads to an underestimation of the recurrent patterns of hierarchisation of difference: at new and existing borders, processes of negotiation still take place in a highly asymmetrical fashion. Focusing on the new quality of borders as instances of negotiation on the one hand de-emphasises the notion of conflict and clash as the main dynamics of civilisations and allows a better grasp of the continuities instead of the cleavages between cultural identities being negotiated. At the same time, such focus runs the risk of reproducing only one

---

3   Isin referred to the first approach as "reverse Orientalism" and to the second as "Occidentalism" (2005: 32). Because these labels are partly overlapping with and partly opposed to the terms of Occidentalism and Orientalism introduced in the previous chapters of this book, for the following analysis, I do not draw on them explicitly, but only on their underlying logic, as summarised above.

212   *Global Inequalities Beyond Occidentalism*

position in negotiation processes, the dominant one, while neglecting the different relations of power at play in them.

In critiques of civilisational analysis, postcolonial theorists have therefore long pointed to the normative and methodological implications that stem from a comparative civilisational approach. In their view, applying the comparative method to the global level requires "resorting to the fiction of independent development, while relationships and interactions hardly come into view (and then only as a direct contact between the units of analysis). Therefore, the comparison of cultures or civilisations tends to emphasise differences over similarities and is more likely to perpetuate the dichotomy between Europe and its Other than to resolve it" (Conrad and Randeria 2002: 14f., my translation). In search of a perspective that would not privilege Western historical experience and trajectories, Shalini Randeria has therefore suggested replacing both the "history of absences" (Mamdani 1996) produced by modernisation discourses and the "history by analogy" created in multiple modernities approaches by a relational perspective which foregrounds processes of interaction and intermixture (Randeria 1999a, 1999b). Her approach, that she labelled "entangled histories of uneven modernities" builds on the work of Nicholas Dirks and Bernard Cohn on British colonialism in India. Independently of Eisenstadt and Huntington and earlier than both, Dirks and Cohn had stressed that "colonial conquest was not just the result of the power of superior arms, military organization, or economic wealth" (Dirks 2001: ix), but also a cultural project of control. According to them, cultural forms in societies newly classified as "traditional" had been reconstructed and transformed through colonial rule and according to its purposes. In turn, allegedly "modern" administrative practices, urban planning measures, and medical experiments had first been attempted in Europe's colonies and their results subsequently exported back to the metropole. Europe's colonies had thus been not only recipients of impulses of the cultural program of European modernity, but laboratories of a global, colonial modernity (see also Stoler and Cooper 1997). Randeria's notion of "entangled histories of uneven modernities" therefore amounts to the plea "to think metropoles and colonies jointly: departing from their mutual dependence and entanglement, metropoles and colonies within empire are analysed as a transnational formation and unit, in which mutually entangled, even though distinct forms and paths of modernity have crystallised during a common history" (Randeria 1999a: 378, my translation).

The reconceptualisation of modernity undertaken in the perspective of entangled modernities makes the history of (violent) interaction and exchange between metropoles and colonies the discursive framework for the construction of both the modern and the non-modern. By viewing Western and non-Western modernities as constituted in and through interaction and structured by the colonial difference, this perspective closely approximates the modernity/coloniality approach to global inequalities, while giving pride of place to the cultural dimension in a non-Occidentalist fashion (see also Boatcă 2013b). At the same time, it explicitly points to the empirical and theoretical consequences that the shift of focus from the uniqueness of Western modernity to the interdependencies characteristic of global modernity entails for sociology as a discipline: On the one hand, sociological theory can no longer build on generalisations made on the basis of a narrow range of societies that the same theory declares to have been unique and exceptional; rather, it needs to engage with and theoretically incorporate the experiences of non-Western societies both in terms of their historical, cultural and socio-structural specificities and in terms of the constitutive entanglement of colonial and postcolonial modernisation in the peripheries with modernisation in the metropoles as reciprocal conditions of global modernisation. On the other hand, Europe's modernisation cannot be analysed only against the background of different phases of capitalist development, but must consider imperialism as constitutive for European modernity and incorporate the various configurations of modernity in Europe as both the prime-mover and the result of the interdependencies established in the context of colonial and imperial rule (Fuchs, Linkenbach and Randeria 2004).

Following a modified entangled modernities approach that draws on insights from the modernity/coloniality perspective, I therefore suggest replacing the notion of a single Europe producing multiple modernities by the one of multiple Europes with different and unequal roles in shaping the hegemonic definition of modernity and in ensuring its propagation. The focus on multiple Europes thus chosen does not aim at re-centring Europe as a continent or reasserting any unique European legacy, but instead involves a reconsideration of the relations of power and the different hierarchies taking shape within Europe itself in the modern era. The systematic entanglements between the West and its multiple Others within Europe on the one hand, and between the multiple Europes and Africa, the Americas, the Arab world, and Asia on the other thereby foreground the historical interdependencies cutting across and underlying any civilisational divides.

The Semitic and Arabic origins of premodern Europe, usually omitted from the supposed unilinear sequence tracing Europe back to a Graeco-Roman and Christian past, have been analysed in detail by Martin Bernal as early as 1987 (Bernal 1987). Others, such as Enrique Dussel and John Hobson, have pointed out that the unilinear diachrony Greece-Rome-Europe is an ideological construct of late eighteenth century German romanticism, which obscures both the Phoenician mythology of the birth of Europe and the influence of the Arab Muslim world in what is defined as "the classical Greek" philosophy (Dussel 2000: 41; Hobson 2004, Dainotto 2007). Likewise, for Anthony Pagden, the idea of Europe has to be reconstructed taking into account the "amnesia of her Asian origins": "an abducted Asian woman gave Europe her name; a vagrant Asian exile gave Europe its political and finally its cultural identity; and an Asian prophet gave Europe its religion. As Hegel was later to observe, Europe was 'the centre and end' of History, but History had begun in Asia" (Pagden 2002: 35).

The same understanding of a Europe ultimately coherent in its main features is apparent in the economic and political project of the European Union, which has been gradually monopolising the label of "Europe" such that only current member states of the European Union, or those about to become members are considered "European" and consequently included in the term. Although the concept of "Europe" has never had a mere geographic referent, but has always reflected both the geopolitics as well as the epistemology of the various historical moments, with the discourse of the European Union we witness what – following József Böröcz's (2005) argument about a "moral geopolitics" of the European Union – one could label a "moral geography" of the continent, with profound implications for the identity politics of the excluded countries. The "moral geopolitics" refers to the civilising discourse which situates the European Union at the top of the value hierarchy derived from the historical legacy and the current political role of its member states, viewed as exemplary in both cases. According to Böröcz, the moral and geopolitical discourse of European exceptionalism obeys the equivalent of what Partha Chatterjee has labelled "the rule of colonial difference" in the European context, and what Böröcz consequently labels the "rule of European difference":

> The rhetoric of European goodness is the centerpiece of the rise of the notion of "Europe" to historic prominence in the civilizational discourse of coloniality. The civilizational rhetoric of European goodness promotes a hierarchical vision of the world, with "Europe" always at the top [...] The cognitive rule underlying it [...] performs two acts of erasing: it wipes away all acts of evil that have taken place within Europe, and sets Europe apart from the rest of the world, occluding the constitutive ties that have since the long sixteenth century linked Europe to locations where evil acts have been committed in its name or service by agents acting on behalf of its states, business corporations, and other organisations rooted in it. (Böröcz 2005: 126)

The discursive construction of this singular notion of Europe thus depends upon the silencing of the historical role of its member states and their predecessors in creating the main structures of global political and economic inequality. As Böröcz and Sarkar point out, the member states of the European Union before its "Eastern enlargement" in 2004 were "the same states that had exercised imperial rule over nearly half of the inhabitable surface of the globe outside Europe" (Böröcz and Sarkar 2005: 162) and whose colonial possessions covered almost half of the inhabited surface of the non-European world. Today, twenty-eight out of the fifty-eight remaining colonial possessions are under the direct control of EU member states (Dependencies and Territories of the World 2013). Not only were the overseas empires of today's EU states such as Britain, the Netherlands, France and Belgium, Spain and Portugal many times larger than the current size of their territories, but the political impetus behind the emergence of the European Union has been closely linked to the loss of colonial empires after World War II. According to Peo Hansen and Stefan Jonsson, the emergence of the European Economic Community as the EU's predecessor went hand in hand with an intellectual, political and institutional discourse that presupposed the transformation of the strictly national colonial projects into a joint European colonisation of Africa (Hansen and Jonsson 2011).

After Uniqueness 215

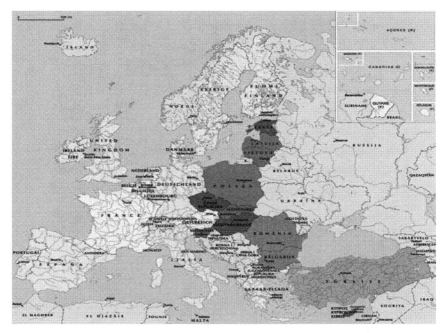

Source: European Commission 2004.

Figure 7.2   Map of EU enlargement 2004 (dark grey), 2007 (light grey) and pending (lighter grey)

The "moral geography" denotes the symbolic representation of the European continent reflecting this discourse. Most telling in this regard were the official maps of the European Union shortly before the 2004 enlargement round, in which the European continent was colour-coded to reflect the "different speeds" of accession and, by extension, the candidate countries' closeness to the European ideal (Figure 7.2). At the same time, Europe's overseas colonial territories, while graphically represented as part of the European Union (i.e., just like the full member states in the map below), played no part in the definition of either the European ideal or the corresponding common identity. However, neither was their non-European location ever mobilised in a discourse of exclusion directed at these territories on account of their cultural, political, or economic difference.

Such geography presupposes an ontological and moral scale ranging from a Western part, whose modern, democratic and pacific character – and therefore superiority – remain unquestioned, up to a backward, violent and inferior part – as such of questionable Europeanness – frequently located in the Eastern part of the continent. However, Eastern Europe and the Balkans only represent the other extreme on the ontological scale of Europeanness, which seems to encompass

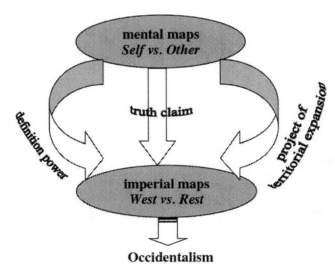

Source: Own drawing.

Figure 7.3   From mental maps to imperial maps

various intermediate degrees. The criteria for one's location in any one position on the scale are nevertheless far from clear.

Although in different forms, both the model of the clash of civilisations and the project of the European Union suggest particular mental maps of the European continent, or rather what Lewis and Wigen have called a metageography, "the set of spatial structures through which people order their knowledge of the world" (1997: ix). While most individual or group-specific mental maps conceptualise differences between the Self and the Other with the help of similar sets of binary oppositions, the truth claims they thereby make tend to remain immanent to their group of origin. In contrast, the mental maps under discussion here combine the typical claim to objective truth with, on the one hand, a territorial project of a colonial or imperial nature that lends legitimacy to the particular representation of the world and, on the other, with the definition power necessary for imposing that representation as valid both to the in-group and to targeted out-groups. They therefore rely primarily on a discursive practice within a power structure – i.e., they are, in Fernando Coronil's words, imperial maps (see Figure 7.3).

During the early modernity of the sixteenth and seventeenth centuries, both the European territorial dominance and the extent of its epistemic power were still partial. In contrast, beginning in the eighteenth century, hierarchies that structured Europe according to principles similar to those applied to the colonial world gradually started taking shape (Boatcă, Costa, and Gutiérrez Rodríguez 2010: 3ff.). As detailed in Chapter 3, after the change in hegemony from the old

After Uniqueness 217

Spanish-Portuguese core to the Northwestern European one, the same principles underlying the spread of Eurocentrism in the non-European world also accounted for the propagation of Occidentalism within Europe. On the one hand, evolutionism served to justify the temporal division of the European continent: while the East was still considered feudal, the South had marked the end of the Middle Ages, and the Northwest represented modernity. On the other hand, the dualism behind constructed categories such as primitive-civilised, irrational-rational, traditional-modern (Quijano 2000a: 543) allowed both a spatial and an ontological division within Europe. The geographically European, (predominantly) Christian and white Southeast of the continent, and especially the Balkans could not be constructed as "an incomplete Other" of Western Europe, as the Far East had been. The region emerged instead as Europe's "incomplete Self" (Todorova 1997). Its proximity to Asia and its Ottoman cultural legacy located it halfway between East and West, thus giving it a condition of semi-Oriental, semi-civilised, semi-developed, in the process of "catching up with the West".[4] In the same vein, the European South, epitomised by the declining Spanish empire and its Moorish legacy, was gradually defined out of the Western core both for its proximity to Islamic North Africa and for its reputation as a brutal coloniser of the New World, constructed as the opposite of England's own benevolent colonialism (Cassano 1995; Santos 2006b).

The construction of the colonial difference overseas thus went hand in hand with the emergence of a double imperial difference in Europe (stretching onto Asia): on the one hand, an external difference between the new capitalist core and the existing traditional empires of Islamic and Eastern Christian faith – the Ottoman and the Tsarist one; on the other hand, an internal difference between the new and the old capitalist core, mainly England vs. Spain (Mignolo 2006). From this moment on, we have at least two types of European subalterns to the hegemonic model of power, as well as the first imperial map of multiple Europes. In light of both the external and the internal imperial difference, we can thus distinguish between what I have elsewhere called decadent Europe (which had lost both hegemony and, accordingly, the epistemic power of defining a hegemonic Self and its subaltern Others), heroic Europe (self-defined as the producer of modernity's main achievements), and epigonal Europe (defined via its alleged lack of these achievements and hence as a mere re-producer of the stages covered by heroic Europe) (see Boatcă 2010, 2013c). While "decadent Europe" and "epigonal Europe" were both characterised by a semiperipheral position, their different trajectories in having achieved this position acted toward disuniting rather than uniting them in their interests: In Spain and Portugal, the memory of lost power and the dominion of imperial languages induced the awareness of a decline from the core, i.e. an imperial nostalgia. Instead, in that part of the continent that had only emerged as "Europe" due to the growing

---

4   Maria Todorova speaks in this context of "Balkanism". Unlike Orientalism, which deals with a difference between (imputed) types, the European (Self) and the Oriental (Other), 'Balkanism' as a discourse treats the differences within one type (Todorova 2004: 235), the civilised Western European and the semi-civilised, semi-Oriental Eastern European.

demise of the Ottoman Empire – i.e., Eastern Europe and the Balkans – the rise to the position of semiperiphery within the world-system alongside the enduring position of periphery within Europe itself made the aspiration to Europeanness – defined as Western modernity – the dominant attitude.

Thus, the subdivisions underlying the imperial map of multiple Europes had served to positively sanction the hegemony of "heroic Europe": France, England, and Germany, as epitomes of what Hegel called "the heart of Europe", became the only authority capable of imposing a universal definition of modernity and at the same time of deploying its imperial projects in the remaining Europes or through them: On the one hand, Northwestern Europe's rise to economic prosperity, during which hegemony was disputed among Holland, France, and England, would use the territorial gains of the first, Spanish-Lusitanian colonial expansion in order to derive the human, economic and cultural resources that substantiated the most characteristically modern achievements – of which the "Industrial Revolution" is a paradigmatic example (Moraña et al. 2008). However, this would occur without integrating the contribution of either the declining European South or of the colonised Americas in the narrative of modernity, which was conceived as being both of (North)Western and of inner-European origin.

On the other hand, and especially as of the mid-nineteenth century, the Western European core of the capitalist world-economy benefited from the end of Ottoman rule in the east of the continent by establishing neocolonies in the rural and agricultural societies of the region and thus gradually gaining control of the strategic trade routes of the Black Sea and the Danube. The subsequent modernisation of the Balkans and the European Southeast through the introduction of bourgeois-liberal institutions and legislation, while pursuing the goal of making the region institutionally recognisable to the West and financially dependent on it, at the same time involved the shaping of political and cultural identities of countries in the region in relation to the Western discourse of power. Consequently, not only Austria, but also Poland, Romania and Croatia defined their contribution to European history as "bulwarks of Christianity" against the Muslim threat, while every country in Eastern Europe designated itself as "frontier between civilisation and barbarism" or as "bridge between West and East". They thus not only legitimised Western superiority, but also fostered the same Orientalism that affected themselves as Balkan, not Christian enough, or not white enough.

Addressing the instrumentalisation of the geopolitical location of "the other Europes" for the purposes of heroic Europe in the long durée helps clarify hierarchies of power within Europe and their impact elsewhere. It thus becomes easier to understand that the Occidentalism directed at the "non-Western" Europes never represented an obstacle to the Eurocentrism that they themselves displayed toward the non-European world. On the contrary: Samuel Huntington accused the Orthodox and Muslim parts of Europe of marginality and passivity with respect to the achievements of modernity, situating them on the other side of one of the fault lines in the future clashes of civilisations. Re-mapping Eastern Europe and the Balkans in the context of a hierarchical model of multiple Europes reveals instead

After Uniqueness 219

that the blindness to the (neo)colonial logic prevalent in these areas' political and identity discourses rather makes them accomplices of the colonial project of power underlying the emergence of modernity (see Table 7.3).

Table 7.3   Multiple Europes

Europe	Prototype	Role in the history of modernity	World-system position	Attitude	Role in coloniality
Decadent	Spain, Portugal	Participant	Semiperiphery	Nostalgia	Founding
Heroic	France, England	Producer	Core	Hegemony	Central
Epigonal	"The Balkans"	Reproducer	Semiperiphery	Aspiration	Accomplice

Such a classification is necessarily incomplete and meant to serve heuristic purposes, not to exhaustively or even partially explain the trajectory of any European region in the longue durée. This has been systematically done a number of times and has yielded widely differing taxonomies, depending on whether the focus of the categorisation were economic or political criteria or a mixture of the two (see e.g. Therborn 1995; Rokkan 1999). On the basis of its most prototypical examples, however, the model of multiple Europes sketched above helps illuminate the impact that the direct or indirect involvement in the extra-European colonial endeavour has had on the definition power associated with a region's structural position within the world-system in general and within Europe in particular. In other words, the further away from the historical experience of "heroic Europe" a part of Europe is or has been, the less definition power it has tended to have with respect to discourses of modernity, European identity, or both. Instead of treating them as structural positions on a continuum of power constantly renegotiated throughout European history, Huntington's model freezes the inequalities of economic and political power around the year 1500 into immutable cultural essences forever divided by civilisational fault lines.

Europeanisation as a Project, a Process, and a Problem

> I admit that it is a good thing to place different civilizations in contact with each other [...]; that for civilizations, exchange is oxygen; that the great good fortune of Europe is to have been a crossroads, and that [...] it was the best center for the redistribution of energy.
>
> But then I ask the following question: has colonization really *placed civilizations in contact*? Or, if you prefer, of all the ways of *establishing contact*, was it the best?
> I answer no.
>
> Aimé Césaire (1950)

220   *Global Inequalities Beyond Occidentalism*

Especially in the wake of the September 11 attacks on the United States and the framing of the terrorist threat as "Islamic challenge" to the entire Western world, Westernisation has increasingly become a matter of taking sides in the clash of civilisations that Huntington deemed characteristic of future global conflicts. On the one hand, the September 11 attacks have overwhelmingly been framed by the US media in terms of a clash of civilisations between Islam and the West, with significant support from some of Huntington's earlier critics (Abrahamian 2003). Recently, *Foreign Affairs* published a twentieth-anniversary edition of Huntington's 1993 article, including prominent responses to its main thesis as well as retrospectives and eulogies (*Foreign Affairs* 2013). On the other hand, Russian support of a division between Western and Eastern Ukraine has triggered a new debate about the validity of the clash of civilisations thesis in both the US and Western European media and academic circles, in which Huntington's views on Ukraine's status as a torn country feature prominently (Hirsh 2014; Schuller 2014; Albrecht 2014).

Apart from its appeal for this type of discourse, the implicit rhetoric of multiple Europes is being reproduced in the majority of the current mental maps of the continent. In this context, the fact that the European Union's current expansion occurs under the heading of "Eastern enlargement" and that incorporation of the Central and South Eastern European countries into the European Union is commonly referred to as a process of "Europeanisation" once again points to the prevalence of the understanding of Europe as a unique set of characteristics, and thus a reduction of Europe to one specific region within it. The unqualified notion of "Europe" used to denote Western and Northern parts of the continent throughout the nineteenth and the twentieth centuries had, until the enlargement round of 2004, which included ten Eastern European countries, become synonymous with the European Union; the Eastern parts of the continent have been recast as a region whose political, socio-cultural, or religious institutions are as many proofs of questionable Europeanness and wanting economic and juridical standards. Likewise, during the 1990s, and with increasing emphasis in the wake of the 2008 financial crisis, Southern Europe's indebted economies have earned Portugal, Italy, Greece and Spain the derogatory acronym PIGS, explicitly meant in opposition to the positively connoted BRICS and implicitly as an accusation of lesser Europeanness. The racial stereotypes mobilised in the process revived familiar eighteenth-century notions of the feudal Catholic South, ailing democracies, and family and clan loyalties preventing the rule of law (Dainotto 2006). At the same time, the remaining colonial dependencies and overseas territories of European Union member states, although largely Christian through colonisation and graphically represented in official European Union maps (see Figure 7.2), atlases, and Euro banknotes, are left completely out of the definition of Europe as well as the question of Europeanness.

The discourse of "Europeanisation" applied to countries with a century-old European cultural and social tradition (from Poland and the Czech Republic to Hungary and Romania) conforms to this very exclusionary logic. On the one hand, it once again instrumentalises the Orientalist imagery to imply that distance from

After Uniqueness 221

the Orient represents the underlying yardstick by which standards of modernity and civilisation are measured. On the other hand, it mobilises the inferiority complexes thus incurred for its own geopolitical projects: As the "Islamic threat" replaced the Communist one in the hegemonic Occidental imaginary, Eastern Europe exchanged its political and economic Second World status for that of a culturally and racially Second World, As such, it remained firmly within the framework of epigonal Europe: By being constructed as (reasonably) white, Christian, and geographically European, but at the same time backward, traditional, and still largely agrarian, epigonal Europe thus reassumes the identity of heroic Europe's incomplete Self rather than, as in the case of Islam and the Orient, its Other (Todorova 1997: 18). In Huntington's model, this shift is portrayed in the replacement of the "Iron Curtain" of politics by the "Velvet Curtain" of culture. While both divides are unbridgeable, the shift additionally creates pathologically "torn" countries that straddled one or both types of borders in the past or do so today.

The fact that the theory and practice of the European Union's "eastern enlargement" act as an "orientalising tool" (Böröcz 2001: 6) becomes apparent in the fact that, for now, the last countries to have achieved admission into the European Union should be Romania, Bulgaria, and Croatia and that among the last to be negotiating it should be Macedonia, Serbia, and Montenegro. At the same time, Turkey, whose application for accession dates almost thirty years, has been repeatedly frozen out of negotiations for membership and currently faces strong opposition from France and, to a significant extent, Germany, who have also repeatedly opposed Romania's and Bulgaria's joining in the Schengen zone (see Chapter 6). Thus, the sequence of the incorporation of new countries into the European Union and its common agreements seems to closely follow the degree of their connection to or overlap with the Ottoman, and therefore Oriental, legacy, constructed as the opposite of politically desirable Europeanness – in turn linked to Western Christianity. The criteria according to which the performance of the Eastern candidates is evaluated poignantly reflect this Orientalist prism: corruption, human trafficking (especially in the form of forced prostitution) and the missing rule of law, responsible both for the belated accession of Romania and Bulgaria during the fifth enlargement round (European Commission 2006), for stalling negotiations with Croatia until 2010 and currently with Turkey (European Commission 2009), clearly belong to the repertoire of Oriental despotism that prominently featured among the images of the Orient constructed in the eighteenth and nineteenth centuries and are now being reproduced in relation to the European East. Singling them out as critical issues in the countries under scrutiny not only renders the applicant states exotic and inferior (Kovács 2001), but, more importantly, traces their problems back to a past which the member states have supposedly overcome. The official rhetoric accordingly bears pedagogical overtones:

> This fifth enlargement of the EU had a political and moral dimension. It enabled countries – Cyprus, the Czech Republic, Estonia, Hungary, Latvia, Lithuania,

Malta, Poland, Slovakia and Slovenia – *which are as European as the others, not just geographically but also in terms of culture, history and aspirations*, to join the democratic European family. They are now partners in the momentous project conceived by the EU's founding fathers. Bulgaria and Romania set out as part of this group, but their entry process took longer. They joined the EU on 1 January 2007 […] Turkey, a member of NATO, with a long-standing association agreement with the EU, applied for membership in 1987. Its *geographical location* and *political history* made the EU hesitate for a long time before replying positively to its application. However, in October 2005, the European Council opened accession negotiations with Turkey. (EU 2009, emphasis added)

The EU accession rhetoric at play in such statements is therefore in line with the logic of both the imperial and the colonial difference: While connections with traditional Eastern empires are a serious impediment to access, but can ultimately be negotiated (if only on Western terms), the possession of former or present colonies by EU member states is not even allowed to surface in accession discourse: The geographical location of the British Virgin Islands, the Dutch Antilles or the French overseas departments in the Caribbean and South America, although much more clearly non-European than that of Turkey, never made the EU hesitate about the legitimacy of their membership. As long as their colonial status remains unaddressed, the political geography of Europe does not need to be redefined. Likewise, academic engagement with the existence of European colonial possessions overseas is unlikely to prompt an official acknowledgment of the fact that the Western borders of the European Union are in the Americas (and have been so for decades).

In turn, negotiations of cultural and racial identities framed in terms of repudiating an Oriental past, stressing one's contribution to European civilisation, and mapping one's integration into the European Union as a "return to Europe" – and therefore as an act of historical reparation – once again dominate the identity rhetoric across Eastern Europe. On the one hand, national elites have referred to the political and economic transition of both Croatia and Slovenia in the 1990's as liberation from "Balkan darkness" (Lindstrom 2003: 319). At the same time, the electoral promise of rejoining Europe both institutionally and economically has been grounded on the emphasis placed on the country's century-old role as "bulwark of Christianity"[5] against the Ottoman threat in both Croatia and Poland (Bakić-Hayden 1995: 922) and has reinforced claims of historical belonging to Central Europe (rather than Eastern Europe or the Balkans) throughout former Yugoslavia (Bakić-Hayden 1995: 924; Lindstrom 2003: 324).

---

5 "antemurale Christianitatis", a title equally claimed first and foremost by Austria, further by Poland and Romania, but explicitly used by Pope Leo X in 1519 in reference to Croatia, in acknowledgment of the role of the Croatian army in fighting back the Ottomans.

After Uniqueness 223

The discourse of historical reparation has also figurely prominently in Spain and Portugal, closely reflecting their enduring position as part of "decadent Europe". The Spanish and Portuguese parliaments have recently approved laws that would grant citizenship to the Sephardic Jews exiled to the Iberian colonies in the Americas or forced to convert to Christianity during the sixteenth century. Applicants have to prove their Sephardic origin, but are not required to take up residence in the country or renounce their current citizenship (BBC News 2013). Although both governments have stressed that the measures aim at "righting a historical wrong" and at recovering their countries' "silenced memory", no similar measure has been approved for Muslims, who have been expelled from Spain during the same period and for the same reasons (see Chapter 3). Some critics see economic motives behind the move of inviting Sephardic Jews – who today number an estimated 3.5 million people living mostly in Israel, the United States, Belgium, Greece, France and Turkey – back to Spain (Kern 2012). However, the resurgence of Islamophobia throughout the world is a more plausible explanation for the renewed exclusion of Muslims within a European matrix of imperial/colonial difference.

The religious, racial or economic focus of the strategies employed by candidates to Europeanness in such negotiations is of little consequence. The primary objective in all cases is the same: ascending from the status of an "epigonal" or "decadent" Europe" to that of "heroic Europe", accomplished only in the case of the respective countries' thorough break with and disavowal of their Islamic, Oriental, or Ottoman legacy. Accordingly, individual strategies of delimitation are contingent upon handing over Easternness, Orientality, and ultimately non-whiteness to newly constructed "others" within the region, thus internally reproducing Orientalism in kaleidoscopic fashion, as Milica Bakić-Hayden has documented for former Yugoslavia:

> while Europe as a whole has disparaged not only the orient 'proper', but also the parts of Europe that were under oriental Ottoman rule, Yugoslavs who reside in areas that were formerly the Habsburg monarchy distinguish themselves from those in areas formerly ruled by the Ottoman Empire and hence 'improper'. Within the latter area, eastern Orthodox peoples perceive themselves as more European than those who assumed identity of European Muslims and who further distinguish themselves from the ultimate orientals, non-Europeans. (Bakić-Hayden, 1995: 922)

Needless to say that, the more the epigonal and decadent Europes emphasise their degree of Europeanness, the more they highlight their difference from heroic Europe and reinforce the imperial map according to which the concept of "Europeanness" corresponds to the dominant Western model. Thus, processes of racial othering in kindred cultural spaces make it possible to include Southern and Eastern Europe in the identity of the expanding European Union as well as to simultaneously exclude them.

"There Is No Safe Place": Open Questions

Can any of the multiple Europes provide the basis for a single notion of Europe, or a unique model for a characteristically European modernity? Given that they all produced imperialist, colonial, nationalist, racist, or totalitarian ideologies at some point in the history of world modernity, there is no geopolitically and epistemologically safe place representing either a European or a modern essence. On the contrary, just as the history of Europe has been entangled with the history of the non-European areas which it conquered, traded with, attacked, and defended itself from, so the history of modernity has been shaped by and become inseparable from colonialism, imperialism, slavery, and warfare. Reducing Europeanness to a triumphalist version of modernity restricted to a handful of heroic "founding fathers" therefore fails to take into account the multiplicity of Europes and their respective (and contradictory) contributions to European civilisation – not the plurality of modernity as such. In an indirect reply to approaches pleading for a unique civilisation to be defended, Walter Mignolo noted:

> The future can no longer be thought of as the 'defense of the Western civilization', constantly waiting for the barbarians. As barbarians are ubiquitous (they could be in the plains or in the mountains as well as in global cities), so are the civilized. There is no safe place to defend, and, even worse, believing that there is a safe place that must be defended is (and has been) the direct road to killing. [...] Dialogue can only take place once 'modernity' is decolonized and dispossessed of its mythical march toward the future. (Mignolo, 2005: xix)

In the context of the self-proclaimed civilising project of the European Union, this however amounts to a renewed race for identity among those Eastern European and Balkan countries situated on the hem of the "Velvet Curtain" that supposedly separates "proper" Christianity from Islam. For them, the race's enduring stake – access to Western markets, employment opportunities, and financial aid – amounts to an exercise in "moral geopolitics" (Böröcz 2005: 115) that involves discarding – or at least downplaying – their "Easternness" while professing a will to Westernisation. For them, sharing in Western privileges thus appears a more urgent task than pointing out the power asymmetries within pan-European political and economic structures and investing effort in restructuring them. It has therefore been suggested that, unlike the clear-cut colonial difference outside of Europe, the ex-Second World situated at the border between the European imperial and colonial powers faces blurredness – of the imperial difference from the West – as well as splitness – between being the West's partial Other and its incomplete Self (Ivakhnenko 2006: 604; Mignolo and Tlostanova 2006: 217; Todorova 1997: 18).

This chapter has therefore pleaded for replacing the idea of a single proper – namely, heroic – Europe, which has generated multiple modernities worldwide, by the one of multiple Europes, whose cultural, political and economic contributions to European civilisation have disproportionately gone into the definition of the specific Western modernity. The heuristic model of multiple Europe proposed here is intended to clarify the multiplicity of historical paths, the geopolitical linkages and the power hierarchies emerged within the European continent since the colonial expansion. Juxtaposed to it is a discursive model of multiple Europes based upon the same historically developed power hierarchies: Each time *the unity* of Europe becomes the object of a programmatic call, as in the identity politics discourse of the European Union, or – the other way around – each time *the historical division* of Europe is set retroactively along cultural and religious lines over the last five hundred years – as in Huntington's idea of the Velvet Curtain of Culture – one of the multiple Europes is hyped up as the only valid. A discursive model that defines Europeanness as unity or as uniqueness, respectively, thereby serves to misrepresent the diversity of postcolonial and postimperial Europe as a limitation and to reproduce, by means of the above-discussed moral geography of the continent, an internal politics of difference which can only result in the opposite of unity.

Chapter 8
Conclusions: For a Sociology of Global Inequalities Beyond Occidentalism

The present book has dealt with the way transregional entanglements characterising the modern world-system since the sixteenth century unsettle the theoretical, conceptual and methodological apparatus of social inequality research developed in the West. I have argued that the Occidentalism (rather than the Eurocentrism) informing much theory-building from sociology's classics up to present-day approaches to national, transnational and global inequalities has led to a systematic neglect, downplaying or misrepresentation of the dynamics of colonialism and imperialism that were responsible for the structural entanglements of power between world regions from the past centuries until today. In so doing, my goal has been to reveal the extent to which the mainstream analysis of social inequalities relies on an *overgeneralisation* of the Western European experience as well as on the *erasure* of non-Western, non-European, and non-White experiences from sociological theory-building.

The twin fallacies of *overgeneralisation* and *erasure* were made possible by two interrelated tendencies of Occidentalist sociological production: First, the historical debt of core categories of the sociology of social inequality, especially class, to the socioeconomic context of Western European industrial society and to the rise of the nation-state, rendered class conflict, proletarianisation, and social mobility within industrial nations more visible than colonialism, the slave trade, and European emigration to the Americas. Second, this differential visibility made for the disproportionate representation of the former processes in mainstream sociological theory as opposed to the latter. The European colonial expansion into the Americas since the sixteenth century triggered a massive dislocation of people, resulting in various waves of ethnic homogenisation of core areas on the one hand and in the racialisation and ethnicisation of the population of peripheral and semiperipheral ones on the other. Disregarding these processes was essential in reproducing a Eurocentric/Occidentalist perspective. The global division of labour in place since the colonisation of the Americas had gradually reorganised the economies, political systems, and social hierarchies of the colonies according to the needs of European colonial centres and in the process decisively transformed and systematically connected both. Neglecting this dynamic was central to the theoretical relegation of colonial societies to a past that Western societies had allegedly overcome. The establishment and maintaining of a sociology of inequality and stratification that neglected race and ethnicity in the West, a sociology of capitalist development that downplayed slave economies, indentured labour, and all forms of non-wage work, and a sociology of migration devoid of both colonisers and colonial subjects until late in the twentieth century were the consequence. Missing from all accounts was the experience of women, to be only partially and gradually corrected by the inclusion of white Western women as objects and, later, subjects of sociological production in the West.

While the critique of sociology's "methodological nationalism" is relatively recent, substantive correctives of such methodological as well as of conceptual blind spots resulted from the erasure of global dynamics of power from sociology's theoretical canon have been applied to it much earlier. They came from at least two distinct directions: On the one hand, feminist theorists have long pointed to the insufficiency of the standard dimensions of class, status, educational level and religious denomination for explaining social inequality, and have argued for the necessity of factoring race, ethnicity, and the North-South divide in the analysis of gender disparities. On the other hand, dependency and world-systems studies, which situated inequality on a global level and viewed class struggle as a conflict between bourgeois and proletarian areas in the world-economy (rather than social strata within a state), have cautioned against positing the nation-state as the unit of analysis for inequality relations. Disclosing the consequences that a methodological shift in the unit of analysis from the nation-state to the world as a whole entails for making visible transregional and transnational entanglements of power has been a central objective of this book. I have however argued that the deficit of mainstream social inequality research is not merely methodological. Instead, a substantive reconceptualisation of inequalities at the global level that transcends the Occidentalism of its core categories also requires systematic consideration of the arguments put forth by both earlier approaches and the insights of more recent theoretical perspectives, in particular worlds-systems analysis, transnational migration research, postcolonial studies, and the decolonial perspective.

In Chapters 1 and 5, I have shown how both Marx' and Weber's theories of class were embedded in larger theories of modernity and capitalism. To these corresponded not only the nation-state framework of their emergence, but also specific theories of social change in the West, as well as an understanding of the dynamics of the processes of class formation behind the production and reproduction of inequality. I have therefore argued that a theoretically informed and methodologically consistent reconceptualisation of inequality that leaves behind the Occidentalist and methodologically nationalist assumptions of the classics' formulations has to take into account the implications of shifts from Western and national structures to global structures in all three dimensions: the upscaling of the unit of analysis, the uncovering of interdependent processes of social change linking Western and non-Western areas, as well as the inclusion of the dynamics of class formation corresponding to both. The previous chapters have illustrated the way in which methodological shifts related to each of these dimensions have been proposed within different theoretical approaches that have nevertheless until now failed to produce a coherent theoretical model. On account of all of their contributions, however, today's sociology of global inequalities does not have to

Conclusions 229

reinvent the wheel in order to account for its wider epistemic and empirical scope, but needs to successfully integrate existing theoretical as well as methodological propositions to this effect.

A strict division between Marxist and Weberian approaches to social inequalities is necessarily artificial today and has been so in the past. As several scholars have noted (and as has been shown in the previous chapters), Marx's and Weber's analyses of capitalism and modernity shared many common points that warrant viewing their approaches to class divisions in the Western world as complementary rather than as contradictory. The overlaps between the approaches of many of their followers additionally reinforce the complementarity argument. Still, if the distinction between Marxist and Weberian positions is not particularly helpful in itself, the consequences derived from the establishment of a Western sociological canon that defined this very distinction as real are all the more with us today: As shown in the case of twentieth-century inequality research, the initial choice between Marxist and Weberian theories of inequality was translated into an intellectual division of labour along the lines of Weber's distinction of class and status: the sociology of social inequality has been entrusted with the analysis of structural disparities, while gender, racial, and ethnic studies have mostly been relegated to the study of "cultural differences" (Weiß 2001). Besides conceiving of gender, race and ethnicity as types of status that result in either second-degree or "new" inequalities, this decoupling of tasks has produced a "culturalisation of sociological analysis" (Eder 2001: 56) that until recently has tended to delegitimise a focus on capitalist structures.

From among the global approaches presented in this book, the ones that most successfully bridge the artificial divide between structure – or the political economy of global inequalities – and culture – as "particularities" of race, gender, ethnicity – have not been explicitly conceived as research agendas for social inequality analysis, but as responses from the Global South to the imposition of Occidentalist concepts from the Global North: The decolonial perspective, presented in Chapter 3, with a background in Latin American dependency theory and world-systems analysis and a history of dialogue with the Indian Subaltern Studies school, was focused on understanding the role of structural dependencies and racial hierarchies in Latin America. Going beyond Indian postcolonial studies' plea to provincialise Europe, its explicit aim was to "globalize the periphery: to recognize the worldwide formation of what appear to be self-generated modern metropolitan centers and backward peripheries" (Coronil 2004). Similarly, the entangled modernities perspective discussed in Chapter 7, with a background in Indian Subaltern Studies, was in part meant as a response to the rise to prominence of the multiple modernities paradigm, but also as a wider intervention in mainstream sociology's Eurocentrism and conceptual nationalism. Although much less elaborated than the decolonial perspective, its thrust went in the same direction of making the constitutive link between modernisation in the metropoles and colonial and postcolonial modernisation in the peripheries the basis for an analysis of the shared histories of entangled modernities (Randeria 1999; Conrad and Randeria 2002). Both approaches thus address sociology's structural imbalance between the West as a subject of study and the holder of the monopoly on theory on the one hand and the non-West as the object of study of most macrosociological paradigms, on the other. The corrective, both in the decolonial and in the entangled modernities approach, is a relational perspective that views colonial and imperial rule as the common transnational context of interaction for both the West and its colonial Others and allows an understanding of colonial and peripheral contexts as laboratories of a global modernity, rather than as mere receptors of Western achievements.

Both the relational perspective and the idea of the colonies as laboratories in which modernity's most characteristic features are tested echo earlier approaches, in turn derived from the experience of the Global South: Among these, Sidney Mintz' notion of the "double linkage of production and consumption" between slaves on Caribbean plantations and industrial workers in Western Europe and Maria Mies' concept of the "double-faced process of colonisation and housewifisation", which structurally and temporally juxtaposes the naturalisation of non-White women in the Caribbean and Africa to the defining of white European women into housewives, are discussed in Chapter 2. To this day, the Caribbean acts as a crucible of economic solutions to the challenges of global modernity, as the example of the earliest citizenship-by-investment programs now being reproduced throughout Europe in response to the 2008 financial crisis has shown in Chapter 6. Similarly, the devaluing of women and nature that led to the social, cultural and theoretical invisibility of women's economic inputs, which Mies and a number of feminists in the Global South as well as the Global North traced back to the onset of agricultural capitalism, has only relatively recently entered global inequality debates as a new phenomenon under the label of the "feminisation of poverty".

From among the approaches explicitly concerned with global inequality and stratification, one of the most successful at exposing the theoretical and methodological implications of a shift in the unit of analysis from the nation-state to the world as a whole and at providing several venues for a sociology of global inequalities is the world-historical model discussed in Chapter 4 (Korzeniewicz and Moran 2009; Korzeniewicz and Albrecht 2013). In particular, the focus of this approach on global inequality patterns provides striking insights into the continued importance of ascribed characteristics such as citizenship for patterns of social stratification of modernity. That globally and longitudinally consistent data to this effect should only be available from non-state actors, as in the case of the Union Bank of Switzerland data used by Korzeniewicz and Albrecht, or the Henley and Partners annual Visa Restriction Index that I discuss at the end of Chapter 6, points to private companies as important transnational actors and collectors of global data sets that social scientific analyses of global inequalities all too often neglect.

By contrast, the comparative-historical analysis of the emergence of the institution of citizenship in different parts of the world in relation to the Western model presented in Chapter 6 fails to target the logic of accumulation at the same time as it reinforces the principle of ascription that underlies it. Ultimately, a

Weberian focus on Western Europe's pioneering role in forging a community of equal citizens channels attention to processes internal to that community and the features that make it unique in comparison to its counterparts elsewhere. Even as it invites a comparative approach, such a focus however prevents an understanding of the interrelations which made the singularity of the original context possible. At its most Occidentalist, the comparative analysis of civilisations replaces the Marxist political economy of class conflict with a Weberian political economy of cultural differences with clearly racist overtones, as becomes clear from the discussion of Huntington's approach in Chapter 7. A global perspective on citizenship however becomes possible when renouncing the comparative focus of units of analysis built on culture. Brubaker's and Shachar's approaches to citizenship as a form of closure and as a form of inherited property, respectively, discussed in Chapter 6, are illustrative in this respect. Also, an understanding of the dynamics of modernity that de-centres the role of West requires relinquishing the notion of multiple modernities emerged through dialectic tension from a Western European original. Drawing on insights from the modernity/coloniality as well as the entangled modernities perspective, I instead propose, in Chapter 7, an analysis of the multiple alterities within Europe which enabled both Western Europe's colonial and imperial expansion and its monopolisation of the definition of modernity.

Instead of heralding global inequalities, transnational migration, or the feminisation of poverty as new phenomena, what is needed is an adequate un-erasure of the history and experience of the non-White and non-European populations as well as non-Western regions from social scientific theory-building. The unerasure of the non-European from mainstream social theory would not only reveal a far more entangled history of multiple Europes than the one we are accustomed to reading, but would also result in global instead of universal sociology. Instead of overgeneralising from the particular history of its own geopolitical location, a global sociology which has moved beyond Occidentalism would be able to account for the continuum of structures of power linking geopolitical locations from colonial through postcolonial times.

References

Abraham, G. 1991. Max Weber: Modernist Anti-Pluralism and the Polish Question. *New German Critique*, 53, 33–66.

Abrahamian, E. 2003. The US Media, Huntington and September 11, *Third World Quarterly*, 24(3), 529–44.

Acker, J. 1992. Making Gender Visible, in *Feminism and Sociological Theory*, edited by R. Wallace. London: Sage, 65–81.

Albrecht, C. 2014. *Europa und die Ukraine: Huntington Reloaded?*, [Online]. Available at: http://soziologie.de/blog/?p=3251, [accessed 24 April 2014].

Alexander, J.M. 1991. Redrafting Morality: The Postcolonial State and the Sexual Offences Bill of Trinidad and Tobago, in *Third World Women and the Politics of Feminism*, edited by C.T. Mohanty, A. Russo and L. Torres. Bloomington: Indiana University Press, 133–52.

Allen, W.R. and Chung, A. 2000. ‚Your Blues Ain't Like My Blues': Race, Ethnicity and Social Inequality in America, *Contemporary Sociology*, 29(1), 796–805.

Althusser, L. 1964. *Marxism and Humanism*. Cahiers de l'I.S.E.A., June 1964, 109–33.

Antón, J., Bello, A., Popolo, F., Paixão, M. and Ranger, M. 2009. *Afrodescendientes en América Latina y el Caribe: del reconocimiento estadístico a la realización de derechos*. Santiago de Chile: CEPAL.

Araghi, F. and Karides, M. 2012. Land Dispossession and Global Crisis: Introduction to the Special Section on Land Rights in the World System. *Journal of World-Systems Research*, XVIII(1), 1–5.

Arjomand, S.A. and Tiryakian E. (eds) 2004. *Rethinking Civilizational Analysis*. London: Sage.

Armer, J.M. and Katsillis, J. 2001. Modernization Theory, in *Encyclopedia of Sociology*, edited by E.F. Borgatta and R.J.V. Montgomery, 2nd ed. Vol. 3. New York: Macmillan Reference USA, 1883–8.

Arnason, J. 2004. Civilizational Patterns and Civilizing Processes, in *Rethinking Civilizational Analysis*, edited by S.A. Arjomand and E. Tiryakian. London: Sage, 103–18.

Arrighi, G. 2002. Global Inequalities and the Legacy of Dependency Theory. *Radical Philosophy Review*, 5(1/2), 75–85.

Arrighi, G., Hopkins, T.K. and Wallerstein, I. 1989. *Anti-Systemic Movements*. London: Verso.

Asian Development Bank 2013. *Gender Equality and Food Security – Women's Empowerment as a Tool against Hunger*. Mandaluyong City, Philippines: ADB.

234 *Global Inequalities Beyond Occidentalism*

Augel, J. 1984. The Contribution of Public Goods to Household Reproduction: Case Study from Brazil, in *Households and the World-Economy*, edited by J. Smith, I. Wallerstein, Immanuel and H. Evers. London: Sage, 173–9

Bader, V.M. 1998. Ethnizität, Rassismus und Klassen, in *Die Wiederentdeckung der Klassen*, edited by Bader, V.M., Benschop, A., Krätke, M.R. and van Treeck, W. Hamburg: Argument, 96–125.

Bădescu, I., Dungaciu, D., Cristea, S., Degeratu, C., Baltasiu, R. 1995. *Sociologia și geopolitica frontierei (2 vols.)*, Bucharest, Floarea albastră.

Baechler, J. 2007. But What Is Sociology? *European Journal of Social Theory*, Vol. 10, Nr. 2, May 2007, 200–205.

Baier, A. 2004. Subsistenzansatz: Von der Hausarbeitsdebatte zur "Bielefelder Subsistenzperspektive", in *Handbuch Frauen- und Geschlechterforschung. Theorie, Methoden, Empirie*, edited by R. Becker and B. Kortendiek, 72–7.

Bakić-Hayden, M. 1995. Nesting Orientalisms: The Case of Former Yugoslavia, *Slavic Review*, 54(4), 917–31.

Balibar, É. 1996. Is There A Neo-Racism?, in *Race, Nation, Class. Ambiguous Identities*, edited by E. Balibar and I. Wallerstein. London: Verso, 17–28.

Balibar, É. and Wallerstein, I. 1996. *Race, Nation, Class. Ambiguous Identities*. London: Verso.

Banton, M. 2007. Max Weber on 'ethnic communities': A critique. *Nations and Nationalism*, 13(1), 19–35.

Bărbulescu, R. 2014. Global mobility corridors for the ultra-rich. The neoliberal transformation of citizenship, in *Should Citizenship be for Sale?*, edited by A. Shachar and R. Bauböck. EUI Working Papers RSCAS, 2014/01, 15–16.

Bartolovich, C. 2002. Introduction: Marxism, Modernity, and Postcolonial Studies, in *Marxism, Modernity, and Postcolonial Studies*, edited by C. Bartolovich and N. Lazarus. Cambridge: Cambridge University Press, 1–17.

Bartolovich, C. and Lazarus, N. (eds) 2002. *Marxism, Modernity, and Postcolonial Studies*. Cambridge: Cambridge University Press.

Bashi Treitler, V. 2013. *The Ethnic Project. Transforming Racial Fiction into Ethnic Factions*. Stanford: Stanford University Press.

BBC News 2013. *EU Shrugs off European Race to Woo Rich Foreigners*. November 18, 2013, [Online]. Available at: http://www.bbc.com/news/world-europe-24940012 [accessed 2 April 2014].

Beck, U. 1986. *Risikogesellschaft*, Frankfurt a. M.: Suhrkamp.

—. 1999. Globalisierung als Unterscheidungsmerkmal der Zweiten Moderne, in *Globalisierung. Ökonomische und soziale Herausforderungen am Ende des zwanzigsten Jahrhunderts, Soziale Welt, special issue 13*, edited by G. Schmidt and R. Trinczek. Baden-Baden: Nomos, 535–49.

—. 2004. *Der kosmopolitische Blick. Oder: Der Krieg ist Frieden*. Frankfurt a. M.: Suhrkamp.

—. 2007. Beyond Class and Nation: Reframing Social Inequalities in a Globalizing World. *British Journal of Sociology*, 58(4), 679–705.

References

Beck, U. and Sznaider, N. 2006. Unpacking Cosmopolitanism for the Social Sciences: A Research Agenda. *The British Journal of Sociology*, 57(1), 1–23.

Bendix, R. 1964. *Nation-Building and Citizenship: Studies of Our Changing Social Order*. New York: Wiley.

—. 1974 Inequality and Social Structure: A Comparison of Marx and Weber. *American Sociological Review* 39(2), 149–61.

—. 1977 *Max Weber: An Intellectual Portrait*. Berkeley: University of California Press.

Bennholdt-Thomsen, V. 1984. Towards a Theory of the Sexual Division of Labor, in *Households and the World-Economy*, edited by J. Smith, I. Wallerstein and H. Evers. London: Sage, 252–71.

—. 1988a. Why Do Housewives Continue to be Created in the Third World too?, in *Women, the Last Colony*, edited by M. Mies, V. Bennholdt-Thomsen, Veronika and C. von Werlhof. London: Zed Books, 159–67.

—. 1988b. Investment in the Poor: An Analysis of World Bank Policy, in *Women, the Last Colony*, edited by M. Mies, V. Bennholdt-Thomsen, Veronika and C. von Werlhof. London: Zed Books, 51–63.

Ben-Rafael, E. and Sternberg, Y. 2005. *Comparing Modernities. Essays in Homage to Shmuel N. Eisenstadt*. Leiden: Brill.

Berger, P.A. 2003. Kontinuitäten und Brüche. Herausforderungen für die Sozialstruktur- und Ungleichheitsforschung im 21. Jahrhundert, in *Soziologische Forschung: Stand und Perspektiven*, edited by B. Orth, T. Schwietring and J. Weiß. Opladen: Leske + Budrich, 473–90.

Berger, P.A. and Hradil, S. 1990. *Lebenslagen, Lebensläufe, Lebensstile, Soziale Welt, special issue 7*. Göttingen: Otto Schwarz.

Bergesen, A.J. and Bata, M. 2002. Global and National Inequality: Are They Connected? *Journal of World-Systems Research*, VIII, I, 130–44.

Bergquist, C. 1996. The Paradox of American Development, in: *Labor and the Course of American Democracy*. New York: Verso, 9–42.

Bernal, M. 1987. *Black Athena: Afroasiatic Roots of Classical Civilization, Volume I: The Fabrication of Ancient Greece, 1785–1985*. New Brunswick: Rutgers University Press.

Bernasconi, R. 1998. Hegel at the Court of Ashanti, in: *Hegel after Derrida*, edited by S. Barnett. London: Routledge, 41–63.

Bhambra, G. 2007a. Sociology and Postcolonialism: Another 'Missing' Revolution? *Sociology*, 41 (5). 871–84.

—. 2007b. *Rethinking Modernity: Postcolonialism and the Sociological Imagination*. London: Palgrave Macmillan.

Blackburn, R. 1988. *The Overthrow of Colonial Slavery, 1776–1848*. London: Verso.

Blakely, A. 2009. The Emergence of Afro-Europe. A Preliminary Sketch, in *Black Europe and the African Diaspora*, edited by D.C. Hine, T.D. Keaton, and S. Small, Chicago: University of Illinois, 3–28

236   *Global Inequalities Beyond Occidentalism*

Boatcă, M. 2003a. *From Neoevolutionism to World-Systems Analysis. The Romanian Theory of 'Forms without Substance' in Light of Modern Debates on Social Change.* Opladen: Leske+Budrich.

—. 2003b. Kulturcode Gewalt, in: *Geschlecht – Gewalt – Gesellschaft*, edited by S. Lamnek and M. Boatcă. Opladen: Leske+Budrich, 55–70.

—. 2006. Die zu Ende gedachte Moderne. Alternative Theoriekonzepte in den lateinamerikanischen und osteuropäischen Peripherien, in *Die Vielfalt und Einheit der Moderne*, edited by T. Schwinn. Wiesbaden: VS, 281–304.

—. 2009. Lange Wellen des Okzidentalismus. Ver-Fremden von Gender, Rasse und Ethnizität im modernen Weltsystem, in *Kritik des Okzidentalismus. Transdisziplinäre Beiträge zu (Neo-)Orientalismus und Geschlecht*, edited by G. Dietze, C. Brunner and E. Wenzel. Bielefeld: transcript, 233–50.

—. 2010. Class vs. Other as Analytic Categories. The Selective Incorporation of Migrants into Theory, in *Mass Migration in the World-System: Past, Present, and Future*, edited by T. Jones and E. Mielans. London and Boulder: Paradigm, 38–54.

—. 2012. Review: Ayelet Schachar: The Birthright Lottery. Citizenship and Global Inequality. Boston: Harvard University Press, 2009. *Critical Reviews on Latin American Research,* 1, 1–4.

—. 2013a. The Many Non-Wests. Marx's Global Modernity and the Coloniality of Labor. *Deutsche Zeitschrift für Philosophie*, special issue 34, 209–25.

—. 2013b. Two-Way Street. Moderne(n), Verwobenheit, und Kolonialität. *Österreichische Zeitschrift für Soziologie* 38 (4), 375–94

—. 2013c. Introduction. Uneasy Postcolonialisms. Easing the Way into a Non-Topic, *Worlds and Knowledges Otherwise* 3 (3), [Online]. Available at: https://globalstudies.trinity.duke.edu/volume-3-dossier-3-uneasy-postcolonialisms [accessed 17 May 2013].

—. 2014. Second Slavery vs. Second Serfdom. Local Labor Regimes of the Global Periphery, in *Social Theory and Regional Studies in the Global Age*, edited by S. Arjomand. New York: Stony Brook Press, 361-388.

Boatcă, M. and Costa, S. 2010. Postcolonial Sociology: a Research Agenda, in *Decolonizing European Sociology*, edited by E. Gutiérrez Rodríguez, M. Boatcă, and S. Costa. Farnham: Ashgate, 13–31.

Boatcă, M., Costa, S. and Gutiérrez Rodríguez, E. 2010. Introduction. Decolonizing European Sociology: Different Paths towards a Pending Project, in *Decolonizing European Sociology*, edited by E. Gutiérrez Rodríguez, M. Boatcă, and S. Costa. Farnham: Ashgate, 1–10.

Boatcă, M. and Lamnek, S. 2003. Gewalt als Phänomen unserer Zeit. *Sozialwissenschaften und Berufspraxis*, 2/2003, 123–34.

Böröcz, J. 1997. Stand Reconstructed: Contingent Closure and Institutional Change. *Sociological Theory*, 15(3), 215–48.

—. 2001. Introduction: Empire and Coloniality in the 'Eastern Enlargement' of the European Union, in *Empire's New Clothes. Unveiling EU Enlargement*, edited by J. Böröcz and M. Kovács. Holly Cottage: Central European Review, 4–50.

—. 2005. Goodness Is Elsewhere: The Rule of European Difference. *Comparative Studies in Society and History*, 48(1), 110–387.

Böröcz, J. and Sarkar, M. 2005. What is the EU? *International Sociology*, 20(2), 153–73.

Brady, H. 2012. *Saving Schengen: How to Protect Passport-Free Travel in Europe.* London: Centre for European Reform.

Britten, N. and Heath, A. 1983. Women, Men and Social Class, in *Gender, Class, and Work*, edited by E. Gamarnikow, D. Morgan, J. Purvis and D. Taylorson. London: Heinemann, 46–60.

Brubaker, R. 1992. *Citizenship and Nationhood in France and Germany.* Cambridge, MA: Harvard University Press.

—. 2004. *Ethnicity without Groups*. Cambridge, MA: Harvard University Press.

Buck-Morss, S. 2000. Hegel and Haiti. *Critical Inquiry*, 26, 821–65.

—. 2009. *Hegel, Haiti, and Universal History*. Pittsburgh, PA: University of Pittsburgh Press.

Burawoy, M., Wright, E.O. 2006. Sociological Marxism, in *Handbook of Sociological Theory*, edited by J.H. Turner. New York: Springer, 459–507.

Bush, B. 1981. White 'ladies', coloured 'favourites' and black 'wenches'; Some Considerations on Sex, Race and Class Factors in Social Relations in White Creole Society in the British Caribbean. *Slavery & Abolition: A Journal of Slave and Post-Slave Studies*, 2(3), 245–62.

Caillé, A. 2007. Introduction to Symposium. *European Journal of Social Theory*, 10(2), 179–83.

Călugareanu, V. and Mogoş, A. 2012. How to Buy an EU Citizenship. *Jurnalul National*, September 12, [Online]. Available at: http://www.jurnalul.ro/anchete/how-to-buy-an-eu-citizenship-623530.htm [accessed 17 May 2013].

Canessa, A. 2007. Who Is Indigenous? Self-Identification, Indigeneity, and Claims to Justice in Contemporary Bolivia. *Urban Anthropology*, 36(3). 195–237.

—. 2012. Conflict, Claim, and Contradiction in the New Indigenous State of Bolivia, *desiguALdades.net Working Paper No. 22*, [Online]. Available at: http://www.desigualdades.net/bilder/Working_Paper/22_WP_Canessa_online.pdf?1367229857 [accessed 26 February 2014].

Cardoso, A. 2008. Escravidão e sociabilidade capitalista. Um ensaio sobre inércia social. *Novos Estudos CEBRAP*, 80, 71–88.

Cardoso, F.H. 1971. Comentario sobre los conceptos de sobrepoblación relativa y marginalidad. *Revista Americana de Ciencias Sociales*, 1(2), 57–76.

Cardoso, F.H. and Faletto, E. 1969. Dependencia y desarrollo en América. Latina. México D.F.: Siglo XXI.

Carver, T. 1998. *The Postmodern Marx*. University Park: Pennsylvania State University Press.

Casanova, J. 2011. Cosmopolitanism, the clash of civilizations and multiple modernities. *Current Sociology*, 59(2), 252–67.

Cassano, F. 1995. *Il pensiero meridiano*. Bari: Laterza.

Castells, M. 1998. *The Information Age: Economy, Society, and Culture, vol. III (End of Millennium)*. Malden: Blackwell.

Castro-Gómez, S. 2000. Ciencias sociales, violencia epistémica y el problema de la invención del otro, in *La colonialidad del saber: eurocentrismo y ciencias sociales. Perspectivas latinoamericanas*, edited by E. Lander, Buenos Aires: CLACSO, 145–61.

Cervantes-Rodríguez, M., Grosfoguel, R. and Mielants, E. (eds) 2009. *Caribbean Migration to Western Europe and the United States. Essays on Incorporation, Identity, and Citizenship*. Philadelphia: Temple University Press.

Chakrabarty, D. 2008. *Provincializing Europe. Postcolonial Thought and Historical Difference* (2nd edition). Princeton and Oxford: Princeton University Press.

Chandler, N.D. 2007. The Possible Form of an Interlocution: W.E.B. Du Bois and Max Weber in Correspondence, 1904–1905. *New Centennial Review*, 7(1), 213–72.

Chatterjee, P. 1993. *Nationalist Thought and the Colonial World: A Derivative Discourse*, Minneapolis, MN: Zed Books.

Chernilo, D. 2006. Social Theory's Methodological Nationalism. Myth and Reality. *European Journal of Social Theory*, 9(1), 5–22.

China Daily 2014. *Migrants Find a Home for Capital in Pursuit of Foreign Residence*. January 31, 2014, [Online]. Available at: http://www.chinadaily. com.cn/china/2014-01/23/ content_17252393.htm [accessed 2 April 2014].

Cleary, J. 2002. Misplaced ideas? Locating and dislocating Ireland in colonial and postcolonial studies, in *Marxism, Modernity, and Postcolonial Studies*, edited by C. Bartolovich and N. Lazarus. Cambridge: Cambridge University Press, 101–24.

CNN Money 2013. *Europe's Golden Visas Lure Rich Chinese*. November 26, [Online]. Available at: http://money.cnn.com/2013/11/26/news/europe-golden-visas/ [accessed 2 April 2014].

Cohen, I.J. 2005. General Editor's Foreword, in *Marx and Modernity*, edited by R. Antonio. Malden, MA, Oxford and Victoria: Blackwell.

Cohen, J., Hazelrigg, L.E. and Pope, W. 1975. De-Parsonizing Weber: A Critique of Parsons interpretation of Weber's sociology. *American Sociological Review*, 40, 229–41.

Collins, R. 1986a. *Weberian Sociological Theory*. Cambridge: Cambridge University Press.

—. 1986b. *Max Weber: A Skeleton Key*. Beverly Hills, CA: Sage.

Connell, R. 1997. Why Is Classical Theory Classical? *American Journal of Sociology*, 102(6), 1511–57.

—. 2007. *Southern Theory. The Global Dynamics of Knowledge in So*cial Science. Crows Nest: Allen&Unwin.

Conrad, S. and Randeria, S. (eds) 2002. *Jenseits des Eurozentrismus: Postkoloniale Perspektiven in den Geschichts- und Kulturwissenschaften*. Frankfurt a. M.: Campus Verlag.

Cooper, F. 2005. Colonialism in Question.Theory, Knowledge, History. Berkeley: University of California Press.

References

Coronil, F. 1996. Beyond Occidentalism: Toward Non-Imperial Geohistorical Categories. *Cultural Anthropology*, 11(1), 51–87.

—. 1997. *The Magical State. Nature, Money and Modernity in Venezuela*. Chicago: University of Chicago Press.

—. 2000. Towards a Critique of Globalcentrism: Speculations on Capitalism's Nature. *Public Culture*, 12(2), 351–74.

Costa, S. 2011. Researching Entangled Inequalities in Latin America. The Role of Historical, Social, and Transregional Interdependencies. desiguALdades.net *Working Paper*, No. 9, 1–26.

Crenshaw, K.W. 1991. Mapping the Margins: Intersectionality, Identity Politics, and Violence Against Women of Color. *Stanford Law Review*, 43: 1241–99.

Curtin, P.D. 1969. *The Atlantic Slave Trade: A Census*. Madison: University of Wisconsin Press.

Curtis, M. 1997. The Asiatic Mode of Production and Oriental Despotism, in *Marxism. The Inner Dialogues*, 2nd edition. New Brunswick and London: Transaction Publishers, 326–75.

Daily Mail 2012. Hungary 'sells EU passports' in return for bailout funds. *Daily Mail*, 31 October 2012.

Dainotto, R.M. 2007. *Europe (In Theory)*. Durham: Duke University Press.

Dalla-Costa, M. and Jones, S. 1973. *Die Macht der Frauen und der Umsturz der Gesellschaft*. Berlin: Merve.

Delanty, G. 2003. The Making of a Post-western Europe: A Civilizational Analysis. *Thesis Eleven*, 72(1), 8–25.

—. 2007. Peripheries and Borders in a Post-western Europe. *Eurozine*, [Online]. Available at: http://www.eurozine.com/pdf/2007-08-29-delanty-en.pdf [accessed 2 May 2014], 1–12.

Dependencies and Territories of the World. 2013. *Worldatlas.com* [Online]. Available at: http://www.worldatlas.com/dependtr.htm [accessed 8 May 2014].

Der Spiegel. 2010. Romanian Passports for Moldovans. Entering the EU through the Back Door. *Spiegel Online*, July 13, [Online]. Available at: http://www.spiegel.de/international/europe/romanian-passports-for-moldovansentering-the-eu-through-the-back-door-a-706338.html [accessed 11 May 2013].

Dirks, N.B. 2001. *Castes of Mind. Colonialism and the Making of Modern India*. Princeton and Oxford: Princeton University Press.

Dirlik, A. 1994. The Postcolonial Aura: Third World Criticism in the Age of Global Capitalism. *Critical Inquiry*, 328–56.

Domingues, J.M. 2000. The City: Rationalization and Freedom in Max Weber. *Philosophy and Social Criticism* 26(4), 107–26.

—. 2006. Amartya Sen, Freedom and Development: A Critical View, in *The Plurality of Modernity: Decentring Sociology*, edited by S. Costa, J.M. Domingues, W. Knöbl and J. Pereira da Silva. München, Mering: Rainer Hampp, 179–94.

Duggan, J. 2013. Income Inequality on the Rise in China. [Online]. Available at: http://www.aljazeera.com/indepth/features/2012/12/2012122311167503363.html [accessed 4 May 2014].

Dunaway, W.A. 2001. The Double Register of History: Situating the Forgotten Woman and Her Household in Capitalist Commodity Chains. *Journal of World-Systems Research*, VII (I), 2–29.

—. 2003. Women's Labor and Nature: The 21st Century World-System from a Radical Ecofeminist Perspective, in *Emerging Issues in the 21st Century World-System, vol. II*, edited by W. Dunaway. Westport: Praeger, 183–202.

—. 2014. *Gendered Commodity Chains. Seeing Women's Work and Households in Global Production*, Stanford: Stanford University Press

Dussel, E. 1995. *The Invention of the Americas. Eclipse of 'the Other' and the Myth of Modernity*. New York: Continuum.

—. 2000. Europa, Modernidad y eurocentrismo, in *La colonialidad del saber: eurocentrismo y ciencias sociales. Perspectivas latinoamericanas*, edited by E. Lander. Buenos Aires, CLACSO, 2005, 41–52.

—. 2001. The Four Drafts of Capital: Toward a New Interpretation of the Dialectical Thought of Marx. *Rethinking Marxism*, 13(1), 10–26.

—. 2004. *La producción teórica de Marx. Un comentario a los "Grundrisse"*. Mexico City: Siglo XXI, first published 1985.

—. 2005. "Ser Hispano": Un Mundo en el "Border" de Muchos Mundos, in *Latin@s in the World-System. Decolonization struggles in the 21st century U.S. empire*, edited by R. Grosfoguel, N. Maldonado-Torres and J.D. Saldívar. Boulder: Paradigm Publishers, 41–55.

—. 2007. *Política de la Liberacíon. Historia mundial y crítica*, Madrid: Trotta.

Dzankic, J. 2012a. The Pros and Cons of Ius Pecuniae: Investor Citizenship in Comparative Perspective. *EUI Working Papers, RSCAS*, 2012/14: 1–18.

—. 2012b. Investor Programs: Attempting to Cure the Struggling European Economies, *Citizenship in Southeast Europe blog*, [Online]. Available at: http://citsee.eu/blog/investor-programs-attempting-cure-struggling-european-economies [accessed 2 July 2013].

—. 2014. The Maltese Falcon, or: My Porsche for a Passport!, in *Should citizenship be for sale?*, edited by A. Shachar and R. Bauböck. EUI Working Papers RSCAS, 2014/01, 17–18.

The Economist. 2012. Gini Back in the Bottle. An unequal Continent is becoming less so. 13 Oct. [Online]. Available at: http://www.economist.com/node/21564411/print [accessed 8 May 2014].

—. 2013. Romania and the EU: Not Ready for Schengen. 17 March [Online]. Available at: http://www.economist.com/blogs/easternapproaches/ 2013/03/romania-and-eu [accessed 2 July 2013].

Eder, K. 2001. Klasse, Macht und Kultur. Zum Theoriedefizit der Ungleichheitsforschung, in *Klasse und Klassifikation. Die symbolische Dimension sozialer Ungleichheit*, edited by A. Weiß, C. Koppetsch, A. Scharenberg, and O. Schmidtke. Wiesbaden: Westdeutscher Verlag, 27–60.

Eisenstadt, S.N. 1966. *Modernization: Protest and Change*. Englewood Cliffs: Prentice-Hall.

—. 2000a. Multiple modernities. *Daedalus*, 129(1), 1–29.

—. 2000b. *Die Vielfalt der Moderne*. Weilerstwist: Velbrück Verlag.

—. 2003. *Comparative Civilizations and Multiple Modernities*. Amsterdam, Brill.

—. 2004. The Civilizational Dimension of Modernity. Modernity as a Distinct Civilization, in *Rethinking Civilizational Analysis*, edited by S.A. Arjomand and E. Tiryakian. London: Sage, 48–66.

Eisenstein, Z. 1981. *The Radical Future of Liberal Feminism*. New York: Longman.

Elwert, G. 1984. Conflicts Inside and Outside the Household. A West African Case Study, in *Households and the World-Economy*, edited by J. Smith, I. Wallerstein and H. Evers. London: Sage, 272–96.

Elwert, G., Evers, H. and Wilkens, W. 1983. Die Suche nach Sicherheit. Kombinierte Produktionsformen im sogenannten informellen Sektor. *Zeitschrift für Soziologie*, 12(4), 281–96.

Engels, F. 1928. *The Mark. Appendix to Socialism, Utopian and Scientific*. New York: Labor News Co.

—. 1992. Letter to Karl Marx, December 15, 1882, in *Marx and Engels, Correspondence*. New York: International Publishers.

Erler, E.J. 2008. Birthright Citizenship and Dual Citizenship: Harbingers of Administrative Tyranny. *Imprimis*, 7/2008, [Online]: www.hillsdale.edu/news/imprimis/archive/issue.asp?year=2008&month=07 [accessed 30 June 2013].

Escobar, A. 1995. *Encountering Development: The Making and Unmaking of the Third World*. Princeton: Princeton University Press.

—. 2004. Beyond the Third World. Imperial Globality, Global Coloniality, and Anti-Globalization Social Movements. *Third World Quarterly*, 25(1), 207–30.

—. 2007. Worlds and Knowledges Otherwise: The Latin American Modernity/Coloniality Research Program. *Cultural Studies*, 21(2–3), 179–210.

European Commission. 2004. *Geo-political and river map of the EU (in yellow) and of the candidate countries (in blue and violet) (situation before the enlargement of the EU in 2004)*, [Online]. Available at http://ec.europa.eu/avservices/photo/photoDetails.cfm?sitelang=en&mgid=38#10 [accessed 8 May 2014].

—. 2006. *Communication from the Commision to the European Parliament and the Council. Enlargement Strategy and Main Challenges 2006–2007*, [Online]. Available at: http://ec.europa.eu/enlargement/pdf/key_documents/2006/nov/com_649_strategy_paper_en.pdf, [accessed 6 May 2014].

—. 2009. *Enlargement Strategy and Progress Reports 2009*, [Online]. Available at: http://ec.europa.eu/enlargement/pdf/key_documents/2009/strategy_paper_2009_en.pdf [last accessed 8 May 2014].

EU 2009. Enlargement and Neighbourhood Policy, in *Europa. Gateway to the European Union*, [Online]. Available at: http://europa.eu/abc/12lessons/lesson_3/index_en.htm [last accessed 14 October 2009].

Evers, H. 1981. Urban and Rural Subsistence Production. A Theoretical Outline (Working Paper 2). Bielefeld: Fakultät für Soziologie an der Universität Bielefeld.

Fabian, J. 2006. The Other Revisited. Critical Afterthoughts. *Anthropological Theory*, 6(2), 139–52.

Federici, S. 2004. The Great Caliban: The Struggle Against the Rebel Body – Part Two. *Capitalism Nature Socialism*, 15(3), 13–28.

Feere, J. 2010. Birthright Citizenship in the United States. A Global Comparison. *Center for Immigration Studies Backgrounder,* August 2010, 1–20, [Online]. Available at: http://www.cis.org/sites/cis.org/files/articles/2010/birthright.pdf [accessed 2 May 2014].

Feldman, S. 2002. Intersecting and Contesting Positions: Postcolonial, Feminist, and World-Systems Theories, in *The Modern/Colonial Capitalist World-System in the Twentieth Century*, edited by R. Grosfoguel and A.M. Cervantes-Rodríguez. Westport: Praeger, 171–98.

Fenton, S. 2003. *Ethnicity*, Oxford: Polity.

Financial Times 2012. *Moscow's rich buy £1m entry into UK*, [Online]. Available at: http://www.ft.com/intl/cms/s/0/a0d6be06-3aff-11e2-b3f0-00144feabdc0.html#axzz2xjXhegYe [accessed 2 April 2014].

Fischer, S. 2004. *Modernity Disavowed. Haiti and the Cultures of Slavery in the Age of Revolution*. Durham and London: Duke University Press.

Focus Online 2013. *"Eintrittskarte in die EU": Zypern lockt Reiche mit Staatsbürgerschaft*. 15 April [Online]. Available at: http://www.focus.de/politik/ausland/eintrittskarte-in-die-eu-zypern-lockt-reiche-mit-staatsbuergerschaft_aid_960645.html [accessed 2 April 2014].

Forbes 2013. *Malta Launches Controversial Citizenship Scheme*. 14 November [Online]. Available at: http://www.forbes.com/sites/carlapassino/2013/11/14/malta-launches-controversial-citizenship-by-investment-scheme/ [accessed 2 April 2014].

Foreign Affairs 2013. *The Clash of Civilizations? The Debate: 20th Anniversary Edition*. New York City: Foreign Affairs Press.

Forsythe, N. 2002. Revisioning Social Change: Situated Knowledge and the Unit of Analysis in the Modern World-System, in *The Modern/Colonial Capitalist World-System in the Twentieth Century*, edited by R. Grosfoguel and A.M. Cervantes-Rodríguez. Westport: Praeger, 147–69.

Frank, A.G. 1966. The Development of Underdevelopment. *Monthly Review*, 18(4), 17–31.

—. 1967. *Capitalism and Underdevelopment in Latin America: Historical Studies of Chile and Brazil*. New York: Monthly Review Press.

—. 1972. *Lumpenbourgeoisie: Lumpendevelopment. Dependence, Class and Politics in Latin America*. New York and London.

—. 1978. *World Accumulation 1492–1789*. London: Macmillan.

Fromm, E. 1956. Foreword, in *Karl Marx. Selected Writings in Sociology and Social Philosophy*, edited by T.B. Bottomore and M. Rubel. New York, Toronto and London: McGraw Hill, xiii-xviii.

Fuchs, M., Randeria, S., and Linkenbach, A. (eds) 2004. *Konfigurationen der Moderne: Diskurse zu Indien, Soziale Welt Sonderband 15*. Baden-Baden: Nomos Verlag.

Fukuyama, F. 1992. *The End of History and the Last Man*. New York: Avon Books.

References 243

Gammelin, C. and C. Hulverscheidt. 2013. SPD sträubt sich gegen Rettungspaket. *Süddeutsche Zeitung*, January 9, [Online]. Available at: http://sz.de/1.1568342 [accessed 11 May 2013].

Geißler, R. 2001. Sozialstruktur und gesellschaftlicher Wandel, in *Deutschland – TrendBuch. Fakten und Orientierungen*, edited by K. Korte and W. Weidenfeld. Bonn: bpb, 97–135.

——. 2002. *Die Sozialstruktur Deutschlands*. Bonn: bpb.

Gerber, J.S. 1992. *The Jews of Spain. A History of the Sephardic Experience*. New York: The Free Press.

Gilroy, P. 1981. You Can't Fool the Youth: Race and Class Formation in the 1980s. *Race & Class*, XXIII(2/3), 207–22.

Glazer, N. and Moynihan, D.P. (eds) 1975. *Ethnicity: Theory and Experience*. Cambridge, MA: Harvard University Press.

Goldthorpe, J.H. 1983. Women and Class Analysis: in Defense of the Conventional View. *Sociology*, 17, 465–88.

Gottschall, K. 2000. *Soziale Ungleichheit und Geschlecht. Kontinuitäten und Brüche, Sackgassen und Erkenntnispotentiale im deutschen soziologischen Diskurs*. Opladen: Leske + Budrich.

Greer, M. 2006. Imperialism and Anthropophagy in Early Modern Spanish Tragedy: The Unthought Known, in: *Reason and Its Others. Italy, Spain, and the new World*, edited by D.R. Castillo and M. Lollini. Nashville: Vanderbilt University Press.

Grosfoguel, R. 1997. A TimeSpace Perspective on Development. Recasting Latin American Debates. *Review*, XX(3/4), 465–540.

——. 2002. Colonial Difference, Geopolitics of Knowledge and Global Coloniality in the Modern/Colonial Capitalist World-System. *Review*, XXV(3), 203–24.

——. 2003. *Colonial Subjects. Puerto Ricans in a Global Perspective*. Berkeley, Los Angeles: University of California Press.

——. 2005. World-Systems Analysis in the Context of Transmodernity, Border Thinking and Global Coloniality, *Review*, XXIX(2), 167–17.

——. 2006. From Postcolonial Studies to Decolonial Studies: Decolonizing Postcolonial Studies: A Preface. *Review special issue*, XXIX(2), 141–13.

Grosfoguel, R. and Mielants, E. 2006. The Long Durée Entanglement Between Islamophobia and Racism in the Modern/Colonial/Capitalist/Patriarchal World-System. An Introduction. *Human Architecture, Journal of the Sociology of Self-Knowledge*, V(1), 1–12.

Gutiérrez Rodríguez, E. 2010. Migration, Domestic Work and Affect. A Decolonial Approach on Value and the Feminization of Labor, New York: Routledge

Habermas, J. 1984. *The Theory of Communicative Action, Vol. I, Reason and the Rationalization of Society*. London: Heinemann.

Hall, S. 1977. The 'Political' and the 'Economic' in Marx's Theory of Classes, in *Class and Class Structure*, edited by A. Hunt. London: Lawrence and Wishart, 15–60.

244 *Global Inequalities Beyond Occidentalism*

—. 1992. The West and the Rest. Discourse and Power, in *Modernity. An Introduction to Modern Societies*, edited by S. Hall and B. Gieben, London: Polity Press, 275–331.

—. 1996. When Was the Postcolonial? Thinking at the Limit, in *The Post-Colonial Question*, edited by I. Chambers and L. Curti. London and New York: Routledge, 242–29.

Hanagan, M. 2002. Gewalt und die Entstehung von Staaten, in: Internationales Handbuch der Gewaltforschung, edited by W. Heitmeyer and M. Hanagan. Wiesbaden: Westdeutscher Verlag, 153–176.

Hansen, P. and Jonsson, S. 2011. Bringing Africa as a 'Dowry' to Europe. European Integration and the Eurafrica Project, *Interventions. International Journal of Postcolonial Studies*, 13(3), 443–43.

Harrison, L.E. and Huntington, S. 2000. *Culture Matters: How Values Shape Human Progress*. New York City: Basic Books.

Hartmann, H. 1981. The Unhappy Marriage of Marxism and Feminism, in *Women and Revolution*, edited by L. Sargent. London: Pluto.

Hechter, M. 1971. Towards a Theory of Ethnic Change. *Politics and Society*, Fall, 21–45.

Hegel, G.H.F. 1995. *Lectures on the History of Philosophy*. translated by E.S. Haldane. Lincoln: University of Nebraska Press, vol. 1, 125–26.

Henley & Partners 2013. *Global Visa Restriction Index 2013*, [Online]. Available at: www.henleyglobal.com/files/download/VISA_Index_2013_Web.pdf [accessed 2 April 2014].

—. 2014, *Why You Need Alternative Citizenship*, [Online]. Available at: https://www.henleyglobal.com/why-alternative-citizenship/ [accessed 2 April 2014].

Hering Torres, M.S. 2006. *Rassismus in der Vormoderne. Die "Reinheit des Blutes" im Spanien der Frühen Neuzeit*. Frankfurt a. M.: Campus.

Hesse, B. 2007. Racialized modernity. An analytics of white mythologies. *Ethnic and Racial Studies*, 30(4), 643–63.

Hill Collins, P. 1999. Moving Beyond Gender: Intersectionality and Scientific Knowledge, in *Revisioning Gender*, edited by M.M. Ferree, J. Lorber and B.B. Hess. Thousand Oaks: Sage, 261–84.

Hine, D.C, Keaton, T.D., and Small, S. 2009. *Black Europe and the African Diaspora*, Chicago: University of Illinois

Hirsh, M. 2014. Ukraine and the Clash of Civilizations. How Putin is proving a 20-year old idea to finally be correct. *National Journal*, March 5, 2014, [Online]. Available at: http://www.nationaljournal.com/white-house/ukraine-and-the-clash-of-civilizations-20140305 [last accessed 24 April 2014].

Hirst, P. 1975. The Uniqueness of the West. *Economy and Society*, 1(4), 446–75.

Hobson, J. 2004. *The Eastern Origins of European Civilisation*, Cambridge: Cambridge University Press.

Hoffman, K. and Centeno, M.A. 2003. The Lopsided Continent: Inequality in Latin America. *Annual Review of Sociology*, 29, 363–90.

Holton, R.J. 2006. *Making Globalization*. Basingstoke: Palgrave.

References

Huffington Post. 2013. *Steve King Introduces Bill to Stop 'Anchor Babies'*. January 4, 2013, [Online]. Available at: http://www.huffingtonpost.com/ 2013/01/04/ steve-king-anchor-babies_n_2411989.html [last accessed 5 July 2013].

Huntington, S. 1968. *Political Order in Changing Societies*. New Haven and London: Yale University Press.

——. 1993. The Clash of Civilizations? *Foreign Affairs*, 72(3), 22–49.

——. 1996a. *The Clash of Civilizations and the Remaking of World Order*. New York: Simon and Schuster.

——. 1996b. The West: Unique, Not Universal. *Foreign Affairs*, 75(6), 28–46.

Hurst, C.E. 2007. *Social Inequality. Forms, Causes, and Consequences*, 6th edition. Boston: Pearson.

Iglesias, F. and Ileana, M. 2011. En torno de los esterotipos respecto a la afrocubana: Construcción y deconstrucción de mitos, in *Afrocubanas. Historia, pensamiento y prácticas culturales*, edited by D. Rubiera Castillo and I.M. Martiatu Terry. La Habana: Coletivo de Autores, 2011, 150–62.

The Independent 2014. *Passports for Profit: British Company to Make 'disgusting amounts of money' from controversial EU passport sale*. January 30, 2014, [Online]. Available at: http://www.independent.co.uk/news/uk/home-news/ passports-for-profit-british-company-to-make-disgusting-amounts-of-money-from-controversial-eu-passport-sale-9094251.html [accessed 2 April 2014].

International Business Times 2013. *The Best Passports To Have For Unrestricted Travel Around The World* [Online]. Available at: http://www.ibtimes.com/best-passports-have-unrestricted-travel-around-world-1422038, [accessed 1 May 2014].

Iordachi, C. (ed.) 2012. *Reacquiring the Romanian Citizenship: Historical, Comparative, and Applied Perspectives*. Bucharest: Curtea Veche.

IPEA – Instituto de Pesquisa Econômica Aplicada 2007. Igualdade Racial. *Políticas Sociais: Acompanhamento e Análise, Edição Especial*, no. 13, [Online]. Available at: http://www.ipea.gov.br/portal/images/stories/PDFs/ politicas_sociais/IgualdadeRacial13.pdf [accessed 14 January 2014].

Isin, E. 2002a. *Being Political. Genealogies of Citizenship*. Minneapolis and London: University of Minnesota Press.

——. 2002b. Citizenship after Orientalism, in *Handbook of Citizenship Studies*, edited by E. Isin and B.S. Turner. London: Sage, 117–28.

——. 2003. Historical Sociology of the City, in *Handbook of Historical Sociology*, edited by G. Delanty and E. Isin. London, UK: Sage, 312–25.

——. 2005. Citizenship after Orientalism. Ottoman Citizenship, in *Citizenship in a Global World: European Questions and Turkish Experiences*, edited by F. Keyman and A. Icduygu. London: Routledge, 31–51.

——. 2013. Citizenship after orientalism. Genealogical investigations, in *Comparative Political Thought: Theorizing Practices*, edited by M. Freeden and A. Vincent. London: Routledge.

Isin, E. and Turner, B.S. 2002. Citizenship Studies: An Introduction, in *Handbook of Citizenship Studies*, edited by E. Isin and B.S. Turner. London: Sage, 1–10.

Ivakhnenko, E. 2006. A Threshold-Dominant Model of the Imperial and Colonial Discourse of Russia. *South Atlantic Quarterly*, 105:3, Summer 2006, 595–615.

Jackson, M. 1983. An Analysis of Max Weber's Theory of Ethnicity, *Humboldt Journal of Social Relations*, 10(1), 4–18.

Jani, P. 2002. Karl Marx, Eurocentrism, and the 1857 Revolt in British India, in *Marxism, Modernity, and Postcolonial Studies*, edited by C. Bartolovich and N. Lazarus. Cambridge: Cambridge University Press, 81–97

Joas, H. and Knöbl, W. 2004. *Sozialtheorie. Zwanzig einführende Vorlesungen.* Suhrkamp: Frankfurt am Main.

Joppke, C. 1995. Toward a New Sociology of the State: On Roger Brubaker's 'Citizenship and Nationhood in France and Germany'. *Archives européennes de sociologie*, XXXIV, 168–78.

—. 2010. *Citizenship and Immigration.* Cambridge: Polity Press.

Kalberg, S. (ed.) 2005. *Max Weber. Readings and Commentary on Modernity*, Malden: Blackwell.

Katz, S. 1990. The Problems of Europocentrism and Evolutionism in Marx's Writings on Colonialism. *Political Studies*, XXXVIII, 672–86.

Kern, S. 2012. *Muslims Angry Over Spanish Citizenship for Jews*, [Online]. Available at http://www.gatestoneinstitute.org/3509/spanish-citizenship-jews [accessed 8 May 2014].

Klinger, C. and Knapp, G. 2007. Achsen der Ungleichheit-Achsen der Differenz. Verhältnisbestimmungen von Klasse, Geschlecht, "Rasse"/Ethnizität, in *Achsen der Ungleichheit. Zum Verhältnis von Klasse, Geschlecht und Ethnizität*, edited by C. Klinger, G. Knapp and B. Sauer. Frankfurt: Campus.

Knöbl, W. 2006. Zivilgesellschaft und staatliches Gewaltmonopol. Zur Verschränkung von Gewalt und Zivilität, *Mittelweg 36*, 1/2006, 61–84.

Knöbl, W. 2012. Imperiale Herrschaft und Gewalt, *Mittelweg 36*, 3/2012, 19–44.

Koch, M. 2003. Closure Theory and Citizenship: The Northern Ireland Experience. *Electronic Journal of Sociology*, 7(4), [Online]. Available at: http://www.sociology.org/content/vol7.4/koch.html [accessed 5 May 2014].

Konno, H. 2004. *Max Weber und die polnische Frage (1892–1920). Eine Betrachtung zum liberalen Nationalismus im wilhelminischen Deutschland.* Baden-Baden: Nomos.

Korzeniewicz, R.P., Moran, T.P. and Stach, A. 2003. Trends in Inequality: Towards a World-Systems Analysis, in *Globalization and Society. Processes of Differentiation Examined*, edited by R. Breton and J.G. Reitz. Westport: Greenwood Press, 13–36.

Korzeniewicz, R.P. and Moran, T.P. 1997. World Economic Trends in the Distribution of Income, 1965–1992, in: American Journal of Sociology 106(1), 1000–39.

—. 2005. Theorizing the Relationship Between Inequality and Economic Growth. *Theory and Society*, 34, 277–316.

—. 2007. World Inequality in the 21st Century: Patterns and Tendencies, in *The Blackwell Companion to Globalization*, edited by G. Ritzer. Malden, MA: Blackwell 565–92

—. 2008. *Rethinking Inequality. A World-Historical Perspective*, paper presented at the the conference "Inequality beyond globalization: economic changes and the dynamics of inequality", University of Neuchâtel, Switzerland, 1–26.

—. 2009. *Unveiling Inequality. A World-Historical Perspective*. New York: Russell Sage Foundation.

Korzeniewicz, R.P. and Albrecht, S. 2013. Thinking globally about inequality and stratification: Wages across the world, 1982–2009. *International Journal of Comparative Sociology* 53(5–6), 419–43

Kovács, M. 2001. Putting Down and Putting Off: The EU's Discursive Strategies in the 1998 and 1999 Follow-Up Reports, in *Empire's New Clothes: Unveiling EU Enlargement*, edited by J. Böröcz and M. Kovács. Shropshire: Central Europe Review, 196–234.

Kowarick, L. 1975. *Capitalismo e marginalidade na America Latina*. Rio de Janeiro: Paz e Terra.

Kreckel, R. 1983. Soziale Ungleichheiten. *Soziale Welt, Special Issue 2*. Baden-Baden: Nomos.

—. 1989. Klasse und Geschlecht. Die Geschlechtsindifferenz der soziologischen Ungleichheitsforschung und ihre theoretischen Implikationen. *Leviathan*, 17, 305–21.

—. 2004. *Politische Soziologie der sozialen Ungleichheit, 3., erweiterte Auflage*. Frankfurt a.M.: Campus.

—. 2008. Soziologie der sozialen Ungleichheit im globalen Kontext, in *Transnationale Ungleichheitsforschung. Eine neue Herausforderung für die Soziologie*, edited by M. Bayer, G. Mordt, S. Terpe and M. Winter. Frankfurt a. M. and New York: Campus, 23–69.

Lacey, M. 2011. Birthright Citizenship Looms as Next Immigration Battle. *New York Times*, January 4, 2011, [Online]. Available at: http://www.nytimes.com/2011/01/05/us/politics/05babies.html?pagewanted=all&_r=0 [accessed 5 May 2014].

Larsen, N. 2002. Marxism, Postcolonialism, and The Eighteenth Brumaire, in *Marxism, Modernity, and Postcolonial Studies*, edited by C. Bartolovich and N. Lazarus. Cambridge: Cambridge University Press, 204–20.

Lehmann, J. 1995. The Question of Caste in Modern Society: Durkheim's Contradictory Theories of Race, Class, and Sex, *American Sociological Review*, 60, 566–85.

Lerner, D. 1958. *The Passing of Traditional Society: Modernizing the Middle East*. Glencoe: The Free Press.

Lewis, M.W. and Wigen, K.E. 1997. *The Myth of Continents. A Critique of Metageography*. Berkeley, Los Angeles and London: University of California Press.

248   *Global Inequalities Beyond Occidentalism*

Lewontin, R. 1968. The Concept of Evolution, in *International Encyclopedia of the Social Sciences*, Vol. 5, edited by S.D. Sills. New York City: MacMillan and Free Press, 202–9.

Liell, C. 2002. Gewalt in modernen Gesellschaften – zwischen Ausblendung und Dramatisierung. *Aus Politik und Zeitgeschichte*, B 44, 6–13.

Light, J. 2013. *The U.S. is Now More Unequal than Much of Latin America*, [Online]. Available at: http://billmoyers.com/2013/01/29/the-u-s-is-now-more-unequal-than-much-of-latin-america/ [accessed 9 May 2014].

Linden, M. van der 2008. *Workers of the World. Essays toward a Global Labor History*. Leiden: Brill.

Lindstrom, N. 2003. Between Europe and the Balkans: Mapping Slovenia and Croatia's 'Return to Europe' in the 1990's. *Dialectical Anthropology*, 27, 313–29.

Linebaugh, P. and Rediker, M.B. 2000. *The Many-Headed Hydra. Sailors, Slaves, Commoners and the Hidden History of the Revolutionary Atlantic*. London: Verso.

Love, J.L. 1996. *Crafting the Third World. Theorizing Underdevelopment in Rumania and Brazil*. Stanford: Stanford University Press.

Lugones, M. 2007. Heterosexualism and the Colonial/Modern Gender System. *Hypatia*, 22(1), 186–209.

McClintock, A. 1995. *Imperial Leather: Race, Gender, and Sexuality in the Colonial Contest*. London: Routledge.

Mackert, J. and Müller, H.P. (eds) 2000. *Citizenship – Soziologie der Staatsbürgerschaft*. Wiesbaden: VS Verlag.

Mackert, J. 2004. Die Theorie sozialer Schließung. Das analytische Potential einer Theorie mittlerer Reichweite, in *Die Theorie sozialer Schließung. Tradition, Analysen, Perspektiven*, edited by J. Mackert. Wiesbaden: VS, 9–24.

Mackert, J. (ed.) 2006. *Staatsbürgerschaft. Eine Einführung*, Wiesbaden: VS.

McLellan, D. 2003. Alienation in Hegel and Marx, in *Dictionary of the History of Ideas, Vol. 1*, edited by P.P. Wiener. New York City: Scribner's, 37–40.

McMichael, P. 1991. Slavery in Capitalism. The Rise and Demise of the U.S. Ante-Bellum Cotton Culture. *Theory and Society*, 20(3), 321–49.

—. 2000. World-Systems Analysis, Globalization, and Incorporated Comparison. *Journal of World-Systems Research*, VI(3), 68–99.

—. 2005. *Development and Social Change*. A Global Perspective. London: Sage.

Mahoney, J. 2003. Long-Run Development and the Legacy of Colonialism in Spanish America. *American Journal of Sociology*, 109(1), 50–106.

Maldonado-Torres, N. 2008. Religion, Conquête et Race dans les Fondations du monde Moderne/Colonial, in *Islamophobie dans le monde moderne*, edited by Mestiri, M. Grosfoguel, R. and Soum, El Y. IIIT Editions: Saint Ouen, 206–38.

Mamdami, M. 1996. *Citizen and Subject: Contemporary Africa and the Legacy of Late Colonialism*, Princeton: Princeton University Press.

Mamozai, M. 1982. *Herrenmenschen: Frauen im deutschen Kolonialismus*. Reinbeck: rororo.

Manasse, E.M. 1947. Max Weber on Race. *Social Research*, 14, 191–221.

References

Mann, M. 1986. A Crisis in Stratification Theory?, in *Gender and Stratification*, edited by R. Crompton and M. Mann. Oxford: Polity Press.

Marcuse, H. 1986. *Reason and Revolution. Hegel and the Rise of Social Theory.* London: Routledge.

Marshall, T.H. 1977. *Class, citizenship and social development: essays.* Chicago: University of Chicago Press.

Martinelli, A. 2005. The European identity, in *Comparing Modernities. Essays in Homage to Shmuel N. Eisenstadt*, edited by E. Ben-Rafael and Y. Sternberg. Leiden: Brill, 581–604.

Marx, K. 1862. in S. Avineri (ed.) 1969. *Karl Marx on Colonialism and Modernization*, Garden City, Anchor Books.

—. 1968. *The Eastern Question: A Reprint of Letters Written 1853–1856 Dealing with the Events of the Crimean War*, edited by E. Marx Aveling and E. Aveling. New York: Ayer Publishing.

—. 1971. *A Contribution to the Critique of Political Economy (1959).* Moscow: Progress Publishers.

—. 1973. Grundrisse der Kritik der politischen Ökonomie. Outlines of the Critique of Political Economy, Notebook IV, [Online]. Available at http://www.marxists.org/archive/marx/works/1857/grundrisse/ch09.htm [accessed 7 May 2014].

—. 1973. *Grundrisse (1857)*, trans. Martin Nicolaus. Middlesex: Penguin.

—. 1978a. Economic and Philosophic Manuscripts of 1844, in *The Marx-Engels Reader*, edited by R. Tucker. New York: Norton, 66–125.

—. 1978b. The German Ideology Part I, in *The Marx-Engels Reader*, edited by R. Tucker. New York: Norton, 146–202.

—. 1978c. Wage Labour and Capital, in *The Marx-Engels Reader*, edited by R. Tucker. New York: Norton, 203–17.

—. 1978d. The Coming Unheaval (From the Poverty of Philosophy), in *The Marx-Engels Reader*, edited by R. Tucker. New York: Norton, 218–19.

—. 1978e. The Grundrisse, in *The Marx-Engels Reader*, edited by R. Tucker. New York: Norton, 221–93.

—. 1978f. Capital Volume One, in *The Marx-Engels Reader*, edited by R. Tucker. New York: Norton, 294–438.

—. 1978g. Manifesto of the Communist Party, in *The Marx-Engels Reader*, edited by R. Tucker. New York: Norton, 469–500.

—. 1978h. On Imperialism in India, in *The Marx-Engels Reader*, edited by R. Tucker. New York: Norton, 653–64.

—. 1997. Critique of Hegel's Philosophy of The State (1843), in *Writings of the Young Marx on Philosophy and Society*, translated and edited by D. Easton and Kurt H Guddat, Indianapolis: Hackett Publishing, 151–202.

Marx, K. and Engels, F. 1962. *Selected Works.* Moscow: Foreign Languages Publishing House.

—. 1968. *A Critique of the German Ideology.* Moscow: Progress Publishers.

—. 1977a. Manifesto of the Communist Party, in *Karl Marx: Selected Writings*, edited by David McLellan. Oxford: Oxford University Press, 245–72.

—. 1977b. The German Ideology, in *Karl Marx: Selected Writings*, edited by David McLellan. Oxford: Oxford University Press, 175–208.

—. 1982. *Collected Works (Volume 38)*. London: Lawrence and Wishart.

Meillassoux, C. 1975. *Femmes, greniers et capitaux*. Paris: Maspero.

Melleuish, G. 2004. The Clash of Civilizations. A Model of Historical Development?, in *Rethinking Civilizational Analysis*, edited by S.A. Arjomand and E. Tiryakian. London: Sage, 234–50.

Merchant, C. 1980. *The Death of Nature. Women, Ecology, and the Scientific Revolution*. New York: Perennial Library.

Mestiri, M., Grosfoguel, R. and Soum, E.Y. (eds) 2008. *Islamophobie dans le monde moderne*. IIIT Editions: Saint Ouen.

Mies, M. 1988a. Introduction, in *Women, the Last Colony*, edited by M. Mies, V. Bennholdt-Thomsen and C. von Werlhof. London: Zed Books, 1–11.

—. 1988b. Capitalist Development and Subsistence Production: Rural Women in India, in *Women, the Last Colony*, edited by M. Mies, V. Bennholdt-Thomsen and C. von Werlhof. London: Zed Books 27–50.

—. 1988c. Class Struggles and Women's Struggles, in *Women, the Last Colony*, edited by M. Mies, V. Bennholdt-Thomsen and C. von Werlhof. London: Zed Books, 131–58.

—. 1996. *Patriarchy and Accumulation on a World Scale*. London: Zed Books.

—. 2007. Patriarchy and Accumulation on a World Scale – Revisited (Keynote Lecture at the Green Economics Institute, Reading, 29. October 2005). *International Journal of Green Economics*, 1(3/4), 268–75

Mies, M., Bennholdt-Thomsen, V. and von Werlhof, C. 1988. *Women, the Last Colony*, London: Zed Books.

Mies, M. and Shiva, V. 1993. *Ecofeminism*. Halifax: Nova Scotia.

Mignolo, W. 1995. *The Darker Side of the Renaissance. Literacy, Territoriality, and Colonization*. Ann Arbor: University of Michigan Press.

—. 2000. *Local Histories/Global Designs. Coloniality, Subaltern Knowledges, and Border Thinking*. Princeton: Princeton University Press.

—. 2002. Colonialidad global, capitalismo y hegemonía epistémica, in *Indisciplinar las ciencias sociales. Geopoliticas del conocimiento y colonialidad del poder. Perspectivas desde lo andino*, edited by C. Walsh, F. Schiwy and S. Castro-Gómez. Quito: Abya-Yala, 215–47.

—. 2003. *The Darker Side of the Renaissance. Literacy, Territoriality, and Colonization*. Ann Arbor: University of Michigan Press.

—. 2005. *The Idea of Latin America*. Malden: Blackwell.

—. 2006a. Islamophobia/Hispanophobia. The (Re)Configuration of the Racial/ Imperial/Colonial Matrix, Human Architecture. *Journal of the Sociology of Self-Knowledge*, V(I), 13–28.

—. 2006b. Introduction. *South Atlantic Quarterly*, 105(3), Summer, 479–99.

—. 2006c. Citizenship, Knowledge, and the Limits of Humanity. *American Literary History*, 18(2), 312–31.

—. 2007. Delinking: The Rhetoric of Modernity, the Logic of Coloniality and the Grammar of De-Coloniality. *Cultural Studies*, 21(2–3), 449–513.

—. 2009. Dispensable and Bare Lives. Coloniality and the Hidden Political/ Economic Agenda of Modernity. *Human Architecture. Journal of the Sociology of Self-Knowledge*, VII(2), 69–88.

—. 2012. *The Darker Side of Western Modernity: Global Futures, Decolonial Options*. Durham and London: Duke University Press.

Mignolo, W. and Tlostanova, M. 2006. Theorizing from the Borders. Shifting to Geo- and Body-Politics of Knowledge. *European Journal of Social Theory*, 9(2), 205–11.

Milanovic, B. 2011. Global Inequality. From Class to Location, from Proletarians to Migrants. *World Bank Policy Research Working Paper 5520*, [Online]. Available at: http://elibrary.worldbank.org/doi/pdf/10.1596/1813-9450-5820 [accessed 9 May 2014].

—. 2012. Global Income Inequality by the Numbers: in History and Now. *World Bank Policy Research Working Paper 6259*, [Online]. Available at: http://elibrary. worldbank.org/doi/pdf/10.1596/1813-9450-6259 [accessed 9 May 2014].

Mintz, S. 1977. The So-Called World-System: Local Initiative and Local Response. *Dialectical Anthropology*, 2, 253–70.

—. 1978. Was the Plantation Slave a Proletarian? *Review. Journal of the Fernand Braudel Center*, II, 1, Summer, 81–98.

—. 1986. *Sweetness and Power. The Place of Sugar in Modern History*. New York: Penguin.

—. 1998. The Localization of Anthropological Practice. From Area Studies to Transnationalism. *Critique of Anthropology*, 18(2) 117–33.

Misra, J. 2000. Gender and the World-System: Engaging the Feminist Literature on Development, in *A World-System Reader: New Perspectives on Gender, Urbanism, Cultures, Indigenous Peoples, and Ecology*, edited by T.D. Hall. Boulder: Rowman and Littlefield, 105–30.

Mohanty, C.T. 1991. Under Western Eyes: Feminist Scholarship and Colonial Discourses, in *Third World Women and the Politics of Feminism*, edited by : C.T. Mohanty, A. Russo and L. Torres. Bloomington: Indiana University Press, 51–80.

Mommsen, W. 1974. *Max Weber und die deutsche Politik 1890–1920*. Tübingen: Mohr/Siebeck.

—. 2005. Max Weber's "Grand Sociology": the origins and composition of "Wirtschaft und Gesellschaft. Soziologie", in *Max Weber's Economy and Society: A Critical Companion*, edited by C. Camic, P.S. Gorski and D.M. Trubeck. Stanford, CA: Stanford University Press, 70–97.

Moran, T.P. 2009. Studying Long-Term Large-Scale Social Change. Concluding Reflections on the Relevant Unit of Analysis. *Journal of World-Systems Research*, XV(1), 115–23.

Moraña, M., Dussel, E. and Jáuregui, C.A. (eds) 2008. *Coloniality at Large: Latin America and the Postcolocial Debate*. Durham: Duke University Press.

Muchembled, R. 1979. *La sorcière au village (XVe-XVIIIe siècle)*. Paris: Julliard Gallimard.

Murphy, R. 1988. Social Closure: *The Theory of Monopolization and Exclusion*. Oxford: Clarendon Press.

Nimtz, A. 2002. The Eurocentric Marx and Engels and Other Related Myths, in *Marxism, Modernity, and Postcolonial Studies*, edited by C. Bartolovich and N. Lazarus. Cambridge: Cambridge University Press, 65–80.

Nye, R.A. 1993. *Masculinity and Male Codes of Honor in Modern France*. New York: Oxford University Press.

O'Brien, K. 2010. A Weberian Approach to Citizenship in a Divided Community. *Citizenship Studies*, 14(5), 589–604.

Ortner, S. and Whitehead, H. 1981. *Sexual Meanings. The Cultural Construction of Gender and Sexuality*. Cambridge: Harvard University Press.

Ostergren, R.C. and Rice, J.G. 2004. *The Europeans: A Geography of People, Culture, and Environment*. New York: Guilford Press.

OXFAM 2013. The Cost of Inequality: How Wealth and Income Extremes Hurt Us All. *OXFAM Media Briefing Jan 18, 2013*, [Online]. Available at: http://www.oxfam.org/sites/www.oxfam.org/files/cost-of-inequality-oxfam-mb180113.pdf [accessed 8 May 2014]

Pagden, A. 2002. Europe: Conceptualizing a Continent, in *The Idea of Europe*, edited by A. Pagden. Cambridge, Cambridge University Press, 33–54.

Pakulski, J. 2002. Towards a Non-Class Analysis of Social Inequality, in *Alternative Foundations of Class Analysis*, edited by E.O. Wright, [Online]. Available at: http://www.ssc.wisc.edu/~wright/Found-all.pdf [accessed 6 May 2014], 217–50.

Parkin, F. 1971. *Class Inequality and Political Order. Social Stratification in Capitalist and Communist Societies*. New York: Praeger.

—. 1979. *Marxism and Class Theory: A Bourgeois Critique*, Cambridge: Tavistock.

Parsons, T. 1965. Full Citizenship for the Negro American? A Sociological Problem. *Daedalus*, Vol. 94(4), 1009–54.

—. 1966. *The Structure of Social Action*. New York: The Free Press.

—. 1970. Equality and Inequality in Modern Society, or Social Stratification Revisited. *Sociological Inquiry*, 40(2), 13–72.

—. 1971. *The System of Modern Societies*. Englewood Cliffs: Prentice Hall.

Patel, S. 2006. Beyond Binaries. A Case for Self-Reflexive Sociologies. *Current Sociology*, 54(3), 381–95.

—. 2013. Are the Theories of Multiple Modernities Eurocentric? The Problem of Colonialism and its Knowledge(s), in *Worlds of Difference*, edited by S. Arjomand und E.P. Reis. London: Sage.

Pelizzon, S. 1998. But Can She Spin? The Decline in the Social Standing of Women in the Transition from Feudalism to Capitalism. PhD. diss., State University of New York at Binghamton.

—. 2002. Writing on Gender in World-Systems Perspective, in *The Modern/ Colonial Capitalist World-System in the Twentieth Century*, edited by R. Grosfoguel and A.M. Cervantes-Rodríguez. Westport: Praeger, 199–211.

Peters, C. 2004. *Women in Early Modern Britain, 1450–1640*. New York: Macmillan.

Pew Research Center. 2013. *Unauthorized Immigrants: How Pew Research Counts Them and What We Know About Them*, [Online]. Available at: http://www.pewresearch.org/2013/04/17/unauthorized-immigrants-how-pew-research-counts-them-and-what-we-know-about-them/ [accessed 6 May 2014].

Pilling, G. 1980. *Marx's Capital. Philosophy and Political Economy*. London: Routledge.

Pries, L. 2008. Transnationalisierung und soziale Ungleichheit. Konzeptionelle Überlegungen und empirische Befunde aus der Migrationsforschung, in *Transnationalisierung sozialer Ungleichheit*, edited by P.A. Berger und A. Weiß. Wiesband: VS, 41–64.

Quijano, A. 1966. Notas sobre el concepto de marginalidad social, *CEPAL*, Octubre 1966.

—. 2000a. Coloniality of Power, Eurocentrism, and Latin America. *Nepantla: Views from South*, 1(3), 533–74.

—. 2000b. Colonialidad del poder y clasificación social. *Journal of World-Systems Research*, VI(2), 342–86.

—. 2000c. El Fantasma del Desarollo en América Latina. *Revista Venezolana de Economía y Ciencias Sociales*, 6(2), 73–90.

—. 2006. El "Movimiento Indígena" y las Cuestiones Pendientes en América Latina. *Review. Journal of the Fernand Braudel Center*, XXIX(2), 189–220.

—. 2007. Coloniality and Modernity/Rationality. *Cultural Studies*, 21(2–3), 168–78.

Quijano, A. and Wallerstein, I. 1992. Americanity as a Concept, or the Americas in the Modern World-System. *International Journal of the Social Sciences*, 134, 549–57.

Randeria, S. 1999a. Jenseits von Soziologie und soziokultureller Anthropologie: Zur Ortsbestimmung der nichtwestlichen Welt in einer zukünftigen Sozialtheorie. *Soziale Welt*, 50, 373–82.

—. 1999b. Geteilte Geschichte und verwobene Moderne,in *Zukunftsentwürfe. Ideen für eine Kultur der Veränderung*, edited by J. Rüsen. Frankfurt a.M: Campus, 87–96.

—. 2002. Entangled Histories of Uneven Modernities: Civil Society, Caste Solidarities and Legal Pluralism in Post-Colonial India, in *Unraveling Ties – From Social Cohesion to New Practices of Connectedness*, edited by Y. Elkana, I. Krastev, E. Macamo and S. Randeria. Frankfurt: Campus, 284–311.

—. 2005. Verwobene Moderne: Zivilgesellschaft, Kastenbindungen und nicht-staatliches Familienrecht im postkolonialen Indien, in *Jenseits von Zentrum und Peripherie. Zur Verfassung der fragmentierten Weltgesellschaft*, edited by H. Brunkhorst und S. Costa. München: Rainer Hampp Verlag, 169–96.

Reiner, T. 2008. The Philosophical Foundations of Gender Equality in Liberalism and Marxism: A Study of Mill and Marx. *21st Century Society*, 3(1), 13–30.

Reuters 2012. *Passports ... for a Price*. February 13, [Online]. Available at: http://www.reuters.com/article/2012/02/13/us-passport-idUSTRE81B05A20120213 [accessed 2 April 2014].

Rokkan, S. 1999. A Model and Conceptual Map of Europe, in *State Formation, Nation-Building, and Mass Politics in Europe*, edited by P. Flora, S. Kuhnle and D. Urwin. Oxford: Oxford University Press, 135–49.

Rostow, W.W. 1960. *The Stages of Economic Growth. A Non-Communist Manifesto*. Cambridge: Cambridge University Press.

Roth, G. 1993. Between Cosmopolitanism and Eurocentrism: Max Weber in the Nineties. *Telos*, 96, 148–62.

—. 2000. Global capitalism and multi-ethnicity. Max Weber then and now, in *The Cambridge Companion to Weber*, edited by S. Turner. Cambridge: Cambridge University Press, 117–30.

Roth, J. 2013. Entangled Inequalities as Intersectionalities. Towards an Epistemic Sensibilization. *desiguALdades.net Working Paper*, no. 43, [Online] www.desigualdades.net/Resources/Working_Paper/43_WP_Roth_Online.pdf?1367229865, [accessed 29 April 2014].

—. 2014. Occidental Readings, Decolonial Practices. A Selection on Gender, Genre and Coloniality in the Americas, WVT: Trier

Rumford, C. 2006. Borders and rebordering, in *Europe and Asia Beyond East and West: Towards a New Cosmopolitanism*, edited by G. Delanty. London: Routledge.

Said, E. 1979. *Orientalism*. New York: Vintage Books.

Sahlins, M. 1960. *Evolution and Culture*. Ann Arbor: University of Michigan Press.

San Juan, E. Jr. 2002. Postcolonialism and the Problematic of uneven Development, in *Marxism, Modernity, and Postcolonial Studies*, edited by C. Bartolovich and N. Lazarus. Cambridge: Cambridge University Press, 221–39.

Sanderson, S.K. 1988. The Neo-Weberian Revolution: A Theoretical Balance Sheet. *Sociological Forum*, 3, 307–14.

—. 2001. *The Evolution of Human Sociality. A Darwinian Conflict Perspective*. Lanham: Rowman and Littlefield.

Santos, B.S. 2004. *The World Social Forum: A User's Manual*, [Online]. Available at: http://www.ces.uc.pt/bss/documentos/fsm_eng.pdf [accessed 6 May 2014]

—. 2006. Between Prospero and Caliban. Colonialism, Postcolonialism and Interidentity, *Review*, XXIX(2), 143–66.

Scaff, L. 1998. Weber's Amerikabild and the African American Experience, in *Crosscurrents: African Americans, Africa, and Germany in the modern world*, edited by D. McBride, L. Hopkins and C. Blackshire-Belay. Columbia: Camden House, 82–96.

References 255

Scheerer, S. 2001. Verstehen und Erklären von Gewalt – ein Versprechen der Moderne, in *Gewaltkriminalität zwischen Mythos und Realität*, edited by G. Albrecht. Frankfurt a.M.: Suhrkamp, 147–64.

Schelsky, H. 1966. *Auf der Suche nach Wirklichkeit*. Düsseldorf: Diederichs.

Schiebinger, L. 2004. *Nature's Body. Gender in the Making of Modern Science*. New Brunswick and New Jersey: Rutgers University Press.

Schiwy, F. 2007. Decolonization and the Question of Subjectivity. Gender, Race, and Binary Thinking. *Cultural Studies*, 21(2–3), 271–94.

Schluchter, W. 1988. *Rationalism, Religion, Domination. A Weberian Perspective*. Berkeley: University of California Press.

—. 2000. Psychophysics and culture, in *The Cambridge Companion to Weber*, edited by S. Turner. Cambridge: Cambridge University Press, 59–80.

—. 2007. Hindrances to Modernity: Max Weber on Islam, in *Max Weber & Islam*, edited by T.E. Huff and W. Schluchter. New Brunswick, London: Transaction Publishers, 53–138.

Schuller, K. 2014. Ost- und Westukraine. Sollbruchstellen durch ein ganzes Land. *Frankfurter Allgemeine Zeitung*, March 2, 2014, [Online] www.faz.net/-hox-7my65, [accessed 24 April 2014].

Schulze, G. 1992. *Die Erlebnisgesellschaft. Kultursoziologie der Gegenwart*. Frankfurt, New York: Campus.

Schwalbe, M. 2000. Charting Futures for Sociology: Inequality Mechanisms, Intersections, and Global Change. *Contemporary Sociology*, 29(1), 775–81.

Schwartz, S.B. 1992. *Slaves, Peasants, and Rebels. Reconsidering Brazilian Slavery*. Urbana: University of Illinois Press.

Scott, J. 1996. General Commentary, in *Class. Critical Concepts*, edited by J. Scott. London: Routledge, x–xxxv.

Seidman, S. 1996. Empire and Knowledge: More Troubles, New Opportunities for Sociology. *Contemporary Sociology*, 25(3), 313–16.

—. 2013. The Colonial Unconscious of Classical Sociology, in *Postcolonial Sociology, Political Power and Social Theory 24*, edited by J. Go. Bingley: Emerald, 35–54.

Sen, A. 1992. *Inequality Reexamined*. Oxford: Clarendon Press.

Shachar, A. 2009. *The Birthright Lottery. Citizenship and Global Inequality*. Cambridge, MA: Harvard University Press.

—. 2014. Dangerous Liaisons: Money and Citizenship, in *Should citizenship be for sale?*, edited by A. Shachar and R. Bauböck. EUI Working Papers RSCAS, 2014/01, 3–8.

Shachar, A. and Hirschl, R. 2007. Citizenship as Inherited Property. *Political Theory*, 35(3), 253–87.

Shiva, V. 1989. *Staying Alive. Women, Ecology, and Development*. London: Zed Books.

Sklair, L. 2001. *The Transnational Capitalist Class*. Oxford: Blackwell.

Smith, A. 2009. *An Inquiry in the Nature and Causes of The Wealth of Nations*. Petersfield: Harriman House.

Smith, A.D. 1995. *Nations and Nationalism in a Global Era*. Cambridge: Blackwell.
Smith, J., Wallerstein, I. and Evers, H. (eds) 1984. *Households and the World-Economy*. London: Sage.
Smooha, S. 2005. Is Israel Western?, in *Comparing Modernities. Essays in Homage to Shmuel N. Eisenstadt*, edited by E. Ben-Rafael and Y. Sternberg. Leiden: Brill, 413–42
So, A.Y. 1990. *Social Change and Development. Modernization, Dependency, and World-System Theories*. Newbury Park, CA: Sage.
Spohn, W. 2006. Multiple, Entangled, Fragmented and Other Modernities. Reflections on Comparative Sociological Research on Europe, North and Latin America, in *The Plurality of Modernity: Decentring Sociology*, edited by S. Costa, K.M. Domingues, W. Knöbl and J. Pereira da Silva. München, Mering: Rainer Hampp, 11–22.
—. 2011. An Appraisal of Shmuel Noah Eisenstadt's Global Historical Sociology. *Journal of Classical Sociology*, 11(3), 281–301.
Stacey, J. and Thorne, B. 1985. The Missing Feminist Revolution in Sociology. *Social Problems*, 32(4), 301–16.
Stam, R. and Shohat, E. 2012. *Race in Translation. Culture Wars around the Postcolonial Atlantic*. New York and London: New York University Press.
Stehr, N. 2000. Da desigualdade de clase à desigualdade de conhecimento. *Revista Brasileira de Ciências Sociais*, 15(42), 101–12.
Steinmetz, G. 2010. Feldtheorie, der deutsche Kolonialstaat und der deutsche ethnographische Diskurs 1880–1920, in *Globale, multiple und postkoloniale Modernen*, edited by M. Boatcă and W. Spohn. Munich: Rainer Hampp Verlag, 219–61.
—. (ed.) 2013. *Sociology and Empire. The Imperial Entanglements of a Discipline*. Duke University Press.
Stender, W. 2000. Ethnische Erweckungen. Zum Funktionswandel von Ethnizität in modernen Gesellschaften – ein Literaturbericht. *Mittelweg* 36(4), 65–82.
Stern, J. 2011. Ius Pecuniae – Staatsbürgerschaft zwischen ausreichendem Lebensunterhalt, Mindestsicherung und Menschenwürde, in *Migration und Integration – wissenschaftliche Perspektiven aus Österreich, Jahrbuch 1/2011*, edited by J. Dahlvik, H. Fassmann and W. Sievers. Wien and Göttingen: V&R unipress.
Stoler, A.L. and Cooper, F. 1997. *Tensions of Empire: Colonial Cultures in a Bourgeois World*. Berkeley: University of California Press.
Swedberg, R. 2005. *The Max Weber Dictionary. Key Words and Concepts*. Stanford: Stanford UP.
Sztompka, P. 2005. From East Europeans to Europeans, in *Comparing Modernities. Essays in Homage to Shmuel N. Eisenstadt*, edited by E. Ben-Rafael and Y. Sternberg. Leiden: Brill, 527–43.
Tambiah, S.J. 2005. Is Hindu-Muslim cleavage the paradigmatic case for conflicts in South Asia?, in *Comparing Modernities. Essays in Homage to Shmuel N. Eisenstadt*, edited by E. Ben-Rafael and Y. Sternberg. Leiden: Brill, 545–52.

Therborn, G. 1995. *European Modernity and Beyond. The Trajectory of European Societies, 1945–2000*. London: Sage.

—. 1996. Dialectics of Modernity: On Critical Theory and the Legacy of Twentieth-Century Marxism. *New Left Review*, 215, 59–82.

—. 2003. Entangled Modernities. *European Journal of Social Theory*, Vol. 6, 293–305.

—. 2006. Meaning, Mechanisms, Patterns, and Forces. An Introduction, in *Inequalities of the World*, edited by G. Therborn. London: Verso, 1–58.

—. 2013. *The Killing Fields of Inequality*. Polity Press: Malden.

Tilly, C. 1998. *Durable Inequality*. Berkeley, Los Angeles and London: University of California Press.

Tiryakian, E. 2004. Civilizational Analysis. Renovating the Sociological Tradition, in *Rethinking Civilizational Analysis*, edited by S.A. Arjomand and E. Tiryakian. London: Sage, 30–47.

Tlostanova, M. 2010. *Gender Epistemologies and Eurasian Borderlands*. New York: Palgrave Macmillan.

Todorova, M. 1997. *Imagining the Balkans*. New York City and Oxford, Oxford University Press.

—. 2004. Historische Vermächtnisse als Analysekategorie. Der Fall Südosteuropa, in *Europa und die Grenzen im Kopf*, edited by K. Kaser, D. Gramshammer-Hohl and R. Pichler. Klagenfurt: Wieser Verlag, 227–52.

Tomich, D. 1991. World Slavery and Caribbean Capitalism. *Theory and Society*, 20, 297–319.

—. 2004. *Through the Prism of Slavery. Labor, Capital, and the World Economy*. Lanham: Rowman & Littlefield.

Touraine, A. 2007. Sociology after Sociology. *European Journal of Social Theory*, 10(2), 184–93.

Tribe, K. 1980. Introduction to Weber. *Economy and Society*, 9(4), 420–27.

Trouillot, M. 1995. *Silencing the Past. Power and the Production of History*. Boston: Beacon Press.

Tucker, K.H. 2002. *Classical Social Theory. A Contemporary Approach*. Malden: Blackwell.

Tucker, R. 1978. Introduction, in *The Marx-Engels Reader*, edited by R. Tucker, New York: Norton and Company.

Turner, B.S. 1990. Outline of a Theory of Citizenship. *Sociology*, 24, 189–217.

—. (ed.) 1993. *Citizenship and Social Theory*. London: Sage.

—. 1996. *For Weber. Essays on the Sociology of Fate*. London: Sage.

Turner, B.S. and Hamilton, P. 1994. General Commentary, in *Citizenship. Critical Concepts*, edited by B.S. Turner and P. Hamilton. London: Routledge, n.p.

Turner, J.H. and Babones, S.J. 2006. Global Inequality. An Introduction, in *Global Social Change. Historical and Comparative Perspectives*, edited by C. Chase-Dunn and S.J. Babones. Baltimore: Johns Hopkins University Press.

Uemura, K. 2006. Marx and Modernity, in *Marx for the 21st century*, edited by H. Uchida. London and New York: Routledge.

United Nations 2005. *The Inequality Predicament. Report on the World Social Situation 2005*. New York: United Nations.

Van Amersfoort, H. and van Niekerk, M. 2006. Immigration as a Colonial Inheritance. Post-Colonial Immigrants in the Netherlands, 1945–2002. *Journal of Ethnic and Migration Studies*, 32, 323–46.

Varga, J.T. 2012. Hungary Provides €250.000 Fast Track into Europe. VJT&Partners highlights the importance of the new Hungarian investment immigration law. *PRWEB* [Online] www.prweb.com/releases/2012/12/prweb10227642.htm [31 March 2014].

Venn, C. 2006. *The Postcolonial Challenge. Towards Alternative Worlds*. London: Sage.

—. 2009. Neoliberal Political Economy, Biopolitics and Colonialism. A Transcolonial Genealogy of Inequality, Theory. *Culture & Society*, 26(6), 206–33.

Vernik, E. 2011. La cuestión polaca. Acerca del nacionalismo imperialista de Max Weber, Entramados y perspectivas. *Revista de la carrera de sociologia*, 1(1), 165–80.

Wallerstein, I. 1974. *The Modern World-System. Capitalist Agriculture and the Origins of the European World-Economy in the Sixteenth Century*. New York: Academic Press.

—. 1979. *The Capitalist World-Economy*. Cambridge: Cambridge University Press.

—. 1991a. Marx and Underdevelopment, in *Unthinking Social Science. The Limits of Nineteenth-Century Paradigms*. Cambridge, MA: Polity Press.

—. 1991b. *Geopolitics and Geoculture. Essays on the Changing World-System*. Cambridge, MA: Cambridge University Press.

—. 1991c. *Unthinking Social Science. The Limits of Nineteenth-Century Paradigms*. Cambridge, MA: Polity Press.

—. 1995a. The Insurmountable Contradictions of Liberalism: Human Rights and the Rights of Peoples in the Geoculture of the Modern World-System, in *Nations, Identities, Cultures*, edited by V.Y. Mudimbe. Durham: Duke University Press, 181–98.

—. 1995b. The Modern World-System and Evolution. *Journal of World-Systems Research*, 1(19), 1–6.

—. 1996. Marx and History: Fruitful and Unfruitful Emphases, in *Race, Nation, Class. Ambiguous Identities*, edited by E. Balibar and I. Wallerstein. London: Verso, 125–34.

—. 1999. The Heritage of Sociology, the Promise of Social Science. *Current Sociology*, 47(1), 1–37.

—. 2000. *The Essential Wallerstein*. New York: The New Press.

—. 2003. Citizens all? Citizens some! The Making of the Citizen. *Comparative Studies in Society and History*, 45(4), 650–79.

—. 2004. *World-Systems Analysis. An Introduction*. Durham and London: Duke University Press.

References 259

Wallerstein, I. and Smith, J. 1992a. Households as an Institution of the World-Economy, in *Creating and Transforming Households. The Constraints of the World-Economy*, edited by I. Wallerstein and J. Smith. Cambridge: Cambridge University Press, 3–23.

—. 1992b. Core-periphery and household structures, in *Creating and Transforming Households. The Constraints of the World-Economy*, edited by I. Wallerstein and J. Smith. Cambridge: Cambridge University Press, 253–300.

Walsh, C. 2002. (De)Construir la interculturalidad. Consideraciones críticas desde la política, la colonialidad y los movimientos indígenas y negros en el Ecuador, in *Interculturalidad y Política*, edited by N. Fuller. Lima: Red de Apoyo de las Ciencias Sociales, 115–42.

—. 2010a. Development as Buen Vivir: Institutional arrangements and (de) colonial entanglements. *Development*, 53(1), 15–21.

—. 2010b. The (De)Coloniality of Knowledge, Life, and Nature: The N.A.-Andean FTA, Indigenous Movements, and Regional Alternatives, in *Alternative Perspectives on Globalization: Status, Regions, and Movements*, edited by J. Shefner and P. Fernandez-Kelley. State College: Pennsylvania State University Press.

Walsh, C., Schiwy, F., and Castro-Gómez, S. (eds) 2002. *Indisciplinar las ciencias sociales: Geopolíticas del conocimiento y colonialidad del poder. Perspectivas desde lo andino*. Quito: Abya-Yala.

Weber, M. 1961. *General Economic History*, New York: Collier.

—. 1971. On Race and Society, translated by J. Gittleman, with an introduction by B. Nelson. *Social Research*, 38(1), 30–41.

—. 1972. Socialism, in *Max Weber*, edited by J.E.T. Eldridge, translated by D. Hÿtsch. London: Nelson, 197–99.

—. 1973 [1910]. Max Weber, Dr. Alfred Ploetz and W.E.B. Du Bois. *Sociological Analysis*, 34, 308–12.

—. 1978a. *Economy and Society. An Outline of Interpretive Sociology, Volume One*, edited by G. Roth and C. Wittich. Berkeley: University of California Press.

—. 1978b. *Economy and Society. An Outline of Interpretive Sociology, Volume Two*, edited by G. Roth and C. Wittich. Berkeley: University of California Press.

—. 1980. The National State and Economic Policy (Freiburg Address). *Economy and Society*, 9(4), 428–49.

—. 1988. *Max Weber: A Biography*, translated by Harry Zohn, with an introduction by Guenther Roth. New Brunswick, NJ: Transaction Press.

—. 1989. *MWG I/10. Zur Russischen Revolution von 1905. Schriften 1905–1912*, edited by W.J. Mommsen and D. Dahlmann. Tübingen: Mohr (Siebeck).

—. 1992 [1930]. *The Protestant Ethic and the Spirit of Capitalism*, translated by Talcott Parsons. New York: Routledge.

—. 1993. *MWG I/4 Landarbeiterfrage, Nationalstaat und Volkswirtschaftspolitik. Schriften und Reden 1892–1899*, edited by W.J. Mommsen and R. Aldenhoff. Tübingen: Mohr (Siebeck).

260   *Global Inequalities Beyond Occidentalism*

—. 1994. *Political Writings*, edited by P. Lassman and R. Speirs. Cambridge: Cambridge University Press.

—. 1995. *MWG I/11. Zur Psychophysik der industriellen Arbeit. Schriften und Reden 1908–1912*, edited by W.J. Mommsen and S. Frommer. Tübingen: Mohr (Siebeck).

—. 1998. *MWG I/8. Wirtschaft, Staat und Sozialpolitik. Schriften und Reden 1900–1912*, edited by W.J. Mommsen, P. Kurth and B. Morgenbrod. Tübingen: Mohr (Siebeck).

—. 2004a. Confucianism and Puritanism compared, in *The Essential Weber. A Reader*, edited by Sam Whimster. London: Routledge, 35–54.

—. 2004b. The distribution of power in society: classes, status groups and parties, in: The Essential Weber. A Reader, edited by Sam Whimster, London: Routledge, 182–94.

—. 2005. *Reading and Commentary on Modernity*, edited by Stephen Kalberg, Malden: Blackwell.

Weindling, P. 1989. *Health, Race and German Politics between National Unification and Nazism, 1870–1945*. Cambridge: Cambridge University Press.

Weiß, A. 2001. Rassismus als symbolisch vermittelte Dimension sozialer Ungleichheit, in *Klasse und Klassifikation. Die symbolische Dimension sozialer Ungleichheit*, edited by A. Weiß, C. Koppetsch, A. Scharenberg and O. Schmidtke. Wiesbaden: Westdeutscher Verlag, 79–108.

—. 2005. The Transnationalization of Social Inequality: Conceptualizing Social Position on a World Scale. *Current Sociology*, 53(4), 707–28.

Wenger, M.G. 1980. The transmutation of Weber's Stand in American sociology and its social roots. *Current Perspectives in Social Theory*, 1, 357–78.

Werlhof, C. von 1984. The Proletarian Is Dead: Long Live the Housewife!, in *Households and the World-Economy*, edited by J. Smith, I. Wallerstein and H. Evers. London: Sage, 131–47.

—. 1988. Women's Work: The Blind Spot in the Critique of Political Economy, in *Women, the Last Colony*, edited by M. Mies, V. Bennholdt-Thomsen and C. von Werlhof. London: Zed Books, 13–26.

Werlhof, C. von, Mies, M. and Bennholdt-Thomsen, V. 1983. *Frauen, die letzte Kolonie*. Reinbek: Rowolth.

Wieviorka, M. 2003. A Symposium on Emerging Issues in the Twenty-First Century World-System. From Marx and Braudel to Wallerstein. *Contemporary Sociology*, 34(1), 1–7.

Wiley, N. 1985. The Current Interregnum in American Sociology. *Social Research*, 52(1), 179–207.

—. 1987. Introduction, in *The Marx-Weber Debate*, edited by N. Wiley. London: Sage.

Williams, E. 1943. *Capitalism and Slavery*. Chapel Hill, NC: University of North Carolina Press.

Wimmer, A. and Glick Schiller, N. 2002. Methodological Nationalism and Beyond Nation-State Building, Migration and the Social Sciences. *Global Networks*, 2(4), 301–34.

Wolff, L. 1994. *Inventing Eastern Europe. The Map of Civilization on the Mind of the Enlightenment*. Stanford: Stanford University Press.

World Bank. 2006. *Equity and Development. World Development Report 2006*. Washington, DC: The World Bank.

—. 2011. *Gender Equality and Development. World Development Report 2012*. Washington, DC: The World Bank.

Wright, E.O. 2002. A Framework of Class Analysis in the Marxist Tradition, in *Alternative Foundations of Class Analysis*, edited by E.O. Wright, [Online]. Available at: http://www.ssc.wisc.edu/~wright/Found-all.pdf [accessed 6 May 2014], 6–40.

Zimmerman, A. 2001. *Anthropology and Anti-humanism in Imperial Germany*. Chicago, IL: University of Chicago Press.

—. 2010. *Booker T. Washington, the German Empire, and the Globalization of the New South*. Princeton and Oxford: Princeton University Press.

Zimmerman, A. 2006. Decolonizing Weber. Postcolonial Studies 9 (1), 53-79

Zubaida, S. 2005. Max Weber's The City and the Islamic City. *Max Weber Studies*, 5(6), 111–18.

Index

9/11 (2001) events, and "clash of civilisations" 220

Africa, social inequality 6
agrarianism, transition to industrialism 11, 13, 14
alienation, Marx on 28
Americas, European "discovery" of 86
Annenkov, Paul, Marx' letter to 42, 43
anti-Semitism 82, 165, 166
Argentina, economy, Weber on 168–9

Bakić-Hayden, Milica 223
Balkans, as Europe's "incomplete Self" 217
barbarians, as Other 83
Beck, Ulrich 125
Bergquist, Charles 120, 121, 122
Bernal, Martin 213
Bielefeld School of development sociology 20, 52, 55–6, 64, 71
Bismarck, Otto von, Germanisation policy 167
blackness, and slavery 95
Bolivia 111, 120, 131
    vivir bien philosophy 112fn29
Bonaparte, Napoleon, invasion of Egypt (1798) 97
Böröcz, József 214
bourgeoisie, in Weber's typology 155, 156
bourgeoisification 66
    in capitalist world-economy 61–2
    proletarianisation, as analogous processes 62
Brazil, social inequalities 6
Brubaker, Rogers, on citizenship 185–8
Buck–Morss, Susan 94
Buddhism 150
bureaucracy, Weber on 152
bureaucratisation 157

capital, labour, relationship 34
capitalism
    and citizenship 178
    and colonialism 37
    and creative destruction 124
    emergence of 145
    and exploitation, Marx on 31
    global
        emergence of 37
        Mintz on 47
    pariah 147
    and patriarchy 71
    plantation slavery in process 59
    primitive accumulation, as basis of 31, 37, 119
    and the Protestant Ethic 145–6
    and rational discipline, Weber on 151, 152–3
    role of sugar in 47
    and social inequality 31–2
    and subsistence labour 52
    USA, Weber's views 170
    Western
        and free labour 148–9
        Weber on 143–4, 145
    women under 32–3
    as world-economy, reframing 66–7
Caribbean, plantations, slave labour 48–9
caste
    notion of 8
    Weber on 158–9
Castro-Gómez, Santiago 103
Chakrabarty, Dipesh 39
Chatterjee, Partha 17, 214
Christianisation, and the civilising mission 93
Christianity
    early, and citizenship 178–9, 182
    Orthodox 209
    Western 209
cities, European, common features 178

citizenship

alternative 195
approaches to 183
as ascribed status 186, 190, 230
by birthright, vs by investment 191–6
Brubaker on 185–8
and capitalism 178
and the civilising mission 129
and class 181
commodification of 191, 193–5, 198
criteria for 103
definition 181
and early Christianity 178–9, 182
economic 192, 193
and equality 21, 99, 177, 181–5
and feudalism 181
and the French Revolution 99–100, 182
global 132–3, 196
and global stratification 130–37
and inequality 130, 132, 198
as inherited property 189–91
Mackert on 188
Marshall on 181
and national identity 130
in Occidentalist discourse 129
rights, extension of 129–30
rise of 177
sale
    Dominica 192
    Hungary 192
    Malta 193–4, 196
    St Kitts and Nevis 192
scheme, Henley & Partners 195–6
second-class 133
Sephardic Jews 223
Shachar on 189–91
as social closure 21, 185–8, 231
transference of 189–90
transnational dimension 184
Turner on 183–4
usurpation strategies 196
and visa-free travel 195
as Western institution, critique 179–80,
    210–11

civilisation

definition 206
"Velvet Curtain of Culture" 208, 209,
    221, 224, 225

civilising mission 84, 109

and Christianisation 93
and citizenship 129
and the Enlightenment 93–104
global design of 106fn24, 114, 115
and progress 97

"clash of civilisations" *see under*
    Huntington, Samuel

class

antagonisms 34
and citizenship 181
commercial classes 154, 155
conflict
    Durkheim on 14
    political economy of 231
and the nation-state 125, 126–7
property classes 154–5
social classes 154, 155
and social inequality 7
status, distinction 14, 157
and stratification 14
structure, Marx on 32, 36
types 154–5
Weber on 153–5
Weber's typology of 155–6
see also stratification

class theory, Marxist, and social inequality
    19, 33, 35
Cohn, Bernard 212
Cold War, end of (1989) 25, 108, 206, 207,
    209
Colombia, identities 111–12
colonial difference, and coloniality 17

colonialism

and capitalism 37
and construction of irrationality 16
and cultural control 212
internal 10

coloniality 115

of being 81
and colonial difference 17
of labour 81
Marx' understanding of 19–20
meaning 107
and modernity 17, 20, 170
of power 81, 107, 108, 118
see also decoloniality

Index

commodity production 27–8, 29, 55, 63, 64, 75
conflicts, typology of 207
Confucianism 149–50
Connell, Raewyn 4
consciousness
  in Hegel's thought 29
  Marx on 27
Coronil, Fernando 81, 85, 109–10, 216
cosmology, evolutionary 94
cosmopolitanism, and "re-bordering" 211
creative destruction
  and capitalism 124
  notion 123
cultural differences
  and Occidental superiority 15
  political economy of 202, 210, 231

Darwin, Charles 94
de Gouges, Olympe, "Declaration of the Rights of Women and the Female Citizen" 99
decoloniality 4, 17, 81, 116, 229
  critique of 115
  see also coloniality
decolonisation 105, 116
  Latin America 107
dependency theory 4, 21, 25, 55
  Latin America 106
  vs modernisation theory 106
development
  alternatives to 114
  and economic growth 105–6
  of underdevelopment 57, 119
developmentalism 105
  and economic growth 105–6
  and globalisation 108
  and the nation-state 106
Dirks, Nicholas 212
discipline, Weber on 151, 152
Discovery Doctrine 88
Dominica, citizenship, sale of 192
Du Bois, W.E.B. 173, 174
  influence on Weber 165
dualism 13, 15, 84
Dunaway, Wilma 74, 77
Durkheim, Emile 201
  on class conflict 14

Dussel, Enrique 18, 213
Dzankic, Jelena 194

economic growth 123
  and development 105–6
  global 108, 114
  and immigrants 131, 132
  and inequality 5, 117, 123
  "The Stages of Economic Growth" (Rostow) 105
  Third World successes 109
Ecuador
  Confederation of Indigenous Nationalities 111
  national plan 112
Eisenstadt, Shmuel
  on modernity 203
  Modernization: Protest and Change 203
  multiple modernities model *see* multiple modernities model
emigration
  and ethnic homogeneity 128
  European, end of 128
  Ireland 128
  to New World 127
"end of history" thesis, Fukuyama 206
Enlightenment, The
  and the civilising mission 93–104
  and European civilisation 93
  and Reason 15
  thought, slavery in 94–5
equality 68, 182
  before the law 69, 177, 181, 186
  as capability 7
  and citizenship 21, 99, 177, 181–5
  male-female, slave populations 101
  political 177, 181
  see also inequality
Escobar, Arturo 111
ethnic groups
  definition 161
  Weber on 160–64
ethnicisation 65
  of the labour force 68–71, 78–9, 82, 89
  and racism 70
ethnicity 158
  history of term 164fn9
  and social stratification 9

266 *Global Inequalities Beyond Occidentalism*

Eurocentrism 37, 82, 229
  critique of 3
  Marx, accusations of 37, 39
  propagation of 13, 84, 97, 217
  see also Occidentalism
Europe
  Asian origins 213
  Central, meaning 222
  colonial expansion, and violence 15–16
  decadent 219, 223
  Eastern, transformation research 109
  emigration, post-1500: 14
  epigonal 219, 221, 223
  and European Union 213–14
  heroic 219, 221
  immigration 14
  imperial dissolution 105
  mental maps 216, 220
  nation-state formation 106
  post-Westernisation 110
  see also multiple Europes
European Union
  accession rhetoric 221–2
  Eastern enlargement 214, 221
    map 215
  and Europe 213–14
  moral geopolitics 214, 215
Europeanisation project 219, 220, 220–21
evolutionism 13, 15, 84, 217
exploitation, definition 42fn5

Fabian, Johannes 96
family
  bourgeois model 102
  as social ideal 90
feudalism 14, 28, 90
  and citizenship 181
  Western, vs Oriental, Weber on 148
Feuerbach, Ludwig 27
Frank, André Gunder 119–20, 123
  on primary accumulation 58–9
French Revolution (1789) 93, 207
  and citizenship 99–100, 182
  and geoculture 67–8
Fukuyama, Francis, "end of history" thesis
  206

gender

equality 12, 33fn4
  hierarchy, and racial hierarchy 90
  and social inequalities 10
  sociology of 12
gender inequality 11
  and Marxism 44–5
gendering
  binary logic of 73–4
  definition 72
  and households 74
  institutionalisation 72
  of Islamophobia 114
  scope 72–3
  as semiproletarianisation of women's
    labour 75, 76, 77
geoculture
  definition 67
  and the French Revolution 67–8
  Occidentalism as 78–9
  as set of ideologies 68
  Wallerstein's notion 78
German Association for Racial Hygiene 172
German Sociological Association 172
Germanisation policy, Bismarck 167
Germanism, and Polonism, Weber on 21,
  167–8, 169, 174–5
Germany
  "Polish question", Weber's views
    169–70
  social inequality 11
  unification (1871) 166
Gini coefficients, and inequality 118–19
global citizenship *see under* citizenship
global financial crisis (2008) 230
  Southern European economies 220
global inequalities
  approaches 136–7
  country rankings 130–31
  of income 5, 21
  longevity of 2
  political economy of 229
  sociology of 18, 228–9
  see also social inequality/ies
Global North 229, 230
Global South 229, 230
globalcentrism 110
globalisation
  and developmentalism 108

and inequality 2, 8, 36, 125
  neoliberal 109, 110, 112
  and social inequalities 2, 5
Glorious Revolution (1688) 93
Granada, Christian reconquest of (1492)
    82, 86
Grosfoguel, Ramón 133
Gulbenkian Commission, report (1996) 2–3

Haiti 68, 100fn20
  see also Saint Domingue
Hansen, Peo 214
Hegel, G.W.F. 213
  consciousness 29
  idealist notion of history 26, 97
  on slavery 96–7
Henley & Partners, citizenship scheme
    195–6
Hinduism 150
history
  "end of history" thesis, Fukuyama 206
  Hegel's notion of 26, 97
  universal 13
Hobbes, Thomas 94
Hobson, John 213
householding 63–8
  in capitalist world-economy 63–4
households
  as agencies for socialisation 69
  classical proletarian 66
  definition 64
  and double-exploitation of women 77
  and gendering 74
  income-pooling 64–5, 72
  semiproletarian 74
  unremunerated activities, as resources 72
Households in the World Economy 53
housewifisation 55, 56, 61
  core working-class household type 66
  effects of 57
  models 65–6
  peripheralised household type 65–6
housewives 20
  economic role 56
  low status 54
  private sphere, confinement to 100
  proletarians, relationship 54
housework

neglect of, in Marxist theory 53
  as non-work 102, 103
  product of capitalist development 65
  and the world economy 52, 53
Hungary, citizenship, sale of 192
Huntington, Samuel 218, 231
  "clash of civilisations" thesis 22, 201,
    205–10, 211
  and 9/11 (2001) events 220
  criticism of 210
  and essence of Western civilisation
    205–6
  Weber's foreshadowing of 201
  "Political Order of Changing Societies"
    205
  "Velvet Curtain of Culture" 208, 209,
    221, 225

identities
  Colombia 111–12
  Latin America 111
  national, and citizenship 130
immigrants, and economic growth 131, 132
income inequalities 10
  and global inequalities 5, 21
India, Marx on 38
Indian Subaltern Studies 17, 39, 229
industrialism, transition from agrarianism
    11, 13, 14
inequality
  Africa 6
  between nations 129
  categorical, relational, distinction 124
  and citizenship 130, 132, 198
  and economic growth 5, 117, 123
  explanations for 118
  and Gini coefficients 118–19
  and globalisation 2, 8, 36, 125
  high 117, 122, 123
    examples 118–19
  and innovation 123
  low 119, 122, 123, 124, 125
  patterns 118–19
  racial 6
  reconceptualisation of 19
  relational, vs distributive 8
  research 122
  as social difference 17

transnational 125, 126, 130
USA 122
varieties of 8
world 127
see also social inequality/ies; world
inequality
innovation, and inequality 123
interculturality
critical 113
examples 113
notion 112
Ireland
British colonial rule 40, 42
emigration 128
Isin, Engin 21, 178, 179, 180, 210
Islam 150
Marx on 38
Weber on 147
Islamophobia 223
gendering of 114

Jews
"pariah people" status 159
Sephardic, citizenship 223
Jonsson, Stefan 214
Judaism, Weber on 146–7

Katz, Stephen 39, 40
Konno, Hajime 175
Korzeniewicz, Roberto P. & Albrecht, S.
131–2
Korzeniewicz, Roberto P. & Moran,
Timothy P. 122, 123, 124, 126, 132
world historical model 21, 117–37,
118, 119, 134–5, 185, 230
Kuznets hypothesis 11

labour
free, and coerced 60
general human, components 52
labour force
ethnicisation 68–71, 78–9, 82, 89
see also non-wage labour; wage labour
labour migration, mass 127
Latin America
agricultural exports 121
decolonial perspective 20, 78
decolonisation 107

dependency theory 106
identities 111
serfdom 107
social inequality 6
underdevelopment 57–8
Lerner, Daniel, *The Passing of Traditional
Society: Modernizing the Middle
East* 105
Locke, John 94
Luxemburg, Rosa 60

Mackert, Jürgen, on citizenship 188
Maldonado-Torres, Nelson 88–9
Malta, citizenship, sale of 193–4, 196
Marcuse, H., on the proletariat 30–31
marriage, as slavery, Marx on 32–3
Marshall, T.H.
on citizenship 181
on social equality 181
Marx, Karl 3, 9, 14, 18
on alienation 28
Annenkov, letter to 42, 43
on capitalist exploitation 31
on class structure 32, 36
on colonial slavery 42–3, 44
colonialist writings, approaches to 39
coloniality, understanding of 19–20
on consciousness 27
Eurocentrism, accusations of 37, 39
on exchange and use value 30
on fetishism of commodities 29–30
on India 38
on Islam 38
on marriage as slavery 32–3
postcolonial criticism of 39
"true Marx", search for 39, 40
"two centuries", differentiation 36
on wage labour 28–9
Weber, common ground 141
works
Capital 37, 44
The German Ideology 44
Grundrisse 28, 43
Wage Labour and Capital 28–9
Zasulich, letter to 40
Marx, Karl & Engels, F., *The Communist
Manifesto* 1, 36, 41, 44
Marxism

Index 269

and dialectics of modernity 41
and gender inequality 44–5
housework, neglect of 53
materialist basis 26, 27
and Orientalism 36, 38
postcolonial criticism of 39
reassessment of 35–6
revival of 44
rise and fall 25, 35
slavery in 49–50
Merchant, Carolyn 90
Mies, Maria 56, 57, 75, 76, 90, 101, 102, 230
Mignolo, Walter 17, 81, 82, 113, 132, 133, 224
migrants, types 133
migration 1–2
intercontinental 2
transnational 2
transregional 2
Milanovic, Branko 1
Mintz, Sidney 76, 230
on global capitalism 47
plantation slavery, study 47–50
works
Sweetness and Power 50
"Was the Plantation Slave a Proletarian?" 47, 50
modernisation, definition 203
modernisation theory
convergence thesis 202
vs dependency theory 106
and traditional structures 117, 123, 136
and US Vietnam defeat 141
writings on 105
modernity
and coloniality 17, 20, 170
decolonisation of 224
dialectics of, and Marxism 41
Eisenstadt on 203
European
impact 204–5
key events 8
indicators of 18
and its Other 15
key events 8
and multiple Europes 213, 224
and progress 17–18
reconceptualisation of 212

and sociology 17, 18
as transformation 12–13
transformative 8–13
and violence 15
Weber's theory of 21, 142–52
see also multiple modernities model
Mohanty, Chandra 57
Moldova, access to Schengen zone, prevention of 197, 198
multiple Europes
model 219
and modernity 213, 224–5
and multiple modernities 213
table 219
multiple modernities
civilisations as 202–5
model 22, 201, 211, 229, 231
USA 204
and multiple Europes 213

nation-state 3, 10, 11, 12, 19, 33, 65
and class 125, 126–7
and developmentalism 106
formation, Europe 106
unit of analysis, shift from 18
Naumann, Friedrich 169
neo-liberalism 108
neo-Weberianism 141
New England colonies 119, 120, 123–4
New World
emigration to 127
European "discovery" of 13, 87
as extension of Christian Europe 88
as female virgin lands 93
non-wage labour 53, 55, 64fn6, 75
wage labour, co-existence of 17
Werlhof on 53
see also wage labour
North-South-divide 10–11

Occidentalism 97, 217, 227
definition 82
emergence of 81
as geoculture 78–9
global designs 114–15
historicised notion of 136
Orientalism, precondition of 81, 82
as overarching metaphor 82

superiority of, and cultural differences 15
and Western Christianity, dominance
of 82
see also Eurocentrism
occupations, wage data 131–2
Orientalism 3–4
and former Yugoslavia 223
and Marxism 36, 38
Said on 38, 79, 102–3
Weber 178, 183
Other
barbarians as 83
and modernity 15
Othering
definition 16
racial/ethnic 82
and creation of world economy 89
religious 82
spatial, of women 91
Otherness
discovery of 13–16
European discourses of 86

Pagden, Anthony 213
Pan-German League 169
Parkin, Frank 164
Parsons, Talcott
on citizenship and equality 181–2
interpretations of Weber 141–2
patriarchy, and capitalism 71
Pelizzon, Sheila 72, 77, 90
plantation slavery 20, 123
in capitalist process 59
Caribbean
industrial production, features 50
Mintz's study 47–51
homeland economies, contribution to 51
in the world economy 51–2
Ploetz, Alfred, Weber, debate 165, 172
political economy
of class conflict 231
of cultural differences 202, 210, 231
of global inequalities 21, 229
identity politics, replacement by 71
Marxist 20, 22, 36, 201, 202
critique of 45
radical 25
of social inequalities 19

Weber on 168
Polonism *see* Germanism, and Polonism
postcolonial
contexts 9
criticism, of Marx 39
critique 13
feminist perspectives 71
immigration 12
migration flows 129
modernisation 213, 229
studies 20, 81
theory 39, 212
poverty 5
feministation of 77
primary accumulation
Frank on 58–9
and gender relations 58
primitive accumulation (of capital) 20, 47, 60
as basis of capitalism 31, 37
colonial 86
critiques of 45, 57
and global inequality 57
vs primary accumulation 58
as process 52, 119
progress
and the civilising mission 97
and modernity 17–18
proletarian, definition 48
proletarianisation, bourgeoisification, as
analogous processes 62
proletarians
housewives, relationship 54
slaves, comparison 50
in Weber's typology 155, 156
proletariat, Marcuse on 30–31
Protestant Ethic
and capitalism 145–6
and world mastery 149–50

Quijano, Aníbal 13, 84, 97, 106–7, 121
coloniality of power, notion 81, 107, 118
and Wallerstein 82, 89

racial hierarchy
and gender hierarchy 90
and religious differences 89
racialisation, spatial 86
racism 79

biological, discrediting of 104
cultural 104
and ethnicisation 70
scientific 102, 128
Weber 169, 175
in world-systems analysis 70
Randeria, Shalini 212
religions, carrier strata 149–50
religious differences, and racial hierarchy
89
Rostow, W.W., "The Stages of Economic
Growth" 105
Roth, Guenther 169
Russian Revolution (1917) 207

Said, Edward 81, 178
on Orientalism 38, 79, 102–3
St Kitts and Nevis, citizenship, sale of 192
Saint-Domingue 120, 129
abolition of slavery 100
see also Haiti
Schengen zone, access, restrictions on 197,
221
Schluchter, Wolfgang 172
Schumpeter, Joseph, creative destruction,
notion 123
Sen, Amartya 7
serfdom, Latin America 107
Shachar, Ayelet, on citizenship 189–91
skin colour, as identity marker 103
slave plantations see plantation slavery
slave trade, Atlantic 2
slavery
abolition of, Saint-Domingue 100
African-American, expansion of 95
and blackness 95
colonial, Marx on 42–3, 44
in Enlightenment thought 94–5
Hegel on 96–7
in Marxism 49–50
as residual feudalism 47–8
southern United States 121
varieties of 49
see also plantation slavery
slaves, proletarians, comparison 50
Smith, Adam 31, 43
social change, as the norm 94
social closure

citizenship as 21, 185–8, 231
formation 159
and status groups 156, 158
Weber on 157–8, 163–4
social difference 17, 115
social inequality/ies
Africa 6
Brazil 6
and capitalism 31–2
and class 7
and economic growth 1
ethnic/racial 5–6, 6
and gender 10
Germany 11
and globalisation 2, 5, 231
Latin America 6
Marshall on 181
and Marxist class theory 19, 33, 35
perspectives 3–4
political economy of 19
research
capability approach 7
inadequacies of 7
methodology 8
Occidentalist bias 4–5, 11, 227, 228
theoretical approaches 7–8
sociology of 4, 10, 227–8
and stratification 16
unit of analysis 2
see also global inequalities
social order, and status groups 153, 159
social stratification
and ethnicity 9
patterns, non-Western 6
sociology
"colonial mode" 12–13
development, Bielefeld School of 52
of gender 12
global, need for 231
of global inequalities 18, 228–9
and modernity, understanding of 17, 18
of social inequality 4, 227–8
Stam, Robert, and Shohat, Ella 88
status
class, distinction 14, 157
stratification of 153, 157
Weber on 156
status groups 146, 156–7

as communities 156
determination of 156
and social closure 156, 158
and social honour 157
and the social order 153, 159
stratification by 153, 157
Weber on 157
stratification 159–60
and class 14
economic 153
emergence of 179
global, by citizenship 130–137
and social inequalities 16
of status 153, 157
by status groups 153, 157
varieties of 153
subsistence labour 20
and capitalism 52
see also housework
subsistence theorists 52, 54, 55, 56, 61, 62,
63, 65, 66, 75
feminist 67, 68, 71, 72, 85, 136
sugar
plantation revolution 76
role in capitalism 47
Sugar Industry Diversification Foundation
(SIDF) 192
sustainable development 112, 114

Therborn, Göran 41, 126, 127
Third World
economic growth 109
modernisation, need for 105
plurality 111
Tilly, Charles 8, 124
Tiryakian, Edward 201, 202
Tönnies, Ferdinand 172
Treitler, Vilna Bashi 88
Tribe, Keith 175
Trouillot, Michel-Rolph 94
Tucker, Robert 29
Turkey 38, 209
EU, application for admission 221, 222
Turner, Bryan 180
on citizenship 183–4

UN
Human Development Index 7

Human Development Reports 7
USA
capitalism in, Weber's views 170
colonial period 121
inequality 122
Mexican border, immigration 198
modernity 204
"Negro question", Weber's views
170–71, 173, 175
see also New England colonies

Valladolid debate (1550) 88
value, exchange and use 30
"Velvet Curtain of Culture" 208, 209, 221,
224, 225
violence
and European colonial expansion 15–16
and modernity 15
Visa Restriction Index 195, 230

wage data, occupations 131–2
wage labour 20
Marx on 28–9
non-wage labour, coexistence 17
see also non-wage labour
Wallerstein, Immanuel 22, 34, 68, 69, 75,
81, 83
geoculture notion 78
on relations of production 60
world-systems analysis 47
see also under Quijano
Walsh, Catherine 112
war against terrorism 114
Weber, Max 3, 9, 10, 18
on Argentina's economy 168–9
on bureaucracy 152
on capitalism
and rational discipline 151, 152–3
in the USA 170
on caste 158–9
on class 153–5
classes, typology of 155–6
Du Bois, influence of 165
on ethnic groups 160–4
Freiburg address 167, 170, 174, 175
on Germanism and Polonism 21,
167–8, 169, 174–5
on Islam 147

Index   273

on Judaism 146–7
Marx, common ground 141
modernity, theory of 21, 142–52
on the "Negro question", in USA
      170–71, 173, 175
on "Negroes" vs "Indians", as workers
      173
Orientalism 178, 183
Parsonian interpretation of 141–2
Ploetz, debate 165, 172
on the "Polish question" in Germany
      169–70
on political economy 168
on the Protestant Ethic 145–6
racism 169, 175
on religions, and carrier strata 149–50
on social closure 157–8, 163–4
on status 156
on status groups 157
on stratification 153
Verein für Sozialpolitik, membership 166
on Western
      capitalism 143–4, 145
      exceptionalism 144
      vs Oriental feudalism 148
      superiority 143
works
      *Collected Essays on the Sociology
         of Religion* 142
      Economy and Society 160, 165,
         172, 177
      General Economic History 143
      "Nationality in Economic Policy"
         (Freiburg address) 167, 170,
         174, 175
      *Protestant Ethic and the Spirit of
         Capitalism* 145, 152, 160, 165
      see also neo-Weberianism
Weiß, Anja 125
Werlhof, Claudia von
   on non-wage labour 53

"The Proletarian is Dead: Long Live
      the Housewife" 47, 53
Westphalia, Peace of (1648) 207
Wiley, Norbert 142
witch-hunting 91–2
   and fight against disorder 92
witchcraft
   as crime against God 92
   and women 92
Wollstonecraft, Mary, "A Vindication on
      the Rights of Women" 99
women
   double-exploitation of, in households 77
   living alone, ordinance against 91
   nature of, debate about 90
   role in European capitalism 85–6
   spatial Othering of 91
   under capitalism 32–3
   violence against 55
   and witchcraft 92
work, cultural attitudes to 171–2
World Bank 5, 56
   "Global Inequality" 1
World Economic Forum, Global Risk
      report 1
world economy
   creation, and racial Othering 89
   and housework 52, 53
   plantation slavery in 51–2
world historical model 21, 117–37, 118,
      119, 134–5, 185, 230
world inequality 5, 59, 123
   and primitive accumulation 57
world-systems analysis 2, 124
   definition 71fn10
   racism in 70
   Wallerstein 47

(former) Yugoslavia, and Orientalism 223

Zasulich, Vera, Marx's letter to 40